PARLIAMENT IN THE 21ST CENTURY

Edited by

NICHOLAS D. J. BALDWIN

POLITICO'S

First published in Great Britain 2005
by Politico's Publishing
an imprint of Methuen Publishing Limited
215 Vauxhall Bridge Road
London SW1V 1EJ

A catalogue record for this book is available from the British Library.

ISBN 1 84275 103 4

Printed and bound by Mackays of Chatham

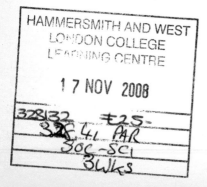

CONTENTS

For my parents

to whom I owe everything

FOREWORD

Rt Hon. Charles Kennedy MP

Leader of the Liberal Democrat Party

Parliamentary democracy is the cornerstone of modern 21st century Britain. It has been the guiding force in Britain's development for many centuries. Through successive generations it has reformed and modernised, bending to the will of its masters – the British people. But its influence is not exclusively within our borders. It has been the guiding force for democracies across the globe and as it continues to evolve and adapt, it remains the uniquely successful and adaptable institution with which we now pride ourselves.

The establishment in Scotland of a national parliament and in Wales of a national assembly has continued to push forward the boundaries of democracy and accountability: delivering their services and expertise closer to the voters and better fulfilling their needs. Just as history charts the evolution of parliamentary democracy, there is no doubt that the 21st century will bear witness to further change and development – pushing forward the boundaries of democracy and government in response to the will of the British people.

Nicholas Baldwin's book *Parliament in the 21st Century* – with contributions from a wide variety of experts and practitioners from across the political spectrum – is not only an important contribution to furthering our understanding of Parliament's often complex activities and procedures but also a valuable contribution to the on-going debate on the role and effectiveness of Parliament within the contemporary British political system.

Charles Kennedy MP
February 2005

PREFACE

The idea for this book grew out of many years of interest in, indeed fascination with, the House of Lords and the House of Commons. This led to my studying and later teaching about – and for a time working within – Parliament.

More particularly, it grew out of having organised more than 50 undergraduate conferences on the subject of Parliament over the past 20 years. These conferences involved members from both the House of Commons and the House of Lords – and I would like to take this opportunity to express my sincere thanks to all those MPs and peers who have lent their support to these conferences over the years.

Although the general theme of this book is 'Parliament in the 21st Century', it may be observed that much of the text deals with the past or the present and not with the future. This is because it is impossible, without some knowledge of the past, to understand the present, let alone look ahead to the future. The intention here is to bring together sufficient information and opinion so as to enable the reader to form his or her own judgement on an ancient British institution in the early years of a new century.

Many people have helped in the preparation and development of the text. First and foremost I would like to express my thanks to all those who have contributed chapters – without them there would be no book! I would also like to thank both Sheila Tofts and Amanda Mabbitt for their typing/computer skills (and endless patience!) as well as John Schwartz and

Emma Musgrave and all at Politico's/Methuen for their encouragement for this project and their support throughout.

I would also like to express my thanks to Vanessa – without you this book might have been completed earlier, but life would not have been such fun!

Finally, I would like to thank my students over the years for their enquiring minds, many questions and endless enthusiasm; this book owes much to all of you.

Nicholas D. J. Baldwin
Wroxton College
Fairleigh Dickinson University
February 2005

LIST OF CONTRIBUTORS

Lord Alton of Liverpool

Local councillor, 1972–80. Liberal/Liberal Democrat Member of Parliament for Liverpool Edge Hill/Liverpool Mossley Hill 1979–97. Created a life peer in 1997. Professor of citizenship, Liverpool John Moores University.

Dr Nicholas D. J. Baldwin

Has written and lectured extensively on British government and British politics. He has been a parliamentary candidate and also served as a special assistant in the House of Lords. Since 1985 he has been Dean and Director of Operations at Wroxton College, Oxfordshire, the British campus of Fairleigh Dickinson University.

Alan Beith MP

Member of Parliament (Liberal/Liberal Democrat) for Berwick-upon-Tweed since 1973. Member of the House of Commons Intelligence and Security Committee since 1994. Member of the Committee of Privy Counsellors on the Anti-Terrorism, Crime and Security Act since 2002. Chairman of the Select Committee on Constitutional Affairs since 2003. Member of the Treasury and Civil Service Select Committee 1987–94. Deputy leader of the Liberal Democrats 1992–2002; deputy leader of the Liberal Party 1985–8. Liberal Democrat home affairs spokesman 1994–9. Liberal Democrat spokesman, Treasury 1987–94. Foreign affairs spokesman 1985–7. Liberal Party Chief Whip 1976–85.

Lord Biffen

Conservative Member of Parliament from 1961 to 1997, during which time he served in various Cabinet positions, including Chief Secretary to the Treasury 1979–81, Secretary of State for Trade 1981–2 and Leader of the House of Commons 1982–7. He was created a life peer in 1997.

Lord Carter

A member of the House of Lords since 1987, he served as Labour Government Chief Whip in the House of Lords from 1997 through to 2002.

James Cran MP

Conservative member of Parliament for Beverley/Beverly and Holderness since 1987. He was a member of the Select Committee on Trade and Industry (1987–92) and a member of the Northern Ireland Select Committee (1994–5). Between 1995 and 1997 he was parliamentary private secretary to the Secretary of State for Northern Ireland. In June 1997 he was appointed as opposition whip with responsibility for the north, and depart-mentally, for the Home Office, Northern Ireland and Agriculture, Fisheries and Food. From June 1998 to September 2001 he served as a pairing whip.

Lord Davies of Oldham

Labour member of Parliament from 1974 to 1979 and from 1992 to 1997.

Created a life Peer in 1997 and a Government Whip in 2000. He has been the Government Deputy Chief Whip in the House of Lords since 2003.

Dr F. Nigel Forman

Member of Parliament (Conservative) for Carshalton and Wallington between 1976 and 1997. During this time he served as a parliamentary private secretary at the Foreign and Commonwealth Office and at the Treasury and was a minister at the Department for Education. He has taught at several universities and is a visiting lecturer at the Civil Service College.

Oonagh Gay

Researcher (Parliament and Constitution), House of Commons Library.

Bruce George MP

Before entering Parliament was a senior lecturer in government at Birmingham Polytechnic. Labour member of Parliament for Walsall South since February 1974. Chair of the House of Commons Defence Select Committee since 1997 (member since 1979). Member of UK Delegation to the NATO Parliamentary Assembly since 1981.

Lord Howe of Aberavon

Conservative Member of Parliament 1964–6 and 1970–92. Holder of various ministerial posts including Chancellor of the Exchequer 1979–83; Secretary of State for Foreign and Commonwealth Affairs 1983–9; Lord President of the Council, Leader of the House of Commons and Deputy Prime Minister 1989–90. Awarded a life peerage in 1992.

Baroness Knight of Collingtree

Conservative member of Parliament for Birmingham Edgbaston 1966–97. Awarded a life peerage in 1997. Vice-chair, Association of Conservative Peers.

Andrew Love MP

Labour member of Parliament for Edmonton since 1997. Parliamentary private secretary to the Minister of State for Health since 2001. Member, House of Commons Public Accounts Committee 1997–2001.

Lord McNally

Political adviser to the Foreign Secretary 1974–6. Head of the Political Office in 10 Downing Street 1976–9. MP for Stockport South 1979–81 (Labour) and 1981–3 (SDP). Member, House of Commons Select Committee on Trade and Industry 1981–3. Appointed a Liberal Democrat life peer in 1995. Following the 1997 general election, he became spokesman on home affairs and in 2001 was elected deputy leader of the Liberal Democrats in the Lords. He was Liberal Democrat spokesman in the Lords on communications and broadcasting as well as home affairs. In 2004 he became leader of the Liberal Democrats in the Lords.

Austin Mitchell MP

Labour MP for Grimsby since 1977. A former parliamentary private secretary, opposition whip, member of the Treasury and Civil Service Select Committees and frontbench spokesperson on Trade and Industry, he currently sits on the Agriculture Select Committee. Previously he was an academic (Nuffield College, Oxford and universities in New Zealand) and a television journalist (BBC and Yorkshire Television).

J. David Morgan

Researcher to Bruce George MP.

Lord Norton of Louth

Director of the Centre for Legislative Studies and Professor of Government at the University of Hull. In 1998 he was elevated to the House of Lords as a Conservative peer and in 1999 was appointed to chair the party's Commission to Strengthen Parliament. He is chair of the House of Lords Select Committee on the Constitution.

Peter Riddell

Political columnist. Peter Riddell is chief political commentator and assistant editor (Politics) of *The Times*, and author of *Parliament under Blair* (Politico's, London, 2000) and *Hug Them Close: Blair, Clinton, Bush and the 'Special Relationship'* (Politico's, London, 2003).

Professor Michael Rush

Emeritus Professor of Politics, University of Exeter.

Dr Meg Russell

Senior Research Fellow at the Constitution Unit, University College London. She is author of *Reforming the House of Lords: Lessons from Overseas* (Oxford University Press, Oxford, 2000) and various other reports and papers on the Lords and its reform. From June 2001 to March 2003 she was seconded on a full-time basis as an adviser to Robin Cook in his role as Leader of the House of Commons, where he was responsible for the government's policy in this area.

Eve Samson

Clerk, House of Commons Select Committee on Transport.

Sir Teddy Taylor

Conservative member of Parliament for Glasgow Cathcart from 1964 until 1979. Following the 1970 general election he was appointed Under-Secretary of State for Scotland. He resigned from the government in July 1971 because of his opposition to Britain joining the EEC. He was again appointed Under-Secretary of State for Scotland in January 1974. Following the general election of February 1974 he became opposition spokesman on trade. In December 1976 he became opposition spokesman on Scotland. Elected Conservative member of Parliament for Southend East in 1980. He had the Conservative whip withdrawn in 1994–5 over the issue of Europe. In May 1997 he was elected as Conservative member of Parliament for Rochford and Southend East.

Graham P. Thomas

Lecturer in politics, Reading College of Technology.

Lord Tordoff

Created a (Liberal) life peer in 1981. Principal Deputy Chairman of Committees 1994–2001. Deputy Speaker since 1994. Deputy Chairman of Committees since 2001. Liberal/Liberal Democrat Chief Whip 1984–94.

Lord Wakeham

Conservative member of Parliament 1974–92. Awarded a life peerage in 1992. Served as government Chief Whip 1983–7 and held various ministerial posts including Leader of the House of Commons 1987–9; Secretary of State for Energy 1989–92; Leader of the House of Lords 1992–4. Chairman, Royal Commission on the Reform of the House of Lords 1999.

Natalie Whatford

Researcher to Bruce George MP.

Sir Michael Wheeler-Booth

Joined the Parliament Office, House of Lords, as clerk in 1960 and worked as an official in Parliament in a wide variety of functions, including serving (from 1991 to 1997) as Clerk of the Parliaments. He has been a commissioner for the Welsh Assembly (1998–9) and a member of the Royal Commission on House of Lords Reform (1999–2000). Since 1997 he has been lecturer in politics at Magdalen College, University of Oxford.

Dr Richard Whitaker

Lecturer, School of Politics, University of Nottingham.

Ann Widdecombe MP

Elected member of Parliament for Maidstone at the 1987 General Election. Member of the House of Commons Select Committee for Social Services (appointed in 1988), and sponsored several Bills on such topics as school bus passes, regional health authorities, abortion and compensation. From November 1990 until May 1993, she was Parliamentary Under-Secretary of State at the Department of Social Security. In May 1993, she was appointed Parliamentary Under-Secretary of State at the Department of Employment. She then served as Minister of State at the Department of Employment from July 1994 until July 1995 and in July 1995 was appointed Minister of State at the Home Office, a position she held until 1997. Elected member of Parliament for the new seat of Maidstone and the Weald in 1997. In July 1997, she was appointed to the House of Commons Standards and Privileges Select Committee. She served as shadow Secretary of State for Health from1998 to 1999 and as shadow Home Secretary from June 1999 to September 2001.

Barry Winetrobe

Worked for many years as a senior researcher on parliament and constitutional matters in the House of Commons Research Service. Seconded to Edinburgh from early 1999 to spring 2000 to help in the establishment of the Scottish Parliament's research and information services. He is currently lecturer in public law at the University of Glasgow.

ONE

The Origins and Development of Parliament

Dr Nicholas D. J. Baldwin

I t is important to place Parliament in its contemporary context, and it is the object of this book to do this. Before doing so, however, some knowledge of the past is necessary, because in order to be able to understand and appreciate the position of the British Parliament within today's constitutional framework, some knowledge of its history and consequent development is essential. In Britain continuity and change have gone hand in hand. Continuity has been the dominant feature of British constitutional development, yet this has not meant the absence of change, as age-old institutions have evolved and adapted to fulfil purposes often very different from those for which they originally came into being or were created. As a result there is often a striking contrast between the theory and practice of the British constitution. Nowhere is this more true than in the case of the British Parliament. Indeed, an important – possibly the most important – feature of the British constitution is its capacity gradually to adapt to changing circumstances. In this respect Parliament is a microcosm of the British constitution, since throughout its long history it has been able to do just this. In contrast to other parliaments elsewhere in the world which have been specifically created with powers and composition clearly defined in basic constitutional documents, the British Parliament is the product of history. It was not created by founding fathers or under a basic law; it has simply developed and changed organically in the soil of British history. This is not to say that its evolution has been linear or continuous; on the contrary, it has been haphazard, spasmodic and uncertain. Yet it has survived and continues to survive, not least of all because of what can be termed its 'evolutionary adaptability'.

Monarch, Lords and Commons

In formal terms Parliament consists of the Monarch, the House of Lords and the House of Commons, with the concept of 'parliamentary sovereignty' resting in all three combined. This fact notwithstanding, however, when the term 'Parliament' is used today it customarily means the two Houses of Parliament, namely the House of Commons and the House of Lords. (In fact – and confusingly – the term 'Parliament' is often used when simply meaning the House of Commons.) With this in mind, it is necessary to be aware of the fact that as the product of evolution rather than deliberate creation, it is not possible to say exactly when Parliament originated, for Parliament as a whole had no single genesis. Rather it came into being gradually 'from the medieval Court and Council where Plantagenet kings consulted the great men of the realm to secure support and offer their people justice'.[1] Nonetheless, it is possible to find the deepest roots of the British Parliament in the consultative customs of the Saxon kings who took periodic advice and support from the Witan.

In Saxon times kings were guided by the Witan or Witenagemot, an assembly of the most important men – lay and ecclesiastical – in the kingdom. The membership was not static and consisted of those individuals whom the King chose to summon to the three or four meetings held annually. As Ronald Butt put it, 'his natural advisers were the elders; the men of strength, standing, influence, experience and knowledge'.[2] Those present included the chief officers of the royal household and others who held high state office, the ealdormen, who represented central government in the shires, bishops and other senior churchmen, and the principal men who held land directly from the King. The functions of the Witan were ill defined, but included 'discovering and declaring' the law, in other words being a consultative and law-consenting assembly. In addition, the Witan sat as the King's supreme court of justice. Its actual power was inversely proportional to that of the King at any given time. Together the King and the Witan were the highest authority in the nation.

A new stage in the development of the nation's political institutions was ushered in when Duke William of Normandy defeated Harold, the Saxon claimant to the throne, at the battle of Hastings in 1066. William the Conqueror (as he came to be known) launched a series of campaigns which, in the fullness of time, left him in undisputed control of the country. It was William's claim that he had succeeded to the throne through inheritance. As a result he laid claim to an element of continuity and sought to maintain many of the laws of his Saxon predecessors. At the same time, however, he brought with him from Normandy a new approach to government, namely the feudal system, whereby the greater part of the country was governed by tenants-in-chief, or barons, who held their land directly from the King on condition that they defended the conquered territory for the King. By the time of the Domesday survey of 1085–6, only about 8 per cent of the land remained in English hands; indeed, of the tenants-in-chief only two appear to have been English.

The Norman barons assembled in the court of their sovereign to regulate the affairs of their tenancies, settle disputes between each other and organise the military subjection of the conquered lands. The tenants-in-chief thus assembled – both lay and ecclesiastical – became known as the *Magnum Concilium* or Great Council. This gathering assisted the King in determining state policy, supervised the work of public administration, acted as the highest court of justice and made or modified the laws of the land. It met only three or four times a year, and then only for a matter of days at a time. For this reason there grew up the *Curia Regis* or Court of the King – an inner circle of the Great Council – whose function it was to assist the sovereign on a day-to-day basis during the long periods when the Great Council was not assembled.

This system of government worked well for a while, but towards the end of the twelfth century tensions between the King and his 'great men' began to increase. Matters were brought to a head by the abuse of autocratic power by King John. Consequently the barons seized an opportunity in 1215, when the King's position was weakened by war and misrule, to force him to sign a *Magna Carta* or Great Charter, setting out some clear principles and safe-guards against further abuse of power by the monarch. The intention of the barons was not to create a new system of government, but rather to ensure better government under the existing system. Consequently *Magna Carta* was not the birth certificate of a new constitutional settlement but, rather, the death certificate of royal despotism (even if this was not apparent to all at the time).

The agreement foreshadowed three of the main principles upon which the development of Parliament was later to be based, namely:

1. the King himself was subject to the law;
2. the King could only make law and levy taxation with the consent of the governed; and
3. the King's subjects did not owe the King absolute or unconditional obedience.[3]

In short, it asserted the limited nature of kingship – the principle of condi-tional or 'constitutional' monarchy which was to be the mainspring of parlia-mentary action against the Crown in the seventeenth century.

Within three months of the King's seal being affixed to *Magna Carta*, however, the concordat which it was supposed to symbolise broke down.

John died in October 1216, to be succeeded by Henry III, then a boy of nine. Henry occupied the throne for the next 56 years, during which time politics were dominated by the struggle between the Crown and the barons. The relationship between the King and the barons deteriorated eventually to the point of armed conflict, in which the barons under Simon de Montfort were victorious. In 1265 de Montfort convened a parliament (literally a 'talking gathering') which was attended not only by the barons, clergy and knights of the shires, but also by two burgesses from each of the boroughs known to be supportive of the baronial cause. This occasion has since been widely recognised as the real beginning of Parliament at Westminster, and it is the recognition of this date which allows the British Parliament to claim that it is one of the oldest parliaments in the world.

During the decades and centuries which followed, the holding of 'parliaments' containing representatives of the counties and towns became the accepted custom and practice and 'Parliament' itself became a feature of the governmental system. At no time was Parliament definitively established, it merely evolved as a consultative forum for the King and the politically important sections of his realm.

Gradually, there took place a realignment of the membership – nobles, greater and lesser clergy, the knights of the shires and the burgesses – into two great groups, one of which became the House of Lords and the other the House of Commons – the one composed of men who attended in response to individual summons, and the other persons who, elected in counties and boroughs, attended in a representative capacity. This bicameral or two-house nature of the arrangement was to become firmly established.

By about 1485 – the beginning of the Tudor period – it may be said that the institutional foundations of Britain's constitutional monarchy had been laid. What came thereafter was in the nature of further growth and development within the existing framework, and, more particularly, the working out of new relationships between institutions, a process which led to altered balances of power and mechanisms of control.

The Tudor monarchs found that there was political advantage for them in having their national policies – such as Henry VIII's break with the Catholic Church or Elizabeth I's determination to oppose the Spanish kings – supported and endorsed by the people's representatives in Acts of Parliament. For this reason no Tudor Monarch sought to dispense with Parliament and each member of the dynasty in turn put its support to good use. However, sessions of Parliament were infrequent and brief. Even during the 45-year reign of Elizabeth I, when Parliament counted for more than had previously been the case, the two Houses (Lords and Commons) were in session on average for little more than three weeks a year. During this period, the House of Lords became predominantly a secular body, while the House of Commons was increased in size by more than a third to about 300 members. By the end of the sixteenth century Parliament had become second only to the monarch as a power in the land.

Constitutional tensions came to the fore under the Stuarts, especially James I and Charles I, who laid claim to the 'divine right of kings' and sought to reduce or deny the privileges acquired by Parliament under the Tudors. The mounting disagreements between Crown and Parliament eventually led to the Civil War (1642–9), the triumph of the parliamentary forces, the execution of Charles I and the abolition of the monarchy itself. For the next few years the country was ruled by Oliver Cromwell in a protectorate. It was not until after Cromwell's death in 1658 that the monarchy was restored, Charles II assuming the throne for the Stuarts in 1660. However, the relationship between the monarch and Parliament was not a great deal better than before the Civil War and matters worsened under James II as he sought to reassert the divine right of kings. The eventual result was that Parliament and people combined against the King, who fled the country in 1688 and was replaced by William of Orange (from Holland) and his English wife Mary – daughter of Charles I – in 1689. This peaceful transfer of constitutional power from one monarch to another – but actually from the monarchy to Parliament – has been described by Whig historians as 'the Glorious

Revolution'. The new constitutional settlement was given statutory recognition in the 1689 Bill of Rights. The 'pretended power' of the Crown to suspend or dispense laws, or to govern without the consent of Parliament, was declared illegal, as was the levying of taxation by royal prerogative without the authority of Parliament. The 1689 Bill of Rights and the 1701 Act of Settlement confirmed the victory of Parliament in the struggle against the Crown. Constitutional monarchy was developed in place of the unfettered rights of kings and queens, and parliamentary supremacy in the government of the country was well and truly established.

From the beginning of the Hanoverian dynasty in 1714, the role of the monarch was reduced still further. George I (1714–27) was a German, speaking no English and knowing nothing of English ideas and ways. George II (1727–60), although more interested in his adopted land, lacked the ability to make himself felt in government affairs. In these circumstances the powers which their predecessors had so jealously sought to preserve fell into disuse or into the hands of the English aristocracy, who effectively ran the country throughout the eighteenth century. George III (1760–1820), perhaps more English than Hanoverian, tried to recapture the royal position that had been lost. His influence on government and politics was far greater than that of his two predecessors to the extent that in 1780 the House of Commons felt driven to declare that the 'influence of the Crown has increased, is increasing, and ought to be diminished'.[4]

After the resignation of Lord North as Prime Minister in 1782, the tide turned back in favour of Parliament, and during the last decades of his reign, the King was discredited by madness. By then a satisfactory way of running the government without the active participation of the monarch had been developed. This fact, soon to be buttressed by successive extensions of the franchise in the nineteenth century, meant that no monarch could turn back the clock. Admittedly, Victoria (1837–1901) occasionally sought to play a partisan political role, but her attempts were increasingly marginalised by a long chain of Prime Ministers who countered her ambitions by variously ignoring, opposing or flattering her. The result is that since Victorian times no British monarch has been seriously tempted to step outside the bounds of constitutional monarchy.

The decline of the House of Lords and rise of the House of Commons

As previously noted, from the late thirteenth century onwards there was a gradual and halting alignment of the membership of Parliament into two principal groups: the House of Lords and the House of Commons – the former composed of men who attended in response to individual summons from the monarch, and the latter of people elected in the counties and boroughs who attended in a representative capacity.

As the principle of representative and responsible government developed in the eighteenth century, the power of control over the executive fell increasingly to the House of Commons rather than the House of Lords. It was to the Commons, not the Lords, that individual ministers and the government collectively came to be held responsible. However, the Lords did not meekly accept the constitutional superiority of the Commons, and the leading territorial magnates in the upper House managed to retain effective control over the lower House by controlling the processes of election to many seats in the Commons, especially the so-called pocket or rotten boroughs. The personification of this manipulative power in the second half of the eighteenth century was the Duke of Newcastle, who, in cooperation with his noble friends and relatives, managed to control between 80 and 100 seats in the House of Commons – enough 'placemen' to ensure that he and his faction either formed or dominated many administrations.

The 1832 Reform Act, which enlarged the electorate from about 3 per cent of the adult population to 5 per cent and which abolished many of the rotten boroughs, deprived the House of Lords of much of the political power which it had enjoyed in the eighteenth century. The Tory peers had strongly opposed it, but in the end were forced to concede to a combination of Liberal reformers in both Houses (led by Earl Grey) and popular pressure from the mob – that is, angry public demonstrations in favour of reform. The monarch, William IV, also played a significant part on the side of reform by indicating his willingness to create a large number of new peers who, if necessary, could have swamped the die-hard opposition in the Lords. In the event, this threat, along with the other pressures mentioned, was sufficient to get the legislation passed.

The expansion of the suffrage and the development of more modern electoral arrangements between 1832 and 1867 gave the House of Commons a growing claim to genuinely representative credentials. At the same time, the power of the landed interest was in decline in the wake of the growth of the industrial towns and, after the repeal of the Corn Laws in 1845, the enormous impact of free trade on the economy and society. These and other factors brought about a gradual shift of political power away from the House of Lords to the House of Commons – for example, the proportion of peers in the Cabinet declined from about three-quarters to about a third of the total. During these years the House of Lords was able to head off challenges to its legal powers and to the hereditary basis of its membership as long as the peers were content to play second fiddle to the Commons. Indeed, in many ways the leading figures in the Lords were careful not to alienate or challenge their counterparts in the Commons for fear of provoking further instalments of constitutional reform which would have weakened their institutional position still more. As Walter Bagehot explained the position of the Lords in 1867, 'the House has ceased to be one of the latent directors, and has become one of the temporary rejecters and palpable alterers' (of legislation passed by the Commons).[5] He went on to describe the House of Lords as a chamber with powers of delay and revision, but little else and concluded that 'its danger is not in assassination, but atrophy; not abolition but decline'.[6]

It was not long, however, before the validity of Bagehot's observations was challenged, since during the last decades of the nineteenth century and the first decade of the twentieth century there was recurrent conflict between the Tory and Unionist majority in the Lords and the Liberal majority in the House of Commons. This finally came to a head in the constitutional crisis of 1909–11. In 1893 the Conservative and Unionist majority in the Lords had heavily defeated William Gladstone's Liberal attempt at Irish Home Rule. In 1906 the Liberal Education Bill had been very drastically amended by the Lords, and consequently abandoned by the Commons. The Lords had rejected the Land Valuation Bill in 1907 and again in 1908, the Licensing Bill in 1908, and finally (and fatefully) the Liberal Finance Bill of 1909. The quarrel between the two legislative chambers – a quarrel in Winston Churchill's words 'often threatened, often averted, long debated, long delayed, always inevitable' – had come to a head at last.[7]

The House of Commons immediately voted to declare the House of Lords action unconstitutional and a breach of privilege. Parliament was then dissolved. In the ensuing general election the Liberals were returned to power, although with a much reduced majority. However, when the Parliament Bill to curb the power of the Lords was introduced into the Commons in April 1910, the Liberals were able to count on Labour and Irish Nationalist support. The first consequence of the new parliamentary arithmetic was that the 1910 Liberal Budget was passed by the Commons and then accepted by the Lords without a vote. However, owing to the death of Edward VII on 6 May 1910, the Parliament Bill itself was not proceeded with. Following the failure of attempts to negotiate an agreed settlement at a constitutional conference, the Liberal government decided that a second general election should be held in 1910 before it could legitimately proceed with the Bill. The Prime Minister, Herbert Asquith, also obtained a promise from the new King, George V, that should the Liberals win the election he would agree to create enough new Liberal peers to overcome the die-hard Conservative opposition to the Bill in the Lords. The new House of Commons (elected in November 1910) was almost identical in composition with the old, so the Liberals remained in office, reintroduced the Parliament

Bill and promptly secured a parliamentary majority for it in the Commons. This time the Lords gave it a second reading, but watered it down in committee. On its return to the Commons, the lower House refused to accept most of the amendments proposed by the Lords and promptly returned it to the peers. On 10 August 1911, after considerable behind-the-scenes activity and argument within the Conservative and Unionist peers, the majority in the upper House were reluctantly prepared to accept the Bill as it then stood as the lesser of two evils. Consequently, the Lords voted not to insist on their amendments by 131 votes to 114, with some 300 Conservatives abstaining.[8]

The 1911 Parliament Act removed the Lords power to reject money Bills, while their powers to veto ordinary public Bills were replaced with a power of delay for a maximum of two years. This meant that if a Bill were approved by the Commons in three successive sessions, it automatically became law at the end of that time whether or not their Lordships were content. Together with the reduction in the maximum permitted span of a parliament from seven to five years, this meant that any Bill passed by the Commons in the first two sessions of a five-year parliament would inevitably become the law of the land if insisted on by a majority in the Commons. Although the Bill curbed the powers of the Lords, the composition of the upper House was not addressed, any more than the whole issue of the appropriate functions for a curtailed second chamber.

The significance of the 1911 Parliament Act was two-fold. Firstly, it created procedures whereby obstruction by the Lords could be overcome and, secondly, and more importantly, it served to act as a deterrent to obstruction by the Lords. It is upon these twin pillars that the activities of the Lords have evolved and developed in the period since 1911, to the extent that the reform, challenged by some at its inception as undermining the entire constitutional edifice of the nation, has come to be regarded as one of the very cornerstones of that constitutional edifice. It can be seen as such because, more through gradual evolution than by design, it led to the development of a chamber which was neither too dependent nor too independent, a chamber which had influence but not authority.

In 1945 the victorious Labour government did not put forward any proposals for reform or abolition of the House of Lords, not least of all because it had many other more pressing legislative priorities – such as the creation of the National Health Service, various nationalisation Bills, and the legislation to bring about independence for India. Furthermore, the Conservative peers under the leadership of Lord Salisbury adopted a deliberate convention of self-restraint under which they did not oppose at second reading any legislative measures emanating from the 1945 Labour manifesto, although they were prepared to press amendments to Labour Bills in the name of 'improving' the legislation. By 1947, however, the mood of the Conservative majority in the upper House had changed and it became clear that, at any rate in relation to the proposed nationalisation of the iron and steel industries, the Conservative peers were prepared to use their numerical superiority against such legislation. Faced with this threat from their Conservative opponents in the Lords, Labour ministers secured approval in the Commons for a further Parliament Bill, designed to reduce the delaying power of the upper House to one year. In spite of efforts to find a compromise between the respective majorities in the two Houses, agreement proved impossible. The government went ahead without all-party agreement, using provisions of the 1911 Parliament Act to ensure the passage of what was to become the 1949 Parliament Act. This effectively, firstly, reduced the period of delay to less than thirteen months; secondly, cut from three to two the number of sessions in which a disputed Bill had to be passed by the Commons; and, thirdly, cut from three to two years the period of maximum delay following second reading in the Commons. Once again, however, the Act did nothing to change the composition or the functions of the second Chamber.

A number of reforms did, however, take place during the late 1950s and early 1960s. In 1957 daily allowances were introduced for travel to and from and attendance at the House of Lords. In 1958 the Life Peerages Act made possible the creation of life peers (that is, peerages which cannot be inherited), including peerages for women in their own right. In 1963 the Peerage Act enabled female hereditary peers to sit and allowed hereditary peers to renounce their titles – while in no way impinging on the rights of their heirs and successors – in order to make themselves eligible for member-ship of the House of Commons. In the wake of these changes, the right of hereditary peers to sit in the House of Lords remained, as did the rights of the House as a whole to reject Bills introduced in the House of Lords, subor-dinate legislation, private Bills and Bills to confirm provisional Orders. In addition, the minimal delaying power which the upper House still possessed gave peers the ability not only to dislocate considerably the government's legislative programme, but also, in the final year of a parliament, to defeat a government Bill in its entirety.

In 1968 the Labour government of Harold Wilson sought to reform both the powers and the composition of the House of Lords through the Parliament (No. 2) Bill. However, the Bill received a critical, even hostile, reception in the House of Commons and, despite never being defeated, the legislation was ultimately dropped. The consequence of this failure was a determination amongst many members of the House of Lords to play a more active role; a determination that bore fruit during the period 1979–90, when members of the House of Lords were seen by many as providing the only effective opposition to some of the policies put forward by Margaret Thatcher's Conservative government.

Following the Labour election victory in 1997 legislation to remove the right of hereditary peers to sit and vote in the House of Lords was brought forth. However, during the passage of what became the 1999 House of Lords Act – indeed, in order to secure its passage – 92 hereditary members were 'reprieved', securing the right to continued membership – at least until promised further reform could be enacted.

The House of Commons and the rise of party government

The Great Reform Act of 1832 – by giving the right to vote to an additional half a million individuals who had not previously had it, and in so doing taking the proportion of the enfranchised population to 5 per cent – extended political power beyond the estates, country houses and drawing rooms of the landed aristocratic elite, creating an electorate of such a size that it could not be influenced solely by personal connection and the power of the nobility (through 'beer and fear', as was remarked at the time). The consequence was the growth of embryonic political organisations such as registration societies and election funds. Yet the 1832 Act did not of itself bring about the transition from aristocratic rule to representative democracy sometimes claimed for it. The period between 1832 and the passage of the 1867 Representation of the People Act still bore many similarities to pre-1832 days, for, as has been pointed out, 'the redistribution of seats in 1832 had been essentially a conservative one, rotten boroughs by no means fully abolished, and the franchise was still highly selective'.9 What the 1832 Act did do, however, was to create conditions which marked out the period from 1832 through to 1867 as a transitional one between aristocratic rule and representative democracy, at least in a very rough form. This was reflected in the choice of government: prior to 1832 it had been chosen by the monarch; after 1867, with the gradual advent of a form of representative democracy, it was chosen – albeit indirectly– by the electorate. In the intervening period governments were chosen by the House of Commons – the so-called 'golden age' of Parliament. The 1867 Representation of the People Act carried forward the principles of the 1832 legislation – that of the extension of the franchise – increasing the electorate to number almost 2.5 million (13 per cent of the adult population). The result was an electorate too large to be contacted other than through highly organised, and in the event fairly centralised, mass membership organisations – namely political parties, and both the Conservative National Union and the National Liberal Federation were created as a direct response to the new political situation. But merely to contact the new voters was insufficient; if their votes were to be forthcoming they had to be promised something. However, party promises could only be kept if party candidates were returned in sufficient number to the House of Commons and, once there, display sufficient voting cohesion.

The position developed whereby MPs were returned on the basis of a party label and, consequently, were expected to support not only the party's leaders but also the party's programme. This led to the development of the theory of the mandate. The 'idea' here is that at a general election each party publishes its programme – its manifesto – outlining in general terms what it proposes to do and what policies it would pursue, if it were to form the government. The assumption is that the voters will read the various manifestos and will make up their minds on how to cast their votes accordingly, based on their assessment of and support for the policies outlined. This process is then presumed to grant to the resulting newly elected government the seal of public approval to implement the policies concerned – the public giving a 'mandate' to the government to act as it said it would. As a result, MPs lost – at least in most instances – the function of legislation.

Consequently, putting these two developments together, the government itself was now not only chosen through the House of Commons at a general election rather than by the House of Commons, but also the government's own legislation – government-initiated legislation – increasingly came to take priority over that from within the membership of the House of Commons as a whole. Government achieved control of the timetable and 'whips' – MPs appointed to keep like-minded MPs informed of business and ensure that they not only turned out to vote but that they voted the same way – became prominent figures in Parliament. As a result

> the task of the House of Commons became one of supporting the Cabinet chosen at the polls and passing its legislation ... By the 1900s, the Cabinet dominated British Government. The House of Commons still

exercised a strong influence, but it did so more as an indicator of public opinion, a warning of what the electors might decide at the next election, than as an authority that might dethrone a Cabinet or reverse its policies.[10]

Because of these developments, by the beginning of the twentieth century party cohesion was a well-established feature of parliamentary life. In short, the era of party government had arrived.

Endnotes

[1] Butt, R., *A History of Parliament in the Middle Ages* (Constable, London, 1989), p. 1.

[2] *Ibid.*, p. 2.

[3] *Ibid.*, p. 60.

[4] The Dunning motion – a resolution by John Dunning in April 1780, approved by 233 votes to 190. See Breeke, J., *King George III* (Constable, London, 1992), pp. 201–18.

[5] Bagehot, W., *The English Constitution* (Fontana, Glasgow, 1963), p. 128.

[6] *Ibid.*, p. 149.

[7] Quoted in Rhodes James, R. (ed.), *Churchill Speaks* (Windword, Leicester, 1981), p. 178.

[8] See Jenkins, R., *Mr Balfour's Poodle* (Collins, London, 1954).

[9] Norton, P., *The Commons in Perspective* (Martin Robertson, Oxford, 1981), p. 14.

[10] Mackintosh, J., *The Cabinet*, (Third Edition), (London: Stevens & Sons, 1977), p.174

TWO

Parliament and its Place in the Constitution

Andrew Love MP

*We live under a system of tacit understandings. But the understandings
are not always understood.*

Sydney Low 1904

Government without a Constitution, is power without a right.

Tom Paine

I n a recent opinion poll commissioned for the British Council, well-
informed young professionals from abroad were asked about the symbols
that best represented their image of Britain. These, it turned out,
included the village pub, bad weather and Margaret Thatcher! But way out
in front were three enduring images - the royal family, comfortably in the
lead, football and, squeezed between the two and symbolically linking them
together, the Houses of Parliament.

This is not coincidental or simply a reflection of the arresting and unique
mock-Gothic appearance of the buildings but is because Parliament is – in
my view – representative of the nation. Nonetheless, not everyone agrees and

there are many who are critical of Parliament and who question its role at the centre of British public life. However, in their criticism a large number show little awareness or understanding of Parliament.

At the time of the 2001 general election only 45 per cent of the electorate said that they were 'broadly satisfied' with Parliament – with a similar number believing that the political system governing Britain 'mainly works well'. In a survey from the year before, 'satisfaction' with the constitution amongst the public topped 50 per cent, although it must be said this higher rating may in fact be the result of a lower awareness and understanding of what the British constitution in fact is and how it regulates the system of government in Britain. This lack of awareness and understanding undoubtedly stems – at least in part – from a confusion that results from the complexity of our constitutional arrangements.

Unlike almost all other countries, Britain does not have a formal, written, codified constitution. Nor, for that matter, does it have an unwritten constitution. Although it is often claimed that the British constitution is unwritten, that is not accurate. In fact the UK constitution can best be described as partly unwritten and partly written but uncodified, for although parts are based in statute, much of the constitution consists of unwritten conventions that have evolved over time with the development of Parliament and our democratic institutions. It has been characterised rather succinctly by Tony Wright MP as 'a great accumulated jumble of statutes, common law provisions, precedents, conventions and guide books. As such it is an awful mess, horrifying to constitutional theorists but an authentic expression of a particular history.'

A constitution is a set of rules, legal and otherwise, which defines, describes and regulates the structure and operation of the state. It can be described as the fundamental law of the state – superior to all other laws. It is the 'legal source of legitimate authority'.

There are a number of important principles that underpin the present constitutional system of the United Kingdom.

The 'separation of powers' is an important concept in constitutional thinking. Put at its simplest, there are three functions of government – the executive, the legislative and the judicial – and those functions should be operated by three different organs with exacting limits placed on any mixing of those functions. To underpin the separation of powers many constitutions incorporate various 'checks and balances' to ensure that no organ of government – executive, legislature or judiciary – can reign supreme over the others. To do otherwise would be a threat to liberty.

In the UK there is some degree of mixing of functions and organs of government, which is often described as a mixed or balanced constitution. The most obvious example is the executive, almost all of whom are members of the legislature. In the Westminster system it is the degree of connection, rather than of separation, that is considered to provide the checks and balances to prevent government tyranny and preserve the liberty of the individual. Whilst differing in the importance placed on the degree of separation, both the classic complete 'separation of powers' reflected in the US constitution (although not as complete as is often thought) and the 'balanced constitution' of the UK share a common belief in limited government. Both have a common approach to the state, which is in the main considered a potential threat to liberty rather than a positive force for collective action. (Although this is not to say that there is not a difference in emphasis in this regard between the two countries.)

The 'sovereignty' of Parliament is the expression of legal sovereignty. This describes where the ultimate source of legal power lies over the state for all purposes. It was described as the 'very keystone of the Constitution' by A. V. Dicey, the famous Victorian jurist and constitutionalist. Parliamentary sovereignty gives Parliament the right to make or unmake any law whatever. No person or body has the right to override or set aside the law of Parliament. The courts are bound to accept and implement any law passed through Parliament and any Act of Parliament is the ultimate expression of the law. This may not be the case in countries with a written constitution, where legislation may be challenged in the courts as unconstitutional. Where legislative power is devolved – as is the case in Britain with regard to Scotland for example – to preserve sovereignty, arrangements are in place for the hierarchical distribution of those powers between the sovereign Parliament and devolved institutions.

No Parliament can bind its successors. As a result it is not possible, in principle, to entrench constitutional change against future amendment or repeal.

For any law to be enacted by Parliament, it must pass through both the House of Commons and the House of Lords and be signed by the monarch (receive royal assent). This process is sometimes referred to as the 'Queen in Parliament'. The courts are entitled to ensure that legislation is an expression of the 'legal' sovereign – that is the 'Queen in Parliament'. Scrutiny by the courts of the 'manner and form' of legislation, it is claimed, will protect Parliament's authority from usurpation by those who are not entitled to exercise it. As a result the courts can judge alleged non-compliance with the rules governing the composition and procedures for the enactment of legislation by Parliament.

Under the British constitution the executive function is divided into the monarchical executive and the political executive, commonly referred to as the government. As the nature of the British constitution has evolved and developed and the powers of the monarch have declined, the powers retained by the monarch have come to be known as prerogative powers – or simply as the royal prerogative. This is defined as the powers and immunities that are peculiar to the Crown. These include the granting – or withholding – of assent to legislation, the power to appoint and dismiss a Prime Minister, the power to dissolve Parliament (call elections), to grant honours, conclude treaties and declare war. Many of these powers have, over time, passed from the personal hands of the monarch to be exercised by the executive – the Prime Minister and ministers – as monarchs sought to withdraw from playing an active part in the day-to-day work of governing.

Few understand the full nature and extent of the powers of the royal prerogative. Legally the Crown cannot invent new prerogative powers but can, to some extent, adapt existing powers to changed circumstances. Occasionally the courts have identified previously little-recognised powers, especially relating to responses to a national emergency. Whilst Parliament can override a prerogative by statute and control its exercise by ministers through use of its powers of supply (funding), government in reality enjoys a wide range of important and far-reaching powers not subject to Parliamentary scrutiny or approval. However, despite being exercised by the executive these powers remain with the monarch and it is for this reason, if for no other, that the matter of the royal prerogative has moved towards centre stage in the debate on reform of the constitution.

The catalyst for this has been the Parliamentary debates on Yugoslavia and – more recently – Iraq. Parliament has no direct, formal role in decisions of war or military intervention as these are currently prerogative powers, although exercised by the Prime Minister.

Many believe that Parliament's role of holding ministers to account could and should be extended to approval of ministerial use of their prerogative powers. Not surprisingly ministers disagree. But debate continues on how best to locate the unaccountable and entrenched powers of the prerogative more firmly in the framework of the constitution.

An important principle that requires those in authority to act in accordance with the law and in compliance with the partly unwritten, partly written but uncodified constitution is the 'rule of law'. This concept ensures the supremacy of regular law and requires those in authority to act in accordance with the law rather than arbitrarily according to their own whim or preference. As well as being ruled by the law, it also encapsulates the notion of equality before the law.

In the UK it is the considered view of many that the constitution is the result of the ordinary law and that liberty and property are best protected by ordinary law rather than via a formal, written, codified constitution and Bill of Rights. Others, both in Britain and abroad, argue that special written constitutional arrangements are necessary to preserve and protect the rule of law. In their view a written constitution and a Bill of Rights are necessary to prevent the loss of liberty that can result either from legislation or the arbitrary actions of governments backed by a parliamentary majority. In these scenarios, the 'ordinary law' basis of liberty can in fact undermine the rule of law, which needs the protection afforded by a Bill of Rights.

The arguments for and against the adoption of a formal Bill of Rights are finely balanced. Those in favour highlight the need to bring the UK into line with most of the rest of the world; it would entrench a flexible and adaptable tool as the legal protection of individual rights and provide the opportunity to develop law and practice beyond what would be likely to occur if left to the executive and legislature. Those opposed raise concerns regarding the precedent set by a Bill of Rights, the powers that would be given to unelected judges and the restrictions that this would be likely to place on Parliament's freedom to legislate. Although the arguments have been set out in great detail and debate has intensified in recent years it remains the case that opinions remain divided as to the best way forward.

The principles enshrined in our constitutional arrangements are only part of the answer to the question of whether or not these rules actually work. Equally important is the practice and how that enhances the role of our democratic institutions. To work the rules must ultimately ensure the sovereignty of the people of the country. This is often referred to as the political constitution.

Parliament is constitutionally charged, on behalf of the people, to legislate and hold the government to account. Parliament has primarily a legislative role – creating, amending or negating the law of the land. It considers legislation initiated by the government.

Parliament provides a forum for national debate on every issue. It grants money to government, a function that used to be central to its activities but is now more often than not a rubber stamp. It scrutinises the policy and expenditure of government departments through the select committee system introduced in 1979.

The rise of the political party has had a dramatic impact on the practice of parliamentary democracy. Running in parallel has been the development of the whipping system, introduced to secure maximum support for each political party in Parliament. The iron discipline of the party whips minimises dissent and ensures that votes reflect the party political balance in Parliament. As a result the government's programme is secured. But the inevitable consequence has been tighter and tighter control of Parliament by the majority.

Bearing this in mind, it should also be remembered that individuals choose to join political parties and stand for election in support of their manifesto. In general members vote to support their party not because of coercion but because they support that point of view. They can and do act independently – on behalf of their constituents, on ethical and moral issues and on matters of important policy and principle. Where a policy is considered controversial or believed not to be in the national interest, members can and do resist the pressures of party or constituency.

Members see themselves as 'representatives' and not 'delegates', recognising the subtle difference that that reflects. They are not elected simply to voice the views of their constituency or other sectional interest but, taking all of these views into account, to represent the wider interest. Often these are not in conflict but where they are the member must balance the contending pressures to reach a decision that reflects the role of being a member of the national Parliament.

At the centre of democratic life lies the constituency, that population of voters living within a tight and distinct boundary. This is the basic unit for election to Parliament. Members represent electors who live within their constituency, some of whom they will assist, and many of whom they will speak for and often vote in Parliament to reflect their views. The link between an individual elector and their member to Parliament is a critically important aspect of British democracy. That link underpins the trust of the electorate that Parliament ultimately responds to their wishes.

The constitutional role of Parliament does not exist in a vacuum. Public attitudes to democratic institutions are continually evolving and demands for change ebb and flow in response to events and Parliament's response to them. The advent of a 24-hour media, the influence of the focus group and much greater emphasis on message (or spin!) have undoubtedly led to a change, some would say a decline, in the influence and centrality of Parliament in today's society. To what extent can Parliament still be considered the forum of the nation?

With parliamentary reporting being replaced by a combination of sound bites and sketch-writing; with Prime Minister's Questions dominating the parliamentary week to the exclusion of everything else and with the increasing competition for the media's attention from ministerial visits, conferences or events, the central role of Parliament is now being seriously questioned. To this we can add serious questioning not only of Parliament's relevance but also whether it retains the confidence of the electorate.

The long-term decline in participation in elections – not least of all the dramatic slump in turnout in 2001 to 59.4 per cent of eligible voters – raises questions of Parliament's relevance to the lives of ordinary people. One of the factors in that decline is a lack of trust consequent upon a widespread perception that politicians are 'only in it for themselves'. Whilst individual members of Parliament are often held in high regard in their own constituencies, there has been a very significant decline in attitudes to parliamentarians in general and, ultimately, in support for Parliament. The public are undoubtedly turned off by loutish behaviour in the chamber, by the rituals of opposition for its own sake or purely for political advantage and by those rows and rows of empty benches during important debates.

Changing attitudes to politics have also led to a partial breakdown of the two-party tradition in Parliament, with the rise initially of third-party politics and more recently of parties representing the nations if not the regions that make up the United Kingdom. The growth in support of independent candidates and the perception that neither major party engages with public concern – along with a decline in voter participation in elections – suggests growing public apathy if not discontent about the role of Parliament in our national life. All of this combines to raise some fundamental questions about how Parliament and government should respond to those changing attitudes and public concerns.

After a fitful start, the constitution has been on the move again in the final quarter of the twentieth century and in the beginning years of the 21st century. This has been led by the widespread demand that decisions should be taken closer to the communities and people affected by them. In the late 1970s plans to create devolved institutions in Scotland and Wales were rejected via referendums by the electorate. Twenty years later, in very different circumstances, that was reversed. The resulting devolution of power to a Scottish Parliament and to a Welsh Assembly represents a fundamental change to the traditional centralised and unitary state.

Reform of the second chamber, the House of Lords, was the great missed opportunity of the twentieth century. The advance of democracy led inevitably to the primacy of the House of Commons, reflected in the 1911 and 1949 Parliament Acts. This curtailed the Lords' ability to reject, and in some cases amend, legislation but little was done subsequently to change the nature or composition of the second chamber other than the introduction of life peers in 1958. Reform really got started with the removal of the hereditary peers in 1999. Only a small rump, elected from amongst their ranks, remained. A royal commission followed, many of whose recommendations were included in the government consultation document 'The House of Lords – Completing the Reform'. That consultation prompted widely divergent views which were subsequently reflected in the options outlined in the report of the joint committee set up to take the reform process forward in Parliament.

The constitutional reform programme has also reached into other, often neglected, parts of the body politic. The culture of secrecy in Whitehall has been challenged with the Freedom of Information Act 2000. Based on the principle of the public's 'right to know', the Act opens a window on the activities of government, the Civil Service and the unaccountable state. In addition campaign finance reform has been introduced, capping expenditure on elections and referendums and creating a new electoral commission. This will oversee modernised rules governing elections and the funding of political parties. The Human Rights Act 1998, incorporating into UK domestic law the European Convention on Human Rights, introduced a fundamental check through the courts on the actions of government and public authorities. Legislation must also be tested for compliance with basic human rights, representing a fundamental revision of what hitherto had been meant by the term 'parliamentary sovereignty'.

One parliamentary tradition that has remained intact is the 'first past the post' electoral system. Strong government is usually the result but at the expense of any proportional relationship between votes cast for a party and the number of its representatives elected. This has helped to preserve the two-party domination of our national politics. In turn it has also strengthened support at Westminster for its retention. Yet change has occurred, with electoral systems long rejected for Westminster being introduced for new as well as established democratic institutions. Multi-party systems have resulted in Scotland and Wales, in Greater London and Europe, using a variety of proportional electoral systems. They sponsor what it is claimed will become a more pluralistic and consensual political culture. Meanwhile change at Westminster remains stalled, apparently immune to the changes that are developing at every other level in the country. Will that eventually undermine the assumptions that currently support the retention of the 'first past the post' system at Westminster? The jury is still out on whether and for how long Parliament will continue to resist change.

One aspect of the constitution that has undergone a remarkable makeover is the role of referendums. Until recently they were seen as inconsistent with and unsuited to parliamentary democracy, in effect a subversive foreign import. Harold Wilson changed all that in 1975 with his referendum on continued

British membership of the European Community. He was primarily motivated by a need to solve a tricky dispute within his own party. Since then there have been two referendums in Scotland and two in Wales (1979 and 1997, both on the issue of devolution), one in Northern Ireland (1998 on the Belfast Agreement, part of the 'peace process'), one in London (1998 on the creation of a directly elected mayor and assembly) and one in the North-East of England (2004 on the creation of an elected regional asembly). In 1997 national referendums were promised on reform of the electoral system used for elections to the House of Commons and on Britain joining the single European currency – although neither of these have, as yet, been held. In 2004 Prime Minister Tony Blair announced that a referendum would be held on the issue of the proposed European Union constitution. It would appear that having opened this particular Pandora's box it could not be shut.

As the 21st century begins to unfold, what can we say with any certainty about the evolution of the constitution and the likelihood of further fundamental change?

After a long period of relative inactivity, an extensive reform programme encompassing devolution, freedom of information and human rights has been introduced. Yet in many ways our constitutional arrangements, especially as they affect Parliament, remain substantially unchanged. For many that will be a source of reassurance and pride. But if Parliament and our political system are to remain relevant both must adapt to the changing times. Whether that should come about through a continuation of the piecemeal procedures of the past or through a programme of constitutional innovation or even a deliberate break with precedent in the form of a formal, written, codified constitution and a Bill of Rights is still hotly contested. We may not know how it will end but there is a remarkable confidence that we will accommodate change whilst retaining continuity with the past and a consensus that it will turn out alright.

THREE (A)

Parliament and the Public:
A View from the Outside

Dr Richard Whitaker

A woman rang me from a hotel in Milan to say her husband had died ten minutes ago and asked what she should do next. I was paged in the chamber by a man who complained that the dustman had left his emptied bin in the middle of his drive. He had been forced to stop his car and move the bin to the side. I asked why he was ringing me. He said he had already rung 10 Downing Street and they told him to contact me. (Flynn 1997: 93–4)

Members of Parliament in Britain receive a wide range of enquiries from their constituents. MPs deal with such requests by holding 'surgeries', in which they make themselves available to see constituents at a local venue. They respond to constituents' letters, they aim to ensure coverage of their activities in the local press and they send out newsletters to inform constituents of their recent actions on behalf of the local area. The public view this type of work as one of the most important aspects of an MP's job. Nearly two-fifths of respondents to a 1996 poll valued the representation of constituency interests above a number of other activities (Table 1). Dealing with constituents' problems was considered most important by nearly one-fifth of respondents (Dunleavy et al. 2001: 82). These public expectations have been reflected in a rise in the amount of correspondence between constituents and their representatives during the postwar period. In recent years MPs have responded to this greater workload through use of the internet and e-mail although these new approaches remain only a part of the range of tools available to MPs for improving their links with the public.

Table 1: Public opinion of the duties of MPs (1996)

	Most important	Second most important
	(% of respondents agreeing)	
Supporting their party loyally in votes in Parliament	8	8
Representing constituency interests	39	27
Taking up individual constituents' problems	17	27
Ensuring government does its job efficiently and honestly	31	30
Voting and acting in line with their own judgement	4	7
Don't know	2	1

Source: Dunleavy et al. (2001, Table 26)

MPs and their constituents

How do MPs go about looking after their constituents? Initial contacts are often made through letters or surgeries held in constituencies. When an issue related to government policy is raised, MPs will frequently write to the relevant minister. Somewhere between 150,000 and 200,000 such letters are exchanged between ministers and MPs every year (Norton 2002: 28). MPs will usually pass the ministerial correspondence on to the relevant constituent. If this does not prove satisfactory, MPs may also arrange to meet with ministers to discuss problems emanating from the constituency. If all else fails, matters might be taken up on the floor of the House, although this strategy is used infrequently. For instance, adjournment debates allow MPs to raise issues of constituency or regional concern with the relevant minister for a 30-minute period. Members can also ask written and oral questions on constituency issues.

The volume of this work has increased rapidly over recent years. For instance, the amount of letters received at Westminster in the mid-1960s was around 10,000 per week. Thirty years later this number had grown to 40,000 per day (Ibid.: 24). MPs' individual postbags similarly expanded from between 25 and 74 letters per week in 1970 to a weekly total of around 190 by 1992, half of these being from constituents (Norris 1997: 30). In addition, MPs must deal with e-mails (see below), although a substantial proportion of these may be from correspondents outside the constituency (Jackson 2003).

Explanations for this rise in demand for MPs' services centre around two themes. First, it has been argued that among younger generations, a process of cognitive mobilisation has taken place during the postwar period. In simple terms this means that due to increased education and greater exposure to the media, citizens have become more aware of the opportunities to participate in the political process. Second, the scope of government has grown in the postwar period particularly through the development of the welfare state. As a result, citizens are more likely to have grievances regarding government actions, the subject of many a letter to the local MP (Norton 1993: 153).

Such increased pressure to engage in constituency work affects the type of representation adopted by parliamentarians. Traditionally the constituency role of MPs was viewed in terms of two categories. The 'trustee' would make decisions independently of their constituents but in the best interests of the constituency and the nation. The 'delegate', by contrast, would provide a voice for constituents at Westminster, faithfully echoing the views of voters back home when speaking in the chamber. However, with so much public demand for MPs' services, members are now unlikely to take on a purely trustee-type role, particularly on matters of local concern. Rather, in line with public demands, they frequently engage with constituents' grievances, taking the views of their constituents forward to ministers. On matters of national policy, MPs are more likely to vote with their political party than to take an independent attitude to each issue. But many members manage to steer a course between the two the modes of representation. For example, one Labour MP described his representational style as dependent on the issue. On a major question that is not constituency specific, such as war in Iraq, he will act as a trustee, taking the decision he feels is right. By contrast, on a matter primarily of constituency concern, such as the problems for the protection of birds brought about by a possible new airport, he becomes a delegate of his constituents and puts forward their views at Westminster. Opinion poll data suggest that the public favour the constituency delegate role above all others. Some 65 per cent of respondents to a 1996 poll agreed that MPs should be most loyal to the interests of their constituents. Only 11 per cent felt that MPs should be loyal to their own conscience, suggesting that there is little support for the 'trustee' approach to representation (Dunleavy et al. 2001: 81).

Given the huge increases in constituency work in recent years and the importance of party in MPs' decision-making, we have little reason to believe that MPs are adopting a trustee approach to their relations with constituents. Rather, parliamentarians choose to respond to issues raised locally by writing to ministers or, less frequently, by raising questions in Parliament or speaking in adjournment debates (Marsh 1985). On the issue of Parliament's relations with the public more broadly, the greater contact between constituents and their parliamentary representatives makes at least some contribution to maintaining the legitimacy of the political system in that constituents have the chance to see their problems taken to the highest ministerial level, even if this does not result in a change of policy. The potential for such contacts between citizens, MPs and ministers has increased further in recent years due to the growing popularity of e-mail and the internet. The following section considers the impact of these developments on Parliament's relations with the public.

MPs in cyberspace: Parliament's electronic links with the public

The internet is a potentially useful tool in furthering Parliament's links with voters. Websites allow members of Parliament to provide information to their constituents relatively cheaply and easily. For members of the public who have access to the internet, e-mail is a convenient method of contacting their representative, and the use of online surgeries allows constituents to air their grievances without having to leave their own home.

Table 2: What people want from their MPs

Internet service	Percentage of respondents in favour
Online surgery	39
E-mail address so that constituents can contact their MP	32
Consultation forum where MP can read constituents' views 22	
E-mail updates sent to constituents on matters of importance 15	
A web site containing MP's daily diary	10
None of the above	15

Source: Coleman (2003)

Survey data collected by the Hansard Society suggest that the public is in favour of greater internet provision from their MPs (see Table 2). Around 85 per cent of respondents wanted their MP to provide at least one of a list of internet-based services. Just under 40 per cent favoured an online surgery and about one-third wanted their MP to have an e-mail address. Among those who already have internet access, support for online surgeries was even higher, at 54 per cent. This demand is likely to increase over time, especially as the proportion of UK citizens with access to the internet continues to rise (Coleman 2003).

In turn, MPs are responding to higher demand for internet contact with constituents. The number of MPs with publicly available e-mail addresses rose from 412 in 2002 to 536 by August 2003. Nevertheless, politicians have not yet completely disappeared under mounds of e-mail printouts; only just over a tenth receive more than 100 e-mails per week. Over half the MPs responding to a survey said the majority of their messages were from outside their constituency (Jackson 2003). Here lies the biggest problem with internet usage, namely that it is not usually constituency specific.

One method of contacting constituents on matters of local interest is to send out newsletters via e-mail. This technique, currently used only by a small proportion of MPs, provides an efficient way of distributing information on constituency affairs and establishing dialogue with interested citizens. Table 3 provides examples of topics covered in a Labour MP's newsletters over two months. Nick Palmer e-mails around one thousand people each week, providing a mixture of views and information on local and national politics, anecdotes and discussion of broader political issues.

Table 3: Coverage of topics in Nick Palmer's weekly newsletters (August–September 2003)

Type of story	Proportion of all stories(%)	Examples
Local issues	52	Reduced unemployment in the constituency; local building developments
Anecdotes and other items	24	Driving too carefully; local discussion on fair trade
National issues	21	Asylum seekers; National Health Service
Broad issues	7	Social class; media

Source: Nick Palmer MP (http://www.broxtowelabour.org)

Not all MPs are equally enthusiastic about the benefits of increasing internet usage in constituent–MP relations. Some argue that Parliament's links with the public could be improved electronically by giving citizens more involvement in parliamentary decision-making. Select committees, for example, could allow the public to contribute to their discussions via the web. The internet might also be used to provide interaction between government and voters on proposed legislation, prior to its introduction in Parliament. Certainly steps have been taken in this direction with the online publication of Hansard and a wide range of government documents (Allen 2003). Others suggest that the internet must remain only part of the parliamentarian–constituent relationship and that MPs must continue to devote time to meeting constituents in person. As Sir George Young puts it, 'if you asked people "Would you rather meet your MP face-to-face for ten minutes over a cup of coffee; or have a chat with him on the web?", even enthusiastic internet users might prefer the former' (Young 2003). The internet serves a purpose as an efficient communication mechanism but, according to this argument, it should not be used at the expense of surgeries and phone calls.

Constituency work: a vote winner?

So far we have seen that MPs are engaged in increasing amounts of constituency work and are embracing new technology in their links with the public. But why do MPs dedicate so much of their time to these activities? In an electoral system where voters choose one candidate per constituency we might expect that constituency work is worth pursuing in an effort to increase vote share at the next election. Certainly, the maintenance of constituency links is often viewed as important in the United States, where a single representative is elected for each district. But in the UK, the electoral benefits gained from constituency activity are subject to debate.

A major motivator for MPs to provide a service to their constituents is simply a sense of duty (Searing 1985). Representing citizens' views in central government has always been a core component of MPs' work and is rooted in one of the original functions of Parliament, as a means of redressing griev-ances (Searing 1994: 122–3). For Searing, members view their parliamentary careers in terms of performing particular roles, for example, as advocates of certain policy areas or as attempting to obtain ministerial office. In line with this approach, some MPs see their role principally as a 'constituency member', concentrating on conducting casework and acting as a delegate of their constituents' views. The motivation for pursuing such a role lies partly in the satisfying nature of constituency work, as noted by one MP: 'Helping individuals is undeniably a terrifically rewarding part – I mean you've no idea what a boost it is on a Monday morning if you actually get a letter from someone saying because of you my life's all right again' (Norris 1997: 41).

Analysis of the 2001 general election results suggests, however, that some MPs were able to cultivate a personal vote. Indeed, Liberal Democrats appear to have been particularly successful as their vote share rose by an average of 6.3 per cent in those seats which the party acquired for the first time in 1997 and where the incumbent MP was standing as candidate. This suggests that such Liberal Democrat members elected in 1997 used their first four years in office to develop a personal vote by representing their constituents' interests at Westminster and defending their constituency where necessary. By contrast, where an incumbent Lib Dem was not defending the seat, the party's average vote share fell by 4.9 per cent. Similar effects can be seen in Labour seats and, to a much lesser degree, in seats secured by the Conservatives (Curtice and Steed 2002: 319). Evidence of a small personal vote can also be found in the 1997 election results among Labour incumbents defending seats they had won from the Conservatives in 1992 (Curtice and Steed 1997).

However, surveys of voters and candidates at the 1992 general election showed that most MPs believed this personal support to be fairly insignificant, on average amounting to little more than 100 votes in a constituency of 70,000. Furthermore, the vast majority of MPs in the study agreed that 'most people vote for the party not the individual candidate' (Norris 1997: 40). Voters' responses corresponded to this with only 1 per cent of those questioned referring to the candidate as either a positive or negative reason for their voting decision, while two-thirds mentioned party as a key determinant. Other factors, such as whether an MP held a frontbench position, the degree of urbanisation and the size of the ethnic minority population in a constituency, as well as an MP's gender, were all found to affect the amount of constituency work taken on (Norris 1997: 46). According to this evidence, then, MPs do not attach much importance to vote maximisation as a motive for constituency work. Nevertheless, they might be inspired to deal with constituents' problems in order to keep local party activists on side. Having a reputation as a 'good constituency MP' may help to ensure that members will be reselected by their local party leadership at the next election.

Conclusions

MPs have increased the amount of time they spend dealing with the public in recent years to the extent that there is more contact between MPs and their constituents through letters, surgeries and via the internet than ever before. While the debate continues as to how beneficial such activities are in terms of votes, surveys of public opinion strongly suggest that citizens want their MPs to act as delegates for their views and problems. Not only do the public want their representatives to support constituency interests above those of political parties, they also favour various additions to the electronic means of contacting MPs. Some members have responded to the challenges of e-politics by making themselves more available on the net while others see this primarily as a tool for deepening Parliament's scrutiny of the executive. In both of these areas the internet remains a key area for future development if the relationship between Parliament and the public is to be improved.

References

Allen, R. (2003) 'Are MPs bold enough to welcome online participation?' in *Democracy Online: What do we want from MPs' web sites?*, Hansard Society, e-democracy Programme report, accessed, July 2003.

Coleman, S. (2003), *Democracy Online: What do we want from MPs' web sites?*, Hansard Society, e-democracy Programme report, accessed July 2003.

Curtice, J. and Steed, M. 'Appendix 2: the Results Analysed', in D. Butler and D. Kavanagh (eds), *The British General Election of 1997* (Macmillan, Basingstoke, 1997).

Curtice, J. and Steed, M. 'Appendix 2: an Analysis of the Results', in D. Butler and D. Kavanagh (eds), *The British General Election of 2001* (Palgrave, Basingstoke, 2002).

Dunleavy, P., Margetts, H., Smith, T. and Weir, S. *Voices of the People: Popular Attitudes to Democratic Renewal in Britain* (Politico's, London, 2001).

Flynn, P. *Commons Knowledge: How to Be a Backbencher* (Seren, Bridgend, 1997).

Jackson, N. 'Vote Winner or Nuisance: Email and British MPs' Relationship with Their Constituents', paper presented at the Political Studies Association conference, University of Leicester, 15–17 April 2003.

Marsh, J. 'Representational Changes: the Constituency MP', in Norton, P. (ed.) *Parliament in the 1980s* (Blackwell, Oxford, 1985).

Norris, P. 'The Puzzle of Constituency Service', *Journal of Legislative Studies*, 1997, vol. 3, no. 2, pp. 29–49.

Norton, P. *Does Parliament Matter?* (Harvester Wheatsheaf, London, 1993).

Norton, P. 'The United Kingdom: Building the Link between Constituent and MP', in Norton, P. (ed.) *Parliaments and Citizens in Western Europe* (Frank Cass, London, 2002).

Searing, D. 'Comment on Cain, Ferejohn, and Fiorina', *American Political Science Review*, 1985, vol. 79, no. 4, pp. 1174–5.

Searing, D. *Westminster's World: Understanding Political Roles* (Harvard University Press, Cambridge, MA, 1994).

Young, G. (2003) 'E-politics is Part of a Total Package', in *Democracy Online: What do we want from MPs' web sites?*, Hansard Society, e-democracy Programme report, accessed July 2003.

Parliament and the Public: A View from the Inside

Sir Teddy Taylor MP

The basic principle of British democracy is that the people are in charge. It is the people who elect the member of Parliament in each constituency and send them to Westminster. They have the opportunity of speaking to all the candidates before the election takes place. But perhaps the greatest power which the people have is that if the elected MP fails to satisfy their constituents with their votes in Parliament, their attendance at debates or their local issues, the people have the opportunity at least every five years to throw out their MP and to elect another one.

However, the situation is not perhaps so simple as the basic democratic principle outlined above would lead one to believe. For a start, the vast majority of MPs are elected on a link with one or other of the major political parties. To become an official party candidate – a prospective MP – an individual has to be approved and accepted as a suitable candidate by a central party committee. After joining the list of officially approved candidates he or she must then be selected as a candidate by the local party. So the candidates being considered by the people, apart from independents or minority groups, have already been through a number of tests.

Of course there are exceptions, and the exceptions are becoming more frequent as dissatisfaction with the major parties is increasing. Indeed, perhaps one of the most worrying aspects of British democracy is that the percentage bothering to vote is declining quite sharply. For example, if we look at the performance of the major parties since 1979, we see that the numbers voting for the Conservative Party declined from 13.7 million to 8.35 million in 2001. The election of 2001 was a great Labour victory, but despite this the actual numbers of voters selecting Labour actually fell over the period from 11.5 million in 1979 to 10.7 million in 2001. The traditional minority party, the Liberal Democrats, actually increased their votes from 4.2 million in 1979 to 4.8 million in 2001. Nationalists increased their votes in both Scotland and Wales from 600,000 to 700,000. 'Others' had the biggest increase of all, from 1.1 million to 1.8 million. A good example of the new trend was the election of Dr Richard Taylor as the Independent MP for the Wyre Forest constituency, which was previously a Labour-held seat, with a majority of 6,946. His sole election theme was campaigning against the downgrading of local health facilities.

The biggest example of the decline in voter participation was in the European Parliament elections in 1999, where the number voting was less than 25 per cent. Although turnout in the European Parliament elections in 2004 went up to 38.2 per cent, the proportion voting either Labour or Conservative declined to only 49.3 per cent of the total. The surprise element in the result was the 16.1 per cent of the vote securing the election of a total of twelve MEPs for the United Kingdom Independence Party, a party which is wholly opposed to Britain's membership of the European Union.

While there are always some who argue that the 'switch-off' of voting interest is related to the individuals in charge of the parties and that it will 'sort itself out in due course', the most worrying aspect of the decline in voter participation is the sharp reduction in the participation of young people.

The decline in voter interest has coincided with a rather dramatic decline in the powers of the Westminster Parliament and the growing realisation that the European Parliament has little control over the new centre of power in Brussels. With the transfer of power to Brussels through the various treaties and conventions, there are many issues which voters care deeply about on which their elected representatives have no control or answerability. For example, the issue of capital punishment or corporal punishment cannot be determined by the British Parliament because of the European Convention and this particular restriction is being incorporated into European law in the proposed new European constitution. Cruelty involved in the export of live cattle is another issue where Parliament is effectively powerless. The situation facing the fishing industry is again a wholly European matter and the same applies to agriculture. The levying of VAT, which is a tax which discriminates against those on low incomes, is something which is a basic European obligation. If voters get angry about the vast sums spent on the subsidising of the growing of high-tar tobacco and its dumping in the Third World, they find that there is nothing their elected representatives can do about it. Perhaps the most ridiculous recent example was the heating allowance which the UK government pays to its pensioners to assist them with coping with the costs of cold winters: The European Commission instructed the UK government that this allowance must be paid to UK citizens residing in the overseas territories of the EU. This means that the British government has to spend about £10 million each year on paying heating allowances to residents in Guadeloupe, the Azores, Martinique and other areas where there is virtually non-stop sunshine, but not to British residents living in Iceland or Canada where snow and freezing temperatures are the winter lifestyle. We had a similar event over measures taken by the UK government to control the funding of political parties. The UK government and Parliament determined that it should henceforth be illegal for foreigners or foreign companies to pay money into the coffers of UK political parties. It was a clear and precise policy until the EU Commission instructed the UK government that the EU had to be exempt from the law. After this initial humiliation, the UK was then advised that the overseas territories of the EU also had to be exempt. This means that if a wealthy person in French Guiana wishes to send £100 to a British political party, there is no problem, but if a resident in the nearby British Guiana chooses to do the same the British party – were it to accept – would be breaking the law.

The basic task of the UK Parliament is to provide a vehicle for the passing of laws and the levying of taxes. It also provides a facility for MPs to question ministers on the effectiveness of their policies and on the need to review them.

The basic principle, unlike in other nations where the executive is separate from the legislature, is that every minister has to be a member of one or other of the two chambers of the legislature, the Commons and the Lords, where he or she is answerable for all the policies of their department. A minister has to introduce and speak for all the legislation his department promotes and he must submit himself not only to regular questioning in the full chamber but also to select committees of MPs or Lords who can initiate reports and enquires on policies or issues for which he or she has responsibility.

The advantage of the House of Lords compared with an elected second chamber is that the Lords do not seek to challenge or overthrow governments. Their powers are limited in that they only have the power to hold up legislation for a year, and their powers do not extend to the imposing of taxes. By and large they only stand firm if a new law is regarded as a threat to liberty or democracy. Used with care, the actual powers of the House of Lords can be greater than they might appear. One example of the Lords using their powers to achieve something were the battles in 2003 over the government's plans to introduce foundation hospitals and to abolish jury trials for complex financial fraud cases. The Lords clearly believed that jury trials were an important part of British tradition, so they continued to debate both Bills right until the end of the session and then, suddenly at the last moment, conceded entirely on the politically controversial issue of foundation hospitals in exchange for the indefinite postponement of the abolition of jury trials.

Bills go through Parliament to become laws in a rather complex procedure. When a Bill is first published it receives its first reading, which is basically its public announcement. This stage provides organisations and individuals with the opportunity of making their views on the proposed measures known to MPs and they can put forward ideas for amendments or fundamental changes. After some time the Bill comes before the House of Commons (if introduced first in the Commons; legislation can be introduced first in the House of Lords) for its second reading. To secure a second reading the Bill must be debated by MPs – usually for a full parliamentary day – and there is then a vote to determine whether it should proceed. If the Bill receives a second reading, it is then sent to a committee of MPs appointed in accordance with the percentage representation of the parties in the House and the committee meets in the mornings and afternoons to go through the Bill line by line and to discuss and vote on amendments. This task, which can take a few weeks, is then reported back to the House of Commons for the report stage. During this procedure, the amendments proposed by the committee are considered and other MPs who were not on the committee can propose amendments. After the report stage is finished, the House then considers the Bill for its third reading and MPs have to consider whether to approve it or not.

Provided a Bill receives its third reading it then goes to the House of Lords, which goes through the same lengthy procedure. If the Bill is approved by the House of Lords, but changes are made in its content, the Lords' amendments are then considered by the House of Commons. If there is substantial disagreement the Bill can go endlessly back and forward between the Lords and the Commons, but the normal procedure is for some compromise to be reached. If both Houses come to agreement, the Bill is then sent to Buckingham Palace, where the Queen signs it – giving it royal assent – and the Bill then becomes an Act of Parliament and becomes the law of the land.

Most legislation is initiated by the government of the day, but time is also made available for private members' Bills, Bills initiated by MPs who are not members of the government. The problem with such bills is securing sufficient parliamentary time, a commodity always in short supply. Having said this, however, it should be noted that many of the issues involving matters of principle or conscience have become law through the private members' Bill route. For example, the Bill to abolish capital punishment was promoted by a solitary MP.

Passing laws is only part of the work of Parliament. Days of debate are also allowed, including for the opposition parties to promote the issues on which they feel strongly. There is also time each day for questions to ministers, with each minister being on duty once a fortnight to answer questions. The exception is the Prime Minister, who answers questions once each week on a Wednesday for half an hour. MPs have to submit their questions in advance and, as there are always more questions than time in which to answer them, there is a ballot each day to determine who will have the right to raise questions in two or three days' time. Each question can have supplementary questions relating to the issue being raised and so there can be a mini debate with four or five MPs participating. To ask a supplementary MPs have to stand in their places after the basic question has been put and look to the Speaker, the chairman of the House, hoping to 'catch the Speaker's eye' – hoping that the Speaker will announce his or her name and allow the question to be asked. Apart from the normal hour-long question period there is an opportunity each day after question time to raise urgent and serious questions. To secure such a question an MP must put in an application to the Speaker's Office early in the morning and the Speaker will determine whether it should be asked. There is also time after questions for ministers to make statements giving details of new policies. One novel feature of the parliamentary day is that no matter when the sitting finishes, there is half an hour set aside for an adjournment debate. MPs can apply each week for an adjournment debate the following week. They can seek such a debate on any subject and a minister must attend to give the government's view on the issue.

One of the most significant changes in the structure of Parliament in recent years has been the reduction in working hours. Parliament used to meet from 2.30 p.m. through until 10.30 p.m., with committees meeting in the morning. Having said this, however, the 10.30 p.m. finish was only a guide and sittings frequently went on much later and often throughout the night. Nonetheless in recent years the hours have been changed dramatically. The

House now normally sits from 2.30 p.m. till 10.30 p.m. on a Monday only and on Tuesdays, Wednesday and Thursdays it sits from 11.30 a.m. till 7.00 p.m. and sometimes till only 6.00 p.m. on a Thursday. On Fridays the House meets in the morning and afternoon although there are quite a few Fridays when the house does not sit at all.[1] In addition the government is now making much more use of programme motions, which restrict the amount of time allowed for committees to consider the details of Bills. This has been rather controversial and has virtually ended the procedure which some MPs used to adopt of speaking for hours and hours simply to hold up a Bill in the hope that it would not be able to complete its full process by the end of the session. These long speeches – known as filibusters – have now become a rarity.

What is it that is special about the UK Parliament? What is the source of its strength? What underpins its power? The first special feature is that the executive comes from the membership of the House and is present in the chamber to answer for its policies. In other nations the executive is separated from the assembly and becomes distant from direct democratic control. Second, the system of election is based on – currently – 659 areas, known as constituencies, the voters in each electing one MP. The disadvantage of this arrangement is that the minority parties get small representation, but the principal advantage is that MPs are answerable to the people in the constituencies rather than to the political parties, who gain the real power in proportional representation arrangements. Third, the second chamber is a non-elected body with limited powers. The advantage of this process is that the power of government is not eroded, as can be the case if there are two elected chambers with different party alignments. Finally, the system is geared to government by party and, in this respect, essentially government by one of two parties, with each party facing each other in the chamber – rather than the circular form of other chambers – and a clear divide between government and opposition.

An essential feature of British parliamentary democracy which contributes to the ability and stability of government is the existence of party discipline and, as part of this, the party whips. On the government side the Chief Whip is a senior figure who attends meetings of the Cabinet. There are also a number of junior whips who have the task of seeking to control the activities of groups – divided by geographical region – of the parties' MPs. The power and responsibility of the whips was set out clearly in *Erskine May*, which states that the whips are:

> concerned with mapping out the time of the session; for applying in detail the Government's programme of business; for estimating the time likely to be required for each item, and for arranging the business of the individual sitting. It is also part of [the whips'] duties to advise the Government on Parliamentary business and procedure, and to maintain a close liaison with Ministers in regard to Parliamentary business which affects their departments. [The Chief Whip] and the Opposition Chief Whip constitute the 'usual channels' through which consultations are held ... about business arrangements.[2]

In addition to the management of the business, the whips also have the duty to seek to persuade MPs from their party to support the policies of their party in Parliament. Each week they send a notification – itself known as the whip – to each MP in their party stating how important each issue is. Some of the business has what is called a one-line whip, which means that MPs don't need to attend at all. Then there is the two-line whip, which means that the MPs are permitted to absent themselves only with the permission of the whips, who can arrange 'pairs' with absentees from other parties. Finally there is the three-line whip, which effectively means that attendance and support of the policy is vital. But do the MPs have to do what the whips instruct them to do, and what powers do the whips have to persuade, cajole and even threaten their MPs?

In a nutshell, the whips have the power of patronage, making recommendations about appointments to committees, visits abroad, and, if of the party in government, promotion within the ranks of government. MPs who ignore the advice of their whips often find that their progress in Parliament is very restricted. The final power which the whips have is to withdraw the whip, which means virtual expulsion from the parliamentary party. An MP in this position can then find that his or her constituency party is asked to replace him or her. I've been through this procedure myself, on a European issue, although happily my local party gave me full support and the parliamentary party had eventually to agree to reinstate not only myself but seven of my party colleagues, who had been expelled over the same issue at the same time. But it was quite an ordeal and it would be unwise to underestimate the power of whips.

The political parties in Britain are substantial organisations. There are local organisations for each party and in addition each party has a national headquarters. The parties hold national conferences and seek financial and other support from business, the trade unions, wealthy individuals and from among the public as a whole. Sometimes life can be easy for parties. For example when Margaret Thatcher was leading the Conservatives, and particularly after her election in 1979 as the first ever woman Prime Minister, she had astonishing support, the party's finances were strong and its membership enormous. However, when there is no clear crusade, the parties can have quite a problem making ends meet. There is no doubt that within all the parties these days national membership is declining. Indeed, the financial problems facing the political parties in Britain have become so serious in recent times that there is a growing debate about the possibility of them securing state funding. Because government parties find it easier to secure funding than opposition parties, steps have already been taken whereby the opposition parties get a form of state funding which assists with the provision of researchers and secretarial help. This is called 'Short money' because it was a minister (a Labour one) called Ted Short who initiated the idea. However, the voluntary side of the parties still provides a substantial part of their necessary spending.

Amongst the two main parties – Labour and Conservative – there have been significant changes in recent years. Both before and immediately after the Second World War, Labour tended to support state control of industry through nationalisation and very costly welfare and other spending. The Conservatives were mainly in favour of minimum state control and low taxation. However, the election of Tony Blair as leader of Labour resulted in the formation of New Labour, which rejects new state control of industry and which in many areas has become even more right wing than Margaret Thatcher. This of course has created a nightmare for the Conservatives, who have been endeavouring to find new crusades. The European Union is also an issue which has created wide division within the parties as the ever-increasing interference and control of the EU has developed.

However, the one thing which does stand out from the history of democracy in Britain is that it has coped well with change, that it has retained the principle of power for the people and that its democratic arrangements still retain the support of the vast majority of the population.

Endnote

1　Nonetheless, despite thse changes – perhaps becasue of them – the House of Commons has decided to revert to later hours following the next general election.

2　May, T. E. *Erskine May's treatise on the law, privileges, proceedings and usage of Parliament* (21st ed.), ed. C. Boulton (Butterworths, London, 1989), p. 202.

FOUR

Parliament and the Media

Peter Riddell

Parliament and the media have always been uneasy companions. MPs and peers have been suspicious of what is written, and more recently broadcast, about them. Yet, for around 180 of the past 200 years, their speeches and questions were at least reported. Parliament set the terms of the relationship. But, for the past 20 years, the tables have been turned. In an ironical reversal of the battles of the late eighteenth century by reporters to gain formal access to Parliament, now it is the MPs and peers who are battling to gain access to the media.

No newspaper any longer carries extensive gallery coverage, or factual reporting, of the exchanges on the floor of either House. Often nothing at all of what has happened at Westminster is reported on the pages of the mass-selling tabloids. The change was symbolised by the decision of *The Times* in 1990 to give up allocating a full page to debates in the Commons and Lords. Afterwards, Jack Straw, then an opposition spokesman, produced a study highlighting the decline in coverage. Between 1933 and 1988, coverage of the Commons and Lords had filled between 450 and 1,000 lines a day on average, and in the *Manchester Guardian* (renamed the *Guardian* in 1959) between 300 and 700 lines. But, by 1992, the average in both papers was below 100.[1] A similar study at the end of the decade for the Hansard Society by David McKie, a former political writer for the *Guardian*, showed how the proportion of parliamentary coverage in newspapers had declined. In 1946,

The Times devoted 4,148 lines to reports about speeches, questions and events in the Commons and Lords in a typical week. This was squeezed into 48 pages in total between Tuesday and Saturday. By the late 1980s, just before the demise of a dedicated parliamentary page, *The Times* carried 3,425 lines of parliamentary coverage in 160 pages over those five days. By 1996 there were just 290 lines of parliamentary reporting in 228 pages per week.[2] By 2004 it was even less.

The decline in reporting of Parliament has been much deplored by MPs and peers. Jack Straw complained in his 1993 study that 'the decline in press coverage of Parliament must have a serious effect on the public's understanding of our democratic system.' Sir Brian Mawhinney, when chairman of the Conservative Party, remarked in a lecture in February 1996 that

> *it is ironic to note that journalists operating without access to word processors or typewriters, without computerized printing presses, without anything more sophisticated than the most primitive from of hot metal, were a century ago able to provide the voting public of their time with a dramatically better account of events in Parliament than any voter can gain today. And since commentators are wont to lament, from time to time, that no modern politician has the public impact of Gladstone or Disraeli, may not a politician occasionally note that no speech delivered in parliament today would receive even a tenth of the coverage given to the Grand Old Man and his rival.[3]*

Yet to focus merely on the decline in the quantity of newspaper reporting of Parliament is to take too narrow a view. This decline is merely a symptom of much broader changes affecting both Parliament and politicians, and the media. Fifty years ago, the extensive coverage of debates in the Commons and Lords was because most political news emerged from Westminster, while broadcasters were severely constrained in what they could report. Ministers announced new initiatives on the floor of the Commons, not in broadcasting studios. Until the mid-1950s, there was a formal rule banning the discussion on radio and television of issues that were due to come before either chamber over the following fortnight. Moreover, no broadcast by an MP or peer might be used between the introduction of a Bill and the time when it either received the royal assent or was withdrawn, or dropped. This rule, a wartime invention, was strongly defended by the two main party leaders, Sir Winston Churchill and Clement Attlee, both products of the late Victorian and Edwardian eras. As significant as the specific issue was the attitude of both. Churchill talked about how it would be 'shocking to have debates in this House forestalled, time after time, by expressions of opinion by persons who had not the status or responsibility of MPs on this new robot organisation of television and BBC broadcasting'. More succinctly, as was his habit, Attlee said the authority of Parliament should be sustained as 'the main forum of discussion'.

Attempts by both MPs and the BBC to abandon the rule were rejected by the government, which issued a formal instruction to the broadcasters. That was linked to a generally more subservient social and working relationship between journalists and senior politicians, an overwhelmingly clublike atmosphere in which much was not repeated publicly or exposed. We had to wait for ministerial memoirs and the disclosure of official papers much later under the 30-year rule to learn about the degree of Cabinet dissension in the final Churchill administration or about the weakening of the Prime Minister's own powers, especially after his stroke in 1953. None of this could have been kept secret now and Churchill would have had to resign immediately.

The fourteen-day rule broke down under the twin impact of the political upheavals associated with the Suez crisis in the second half of 1956 and the end of the BBC's monopoly in the mid-1950s after the arrival of independent television. A more adventurous style of reporting and interviewing developed, along with a greater number of news and current affairs programmes. So over the following two decades, more political issues were discussed on radio and television first. Politicians were promoted who were seen as 'good on the box'. Their comments on the BBC *Today* programme in the morning or on what eventually became *Newsnight* in the evening were more likely to be talked about at Westminster than most speeches made on the floor of the chamber.

The shift of political debate from Westminster to the broadcasting studio was matched by a perceived move in power away from Parliament itself. The two developments were linked. Much of the discussion about the 'decline' in Parliament is oversimplified. But that does not mean it is entirely wrong. It is not just the power of the executive – Whitehall as opposed to Westminster. Alternative power bases have emerged, or strengthened. Some are constitutional – such as Britain's membership of the European Community (later Union); devolution to subsidiary (but, in practice, quasi-independent) parliaments since 1997; the increased use of referendums on tricky issues; and the greater role of the judiciary, via the growth of judicial review and the constraints of the Human Rights Act. Other changes have involved a shedding of power by ministers to arm's-length bodies: notably the Bank of England being made responsible for setting interest rates after 1997, or, earlier, the growth of regulators overseeing the newly privatised utilities in the 1980s. In all cases bar Britain's membership of the EU (with the resulting acceptance of the primacy of European laws), formal sovereignty has remained with Westminster. Parliament could repeal the Scotland Act of 1998 and abolish devolution, just as the Greater London Council was removed by Act of Parliament in the mid-1980s. But merely to write that sentence shows how inconceivable such an action would be, unless it was demanded by the Scottish people and approved in a referendum. Moreover, ministers remain accountable to the Commons for all the many regulators and quangos, though, in practice, the Chancellor of the Exchequer also refuses to comment on interest rate decisions, saying that is a matter for the Monetary Policy Committee of the Bank of England.

Westminster has appeared – often to an exaggerated extent – to be at the margin of events. The decline in formal reporting of debates has been both a response and a cause. Ministers and shadow spokesmen have preferred to make announcements outside the chamber, knowing that they will get more coverage either directly via a newspaper article or a broadcast interview. This, in turn, has further shifted the political debate away from Westminster to the broadcasting studios. One of the many paradoxes of the arrival of the cameras in the House of Commons in 1989 is that the creation of a new centre for television and radio studios at 4 Millbank to handle broadcast coverage has led to an increase in the number of ministers, spokespeople and MPs being interviewed there, rather than a big rise in reports from the floor of the chamber. There are exceptions, of course: Budget day or the big Iraq debates of February and March 2003, which were extensively reported in several newspapers and broadcast live on terrestrial channels.

At the same time, the media – both newspapers and, increasingly, television – have been subject to increasing competitive pressures. How far this has led to 'dumbing down' is open to dispute. Many news reports, columns and features are as high quality, if not higher quality, than in the past. Rather, space is at a premium and gallery reports of debates from Parliament are neither cheap nor widely read. Simon Jenkins as editor of *The Times* ended the paper's dedicated parliamentary page in 1990 and later justified his decision in typically dismissive terms: 'I stopped it because I couldn't find anyone who read it apart from MPs. We are not there to provide a public service for a particular profession.' And much of the contents of the old parliamentary pages was dull and badly written. On many days, parliamentary journalists looked for material to fill the space. Sir Max Hastings, editor of the *Daily Telegraph* at this period, argued that the televising of Parliament was the main reason why newspapers no longer needed to cover what was said in the chamber. Both points are as much excuses as explanations. Commercial pressures were as important. At the turn of the millennium, before and after the 2001 general election, the *Independent*, the *Daily Telegraph* and *The Times* temporarily revived partial gallery coverage, in a deliberate attempt to provide a public service. But these initiatives soon petered out as gallery stories got squeezed in length or pushed out altogether by more 'newsworthy' or 'sexier' political stories. News executives had little time for high-minded coverage in face of competitive pressures and a squeeze on space, especially as advertising fell in late 2001 and 2002 and the papers shrank in size.

It is wrong to view the media's relationship with Parliament purely in terms of the quantity of coverage in reporting debates. The nature of political journalism began changing along with the decline in gallery coverage. The traditional distinction between straight gallery stories and background lobby reports disappeared during the 1980s. The sharp contraction in gallery coverage since the late 1980s has been partly offset by an expansion of other political coverage. (These changes are well discussed in Andrew Sparrow's thorough, entertaining and balanced history of parliamentary journalism, *Obscure Scribblers*.4) Often, what is said in the chamber is only part of a broader political story, also including remarks in a television or radio interview, a lobby (that is, unattributable) briefing or conversation with a minister, civil servant or special adviser, all linked in a more interpretative manner. The non-gallery parts of the story are often as important as, if not more important than, what is said in the chamber. Indeed, in the world of the 24-hour news cycle, a Commons statement or speech is often only part of a developing story, instead of the main one. Ministers will have appeared on the *Today* programme, and possibly also have given evidence to a Commons select committee.

Tony Blair's twice-yearly appearances before the Liaison Committee, consisting of chairmen of select committees, are as important a parliamentary occasion as his rare speeches opening full-scale debates. The questioning over two and a half hours has so far seldom put him under pressure but his answers have often been more revealing than the ritualised exchanges during Prime Minister's Questions every Wednesday. So these sessions are not only televised on cable news channels but are often fully reported.

In that sense, the mix of gallery and non-gallery reporting can offer readers a much fuller picture of what is going on in politics. Readers now know more about the discussions inside government and behind the scenes in Parliament than 40 or 50 years ago, when coverage was mainly from the press gallery. Assiduous political journalists, often working closely with specialist correspondents, provide fuller reporting and analysis of developing issues than in the past. The debates over the euro within the Blair Cabinet, and between Tony Blair and Gordon Brown, have been more fully and accurately reported than, say, the discussions over exchange rate policy in the 1950s. Moreover, the moves towards greater attribution of stories – developing in stages since the late 1980s – have been linked with a greater opening up of the whole system. Politics is generally less secretive and more transparent.

These positive developments have to be heavily qualified. Despite an expansion of non-gallery stories, the space devoted to overall political coverage in most papers, particularly the mass market tabloids, has been under severe pressure. The search is on to attract new, younger readers, who are believed to be uninterested in conventional Westminster-based political stories and party politics. Hence there is an emphasis on scandal and misconduct, on personality stories rather than analysis and procedure. This is linked with a soundbite culture and the carefully crafted 'spin' or presentation of all policies and announcements by politicians. Infinitely more column inches and broadcast minutes (or days) have been devoted to allegations about spin than to the substance of Bills being considered by Parliament. Coverage increasingly focuses on a few leaders and colourful personalities. Ordinary backbenchers and small parties are largely ignored. Previous taboos on probing the private life of politicians have been forgotten. Nothing is out of bounds to the tabloids – spouses, children and past indiscretions.

Consequently, as I argued in my book *Parliament under Blair*, 'the coverage in most papers lacks depth and context, as well as being squeezed in size. Personality differences are exaggerated. Every dispute becomes a split. Every small shift in position becomes a humiliating climb-down. Stories about policy developments, the activities of backbench groups, the work of think tanks … are given a low priority. There is little consistency or follow-up. Readers may be told about a story for a few days when it is big news in conventional terms – of a row, scandal or possible ministerial resignation – but they are seldom told what happens then.'[5]

As worrying is the increasing blurring of the distinction between news and comment. Many British newspapers have always taken a strongly partisan approach. But these allegiances have increasingly influenced the news coverage, even at the top end of the market in what used to be known as the broadsheets. Hence, in several Eurosceptic newspapers, reporters have been encouraged to find anti-Brussels stories and the pro-European viewpoint has been largely ignored. The same was true in the run-up to the Iraq war as both strongly pro and anti papers slanted their news. The controversy surrounding the publication of the Hutton report in January 2004 highlighted the partisan nature of much reporting, not only in newspapers but also in parts of the BBC.

These faults have undermined both the quantity and quality of coverage of Parliament. In many papers, the main place that Parliament features is in the daily sketches by 'colour' writers such as Matthew Parris in *The Times* during the 1990s, Frank Johnson in the *Daily Telegraph* and Simon Hoggart in the *Guardian* on various occasions over the past 25 to 30 years. Their vivid and rightly praised writing often captures the mood in Parliament, but, by definition, does not attempt to report on what is said in a broad or balanced way. In many ways, the rise and prominence of 'star' sketch writers contributes to the personality-driven view of the Commons.

More broadly, the media are often accused of feeding a mood of cynicism about politicians and Parliament. Of course, generalisation is misleading. But the previous deference has gone. Many political journalists have been educated as well as, if not better than, ministers and MPs, and they mix as social equals. There is no longer any sense of deference. Even a casual glance at a range of newspapers over a week would reinforce the impression that 'all politicians are liars' and that 'MPs are out for themselves' – either personally on the fiddle or using taxpayers' money to go on wasteful trips by committees or all-party groups. So a lack of interest in the affairs of Parliament is reinforced by a generally negative coverage of politicians. Because the solid, worthy work that goes on in both chambers is largely ignored, the public knows only about the rows and the scandals. However, repeated polls have shown a distinction between a generally hostile view of politicians as a class and Parliament as an institution, and a much more positive view of their constituency MPs. The big increase in constituency casework undertaken by MPs has affected the attitudes of the public, if not necessarily their votes.

But the picture is not one sided. MPs and Parliament as an institution have contributed to this shift in the balance. Ambitious MPs and party media managers have deliberately bypassed the Commons chamber and gone straight to newspapers and broadcasters to get over their viewpoints. This has prompted complaints from Speakers of the Commons about statements being trailed on the *Today* programme or in the morning newspapers before they are announced to the Commons. Moreover, many of the procedures of the Commons are obscure, and often unintelligible to outsiders. It takes some time for any newcomer to Westminster to learn how the place operates. There is still at times a sense of the pre-mass franchise attitude of fear mixed with contempt for the public 'out of doors', as the Victorians put it. Many older MPs, of all parties, quite like to maintain a distance and do not like the media to pry into their affairs.

Moreover, the format of proceedings is increasingly out of line with how people outside conduct their lives and their businesses. We no longer live in an era where millions of people spend an hour on a Sunday listening to a sermon or attend public meetings where a politician makes a lengthy speech. Hence a six-hour debate in which MPs stand up and address each other is an alien, unfamiliar means of communicating for many voters. Add to that the raucous yah-boo politics of Prime Minister's Questions, still the most watched part of the Commons, and it is not hard to understand why many, especially younger, voters feel alienated from Westminster politics. They are suspicious of confrontational party politics.

There is a lot that Parliament could do, beyond deploring media attitudes. However, the use of the word 'modernisation' by the Blair government since 1997 to cover the debate about changing the procedures and practices of the

Commons grates and has alienated many MPs, both Tories and older Labour members. Talk of 'family-friendly hours' and the like has annoyed many MPs with families hundreds of miles from London. But the attempt to remove some of the mystery is correct. Members of the Lords often talk and behave as if they were in a private club, and a pretty complacent one at that. Members of the Commons are usually more subtle, but, in both Houses, there is a deeply ingrained conservatism towards outsiders. Of course, several changes have been introduced, more than is commonly appreciated. Leaving aside substantial changes in the work of select committees and in the scrutiny of legislation, several of the more noticeable public aspects of Parliament have altered. The format of oral questions is now more intelligible, the order paper has been simplified and, during recess periods, members of the public can visit where their representatives work.

But more needs to be done. Various proposals have been examined by the Modernisation Committee to break down the barriers between the public and Parliament. Westminster could do worse than look at the innovations introduced by the devolved bodies. Both the Scottish Parliament and the Welsh Assembly are much more voter friendly, not just in the formal sense of physical access but also in encouraging direct communication between voters and representatives.

The public can gain direct access to the proceedings at Westminster though the Parliament Channel, now run by the BBC. This provides gavel-to-gavel coverage of the Commons to cable subscribers. When the Commons is not sitting, the channel shows select committee hearings and Lords debates. About a dozen committees are televised each week. In addition, both Houses have a webcasting service which offers people an alternative to traditional broadcasting.

The key is the internet. This effectively bypasses the conventional mass media of broadcasters and newspapers. In many respects, it matters much less that newspapers have abandoned their gallery coverage of the Commons and Lords when the full Hansard reports are available on the Parliament website the following morning. The annual report of the House of Commons

Commission noted that 'demand for Hansard on paper continues to decline, although there has been increasing demand for the publication online.' In 2002/3, there were 14.6 million hits on the Parliament website, 'demonstrating the extent to which, for many members of the public, the website is the preferred medium for accessing information about the House'.[6] The proceedings of standing committees are also on the website, along with reports of select committees at the time of publication. In addition, uncorrected records of oral evidence sessions with Cabinet ministers are usually put on the website within a day or two of the committee hearing. Other evidence appears after a short delay, though the Lords has been much slower in making the evidence of its committees easily accessible online.

The Parliament website was redesigned in July 2002 to become easier to use for the non-specialist. The home page provides direct links to the order paper, Hansard, current Bills, select committees, early day motions and the Register of Members' Interests. Yet still more could be done to make the website more accessible. The news section could be expanded to become a continually updated noticeboard for forthcoming statements and announcements by government departments. For instance, if a spokesman for 10 Downing Street trails an announcement at the 11 a.m. meeting with journalists, the news could simultaneously be put on the Parliament website. This would overcome some of the resentment of MPs at journalists learning about government initiatives first.

But the internet can also be used much more actively as a two-way means of communication. Thanks to the work of the Hansard Society and Professor Stephen Coleman, online consultations have been held by a number of select committees and by the Joint Committee of both Houses on the draft Communications Bill as part of its prelegislative scrutiny. This practice could be extended if there was more scrutiny of draft Bills and as part of the routine work of select committees. In addition, the Scottish Parliament allows voters directly to petition on matters of concern via the internet. At Westminster, petitions are largely ignored after being presented by a member of the

Commons. But in Edinburgh, the Petitions Committee sifts through them and holds hearings on those judged to be of importance. This procedure has produced changes in both administrative practice and in legislation.

Parliament's relations with the media are too often seen in negative terms. But if you look more closely, there are several positive aspects. After analysing the decline in gallery coverage, David McKie concluded his report for the Hansard Society on a more optimistic note because of the internet.

> *There is no point in lecturing newspaper editors on their dereliction of public duty in abandoning Westminster coverage, those days are not going to come back; they don't even need to. If people are eager to know what the Commons and Lords are saying and doing, they'll have all the access they need. Whether Parliament can succeed in commanding the people's attention then is, of course, a quite different matter.*[7]

Endnotes

1   Straw, J. 'Democracy on the Spike', *British Journalism Review*, 1993, vol. 4, no. 4.

2   McKie, D. *Media Coverage of Parliament* (Hansard Society, London, 1999).

3 '   Government, Politics and the Media', lecture at Manchester Business School, 28 February 1996.

4   Sparrow, A. *Obscure Scribblers: a History of Parliamentary Journalism* (Politico's, London, 2003).

5   Riddell, P. *Parliament under Blair* (Politico's, London, 2000), p. 173.

6   *Twenty-fifth Annual Report of the House of Commons Commission*, HC 806.

7   McKie, *Media Coverage of Parliament*.

The Parliamentary and Constituency Roles of an MP: The Backbencher's Lament

Austin Mitchell MP

Backbenchers are in theory the power elite in a British constitution built on the supremacy of Parliament which they constitute, but in practice they are the workhorses of the system. In theory Parliament can do anything. In practice its power is controlled by the executive in a system in which government is by and through party backbenchers, who are the infantry, obeying their leaders and tramping through the lobbies to support or oppose the executive. The representatives of the people have been harnessed to the chariot of party.

Backbench life is more interesting in opposition because it's the life of guerrillas and sharpshooters as compared to the discipline of a government army, in which backbenchers are the foot soldiers so duty and square-bashing drive out fun. They are nevertheless essential, for no government can continue without the votes of its backbenchers. No legislation passes without their consent and no money is granted. Instead of using these powers to influence the executive or exercise a degree of control over it, they are controlled by it and mostly in its power. Government can count on the votes of its majority but in practice they are relegated to doing the dirty work and heavy lifting of the constitution. The system works because they have surrendered their power.

To keep these truths from constituents who might be less likely to vote for dogsbodies, they give the impression that they go down to London to do a spot of governing the country before coming back to the constituency to tackle the problems that really matter. To describe their role many revert to Bagehot's picture of men of independent judgement, articulating the views of constituents, and holding governments to account. When Bagehot wrote that in the 1860s the picture was almost true. Yet government only listens if it fears being thrown out. In Bagehot's day governments fell as a result of votes in the House but the development of mass political parties since then has transformed parliamentary government into government by party, and MPs from senators to servants. The executive, the leadership of the majority party, controls Parliament. MPs are spectators of the great game of power, not participants on the field of play.

These bit part players of the constitution don't, however, have just one defined task with a clear job description. MP is several mini roles rolled together and paid at a rate of £57,485 a year. None of the roles are obligatory and MPs tackle as many or as few as they want, for the title is a status, a place on a platform with a ticket requiring renewal every four or five years. In that period what they do, how many of their tasks they tackle, what use they make of the platform, is largely up to them.

The most basic role is the original one. They began as knights of the shire or burgesses of the boroughs selected by the county or borough court and they still have a civic role as the embodiment of a constituency, marching behind the mayor, sheriff or Lord Lieutenant at civic ceremonies, remembrance days and religious occasions. Councils, chambers of commerce, voluntary organisations, hobby and sports clubs, schools and local societies look to their MP as focus, representative at Westminster and local figurehead.

Originally the job as local representative was to convey the grievances, pleas and petitions of constituents to the King and give consent to the money and legislation he asked. Its essence remains the same today, though we do not necessarily come from the constituencies and we represent parties as well as places. The views we relay are more numerous and complicated, embracing the needs and complaints of constituents, of companies, of local bodies, and the area's needs in terms of aid, grants, help, facilities and government action. All this is transmitted not only via Parliament but directly to government ministers and departments, not to mention all the ad hoc bodies, authorities, agencies and quangos, as well as via the media. In an age of competition for jobs, companies and development aid the MP has to be a local booster and propagandist too.

All this takes MPs into media hype, development promotion, even the pork barrel, though usually in reverse as MPs fight to save or protect facilities in their constituencies. At cliffhanger time the power can be used positively. When in 2004 New Labour got itself into a panic about the vote on university tuition fees I traded my vote for the payment of £2 million of medical expenses incurred by a failed asylum seeker and an enhancement of the status of Grimsby College. This prompted a letter to *The Times* complaining that a vote on war could be held up until government agreed to a public lavatory for Grimsby.

Transmission is a two-way process. Just as the first MPs relayed the King's views back, so we now relay Westminster's views and news, the policies and plans of the executive and the party, acting as the representative of Much Twittering in London and Whitehall in Much Twittering.

'All politics are local,' said US House Speaker Sam Rayburn. So is the work of MPs. Government covers many areas so that MPs have become local ombudspersons, someone with whom constituents can raise their problems with the machine, its departments and business. This brings in a tide of problems on social security benefits, tax, health services or the simple inefficiencies of agencies dealing with driving licences, prisons, passports and immigration, including asylum. Asylum seekers have no votes but are dispersed round the country and have problems which the legal profession is loath to tackle without fees. So they, too, turn to MPs.

This work has grown exponentially.[1] Today's backbenchers are in their constituencies more, more likely to live there, and more exposed to campaigns from pressure groups who have learned the American trick of mobilising mail from constituents. Overwhelmed by the scale of all this, government has tried to exclude MPs from some areas by removing discretion, toughening up rights, privatising and creating agencies to be dealt with directly rather than through ministers (though some, like Gerald Kaufman, still insist on going down that track). Yet at the same time government has created its own messes through computer failures and badly prepared strategies, producing tax credit chaos, the passport mess, social security and computerisation problems and, biggest work producer of all, the Child Support Agency. All these produce ever more complaints to MPs, who then have to be given special hotlines for an access Joe and Jill Public can't get.

This 'ombudsman' role extends even to local government. Enoch Powell sensibly refused to deal with matters such as council housing and any sensible MP stays out of planning matters unless on a 'not in my backyard' basis. Yet most do pursue what are strictly council matters, such as housing, rubbish collection, rate demands, education access and council services, as well as being brought into the constant arguments between central and local government about finance, priorities, privatisation of council services and the vast consultancy industry councils must employ to tell them their jobs.

The role is valuable as a check on the system. If the machine isn't working well, MPs get the fall-out of complaints and problems. Their status entitles them to go up the hierarchy to managers and ministerial level where decisions are reviewed, a process which produces change in a minority, although perhaps up to a fifth, of cases as well as explanations which satisfy others because they feel that they have at least been heard.

Most tackle all of this out of a sense of duty, though some undoubtedly feel that it brings a reward in terms of votes received. There is, however, little evidence for this. In the USA the incumbency effect brings both votes and money. Here it brings only exposure, showing constituents that the MP is still alive, and a word-of-mouth reputation. Yet the only real effect comes at the end of a newcomer's first parliament, when being better known helps and brings in some votes. That appears to be the end of the affair, even for those who sit on forever, aiming to be not just the Father of the House but its grandparent. Helping doesn't win votes, partly because the people helped are the inadequate, who often don't vote anyway. There is no evidence of a positive result but, equally, no evaluation of any negative consequences befalling MPs who don't go in for local service. Do they lose votes?

MPs represent a party as well as a place. They are elected because of their party label, not their own charms, fame or endearing personality, and they lose their seats through no fault of their own but simply because their party fails. They have little control over their own destinies, not even Liberals and nationalists, who have to work harder, particularly at pavement politics, but still benefit (or lose) primarily because of their party's standing as a vehicle for protest. Only the independents owe it all to themselves, helped usually by very rare circumstances. Party is the key to victory and beyond that to office and promotion. It is the ladder which the ambitious climb and the organising principle of parliamentary life. Backbenchers are party people, the foot soldiers of the party army. However independently minded (and that's becoming a good thing to be), they believe at bottom that however little their potential has been recognised, their party still deserves power more than any other. Dissent is growing because parties are looser and more divided with more cross-cutting issues, such as war and peace, Europe, fox-hunting, animal rights and economics. Yet however great and noisy the angry gestures and however much they are exaggerated by a media hungry for sensation, rebellions have never, since May 1940, been taken so far as to bring down the government.

Labour's 1974–9 government survived first with the barest of majorities and then as a minority before finally being defeated – by only one vote – in a vote of no confidence in March 1979. Similarly, the bitter divisions among the Tories after 1992, although creating an image of disunity which damaged it electorally, did not bring the government down. Cliffhangers should have ended with New Labour's huge majority, among whom loyalty was almost a cult religion copiously scripted with briefings, hymn sheets and 'bullet points' prepared by a large new resource centre. Old Labour MPs were not as enthusiastic and when first public sector and benefit reforms and then Iraq began to divide the party, revolts developed, bigger because a large majority made them safer. It demands real incompetence for a government with a majority of 164 to get its majority down to cliffhangers of five and fifteen. Labour has managed this, but has nonetheless never been in real danger of being brought down.

The parties which dominate the lives of backbenchers are decaying at the roots but paradoxically getting more powerful in Parliament. Class conditioning has faded, the parties are blander. Membership shrinks. MPs are forced to take on responsibility for keeping local parties alive and supporting them through office facilities and allowances and by taking on the work that agents and members used to do. Yet the system is also becoming more presidential and career politics are now the pattern so parties become more important as the president's pedestal and members are forced to attend by constant three-line whips – something which was once rare.

In Parliament MPs compete for publicity and promotion. They demonstrate their abilities, even their sycophancy, and try to attract attention in a competitive game. They compete, too, to serve the party, to campaign and to draw attention to themselves outside the House, though too many appearances on TV, even in their underpants, provoke jealousy. The rules of ascent have changed. Dissent and rebellion, once the path to the top for such giants as Churchill, Bevan, Strachey and Macmillan, is now a dead-end street, even the road out. Aspirants for promotion must now ingratiate and offer themselves as ideological blank slates on which the leadership can write whatever messages it currently has: anti-EU in the 1970s, vacuously pro in the 1990s, bemused in the new century.

All backbenchers are potential trainees for office because they constitute the limited pool of talent from which ministers must be drawn. The opportunities for getting on are increasing as the number of junior ministers and parliamentary private secretaries grows. These are the training grounds, designed, like parade drill in the army, to break independent spirit in preparation for comparatively unimportant jobs whose holders are bound to vote the Cabinet line without having any say in deciding it. The PPS job is to be a minister's messenger boy or girl or, in public school parlance, a 'fag', though that might not be politically correct today. It involves doling out 'spontaneous' questions and biased briefings, relaying reports from the troops and fixing meetings. None of this is important. The appointees are trusty dullards striving for promotion and told that their job is the first step on the ladder. For most that is as far as they get, so a prolonged constriction can become irritating.

The number of junior ministers has grown to bring the 'payroll vote' up to 130 in a party of 406. They, too, are on probation but allow the government to appear to bring in younger ministers and more women when it is really relegating them to a dogsbody role of doing the department's dirty work. They get a ministerial car (of inferior type) but can do little, being managed by the civil servants who answer their letters, tell them what to say and ensure they never step out of line. This is called probation but it has more in common with protective custody.

Junior ministers are a protective cushion round senior ministers, designed to fob off interest groups and backbenchers and routinely defend the indefensible. Women are particularly useful at this because they can't be hit as hard. So Dawn Primarolo defends VAT, private finance initiatives and the failures of the tax–benefit system, Melanie Johnson does likewise for DTI and Health enormities, and Beverley Hughes less successfully for immigration and asylum chaos. Lack of perceived intelligence and a dogged ability to stick to a brief are major assets.

Whips, enforcers of policies they don't understand and haven't influenced, are a third probationary grade. The office was once a dumping ground. Now more people are shuttled through to be dropped later rather than promoted. Questioning minds like Graham Allen go no further. Dullards dominate. So the range of recruitment is minimal because thuggery isn't a transferable skill.

These intermediate jobs have a mediating role between leadership and the rank and file but in presidential politics their task is heavily loaded to the leadership. Prospects of a rise to real power are illusory for the great majority of ladder climbers. With power confined to a coterie at the top, not a lot trickles down to Cabinet and nothing to junior ministers, who have office without responsibility, ministerial cars but no real role.

Nevertheless most backbenchers want jobs. Few hesitate to accept when one is offered, a powerful inducement to loyalty even though so many have been through the mill only to be ignominiously thrown out after being used for a couple of years. No one, except Chris Mullin, has stood down voluntarily – and even he later went back. Rejection is a learning process. The experience of being sent back to the back benches has contributed to the rising tide of discontent as the rejects discover a sudden squeamishness about causes they promoted as trustees.

MPs are legislators, a job which takes nearly half of Parliament's time but is their least satisfactory role. Government MPs are not good law drafters, critics or amenders, all minor roles which can be left to the Lords. They are brute votes pushing legislation through and allowing the government to alter it as it goes along. Standing committee debates are not a useful testing process. Government backbenchers serve by sitting and staring. They're discouraged from speaking. Opposition MPs amplify any criticisms they can dredge up, though the old art of the filibuster is now less useful because most Bills are programmed. With government in tight control committees have become tame affairs. Dissenters or government members with expertise or doubts are no longer appointed, so the kind of splits which allowed the modification of the Financial Services Act and the television legislation of the 1980s don't now occur. As for report stage, the last chance for backbenchers not appointed to the committee to change the Bill, it is a rushed and confusing affair, compounded by the grouping of amendments so that only the devoted can follow it and few amendments are successful – apart, that is, from the final dribble of government afterthoughts.

In 1979 MPs were given a new weapon in the specialist select committees, each covering the work of one or more departments. They are far more satisfying because they educate MPs, give them an edge of specialisation and expert advice and plug them into the specialised opinion which governments do listen to. All are valuable new strengths but the power of the American committees on which they were based eludes them. Because government has a built-in majority ours can't influence policy, change legislation or hold dramatic inquiries. Congressmen are more powerful and independent but our all-powerful executive won't tolerate thorns in its own flesh. So the select committees were emasculated by the efforts of the whips and ministers to manage and control membership and decisions.

Gradually more work has been loaded onto the select committees to the point that they are now unable to keep up with departmental reports, budgets, Euro-regulations, prelegislative scrutiny, policy changes and all the other issues heaped on them. Yet if they don't and can't reject government policy they can question it, examine the intellectual basis on which it rests, hear the arguments and publish the evidence. All these are useful devices through which both public and backbench education can be achieved. Intellectual review was particularly valuable when Thatcherite policies were formulated on an instinctive basis, and where New Labour is lumbering into a constitutional mish-mash by failing to think through and coordinate its approach to the new politics. Ideological policies, such as monetarism and council house privatisation in the 1980s or, more recently, the private finance initiatives, have been severely criticised and the processes both informs and educates MPs. The committee inquiries have, however, become poor persons' royal commissions. Royal commissions bring together the great and the good to reach consensus conclusions. Select committees are more assertive, more populist and less well-researched attempts to follow fashion. Yet they are still useful because they highlight an issue, feed a media debate and put government on the spot – as such topical reports as those on gangmasters, obesity or the honours system all have done. Consequently, they can give considerable satisfaction to the MPs who take part.

In the so-called 'Golden Age' of the House of Commons MPs were supposed to 'warn the executive up with what the people would not put'. Up to the1970s such warnings from the country gentlemen in the Tory Party or the trade union loyalists in Labour were always treated seriously. It was their reaction to the 'In Place of Strife' proposals that changed the Wilson government's policy on industrial relations. Yet gradually the stolid ballast tanks have emptied. 'We're all careerists now' with few content to take a back seat as repositories of party wisdom. Nor do MPs still have a real role in relaying lay opinions or the views of constituents. Through polls and focus groups ministers are in better touch with the nation and those reactions that matter electorally than are MPs. They still make mistakes, such as the poll tax or Iraq, but only where ideology takes them off carefully triangulated courses.

The generalist has been driven out by the specialist and instincts by research. MPs come in younger, usually without having pursued a real career outside politics. So the numbers with employment expertise – as farmers, teachers, councillors, doctors, academics, manual workers – are less, even though backbenchers are better educated, better able to get access to specialised knowledge and expertise and fast, if superficial, learners. Which makes the select committees an appropriate tool for the new generation, allowing them to specialise in a limited number of areas. Particularly those which affect constituencies.

This is parliamentary adult education, a process strengthened by the proliferating all-party groups and the increasing trend for pressure groups to work and enlist support through Parliament. Most departments have a cluster of pressure groups round them. Others agitate outside the charmed circle of influence to win public support. Some work a three-ring circus seeking influence, with government, in Parliament, and with the wider elec-torate. So many pressure and interest groups now seek to educate or influence MPs by providing information and propaganda, by backing and support for the proliferating all-party groups, by providing evidence and expertise to select committees, and by pressuring MPs through their constituents. MPs are the gatekeepers of all these processes. They have the power to help and participate with questions, early day motions, adjournment debates, or by writing or taking delegations to ministers. They can even become players as paid consultants to industries, causes and groups. The path was pioneered by Brian Walden, who took a retainer of £5,000 from a bookmaker ('best paid bookie's runner in the country', Dennis Skinner called him). Since then many others have wandered profitably down the same path and though interests and consultancies must now be declared in the Register of Interests, backbenchers who don't reach office can find both a useful role, even a financial bonus, via this opening.

MPs have almost automatic access to their local newspapers and radio stations, particularly BBC local radio, which has a greater sense of public service responsibility. They use this partly to inform, mainly to show constituents that their MP is alive and well though living (apparently against his or her will) in Westminster. They also put across their and the party's arguments and policies. Here they are now excessively well briefed, which can leave them all saying the same thing or contradicting earlier claims when policy changes, as it did on the referendum on the European Constitution.

Some would be better advised never to appear on TV, though all want to, for backbenchers have a love–hate relationship with television: love it when they're on, hate it when they're not. Which is most of the time. With appearances on national programmes based on expertise and standing most backbenchers are excluded and appearances on local magazine or political programmes are much fewer because ratings come from celebrities, reality shows, cooking, gardening and house renovation programmes, not politics, which is, in contrast, seen as the kiss of death, to be administered only through such duty programmes as *Question Time* or *Newsnight*. These are dominated by ministers and shadow ministers. TV opportunities for the average backbencher are now few and far between. Except on satellite channels, which don't pay and no one watches.

When I was first elected an old mining MP told me not to bother replying to letters: 'If it's important they'll write again.' An office in the constituency was equally unnecessary: 'They know where I live and if they want me they'll come round to the back door.' That is no longer true. The government machine is less generous, administrative glitches more common. Constituents are better educated. Tasting power as consumers they seek it as citizens and want to be heard. The MP is the only part of the huge impersonal machinery of government who can provide the ears they need. Couple this with an expanding workload through more legislation, more complex issues, more media, and it's clear that MPs can't do it all unaided. They need staff, secretarial and with social worker skills and an interest in political issues, perhaps even a political career. Members still abuse the privilege by employing wives or relatives or, more justifiably, by taking on people from home, such as students, local activists, relatives of council officers or party members – as even American senators and congressmen do with their far larger staffs – but the growth in the volume of work ensures that those who don't employ the best and the most staff perform less adequately.

MPs are on a treadmill that is running faster against them as the work, the travel and the parliamentary duties all increase. Those who try to fulfil all the roles in their portfolio must fail because it can't be done. Driven by duty rather than hope of reward most will do as much as they can, neglecting some roles to concentrate on others. A few won't bother much with any. The only audit is their own conscience, the only driver their own sense of duty. It is possible in a safe seat to do next to nothing and survive, unless a much-imposed-on local party is driven to deselect. The days when his Sheffield party wrote to George Darling to say that in view of his appointment to the important job of PPS they would free him from his obligation to visit them monthly are gone, though those of easy deselection have gone too. As long as an MP keeps the local party mildly gruntled tenure is secure.

There is no 'audit of performance' by which anyone can know how well or badly an MP is doing the job or how lazy or dynamic the member is. The lobby correspondents, national and local, may know who's up to the job, who's not, who's competent, who's failing, who drinks too much and who works too little, but lobby conventions prohibit them from publishing. Few local newspapers want to endanger their relationships by reporting derelictions and failures. Constituents can't tell. Indeed a majority don't even know their MP's name. So how can they judge his or her achievement or the lack of it? Most don't see them and few have information or standards of comparison, unless they are physically assaulted by the MP or see their member lying drunk in the road.

Party members know more but don't want to rock the boat. Deselections – rare now – are usually for ideological reasons rather than performance, such as the Tory purge of 1956–7 when MPs opposed to the Suez invasion were deselected spectacularly or quietly dropped, or during Labour's nervous breakdown of 1979–83 when left-wing parties deselected a dozen right-wing (and usually lazy) MPs, and 20 more left the party rather than face a challenge. Conservative Euro-enthusiasts have also faced difficulties. Yet MPs always exaggerate the threat and the numbers actually deselected have been small. Particularly compared to the numbers of those who should be, on grounds of indolence, insanity or incompetence.

In theory whips are the puppet masters, keeping careful eyes on the abilities, work habits, even sex lives of MPs to assess them for promotion and to report on them to the leadership. Their real power is far less than they pretend. Prospects of promotion are dangled as an incentive to good behaviour, not because whips decide it. Over the majority who won't end up in office, even as PPS, they have neither influence nor control. Rebels may not get overseas trips or membership of interesting committees. They may not even get home early on a Thursday. Yet these are not powerful disincentives and no use at all in the face of a mass revolt. Indeed, some see the disapproval of the leadership as something of a campaign medal: 'For Awkwardness'. Whips report to constituency parties before reselection on the number of times members have voted against the government, but with many local parties alienated from party policy MPs can see this as an incentive not a deterrence. When government creates its cliffhangers the whips can only cajole and con. In March 2003 they used reports that Tony Blair would resign over Iraq if a majority of Labour MPs voted against war. Perhaps a dozen Labour MPs were persuaded to change their minds and a score of others to abstain. It was just enough.

Backbenchers are the pool of talent from which ministers are chosen but the range of choice is not wide and may even be narrowing. People with specially needed skills, lawyers or economists or Blair favourites, can be parachuted in, but the best and the brightest, such as Oxbridge firsts, are no longer attracted to politics. Those who do come, such as David Miliband, Ed Balls or Peter Mandelson, all have their path smoothed. Once in, all must compete, though not with equal chances, to catch the eyes of leaders and whips, to highlight their abilities, and to get on the promotion ladder. Some never make the first rung, most reach no higher than the marshy middle ranks, where many are called but few are chosen. For the majority promotion is largely a matter of luck and timing.

The professionalisation of politics has widened the gulf between the elite, the people of destiny or 'ministrables' who are rocket assisted to office or parachuted to seats, and the rest, the parliamentary also-rans, destined never to reach ministerial ranks. There are perhaps 50 top 'players' on the government side, above the protective shield of junior ministers and PPSs, 150 or so in the buffer zone to fob off backbenchers. Below them are the rest, the also-rans, the pioneer corps of the party.

Is that job worth doing? Much is now routine, bogged down in social work or minutiae which competent staff or caseworkers can, and do, take care of, usually more competently. The public platform is exciting for those who've known nothing like it before. Yet it stands in a political ghetto. Serving a community is satisfying and fulfilling. But can also be frustrating. Essentially the job is a minor one which must be done if the people are to have the channel of communication and representation they want and need, but what comes through it is confusing, conflicting and difficult to do anything about.

Because the workload has been increasing as respect for politicians and parties has declined, a strong sense of duty is needed to shoulder burdens which are bigger but more mundane. Most backbenchers have it. Some do the job only as a necessary purgatory for what they really want: power and influence, to be a player in the game, not a backbench spectator. Though not all can get into the game most want to, and feel they have the magic boots in their bag. If only they'd been allowed to play. Sadly several of those who are allowed find the boots don't fit. A quarter of those who go through the ministerial mill come out the other side resigned or damaged. Several of them then use the backbenches as a base to stir up trouble and take revenge or sit there dissatisfied and unhappy, seeking a way out.

The backbench job is worth doing, and even those who don't particularly enjoy it eventually resign themselves to carrying on. The life's comfortable and, more important, there is no alternative. Diminishing numbers do another job as well. A few step down. Some, like George Morton or Tim Smith, are forced out by scandal, others, like George Galloway, are dumped by the party, while some dump it. A few Scottish MPs, such as John Maxton and John Hume Robertson, opted for the smaller but more interesting Scottish and Welsh stages; others, such as Bryan Gould, Matthew Parris or Terry Davies, go on to more profitable or interesting fields. Yet most of those who leave are thrown out. They then find that ex-MPs are not easily saleable. Plum jobs such as a High Commission in Australia or a commission in the EU are few. Parliamentary skills are marketable only in lobbying.

So there is a built-in tendency to linger on listlessly. It should be made easier to move in and out by making it more financially rewarding to step down and better pension arrangements go a little way towards this. Yet until a scheme with generous golden goodbyes for early exit is developed we will not know how satisfying the job of backbencher really is. My guess would be that most would still go on. So we can only take those who stay, proclaiming their satisfaction and delight in service, at their own word.

74

The job could, and should, be made more interesting and satisfying by reform of Parliament. The attempt to do this has been the preoccupation of the last 40 years. Originally aimed at restoring the power and authority of Parliament, improving the lot of MPs was an essential part of reform. It has made great strides, yet, paradoxically, the more it has been reformed the more the influence of Parliament and backbenchers has shrunk. This sad 40-year failure is explained by changes in both the nature of the political system and in MPs.

The key reform, however, is one which would break the dominance of party and end the elective dictatorship. Only reform of the electoral system through the introduction of a system of proportional representation for elections to the House of Commons can open up the Commons, force parties to deal with each other, give backbenchers a greater influence and role, force government to listen to Parliament and require it to build cross-party agreements. All this has resulted from PR in New Zealand. It would do so here if government would accept it and if MPs didn't think that the system which elected them must be the best in the world. In opposing it backbenches are damaging themselves because making Parliament more genuinely representative would make it more powerful and influential and give it a more satisfactory role by ending the easy ride our winner-takes-all electoral system gives to the presidential dictatorship. It would make the job of the executive and ministers far harder. Anything which does that helps backbenchers.

'All political careers end in failure,' said Enoch Powell. The backbenchers' starts there as well, though only on the assumption that office and power are the only jobs worth having so that those who attain neither have failed. Many in that situation do in fact feel that intermittently or full time but many don't and the job of backbencher will still be worth doing without going any further. It is neither mute nor inglorious, though certainly less heard than ministers. It will still provide a – shrinking – platform, a ringside seat and a useful social and political role. Yet the job will still be done by the dull and dutiful, not the first-class brains, the trainee statesmen or those with a major contribution to make in the great game of power. The colourful, the best and the brightest, the ambition driven, will be attracted into the media, if they have not been already, not to the dull and deep political role of Parliamentary Hack.

Endnote

1   Phillip Williams estimated in his biography of the Labour leader Hugh Gaitskell that he received around 50 letters a month from his Leeds constituency. Today the average MP would get that in less than a week, to say nothing of holding frequent surgeries and receiving visitors to their offices in the constituency – offices which most MPs now have.

The Parliamentary and Constituency Roles of an MP: An Opposition View

Ann Widdecombe MP

The role of a member of Parliament is, like all Gaul, divided into three parts. He must represent his constituents at Westminster, hold the executive to account and help to pass coherent law. Each of these functions has changed massively over the course of the last century and indeed in the seventeen years in which I have served in Parliament.

Probably the biggest change has been in the first part of the role – constituency work. Long-serving members often recall days when the postbag was some 30 letters a week and could be dealt with by hand in the library after lunch. Indeed, when I first arrived I had no desk for two weeks, nor did the authorities think it reasonable for me to need one. I shared an office with three other MPs and many of my colleagues shared secretaries.

Today the caseload is such that each member has a sufficient allowance to employ two full-time secretaries and is equipped with three computers, a laptop and his own office. The greater confidence of the public in writing to MPs, the huge growth of pressure groups and the 'issue'-dominated media have seen to that.

It is difficult now to isolate the role of MP. Not only are we increasingly social workers and mediators but we also perform the tasks which properly belong to other elected individuals. We, in addition to – or more often instead of – local councillors, write to the heads of local authority housing departments, social services and borough treasurers to reinforce the complaints of our constituents about their places on the housing list, the absence of meals on wheels or incorrect council tax calculations. If I were to refuse to deal with any complaint which should properly be dealt with by someone else, my postbag would halve – and I would be perceived as idle by those who elect me to represent them at Westminster.

Any complaint which relates directly to a government department or the workings of the law is sent to a minister or, if it is about policy, both to a minister and to a shadow minister. Sometimes the complaint is passed on in the hope that it might influence the development of opposition policy, sometimes to find out what the policy is or, indeed, is not. Sometimes it is passed on as an illustration of whatever the opposition is denouncing or proposing. When I was shadow Secretary of State for Health my colleagues regularly passed me letters from people who had waited years for an operation or spent days on trolleys. It was more convincing than any statistic.

When letters to ministers draw an unsatisfactory response it is the role of the MP to step up the pressure. He may table a question or raise the matter in debate or initiate his own debate. In opposition there may well be a political as well as constituency angle to such activity with debates designed as much to draw attention to government policy failures or incompetence as to individual cases. Most MPs will have at any given time half a dozen cases which might be suitable subjects for debate but will be able only to choose one.

The easiest way of raising cases in debate is by applying for an adjournment debate, a half-hour business at the end of the parliamentary day, usually attended only by the minister and the member raising the debate. Unfortunately such debates are allocated by lottery and it can take weeks to obtain one, so it is an uncertain instrument in any event and unacceptably risky where there might be any urgency.

Otherwise the member can simply apply to speak during a debate on a particular Bill or topic, using his constituent's circumstances to illustrate his argument. In his own adjournment debate he will have fifteen minutes to present his case, or more if he is prepared to limit the time for the ministerial reply, but in a main debate he is likely to be limited to ten minutes.

One of the main purposes of any such debate is publicity for the cause being espoused. Raising an adjournment debate and issuing a press release will raise interest locally but no national reporter is likely to stay around to listen, whereas speaking in a main debate might just spawn a wider interest.

Constituency interests of course go beyond individual complaint: the closure of a hospital, the construction of a railway line, the reduction of a regiment, a proposal to build a large number of extra houses will all generate enormous local feeling and create pressure for the MP to make a difference, preferably by bringing about a policy reversal but at the very least by limiting its damage. Indeed the only Independent MP to be elected in the 2001 general election was a doctor who led a local campaign to keep open a hospital.

In government the MP will exert huge private as well as public pressure on ministers. In theory all MPs have access to ministers but in practice it is vastly easier if your own party is in power. Ministers will want to help backbench colleagues if they can and the opportunities for meeting are informal as well as formal, including the lobbies, the tearoom and dining rooms, where MPs take refreshment in strictly segregated areas.

In opposition, access to ministers is more limited and more formal but there is a different type of opportunity, not available to government backbenchers, whose ministers' policies are often set in tablets of stone and cannot be reversed without major complications: an opposition MP can seek from his party a pledge to reverse whatever is in question. Sometimes, especially where his is not the only constituency affected and there is a national dimension, he may be successful. Even if he is not he will usually be given the comfort of a promise to look again at the matter in government or if reversal is impractical there may be some sugar to sweeten the pill – such as delay or compensation or fresh consultation.

An opposition MP generally has more opportunity to represent his constituents in public, because government backbenchers do not like embarrassing ministers, but in private an MP from the governing party probably gets more attention because ministers do not like embarrassing their backbenchers.

An opposition MP probably also has more time to be among his constituents although this does not necessarily hold true if the governing party has a vast majority and can release its MPs by rote or if the opposition is particularly effective at harrying the government and requires its army at full strength on a regular basis.

Holding the executive to account is, constitutionally, the duty of all MPs but, in practice, it will fall largely to the lot of Her Majesty's Loyal Opposition. In recent years various measures have reduced the effectiveness of this function even though there were already serious constraints.

One such obvious constraint is the composition of select committees, which, by tradition and convention, have a built-in government majority in proportion to its majority in the House of Commons. Where that majority is large government backbenchers swamp the committees, ensuring that, for example, opposition policy is unlikely to be reflected in their reports, that criticism is accompanied by damage limitation and that philosophically the view of the committee will always be nearer to government thinking than to any other strand of thought.

That is not to say that committees never produce damning reports – some have been sensational – but there is a built-in sympathy with government which can cramp the style of others on the committee. Most committee chairmen will strive hard for unanimous reports and opposition MPs can often effect change by threatening a minority report but no select committee, dominated by the governing party, is going to embarrass the Prime Minister directly.

Another limitation to the effectiveness of select committees is the introduction of prelegislative scrutiny, which at the same time both expands the role of a select committee and limits it. Where a government department has a large legislative programme the committee can become so bogged down in examination of proposed Bills that it is restricted in the development of its own programme of work and finds its agenda driven by government priorities rather than its own.

Balanced select committees devising their own agendas would be vastly more powerful watchdogs over the executive. Yet they are not and never were designed to be policy forums and were originally intended to monitor the effectiveness of individual departments rather than to second-guess the decisions of the House. They have somewhat strayed from that role over the years and might be sharper if they returned to it.

One of the few weapons available to the opposition used to be delay. Delay would not kill a Bill but it was a useful counter to have on the board in any bargaining process. Opposition parties used it and individual MPs also availed themselves of it. The routine guillotining (euphemistically now called 'timetabling') of every stage of every Government Bill has removed that weapon pretty well completely, but it has also done something vastly more serious, as you and I are now governed by increasing tranches of law which have never even been debated by Parliament, let alone voted upon.

It is the duty of opposition to scrutinise legislation, to understand its effects, to disseminate that understanding and amend it to produce coherent law. The committee stage of a Bill used to be the place where most of the serious work was done and where, even though the government has a majority, changes could be wrought by reasoned and diligent argument. A Bill made progress through committee by means of agreement with the whips, with the opposition indicating where they wanted lengthy examination and where they were happy to progress clauses rapidly. A guillotine at committee stage was a rarely used device and was only imposed if there was a genuine filibuster taking place.

Now it is not unknown, where a Bill is divided into several parts, for an entire part to escape scrutiny. It was in response to just such a phenomenon that the author of this chapter staged a 'sit-in' during one committee. The Police and Criminal Justice Bill was on its last sitting in the committee stage with no examination having been given to the Police half of the Bill so I, along with senior opposition whips, occupied seats reserved for members of the committee in order to prevent the session from ending so that the committee would have to reconvene the following day, thereby allowing a further sitting. The government's response was simply to table a motion 'deeming' that the committee had completed its examination and reported back to the House!

Guillotines are routine also at report stage as well as at the principal stages and there is no room for manoeuvre even if an extra hour or so could make the difference between a clause being examined or passed without scrutiny. It is not a reassuring picture of a legislature at work.

The routine use of guillotines was presented to Parliament as the price of shorter hours. In other words less time in the House equals less scrutiny, which in turn equals the executive being held less to account. The hours themselves have truncated debate and made the role of the backbencher a more frustrating one. It is worth digressing a little to examine their effects.

It is difficult to see who, other than London MPs whose constituencies are just a few miles from the House, has benefited from the change. Members whose seats are in the Home Counties were formerly able to be in their constituencies in the mornings and still be in the House for the start of the day's business at 2.30 p.m. Under the current arrangements, with the House commencing business at 11.30, this is no longer possible, but equally MPs cannot use the evenings instead because voting does not begin until 7.00 and by the time this is completed it is too late to get to a station, catch a train and still be in time for a function.

Those with further-flung seats are not affected either way but it is difficult to see the merits of a system which disadvantages some members without any compensating advantage to others. Nor is there any benefit to families as most do not live in London. It is geography, not hours, which prevents parliamentary life from being family friendly.

Meanwhile committees sit at exactly the same time as ministers are answering questions in the House, thus presenting many a backbencher with a choice between holding government to account in the chamber or upstairs in committee.

A little-appreciated effect of the change is the impact on *esprit de corps* and the diminution of camaraderie amongst members of the same party. Members now go home on Wednesday night, with Thursdays and Fridays sparsely attended, and, released at 7.30 or thereabouts, leave the House on Tuesdays halfway through the evening. In the days of long hours and late-night sittings and even when those sittings ended at 10.30, MPs socialised with each other in the bars, restaurants and tea room. They met all members of their party, getting to know each other, exchanging views, hatching schemes.

Another culprit is the supply of live feed television to all offices. It is now no longer necessary for an MP to be in the chamber to hear a speech. He may simply put down his pen, look up and watch it on television. When I first entered Parliament the chamber would still fill up when a speaker of note was performing or when a highly controversial amendment was being put forward. Now MPs rarely attend unless they are participating in the action. It is a situation which may suit government but it does not contribute much to the role of holding that government to account.

The difference between a government minister and an opposition spokesman is that the minister gets up in the morning wondering 'what am I going to do today?' and the opposition spokesman wonders 'what am I going to say today?'. Yet for the backbencher the opportunity to contribute to policy is probably greater in opposition than in government.

Ministers are limited by existing baggage, by crisis management, by manifesto commitments. Oppositions can go back to the drawing board, can initiate consultations, can amend or drop proposals, float ideas and generally be imaginative. If government trails an idea there is an immediate expectation that the idea will be turned into law: the Civil Service cranks up its machinery to deliver and pressure groups are galvanised into action both for and against whatever is being floated. If the idea is then dropped there are cries of 'U-turn'. In opposition, however, debates can be freer and in the early years at least they can be more daring. No one seriously expects such ideas to become law in the near future and there is therefore a more relaxed approach to the examination of their merits.

Opposition spokesmen, looking for policies and lacking a Civil Service, will turn to a wide range of thinking including that of its own backbenchers. Ideas, especially where backed up with experience, will be hugely welcome. Thus a backbencher, who may never reach the ranks of minister, may nevertheless have a genuine influence on future law.

Meanwhile he can have an influence on current law through the private members' system, which allows the introduction of 20 Bills each year, determined by lottery. In reality only the top seven will attract a second reading but a Bill lower down which is uncontroversial may pass through its stages formally into law. No controversial Bill, whether in first or twentieth place, can pass into law through this system, for in it Bills are not guillotined and they can therefore be talked out or indeed, in the case of Bills other than the first seven, can be killed with a single cry of 'object!'.

A member with a Bill in the first seven has a choice: he can choose something wholly uncontroversial and which has government blessing and stand a real chance of getting a Bill on the Statute Book or he can decide to introduce something highly controversial which will not become law but which will make a point and force an issue into public consciousness. The Alton Abortion Bill and the Foster Hunting Bill are good examples of the latter approach.

Occasionally government may give extra time to allow a Bill to proceed or it may commit to dealing with the matter in its own legislation. The Leo Abse Bill to make homosexuality legal is an example of the first, the Foster Hunting Bill an example of the second. Sometimes there will be such an undertaking from government from the outset but sometimes a Bill generates such strong feeling that government is obliged to intervene where it had not intended to tread at all. The Alton/Widdecombe Abortion Bills of the late 1980s resulted in the then government tagging abortion votes onto its own Human Fertilisation and Embryology Bill.

The only other option which exists for backbenchers to legislate is the ten-minute rule Bill. Its advantage is that it relies on queue not lottery but its overwhelming disadvantage is that it can make no progress if opposed as it goes to the back of the line of private members' Bills. A small number of ten-minute rule Bills do become law but their principal virtue is that they are moved in prime parliamentary time after questions and before the main debates, thus allowing the issue a prominent airing.

An active backbencher will use all the above devices: questions, debates, adjournment debates, private members' Bills and ten-minute rule Bills, but these days he is more likely to win attention for his cause if he airs it in the press and media.

There has been a sea change in the importance attached to parliamentary proceedings in both press and media reportage over the last 30 years. There is now little interest in debate and especially in backbench contributions, the exception possibly being Radio 4's *Today in Parliament*. There is, however, plenty of appetite for drama and if a backbencher can produce a good story it will attract attention. The current government has not been slow to recognise that a judiciously timed press announcement will guarantee headlines whereas a statement to Parliament will give too much opportunity to the opposition to influence those headlines.

Inevitably the decline in reporting of debates has led to complaints from opposition that its policies and pronouncements attract too little attention and this is almost certainly justified as the press now plays censor – deciding what it will or will not report, from what angle it will report, how selectively it will report and against what agenda of its own. Indeed one wonders how accurate the verb 'report' is when applied to modern press coverage.

Television is even more superficial with discussion of major topics dismissed in seven or eight minutes and considered poor viewing unless delivered in confrontational format. Yet the scope for pushing an MP's or an opposition's own agenda is considerable if managed properly. It needs only a victim willing to be named, suitably dire circumstances and an unpopular government to turn any issue into a story.

It is popular wisdom that backbenchers use their local media and ministers and spokesmen the national media but such an approach has cost many an opposition spokesman an ideal opportunity. An interview on the *Today* programme may be considered prestigious and if the issue takes off then it can set the day's news but if an opposition spokesman instead does twelve local radio interviews back-to-back he (a) reaches many more people, (b) reaches people who never hear the *Today* programme and whose primary interest is not politics and (c) gets a better chance to explain his policy or point because the interview style is likely to be less aggressive. Intelligent use of the media as well as of parliamentary opportunities is therefore crucial to the effective functioning of an MP.

There is an overlap between the role of backbencher and frontbencher in opposition which does not exist in government. Opposition frontbenchers may raise adjournment debates, participate in general debates other than their own, put down questions and take up private members' Bills. Junior spokesmen are not restricted to their own briefs provided they do not stray from the party line. In government the line between executive and backbencher is strictly drawn and may not be crossed.

The flexibility in opposition is especially important where the governing party has a large majority and there are sufficiently few members on the benches opposite to make multitasking essential. In such a case competent MPs will often find themselves promoted into the ranks of spokesmen at an earlier stage than usual and the overlap between the roles means they can learn both at once.

Members of Parliament have threefold loyalties – to their constituents, to their parties and to their consciences and beliefs. Accordingly rebellion against a party line can sometimes be both necessary and desirable. In government a serious rebellion can augur defeat and the collapse of a Bill's essential purpose. In opposition a rebellion can mean the loss of opportunity to defeat the government of the day and is therefore almost equally unwelcome. A competent opposition is always vigilant for opportunities to exploit conscientious dissent in the government ranks for its own advantage.

Party games have destroyed parliamentary opportunities as much as they have created them. Earlier last century questions to the Prime Minister were put down by members who had some genuine constituency or other concern. Then it became obvious that here was wonderful scope for embarrassing the Prime Minister rather than just divining his intentions. So opposition MPs began flooding the order paper with questions and government backbenchers began competing for the same space with the sole objective of stopping them. The result is the weekly circus we now call Prime Minister's Questions, in which questions are allocated by lottery and genuine ones get squeezed out altogether.

A similar game was played with ten-minute rule Bills. When I first entered Parliament they were the property of backbenchers rather than the party machines. If you wanted such a Bill you queued in the small room opposite the clerk's office and presented him with your Bill at 10.00 a.m. on Mondays and Tuesdays. All you had to do was be first in the queue, which meant turning up very early in the morning. Then the whips thought what a good idea it would be if their own backbenchers won the ten-minute rule slots and introduced proposed Bills which would embarrass the government.

At once rotas were organised and the other side retaliated. The result was that for a Tuesday Bill you had to start queuing on a Sunday night. In charge of the rota, I spent many a Sunday night sleeping in the little room as I kept a place for the Conservative member who would take up the Bill at 10.00 a.m. on Tuesday. It was a madness that could not continue and eventually the two big parties agreed to divide the Bills out evenly between them, which was unfair to the smaller parties and to an MP wanting to move a Bill on his own initiative.

Once the parties have altered the character of parliamentary proceedings the change is irrevocable. Prime Minister's Questions will not revert to its old character, nor will other ministers' question times and nor will ten-minute rule Bills. The role of an MP may be a constant but the way he discharges it is at the mercy of the party machines.

The trends for the current century are not hard to predict: the chamber will continue to decline in importance, MPs will grow remoter from their colleagues, perhaps even voting electronically, and the parties will continue to bend all parliamentary devices and opportunities to their own advantage.

There is another trend which may have very considerable significance not for the functions but for the quality of our MPs and that is what President Clinton described as the politics of personal destruction. It is now a mark of success to bring about a resignation, to 'get a head'. The press play the same game not merely with politicians themselves but with their families too. The indiscretions of sons and daughters are splashed across our newspapers merely because their parents are politicians. It is impossible to imagine a young man drunk in Leicester Square attracting two lines in a local paper but if he happens to be the Prime Minister's son his petty lapse from grace will be the subject of banner headlines in all the national press.

The effect must be to give pause for thought to serious achievers who want to round off their careers by 'giving something back'. Once Parliament and the public service it represents would have been a natural choice but the culture of contempt and the destruction of family members are now real obstacles to such a choice. Over time it can only mean we will have fewer MPs with a record of success in the outside world and more career politicians who go from university to their party headquarters as researchers and thence to Parliament.

Perhaps the role itself will also diminish in quality and importance with the increasing part played by European institutions, the tendency of the judiciary to overrule government and the prospect on the horizon of an elected or partially elected House of Lords and still further devolution. Those of us who were politicians in the twentieth century have probably been privileged to witness Parliament at the height of its power and influence.

FIVE (C)

The Parliamentary and Constituency Roles of an MP: A View from the Third Party

Alan Beith MP

The House of Commons entered the 21st century still looking like a two-party chamber, with its facing blocks of seats and its weekly staged confrontation between the Prime Minister and the statutorily recognised and salaried leader of the opposition. For 30 years after 1945 the party system itself seemed to be resolving itself into a duopoly. Procedure in the Commons reinforced this assumption and to a large extent continued to be based on it.

With a longer perspective, the reality is different. For most of the last two centuries, the Commons was a three-party chamber. The Irish party maintained a substantial presence from the mid-nineteenth century until the 1918 general election, when Sinn Fein replaced them but boycotted the Westminster Parliament. The rise of the Labour Party as a force separate from the Liberals ensured that there was still a three-party system. Although the Liberals then divided, they showed enough signs of recovery with their Yellow Book programme to ensure that three-party politics continued for a little longer. The wartime coalition returned Liberals to an involvement in government, and the wartime electoral truce preserved their limited parliamentary strength until it was almost eclipsed in the 1945 and subsequent elections. After an initial Liberal revival under Jo Grimond the two-party hegemony reasserted itself in 1970, but after a series of by-election gains the 'third party' maintained a viable and increasing parliamentary force, rising from thirteen seats in 1974 to 54 in 2004. At the same time, other parties became established on the parliamentary map, as Ulster Unionists ceased to be allied to the Conservatives and subdivided, and Scottish and Welsh nationalists established a parliamentary presence. The point was reached when there were ten parties represented in the House by at least two members.

The first-past-the-post system has, of course, tended to bolster and perpetuate the two-party system, (except in pre-1922 Ireland and post-1922 Northern Ireland). The reference to third and other parties as 'minority parties' tended to conceal the fact that no party enjoyed majority support. The February 1974 election left no party with a parliamentary majority even under the first-past-the-post system; as the Liberal leader of the time, Jeremy Thorpe, accurately observed, 'we are all minorities now.'

Despite the long Commons experience of three-party politics, a newly arrived third-party MP taking his seat at any time in the last half of the twentieth century was confronted by procedures which seemed so exclusive that they invited a 'guerrilla' approach to politics. Those MPs who came in during the 1960s and 1970s found themselves in a House in which the entire timetable and the structure of debates and the availability of many facilities were entirely in the hands of the front benches of the two largest parties. Indeed they would regularly and gleefully combine to resist any change in their comfortable duopoly. The 'usual channels' at that time wholly excluded the third party, and the Speaker and his three deputies were – and still are – all from the two larger parties. The 'official' opposition, even when it represented roughly the same proportion of the voters as the third party, has had a salaried leader equipped with government car and driver, salaried whips and civil servants to run its whips' office. The arrival of funds for opposition parties in Parliament ('Short' money) reduced the disparity, but it remained significant. If politics had been subject to the Office of Fair Trading, the prevailing arrangements would have become a textbook example of the unacceptable.

As if this were not sufficient incentive to adopt a 'guerrilla' approach, Liberal and Liberal Democrat MPs had an added incentive. A further consequence of the first-past-the-post system is that the party's Westminster success depended more on the ability of individual candidates to win and hold seats than it did on the party's ability to build up votes across the country. Vigorous campaigning on behalf of their constituents was absolutely essential to the success and survival of third-party MPs, so nothing could be allowed to displace the primary role of the constituency. It was, and to a large extent still is, a Darwinian process of natural selection – you only become and remain a Liberal Democrat MP if you are an effective constituency representative, and that colours your perception of what Parliament is about. Only parties which can think of seats as 'safe' – which is not always a wise thing to do – have a place for the sort of member whose constituency work either locally or in Parliament is a minor consideration alongside national political aspirations and other interests. I remember discovering a backbench Labour MP whose only appearance in the Hansard index for a whole session was a single written question which did not have any particular bearing on his constituency. My own Conservative predecessor never held anything resembling a constituency 'surgery' in his entire tenure of the seat, which lasted over 20 years.

The practical consequences of this sense of exclusion and of this priority for constituency work are numerous. They result in working priorities which are, of course, not unique to third-party MPs – there are conscientious constituency MPs and campaigners in all parties – but they are the accepted priorities of the Liberal Democrats as a group, and failure to live up to them is much more a subject of peer pressure than it would be in the other parties.

In day-to-day terms, this approach means that the effective organisation of constituency casework and the effective use of parliamentary time to raise constituency issues have first claim on a third-party member. Getting oral questions, urgent questions, adjournment debates and debate interventions on issues of constituency concern is a priority. Where the system denies opportunities, a campaigning MP will challenge the system through points of order or other procedural devices to make the point. Falling foul of parliamentary rules is rarely a problem in the eyes of constituents. I recall the late David Penhaligon feeling distressed because he had been shouted down by both the other parties for getting the procedure wrong when raising a constituency point. When he telephoned his wife to admit his misjudgement he discovered that it was headlines on the news in Cornwall, where his defiance got him treated as a hero.

When parties and individuals are denied a voice, parliamentary procedure has always left opportunities for disruptive tactics to draw attention to a grievance, and Liberal Democrats have used them. Tabling large numbers of amendments to a Bill expected to be uncontroversial, insisting on extra divisions, blocking motions which the front benches want to get through 'on the nod' – all are part of the armoury. But, as the Irish party eventually found, every use of a procedural weapon runs the risk of retaliation, which makes it unusable in the future. Delaying Bills (other than at the end of a session) is now largely prevented by rigid timetabling. A decision by the Commons to reject a Lords amendment requires a specially appointed committee to draw up reasons for the rejection, a procedure which is usually a bizarre formality. Liberal Democrats have used motions to appoint a 'reasons committee' on a Lords amendment to stop Bills being rushed back to the Lords – in one case causing the reasons committee to sit for several hours – but that avenue has now been closed off by including the reasons committee in the timetable motion. Guerrilla tactics have to be used sparingly, and in circumstances where the public outside the Commons can see and sympathise with the reasons for the action. Every successful action risks a further tightening of the rules to prevent it being attempted again.

If Britain's third party were a regional or narrowly sectional party, that might be the end of the story. It could be a force of guerrilla fighters using every available parliamentary opportunity to promote and bargain for the interests of the constituents of its individual MPs, and those of the region or section upon which it could rely for its electoral base. But the Liberal Democrats are a broadly based party, with voting support throughout Britain and aspirations to win seats in all areas. It has to have and promote views on the whole range of political issues. It has to engage in national political debate across the board. It has to have spokesmen and spokeswomen to cover the same political ground as the other parties, and it needs and demands a fair share of media coverage to reflect the distinctions of its views and the large number of people who vote for it. So, when the parliamentary party of the 1970s found that it represented up to 23 per cent of those who had voted, Monday's guerrilla fighter had to be Tuesday's shadow Chancellor or shadow Foreign Secretary. Covering the whole range of government when the party had only thirteen MPs was like putting on a performance of *Aida* with a very small opera company – just as the same soldiers would reappear in the Grand March several times with different hats on, so Liberal spokesmen would shadow several departments. Growth to over 50 members has changed the pattern totally, because it allows room for a shadow Cabinet, for other front-bench spokespeople, and for some members to take on purely backbench roles including select committee chairmanships. The majority of Liberal Democrat MPs carry out a spokesmanship role on behalf of the party and have to balance that with the commitment to constituency campaigning which is expected of them. Even with a membership of 54, the parliamentary party is still able to function as a coordinating and debating forum in which all MPs can contribute to discussion on controversial topics and feel some sense of ownership of the collective decisions which are reached. Whether this collegiality could survive in a larger parliamentary party of over 100 is a question the party may have to face in the future.

There is another aspect to the tension which third-party MPs experience in their parliamentary role. The Liberal Democrats are a party of reform, who have high aspirations for Parliament. They have long advocated and voted for

Lords reform, electoral reform and reform of parliamentary procedure in order to make the Commons more effective in controlling the executive and scrutinising legislation. One of these reforms, that of the electoral system, would undoubtedly strengthen the Liberal Democrats' position, because the party's vote is massively underrepresented in parliamentary seats. A number of the others, however, have been potentially contrary to the party's short-term interests as it has sought to make the most of its limited parliamentary strength. The party has supported the timetabling changes which make it virtually impossible for opposition parties or dissident groups of backbenchers to use delay as a bargaining counter to secure changes in legislation. Under a reformed electoral system without artificial majorities, there would be a premium on achieving consensus, and no need to use delay rather than substantive votes to prevent measures from being railroaded through. In the absence of electoral reform, Liberal Democrat support for timetabling has removed an occasionally useful weapon from the party's armoury in the short term. It is a stance based on a desire to allocate time rationally to the various parts of a Bill – a worthwhile objective which is not always achieved under the new system. It was part of a programme to end the all-night sittings and tedious filibusters which undermined the public credibility of the Commons and did nothing to ensure that laws are properly drafted and examined.

Similarly, Liberal Democrats have been strong backers of the expansion of the select committee system as a means of scrutinising and challenging the executive. But when the party's numbers were significantly smaller, time spent by members in the relative anonymity of select committees was time not available to promote constituency needs on the floor of the House or to present the party's case in the media. Select committees are at their best when, through judicious choice of subject and approach, they can take a critical line without dividing on party lines. The result is often welcome to Liberal Democrats, but the process is one which confers few benefits on a third party with small numbers. Increased numbers have significantly reduced this dilemma by freeing more MPs for select committee work, including chairmanship.

Despite the short-term divergence between the parties' ideals for the political system and the tactics and advantages which are relevant to its third-party status, the Liberal Democrats have tended to stick with the ideals. Moreover, their political ideals would not be met by a situation in which the party took over the role of one of the larger parties and merely replaced it in a continuing two-party system, as Labour very nearly did to the Liberals in the mid-twentieth century. The ambitions of Liberal Democrats are for a pluralist political system which recognises the diversity of opinion. Two-party systems tend to ossify old divisions which do not reflect current reality. Electoral reform presumes multi-party politics and governments made up of more than one party. It is a road that the party has showed its willingness to follow, not only in Scotland and Wales but also in the Lib–Lab pact of the 1970s, which chalked up some achievements and, despite a very hostile media reaction, served the party's short-term electoral interests at the time. It also educated its members about some of the demands of government.

If Liberal Democrats had not insisted on electoral reform as a condition of setting up the Scottish Parliament, the Conservatives – who opposed it – would have been completely obliterated at the first elections to it. But that was not the point – Scotland had four-party politics, and that needed to be reflected in representation at Holyrood. Indeed, a wider range of opinion is now represented there than was represented by Scottish MPs at Westminster. The consequent need to form coalitions is seen by the Liberal Democrats as an appropriate response to the need to find a way of reconciling different points of view in a democracy.

What will be the role of the third-party MP in a 21st-century Parliament (whichever party turns out to occupy that role)? That depends on the extent to which reforms of the kind which Liberal Democrats support are carried through to completion. Some have happened already, some are projected and are likely, while others are less certain. If Liberal Democrats had their way, a number of things would significantly affect the role of an MP. Electoral reform would make it unlikely that single parties would form majority governments: coalitions would mean that third parties would not be permanently excluded from power, and that in some instances governments would have to look beyond the administration's declared supporters to win votes. When that happens, the chamber of the House of Commons ceases to be a place of mere ritual, and becomes a forum in which support has to be won: the role of the individual MP is consequently a stronger one. Legislation would be more seriously open to amendment, and could be dealt with in specialised committees rather than ad hoc Bill committees.

Devolution, not only to Scotland and Wales but, increasingly, to the English regions, would mean that many issues would fall outside the jurisdiction of Westminster MPs (as is now the case for Scottish MPs). There would be no need for such a large House of Commons – much larger than almost any other democratic legislature – if regional assemblies were doing so much more of the work now done at Westminster. Devolution would also make it possible for the Commons to sit at Westminster for fewer days, making it easier for MPs to maintain contact in their constituencies and for those with constituencies and homes away from London to have a normal family life, which in turn would widen the range of potential candidates.

Involvement in select committee work would be significantly more attractive if committees had stronger powers to get at all the papers and witnesses needed to scrutinise government effectively. Once the limitation on access to 'advice to ministers' is removed, it becomes possible to establish clearly why or whether something is going wrong, and whether alternatives in policy or strategy have been properly considered. New technologies will facilitate the direct involvement of individual constituents and groups in the consultative process around both legislation and scrutiny of the executive. A more secure and independent role for local government, with its own tax base, would free Westminster MPs from the minutiae of local services and from endless arguments about the level of government grant for each individual local authority.

These changes would affect all MPs, not just third-party MPs – indeed, they would reduce the distinction between 'government' and 'opposition'

MPs because all would have a significant role. In a reformed Parliament, all members of a much smaller House of Commons would have the potential to be seriously and significantly involved in each of the key functions of Parliament:

- forming and sustaining a government;
- scrutinising that government;
- presenting the case for an alternative government and policy;
- seeking redress of grievances for constituents individually and collectively.

SIX (A)

The House of Lords from the Inside:
A Conservative View

Baroness Knight of Collingtree

For at least 200 years prior to 1958 it would have been a pretty
straightforward matter to write a treatise on the House of Lords and
the duties of those who sat in it. A few changes had taken place, such
as the Acts of Union of 1707 and 1800 with Scotland and Ireland (which
entitled first Scottish and then Irish peers to elect representatives to sit in the
House of Lords) and the 1911 Parliament Act, allowing a Bill to pass without
Lords consent, with certain provisos. There were also laws which restricted
the powers of the Lords to delay Bills. But in the main, Parliament sailed
along, largely as it had always done, with the Commons mostly initiating
legislation, and the Lords carefully scrutinising it and suggesting deletions or
amendments where those seemed wise. Second thoughts, and especially those
emanating from a chamber generally more independent in character, proved
to be beneficial.

The 1958 change was a profound one. For the first time, in addition to
the hereditary peers, the Law Lords and 26 bishops, there were to be members
appointed for life: life peers, men and women who had considerable experience of the House of Commons and had served as senior government
ministers, ex-Prime Ministers, persons who were considered to have made
outstanding contributions in a variety of fields such as industry, the arts,

medicine or the military, joined those members who were there by right of birth. This change has worked well, often providing specialist expertise to our debates and an extra dimension of knowledge which is extremely valuable.

Since the passage of the House of Lords Act 1999, however, it has been almost impossible to see which way the House of Lords is heading. Are all the hereditary peers to be banished and, if so, when? Will there be a half – or even fully – elected House? Are there to be age limits imposed? Is the House to have a Speaker? What is to happen to the Lord Chancellor's role and when? What of the Law Lords? What of the bishops? As I write these words, no one knows the answer to any of these questions.

Let me now turn to examine the function, duties and place of the House of Lords in our legislative system.

The British Parliament has three distinct and different parts – the House of Commons, the House of Lords and the Queen (the Crown). No Bill can pass and become a statute without the involvement of all three. But the primary power rightly lies with the House of Commons, not least of all because it is the only one of the three which is elected by the people. Most Bills (though not all) are introduced in the Commons by the government of the day, which has been given its powers through democratic election. When all of the first stages of Bills have been completed there, they come to the House of Lords for scrutiny and consideration. It is currently a matter of considerable concern to peers that so many important Bills come to us without having been fully debated or considered in the 'other place'. Indeed, sometimes whole chunks of a Bill might not have even been discussed there at all! All the more vital therefore that the House of Lords does its business, for if we did not, Parliament would not be doing its duty and the British people would have some extremely raw and ill-considered legislation thrust upon them. The peers, then, have much work to do. They make alterations, and put forward suggestions to improve legislation where they think this is advisable. That legislation then goes back to the Commons, where the government – using its majority – either accepts or rejects the changes made. If rejected (or accepted with amendment) the Bill in question then returns to the Lords. Sometimes the peers will resist the rejections, but more often than not they accept them, for we are very conscious that MPs are elected, while we are not. Finally, the completed Bill will go to the Queen. Her signature – royal assent – has to be on all legislation before it can become law.

There have been numerous recent instances of the Lords improving government Bills substantially. Following the foot and mouth outbreak in 2001, when thousands of farmers lost their herds and their livelihoods because so many cattle were slaughtered, it was their lordships who insisted, in the Animal Health Bill of 2002, that a vaccination policy, rather than one of killing, should be adopted. The anti-terrorism Crime and Security Bill of 2001 has provisions to ensure an appeal mechanism against deportation, solely because of the work of the Lords, while the government was forced to compromise on the issue of limiting trial by jury in order to get its flagship Criminal Justice Bill onto the Statute Book in 2003. A look at the figures officially compiled bears out the claim that the House of Lords works extremely hard on improving legislation that comes before it: Between 2001 and 2002, no fewer than 8,813 amendments were tabled by their Lordships, of which 2,557 were adopted.

Some government-backed Bills, such as the one to abolish fox- and deer-hunting and hare-coursing with dogs in England and Wales, have caused running battles between the Houses, with the Commons voting with huge majorities to end the activity, and the Lords voting just as determinedly to try to keep it. There may well be a division of area understanding and sympathy here with the present huge Labour majority in the House of Commons. Big cities and many urban areas are mostly represented by Labour politicians, while scores of their Lordships either live in the country or have a special fondness for and understanding of it. We have now experienced the cudgel of the Parliament Act to ensure that the Commons got its way. However, there will be further trouble, not least of all because the Parliament Act was never brought in to deal with issues such as this.

Apart from revising legislation, the House of Lords has an important duty to act as a watchdog, to hold the government to account and to force ministers to explain their actions and decisions. A spokesman for the government will frequently repeat in the House of Lords a statement made earlier in the day in the House of Commons. Their Lordships on all sides of the House will respond, questioning the minister closely, picking up any doubtful points like bloodhounds on a scent. Many a minister looks embattled after a session of this kind, for there are no holds barred.

Another way in which their lordships probe the actions of government, or apply pressure for improvements, is to put down oral questions. In the Commons, a particular minister answers for his or her department on a particular day. All questions on health matters, Treasury business, foreign affairs and so on are grouped together and answered in a bunch. In the Lords, there are often as many departmental subjects covered as there are actual questions on the order paper. You can have a question on housing, then one on health, then one on any other matter on which a peer may be exercised. The minister responsible will know the words of the main question he has to answer, but have no idea quite what supplementary the questioner intends to put. Both attacker and attacked have to be adroit and (preferably) quick witted. While it may well be that all ministers have a number of civil servants trying to figure out just what supplementary the questioner intends to put, it is always a test for the man or woman who has to reply from the government front bench. Particularly since any peer may rise and put his own supplementary, at least until the Leader of the House decides that time is up, and the House must move on to the next question. I was once told that one should never put down a question on the order paper unless one knew the answer: wise advise, for one is often not searching for knowledge so much as exposing weakness, or even perhaps a scandal.

A further important task carried out by the Lords is to man the select committees, which are investigative, and exist to examine a very wide range of matters of public concern. They regularly produce reports of their findings. I currently sit on two – firstly that section of the European Union committee which deals with social affairs, education and home affairs. Recently, that committee has been concentrating on immigration – a difficult subject. The public have indicated their extreme concern about it, not least by electing as local councillors members of the fascist British National Party in some parts of our country, which would have been unthinkable only a few years ago. Our committee has studied the subject in a great amount of detail, taking evidence from a wide range of interested groups, though not the BNP, I might add. We went to Germany and Poland in 2003, to study the methods of border control in place, which is a matter that concerns me greatly, for the way Europe is progressing (some wish to make it a federation, and most look to a sort of United States of Europe for the future) means that, once a person has got through the outside edges of the European Union, he can travel anywhere he likes within it. Thus, unless the whole range of different countries in Europe operates a strong system of border controls at their outside edge, pretty well anyone will be able to get in, and travel to Britain, or any other part of the European Union, without let or hindrance.

My second select committee is one which has just been set up to study the draft of the new Mental Incapacity Bill. This is a new idea for, up until now, it has been accepted that there are plenty of opportunities to scrutinise the contents of Bills during the second reading and committee stage debates. If the Bill was a very contentious one, the government of the day would produce a Green Paper, which would then be available for every interested group to comment on or put objections to. After that, there would be a White Paper setting out the government's intentions. Recently, however, it has been decided by the powers that be that this is not enough. A select committee process may now be put in place, witnesses can be called and questioned, and the committee will produce a report on the wisdom (or otherwise) of taking the matter in legislation.

There are currently over 70 peers sitting on the various select committees, and these committees take up many, many hours in each week. And it is not only the actual sittings – the thick pile of papers which have to be read and digested before each meeting is daunting. I estimate that I must find at least two hours (often more) before each meeting, to get through all the necessary papers so as to be thoroughly briefed on the business we are going to discuss, decide what questions I want to put to witnesses and what points I consider need elucidation.

Any peer can introduce a matter for debate simply by putting down his or her name for a vacant spot, and many do. The dinner hour is available on most sitting evenings, and there is also the power, individually, to introduce a Bill. The normal debates give opportunities for peers to speak. Unlike the Commons, anyone who puts his name down on the list for debate (or debates) of the day will get the chance to voice his opinion. However, if a very large number of names go down, the length of time each peer may speak will be very limited. The House takes extremely seriously its duty to debate each Bill, whether it is one sent up by the Commons or one introduced by a colleague. The latter involves much work for the peer who chooses to take this step but it gives a chance to alter a bad situation. I recently had such a Bill before the House: the Patients' Protection Bill, which sought to ensure that sick people are given food and liquid when in hospital. I had a worrying number of cases on file where this had not been happening.

In addition to all these duties, the House of Lords, through its Appellate Committee, is the highest court of appeal in the land, except in Scotland, which has a different system. This work is separate from the legislative and scrutinising functions which I have already described, and ordinary peers have little or no involvement in it. I mention it simply because it is an important part of the function of the House of Lords, but it has its own rules. It does not necessarily sit at the same time as the Lords, being matched not with parliamentary sessions, but with the legal year. Law Lords hear appeals, and give judgments from Mondays until Thursdays, starting at 10.30 a.m. and ending at 4 p.m. They are frequently called upon to chair special public inquiries, such as the one chaired by Lord Hutton into the circumstances surrounding the suicide of Dr David Kelly. The Law Lords get paid – we do not.

Considering all of these differing and heavy responsibilities, it will be no surprise to hear that the British House of Lords is one of the busiest Parliaments in the world. Its preservation and continuance is, without doubt, of crucial importance to the people of our country. Why, then, has the present government embarked upon a course which weakens and emasculates it? The first salvo came with the abolition of the hereditary peers in 2002 – a move which seemed to be based purely on spite, class hatred and the determined pursuit of egalitarianism. It was certainly not because the hereditary peers had not been doing their duty, or in response to a public outcry for this change. In all my years as an MP, I never had a single letter or interview indicating a demand for it. Nobody has ever organised a march for it, waved banners screaming for it, and nor, unless I am much mistaken, has any newspaper campaigned for it. If it came about because the Labour government detested the fact that so many hereditary peers were Conservative, and feared votes in the Lords would always be cast on a party political basis, they should have studied the voting records of the House of Lords in recent years, which shows that there is a strong individualist element in play when Lords have to vote. They make their own minds up without any pressure from constituents, of whom they have none. Measures sent to the Lords by Conservative governments throughout the 1980s and 1990s were frequently thrown out by the peers, and when they were not, it was always the case that the elected House got its way, as all elected British governments will.

The House of Lords from the Inside: A Labour View

Lord Carter

T
he parliamentary role of Labour peers is conditioned entirely by the fact that the Labour Party has always been substantially in the minority in the House of Lords. When I joined the House in March 1987 there were 107 Labour peers in a House with a nominal strength of about 1,180. The nominal strength of 1,180 included 792 hereditary peers, a large number of whom could be brought in for important votes – the so-called 'backwoodsmen'.

When Labour came to power in May 1997 there were 116 Labour peers compared with 477 Conservatives, 57 Liberal Democrats, 417 crossbenchers and 26 bishops. The addition of the 43 working peers announced in 2004 will result in a House composed of 204 Labour, 207 Conservative, 71 Liberal Democrats, 203 crossbenchers and 26 bishops. For the first time ever in the history of the House of Lords – and seven years after coming to power in 1997 – Labour will have rough parity with the Conservatives. (Ironically the removal in May 2004 of the Conservative whip from five peers who supported the UK Independence Party means that Labour actually had two more peers than the Conservatives). Labour will still have only 29 per cent of the total vote in the Lords.

I have set these figures out in some detail because they underline the fact that to be permanently outnumbered whether in government or opposition is and has been the daily experience of Labour peers and totally conditions their parliamentary role. Loyally supporting a Labour government which has a massive majority in the House of Commons but is substantially in the minority in the Lords – or trying to perform a proper role in opposition when massively outnumbered – requires a particular blend of patience, optimism and parliamentary skills.

This rather strange constitutional and legislative situation is not always understood or appreciated by Labour colleagues in the Commons. Although the two chambers are a minute's walk apart, the gulf in understanding is considerable. As government Chief Whip briefing MPs who were coming to the Lords, I became used to the remarks 'I had absolutely no idea how the Lords operates' and 'how on earth does a Labour government ever get its legislation through the Lords?'. I always replied that Labour peers preformed an effective parliamentary role as the result of the exercise of charm and persuasion by the Chief Whip and an immense amount of loyalty and goodwill from colleagues on the Labour benches.

The Lords sets great store by the fact that it is 'self-regulating'. The House has no Speaker and so there is no such thing as a 'point of order' in the Lords, as there is no one to rule on order. The House is responsible for its own order and the proper conduct of the House relies entirely on all its members observing the conventions of the House. Add to this the fact the government is substantially in the minority among the membership of the House as a whole and therefore has to rely on the cooperation of the opposition parties and other groups to obtain its programme of legislation and it will be evident that the House of Lords is a unique parliamentary chamber.

The frustration of Labour peers trying to perform an effective parliamentary role in the situation I have described when the Labour Party had won two parliamentary elections – 1997 and 2001 – resulting in Labour governments with massive Commons majorities can be understood. Having said that, it is only fair to point out that the government has obtained its programme of legislation, albeit with very substantial concessions on a number of Bills. The Parliament Act has been used only three times since 1997 – on the Sexual Offences (Amendment) Act 2000 (which was subject to a free vote), the European Parliamentary Elections Act 1999 (which was a very special case) and the Hunting Act 2004 (which banned fox- and deer-hunting and hare-coursing with dogs in England and Wales).

The difference in the behaviour of the Lords between periods of Conservative government and Labour government can be demonstrated by the record of government defeats. In the five years between 1974 and 1979 the Wilson and Callaghan governments were defeated about 60 times a session. In the eighteen Conservative years from 1979 to 1997 the Thatcher and Major governments were defeated about thirteen times a session.

In the two parliamentary sessions before the removal of 90 per cent of the hereditary peers in November 1999 the Labour government was defeated 70 times – an average of 35 times a session. Since November 1999 (to the time of writing) the government – in the reformed House – has been defeated 227 times – an average of more than 50 times a session.

Another measure of the relative power of the Lords and the Commons is the number of times Bills go between the two Houses during a procedure often referred to as 'ping-pong'. This is the procedure by which a Bill goes back and forth between the two chambers until the two Houses reach agreement. In the eighteen Conservative years from 1979 to 1997, three Bills were subject to more than two rounds of ping-pong – one every six years. In the Labour years since 1997, fourteen bills have had more than two rounds of ping-pong – one every six months.

An alliance of Conservative and Liberal Democrat peers now routinely defeats the Labour government and this makes the parliamentary role of Labour peers very difficult. Conservative MPs do not have the numbers to defeat the government in the House of Commons. The Liberal Democrats do not expect to form a government. This is a potent combination when the only place where the government can be defeated is the House of Lords. The government has not lost a single division in the Commons in the seven years since 1997. It has been defeated 297 times in the Lords in the same period. This compares with 241 defeats of the Conservative government in the eighteen years 1979–1997.

Some might argue that this merely demonstrates that it is the Lords and not the Commons which is holding the executive to legislative account. Others would argue, perhaps more persuasively, that since 1999 and the removal of 90 per cent of the hereditary peers the Lords has claimed and acted on a perceived increase in its legitimacy without there being a clear definition or understanding of the relative roles, powers and functions of the two chambers of Parliament.

For ten years, between 1987 and 1997, I served on the opposition front bench as spokesman on agriculture and rural affairs, health and social security. I was also a whip and then Deputy Chief Whip. Looking back on that period it is quite remarkable just how effective an opposition we were. We were denied adequate reinforcements. Despite the effective Conservative majority in the Lords, Margaret Thatcher and John Major created twice as many Conservative life peers as they allowed Labour, thus increasing the imbalance. It has taken seven years and the passage in 1999 of the historic House of Lords Act – the removal of most of the hereditary peers – for Labour to come to rough parity with the Conservatives.

The only way for Labour peers to get victories while in opposition was to form an alliance on an issue with the Liberal Democrats, the crossbenchers and dissident Tories. Significant victories were occasionally obtained but these were usually overturned in the Commons and when the Bill returned to the Lords the Conservative majority would prevail. This often resulted from bringing in the 'backwoodsmen', hereditary peers who rarely came to the House except when persuaded by the Conservative whip to come in for important votes.

The unfamiliarity with the procedures of the House of some of the back-woodsmen is illustrated by the true story of the rarely seen hereditary peer who came in to register to enable him to vote in his party group in the election of hereditary peers (procedures introduced as a result of the 1999 House of Lords Act). While he was registering there was a loud and prolonged noise. He turned to the clerk and asked: 'What on earth is that noise?' 'That, my Lord, is the Division Bell' was the reply.

I have referred to the self-regulating nature of the Lords, the absence of a Speaker and the reliance on conventions to ensure the proper conduct of the House. This means that a handful of peers, probably no more than half a dozen, could bring the business of the House virtually to a halt by ignoring the conventions, but without contravening a single standing order.

For example, the grouping of amendments to Bills in the Lords is entirely voluntary. Any peer can demand that amendments he or she has tabled be debated separately, even to the extent that amendments can be degrouped in the chamber during debate. (In the Commons amendments are selected for debate and grouped under the authority of the Speaker and cannot be degrouped.)

It would be within the standing orders of the House but completely outwith its conventions for a small number of peers to table vast rafts of amendments, insist on each being debated separately and then call a vote on each amendment. Instead of the normal 20 or 25 groups of amendments being dealt with in a day the House might manage to debate only a handful of groups. The only way to stop the process would be to move 'that the Noble Lord be no longer heard', which is itself a debatable motion.

With these tactics available, it might be asked why Labour peers did not employ such stratagems in the long years of opposition. The answer is twofold. Firstly, there was an innate sense of parliamentary responsibility in the House. Add to this, not only the hope of Labour peers that Labour would form the next government, but the knowledge that if such a precedent had been set then the very same tactics could – indeed would – be employed by a Conservative opposition and that this would wreck any future Labour government's programme.

It was also the case that many hereditary peers recognised the constitutional illegitimacy of their position compared to the elected House of Commons, although it is unlikely that they would have spelt it out in those terms. It was not just the weight of Conservative votes that caused only three Bills to be returned to the Commons more than twice between 1979 and 1997. There was also the unspoken assumption that, although the Commons might be wrong, they were the elected chamber and should therefore have their way.

There was an uneasy truce or stand-off between Conservative and Labour in the period 1979 to 1997. The Conservatives did not push their numerical superiority too far, knowing that they could always get their way in the end if the business was vital to the government. Labour peers did not want to create a precedent by using wrecking tactics which would rebound on them when Labour came to form the government. It is also possible that hereditary peers, knowing that their days were probably numbered, tried not to assist the argument for their removal by too blatant a use of their voting power.

Since completion of the first stage of reform towards the end of 1999 the culture and behaviour of the House has certainly changed. The removal of the hereditary peers has created an increased feeling of legitimacy and the boundaries of the conventions have been regularly tested. Since November 1999 the Lords have voted down Statutory Instruments for the first time since 1968; passed a dilatory amendment to slow down the passage of the Animal Health Bill, a procedure not used since the nineteenth century; amended the traditional message to the Queen following the Queen's Speech for the first time since 1914; and sent the Constitutional Reform Bill to a select committee, only the second time a Bill has been delayed in this way since 1917. Wrecking amendments to Bills are now more common. For example, the Civil Partnerships Bill was wrecked by totalling redefining 'civil partnership' in such a way that the Bill as drafted was virtually meaningless.

All of these devices exploit the fact that the government is substantially in the minority in the Lords. All the current proposals for reform of the composition of the House of Lords accept as given that the government of the day will always be in the minority in the Lords. If the long-standing conventions of the House continue to be flouted there will have to be some new understanding or concordat between the parties in the Lords regarding the proper conduct of the

House. This will be as much in the interest of the Conservative Party as Labour because when the Conservatives do come to form a government the combined opposition of Labour and Liberal Democrat peers is likely to be a much more potent weapon than the present rather uneasy relationship between the Conservatives and the Liberal Democrats in the House of Lords.

Besides the Salisbury/Addison convention that the Lords do not vote against a Bill at second or third reading if the Bill was in the manifesto there are two further fundamental conventions which have governed the behaviour of the Lords in the past: the government is entitled to get its business without unreasonable delay and the elected chamber should finally have its way. The first convention has been challenged by the deliberate delaying of the Animal Health Bill and the Constitutional Reform Bill. The second is more or less holding but at the price of the government having to accept major concessions to some of its Bills rather than have them delayed for a year by invoking the Parliament Act. If the 2004 Lords Reform Bill had been introduced Lord Strathclyde, leader of the opposition in the Lords, made it clear that delaying or wrecking tactics would have been employed on other Bills in the programme. Since the Bill was not introduced we shall never know if the threat was real.

Whatever the eventual reformed composition of the Lords, whether appointed, elected, or a mixture of the two, the powers, procedures and conventions of the Lords will have to be re-examined. The Lords still does a good job of revising and scrutinising legislation and holding the executive to account through questions and debates. The work of its select committees is generally acknowledged to be excellent. There has to be a balance between the right of the Lords to revise and scrutinise legislation and the right of the elected government to obtain its programme of legislation.

A settlement between the political parties and the two chambers setting out the agreed modalities of the legislative process will have to be reached. To codify such a settlement completely in legislation is possible but this would be an inflexible solution, although some revision of the Parliament Act may be necessary. It would be better to reach agreement on a concordat setting out the relative powers of the two chambers of Parliament and the conventions which should govern the proper conduct of the Lords. Without such an agreement and understanding the House of Lords will have the considerable power of a House where the government of the day is always in the minority without responsibility or accountability of an elected House where the majority party forms the government. It should not be beyond the power of responsible parliamentarians to find a solution which firmly establishes the scrutinising, revising and eventual delaying powers of the Lords while allowing the elected government to obtain its programme of legislation.

The House of Lords from the Inside:
'An insuperable reluctance'
A Liberal Democrat View

Lord McNally

I n 1909 the then Prime Minister, Herbert Asquith, received the following assessment of prospects for reform of the House of Lords from his parliamentary private secretary, Edwin Montagu:

> *The history of all former attempts at coming to close quarters with the House of Lords Question shows a record of disorder, dissipation of energy, of words and solemn exhortation, or individual rhetoric and impressive* ipse dicits *without any definite scheme of action.*

It would not be too unfair 95 years later to send a similar memo to Tony Blair. In spite of a century-old commitment by the Labour Party to reform and democratise Britain's second chamber, Lords reform has once again been put on the back burner as a matter to be dealt with in the next parliament, after another general election. It seems hard to believe that a Labour government with two successive landslide victories (in 1997 and 2001) under its belt should have failed to deliver on so fundamental a commitment. To be sure, the House of Lords Act 1999 did remove the right of all but 92 hereditary peers to sit in the Lords. As a result the number entitled to sit in the upper House came down from nearly 1,400 to a little under 700. However no one doubted that this was no more than an interim measure and a compromise. The real prize was, and is, the creation of a Lords which is both more democratic and more representative than the Lords as now constituted. The Royal Commission on Lords Reform, chaired by Lord Wakeham, said as much in its report of January 2000 and that view was endorsed by the Labour Party general election manifesto of May 2001. Yet it seems that the limit of the Prime Minister's ambition is now to have a fully appointed second chamber with its ability to delay legislation severely curtailed. Instead of seeking a consensus which could be sustained for a considerable length of time the Prime Minister seems intent on achieving a short-term fix which would satisfy no one but his party business manager.

The reasons for the failure to achieve consensual reform thus far are mixed and complex. There is a genuine fear in the House of Commons that a House of Lords fully reformed and with a popular mandate would challenge the ultimate authority of the lower House in a way that an unreformed Lords would not dare to do. There are also those who feel that the House of Lords does a very good job. Why, they ask, should we contemplate changing something that works very well? Or, as the great parliamentarian Edmund Burke opined more generally on reform, 'I have an insuperable reluctance in giving my hand to destroy any established institution of government upon a theory, however plausible it may be.'

The House of Lords spends two-thirds of its time revising and processing legislation. It can also question ministers on government policy. All government departments have a spokesman in the Lords. It can initiate debates both on issues of the day and on broader-based strategic themes. Its committees have the same power to call for papers and summon witnesses as those in the Commons; but are able to cross departmental lines in their inquiries, whereas the Commons select committees have oversight of a particular government department.

It can, and does, defy the government and it is this defiance which gives the government most grounds for complaint, notwithstanding the fact that the government still has in its armoury the Parliament Act, which allows the Commons to override the will of the Lords after a year's delay.

For the most part, however, the main influence of the Lords is not in delay but in tweaking and improving legislation. Because the government cannot impose timetable motions in the House of Lords as it can in the Commons many issues get a more thorough airing in the Lords. It is easier for amendments to be put down and debated. As a result the Lords often proves more fertile ground for the activities of outside lobbyists and pressure groups. To safeguard against abuse of this greater flexibility in process a tough regime is in place to prevent peers having undue influence in areas where they have outside commitments or interests.

All legislation has to go through the Lords with parallel procedure to that of the Commons (formal first reading, second reading, committee, report, and third reading). Any peer may table, and have debated, as many amendments to a Bill as he or she wishes and there is no guillotine to a cut a speech short. It sounds like a wrecker's charter; but the Lords use these powers wisely and a Bill which has the clear support of the Commons is rarely wrecked or frustrated in the Lords. Indeed the Salisbury Convention, worked out when a Labour government was first elected with a large majority after the Second World War, specifically prevents the Lords from frustrating manifesto commitments, which carry the weight of a democratic mandate.

As well as government Bills there are private members' Bills. Any peer may introduce a Bill and all Bills are given time for debate. The snag is that Lords private Bills have little chance of finding time in the Commons.

There are also Statutory Instruments, the secondary legislation which flows from the broad powers given to the government by primary legislation. All Orders requiring a motion of approval by both Houses are debated on the floor of the House and any peer may speak in the debate. Negative Orders, which pass through by virtue of being before it for 40 days, are debated on the floor of the House if any peer 'prays' against the Order. Although Orders are not voted on it is a useful way of exposing government action to scrutiny. However, there is a growing volume of secondary legislation and a growing concern that the present parliamentary machinery is inadequate to monitor and scrutinise it. Against this backdrop a committee of the House is now working on ways of improving the scrutiny of secondary legislation.

The House of Lords also has an influence via its non-legislative strategy debates. The three main parties plus the crossbenchers are allotted time each session for debates on specific topics. The debates often see the Lords at its best, when peers with real expertise speak on their subject. It is open to lobby and interest groups to suggest their topic for debate. Education and overseas development groups are good at doing that and then briefing peers for the ensuing debate. There are also balloted debates. Any backbench peer may enter the ballot for a chance to introduce a short debate on a topic of their choice.

Another opportunity to raise issues is the unstarred question. This is a mini-debate which is centred around a question to the government. It is not unlike the adjournment debate in the Commons in that it allows a specific issue to be raised and bring forth a ministerial reply.

There are also starred questions. This is the Lords' Question Time. A peer can put down a question for oral answer by a minister and there then follows about seven minutes of general questioning on that topic. Four or five such questions are allowed at the beginning of business each day. It is an excellent session when issues are raised in a probing and civilised way.

There are two main select committees in the Lords: the European Union Committee, which operates through six subcommittees, on which about 70 peers now serve, and the Science and Technology Committee.

There is a determination both by the European Union itself and by the British government to improve the scrutiny of European legislation by national parliaments. There is, as with secondary legislation, a strong case for giving this responsibility to a reformed Second Chamber.

Meanwhile the Science and Technology Committee can produce an awesome array of talent to look at matters as diverse as management of nuclear waste and arguments for the use of cannabis for medical and recreational purposes. There are also committees on the constitution, economic affairs and human rights. The House also has the power to set up ad hoc select committees. I have served on two such committees, on freedom of information and the public services. Lords also sit on joint House of Lords and House of Commons select committees, which are increasingly being used for prelegislative scrutiny.

Funny, anachronistic, undemocratic: all these descriptions fit the House of Lords and a few more besides. There is a clear case for modernisation and reform. Yet even in its present form it regularly outpolls the Commons in terms of public esteem, and most observers think that the work that the House of Lords carries out on legislation is both thorough and effective.

What then is the case for reform and what should a reformed House of Lords be asked to do?

First of all it has to be said that there is an equally strong case for reform of the House of Commons. As someone who has sat in both Houses, I can honestly say that legislation is handled more thoroughly in the Lords than in the Commons. Reform of the Commons which just twiddles with the timetable and makes it a more family-friendly place fails to address the central issue: that we have an overpowerful executive and an underperforming legislature.

The Lords must be reformed as part of a package of measures designed to modernise Britain's system of governance in the 21st century. The House of Lords has survived many winds of change over the centuries and I am sure that it will survive Mr Blair's zephyrs of radicalism. What is in its interest and that of the country as a whole is that those functions that it does so well are retained so that both government and country benefit from its advisory and revisory wisdom without carrying with it the overtones of class and privilege which make it an anachronism in a modern democracy.

The delay in bringing forward the next stage of reform is a disappointment. The Prime Minister's recipe of patronage appointment and curtailment of power cannot be the end of the matter. Reform enthusiasts in the Lords and elsewhere see reform as an opportunity to give the Lords a range of new powers and responsibilities which will fill the democratic and legislative deficits they perceive in our present system. There have been suggestions, for example, that the Lords might prove to be the linchpin of national unity between Westminster and the devolved assemblies and Parliaments emerging in Scotland, Wales, Northern Ireland and the English regions. As I have already indicated, there is a feeling that a job the Lords already does well, scrutiny of European legislation, should be expanded and that it should also have some role for liaison with the European Parliament.

The select committee system, which I have already described, could be expanded. If more powers are to be transferred to local government the Lords could play an important liaison role there so that there would be a genuine dialogue too often lacking between local government and Westminster.

On a more radical tack, the Lords could be given powers to advise and consent on public appointments and scrutinise treaties, powers which in the past under our system have been jealously guarded by the executive.

I do not want to see a Second Chamber which will challenge the pre-eminence of the Commons. However, both Houses of Parliament are too big. As devolution takes hold I see no reason why both Houses should not have a maximum of no more than 450 members each.

The policy of my party is for a directly elected second chamber, elected from the regions by a system of proportional representation. There is no doubt that that would immensely strengthen the legitimacy of the Lords and, consequently, be seen as a threat to the pre-eminence of the Commons. As such it may be too much for the Commons to swallow.

However, there are no shortages of tasks for a reformed House of Lords to undertake. We need to revitalise our democratic system and re-engage it with the people. We need to have a parliamentary system which can check and make accountable the power of the executive in both Whitehall and Brussels. We need to put in place machinery to preserve national cohesion whist pressing ahead with devolving power from an overpowerful centre, to both local government and the regions.

What we must not allow to happen, either by accident or design, is for the pressure for reform to lose momentum.

The historian Janet Morgan, writing about Lords reform 30 years ago, highlighted the dangers:

> *On summer evenings and winter afternoons, when they have nothing else to do, people discuss how to reform the House of Lords. Schemes are taken out of cupboards and drawers and dusted off, speeches are composed, pamphlets written, letters sent to the newspapers. From time to time, the whole country becomes excited. Occasionally legislation is introduced. It generally fails.*

Chilling words indeed for those who believe modernisation of our constitution is an essential part of – indeed, prerequisite for – modernising Britain, especially if combined with that other warning from the past which W. S. Gilbert wrote over a century ago:

> *With all our faults,*
> *We love our House of Peers.*

The House of Lords from the Inside: 'Finding somewhere for the birds to sing' A View from the Crossbenches

Lord Alton of Liverpool

People take various routes into politics. Mine was the well-trod path from local government into the House of Commons. I now sit on the crossbenches – as an independent – in the House of Lords.

Throughout the 1970s I served as a member of Liverpool City Council and the now defunct Merseyside County Council. Beginning life as the council babe – a precocious 21-year-old student, and the council's youngest member – at various times I served as the council's deputy leader, as Chief Whip and chairman of the Housing Committee.

Election to Parliament, in a bizarre by-election held the day after the Callaghan government lost a vote of confidence, sent me to the House of Commons, once again as the *enfant terrible*, but also as the shortest-serving MP. Only six days elapsed before the House was prorogued and MPs headed off to fight the 1979 general election that brought Margaret Thatcher to power. Four weeks later, having endured two election campaigns and two election counts, I was one and a half stone lighter, and finally able to take stock of my new role: member of Parliament for Liverpool's Edge Hill division, and one of just eleven Liberal MPs, the rump of what was left of Mr Gladstone's patrimony.

I was struck by the powerlessness of the backbench MP in a tiny minority party. Margaret Thatcher enjoyed a working majority, the desultory Labour opposition was in a state of collapse and Marxist neophytes, in cities like my own, were beginning their long campaign of attrition to seize control of Labour. Meanwhile, the former Liberal leader, Jeremy Thorpe, was before the court on charges of conspiracy to murder, and it seemed very unlikely that a handful of die-hard Liberals could make much difference in Parliament.

I compared the resources that I had enjoyed in my local government role with those available to me as an MP. As housing chairman, and as the council's deputy leader, I had access to officials and resources: decisions I promoted through the local authority (on issues such as building low-cost homes for sale on inner-city sites, promoting housing cooperatives, designating the biggest housing action area programme in Britain) made a real difference in the lives of underprivileged people. The contrast between being able to deliver inside sanitation and hot water to homes that had previously been without them (50 per cent of the homes in my council ward were without these basic amenities) and the ineffectual banalities of political slanging in the House of Commons could not have been greater.

My part-time secretary, a dingy office, wholly inadequate resources to properly service the needs of constituents who deluged me in the desperate hope that I could put right some injustice, seemed a poor substitute for the realities of local government. And yet, and yet …

Early on during my time in the Commons I decided that as well as playing a role in my party, I should simply take the opportunity that the Commons offered to pursue the causes about which I cared and to relate the symptoms I saw on the ground in my constituency to the legislative causes: to become 'a good constituency MP' and 'a good parliamentarian'. In short, to use whatever time I had in the House to achieve small things.

In retrospect, this was the right decision. Too many people now seem to go into Parliament in the mistaken hope of becoming something else – one of the great political panjandrums, climbing ladders that with another roll of the dice take you back to where you started. The parliamentary game has many more snakes that propel you down than ladders to take you up.

Enoch Powell was broadly right when he said that political careers end in failure, and the parliamentary landscape is littered with the wreckage of frustrated and failed ministerial careers. Festering bitterness followed by years of back-stabbing seems a poor substitute for the satisfaction and fulfilment enjoyed by 'campaigning' MPs.

Parliament is also better for having more independent voices. The post-1997 parliaments have been characterised by a slavish, unquestioning adherence that it took a war in Iraq to end. This is not healthy for a parliamentary democracy. They say that for the pearl to emerge from the oyster a bit of grit has got to enter in. We need many more bits of grit in our House of Commons.

E. M. Forster says in *Two Cheers for Democracy* that the saving grace of our parliamentary system is the cranky, often idiosyncratic MP who by dint of effort perseveres and gets some injustice put right. No doubt dictatorships are easier systems to operate but totalitarianism has little else to commend it.

Democracies can be judged by the vigour and effectiveness of their oppositions: when the Loyal Opposition is in disarray and consumed by internecine warfare (as was the case with Labour in 1979 and with the Conservatives in 1997) it weakens the process of accountability. When, during those same periods, internal opposition within the governing parties is stifled by the unedifying sight of aspirant career politicians waiting in the queue for Buggins' turn as a parliamentary under-secretary of state, it makes matters even worse. If the unhappy soul, the aspiring politician, only finds their voice when they have been passed over for the umpteenth time or sacked to make way for someone else, it isn't usually conducive for the credibility (or for the quality) of the views they then express. And hell knoweth no fury like a politician spurned.

I am not arguing that there is no point in taking on arduous responsibilities in politics, and that no one should ever leave the back benches. Quite the reverse. If parties did not exist bands of independents would rapidly coalesce and form them. Alliances are the only way to create majorities capable of delivering votes and priorities. Independents inevitably have to sacrifice something from their own agenda in order to gain acceptance for a key objective: it is often described as the clash between purity and power but it is much more subtle than this and perfectly honourable. The sin is to surrender every last principle for the unalloyed pursuit of power and to forget why you probably came into politics in the first place.

Phrases like 'serving the people', 'public duty' and 'civic responsibility' are now routinely scoffed at; but when I first entered Parliament there were a lot of members (many of whom came into the Commons after serving in the forces during the Second World War) who genuinely and passionately believed in those virtuous reasons for engaging in politics. And who will say that the MPs who appeared before the House of Commons Privileges Committee during the 1990s, when I served as a member investigating the 'cash for questions' scandal, were driven by higher ideals?

Although I am no longer a member of a political party I do not despise party politics. I do not condescendingly see it as 'a necessary evil'. Parties are an indispensable part of the political architecture. If you can find one in which you can happily live, you should join a party and, if you are fortunate enough to hold elected office, work through the party to serve the needs and interests of your constituents. Churchill – who was a Conservative, a Liberal and a Conservative again – said a man should not be without a party for too long. I agree but would simply add the caveat that it is not worth staying in a party at all costs.

I measure politicians by their causes – not by whether they are left, right, or centre. If they don't have a cause of any kind then they are usually there for all the wrong reasons. And if they surrender or forget their causes, simply to make political progress, it isn't usually good for them or, in the longer term, for their party or democracy generally.

For 30 years I was myself a party member. At various times, as Liberal Chief Whip, chairman of its Policy Committee, its Finance Committee, its By-election Unit, and its Candidates Committee – and as its parliamentary spokesman on a whole raft of issues – I worked hard for its progress.

As a parliamentary spokesman on the Home Office, the environment, local government, Northern Ireland and other portfolios, I did my fair share of 'frontbench' jobs in the Commons. On numerous standing committees – where I served as a lone minority member – I shadowed vast Bills on everything from telecommunications to immigration. Getting the balance between these duties and being a 'good constituency MP' – as well as pursuing non-party causes – was always difficult but one activity fed into and cultivated the other. I often found that the personal issues I was hearing about at weekly advice centres (which would often last for most of a day) would form the basis of an amendment to a Bill or a campaign.

The more that politics is about a sheltered Westminster existence – informed only by the chatter of the Islington dining rooms and where PC stands for political correctness rather than political conviction or political courage, the less likely it is that politics will be relevant to ordinary people.

If you want to know why only 6 per cent of the people bothered to vote in a local government by-election, why only one in three voted in one inner-city constituency at the 2001 general election, and why we have see the rise of groups such as the British National Party – it is because politicians have abandoned grassroots affinities with local communities and replaced day-to-day contact with real life and real issues with marginal fringe concerns. Politics has become obsessed with tick-box agendas driven on by well-financed little lobby groups who pursue issues that are largely irrelevant to the vast majority of British people.

I began my own interest in politics at seventeen as the chairman of my local Young Liberal branch, and later I became the Federation chairman and President of the National League of Young Liberals. I was also involved in the student movement and my college student union. The issues of the day – the Soviet oppression of the Prague Spring, Vietnam, British troops in Northern Ireland, famine in West Africa, and domestic legislation such as the 1967 Abortion Act – were all questions that fired my conscience and engaged me in the life of politics. And then came my engagement in inner-city community politics, getting elected to the city council while I was in my final year at college.

My first real clash with my party came when I was 23 and fighting my parliamentary seat for the first time. A local councillor (one of our own) used his position to advance applications for housing grants and planning permissions on properties he owned. I exposed this and a motion was moved to expel me from the party. No action was to be taken against the miscreant. Happily, the local members saw the paradox and voted with me, against the party leadership, but it was nevertheless a useful baptism of fire.

During the years that followed I rarely had any major differences with my colleagues over issues of principle. As Chief Whip I insisted that members had the right to follow their conscience but that if they intended to vote against the spokesman's position they had a duty to come and explain that to him and to me in advance. This worked very well and most of the time we were able to be reasonably united without stifling independence. That said, I never lost sight of the good advice that my old friend Sir Cyril Smith – then MP for Rochdale – had given me when I was first elected to the Commons: 'Don't ever forget, David, over there sit the opposition; and all around you, that's the enemy.'

This period – the 1980s – was a less happy time for members of the Labour Party, which had become riven by left–right warfare on a whole range of ideological issues. In the end, significant political players, such as David Owen, Shirley Williams and Roy Jenkins, left Labour to found the Social Democrats. They were unable to accept any longer the attempts to coerce them into unacceptable gyrations on key questions such as the operation of a social market, Europe and defence.

As Liberal Chief Whip during much of the period of the Liberal–SDP Alliance I saw, at close quarters, the destructive effect that Labour's attempts to impose an ideological straitjacket had on many of their own members. It also subverted the role of an MP. Many of them returned to their constituencies only to be confronted by small gaggles of activists attempting to intimidate and deselect them on a regular basis. The Birkenhead MP, Frank Field, spent most of the 1980s doing nothing other than fighting members of his local party who were determined to remove him as their MP. These battles threw into sharp relief Edmund Burke's old question about whether an MP is a delegate or a representative.

Ironically, although groups like the Trotskyite entryists the Militant Tendency were ultimately defeated by Neil Kinnock, John Smith and Tony Blair, New Labour is also prone to move power away from constituents into the hands of party activists, albeit more surreptitiously and subtly. For instance, Labour's decision to elect members of the European Parliament by the closed party list system vests huge power in the hands of a few hundred party activists. The electorate, for the very first time, have to vote for a take-it-or-leave-it party list and can no longer vote for individual candidates. This subverts Burke's dictum and entrenches the hold of a party over their delegate. It dangerously erodes democratic accountability and saps the independence of the MEP. Many in the Labour Party have indicated that they would like to see the same system replace the first-past-the-post constituency system for Westminster. This will merely entrench the power of the parties and the alienation of the voters.

Blind allegiance to a political party should not be the bedrock of our political life but there is no great virtue in staying outside the flow if you can comfortably feel you can enter it.

Historically, there have been a whole host of political players who have left their parties over shifts to left or right or because of individual issues of principle. Our two greatest Prime Ministers, W. E. Gladstone and Winston Churchill, were amongst them.

In trying to square political realities – pragmatism – with some sense of principled politics, I have personally adhered to what might be called the '50 per cent plus one' rule: that is, if you can broadly agree with a majority of a party's platform it is possible to remain a member but when you find yourself in disagreement with a majority or significant part of its policies – or a particular issue of principle – then it is time to go.

In 1992 I was faced with a dilemma that led me out of party politics. For the first time, the party decided to make abortion a matter of party policy. Unable to accept this, I announced that I would stand down and when that Parliament expired I did not renew my party membership. Having kicked off the dust from my shoes and accepted a chair at Liverpool's John Moores University – where I have been director of their Foundation for Citizenship – I was startled to be offered a life peerage by John Major in the dissolution honours list in 1997. I opted to sit as an independent crossbencher.

The upper House was just about to be 'reformed', so the ensuing years have given me plenty of food for thought about the role of the second chamber and its members.

One of the traditional attractions of the Lords is that those who sat there – whether hereditary or life peers – had a healthy independence and willingness to send back Bills to the House of Commons. During Margaret Thatcher's years the only time she suffered parliamentary defeats was at the hands of the unelected House of Lords. Tony Blair, on issues such as trial by jury and fox-hunting, has suffered the same fate.

Labour had a manifesto commitment to abolishing the hereditary peerage. Their failure to say what they would put in its place led some of us to vote against giving them a blank cheque until they spelt out what reform would mean.

The Prime Minister's attachment to an all-appointed House vests great power in the hands of politicians who will generally use their patronage merely to reward 'services rendered' – everything from donations to party coffers to unquestioning loyalty. Clearly this will not deliver independence or a robust bicameral legislature. I voted against such a system and voted, instead, for a fully elected House. Of the various options on offer (in all, seven variations, all of which were rejected by the House of Commons), a small elected House, modelled on the US Senate, perhaps with a one-term membership of seven to ten years – would be better than a House lampooned for 'cronyism'.

It would be absurd, though, to suggest that the Lords has proved incapable of change or evolution.

Until the seventeenth century peers sat in the House in strict order of precedence – the Lords spiritual on the right of the throne (and Church of England bishops still sit there to this day) and the Lords temporal on the left. Increasing membership led the authorities to put in more seats to accommodate the newly arrived viscounts and barons of the day.

In 1876 the Appellate Jurisdiction Act allowed Law Lords to sit as life peers and in 1958 the introduction of life peers created a permanent change in the composition and balance of the House. Earlier, in 1911, the Parliament Act – following a confrontation between the Liberal government and the Lords – had seen its powers emasculated. The changes made by the Blair government in the 1999 House of Lords Act – ending the automatic right of hereditary peers to sit and vote – were only the latest of these changes.

Once they have evicted the remaining 92 hereditary peers I do not believe that we will see any further 'reform' because, by a process of stealth, the political establishment have achieved their fully appointed House without ever being given a mandate for it either by the electorate or by Parliament. Personally, I am always saddened that, beyond the debate about political legitimacy, so little is ever said about the role played by individual hereditary peers, who have often given devoted and non-partisan public service. I am also cynical about an argument for abolition that rested on democratic legitimacy and replaced hereditary peers with appointed peers. Owing your seat to a dead ancestor may even make you less biddable than owing your seat to a living Prime Minister.

In a fully appointed House the role of the independent crossbench peers will be especially important in trying to hold to account the political machines and government.

In January 2000 the Royal Commission on the Reform of the House of Lords, chaired by Lord Wakeham, published its findings and pointed to the pivotal influence of the crossbenches. Many peers believed that the built-in majority that the Conservative Party had always traditionally enjoyed in the Lords was no longer tenable, but that if this was not simply to be replaced by a Labour Party ascendancy, the best way to proceed was with the creation of roughly equal numbers between government and opposition with the crossbenches holding the balance.

So who exactly are the crossbenchers?

Peers in the Lords who do not take a party whip (i.e. are not told how to vote by a political party) sit on the crossbenches. They are well known for their independent, non-party political stance. They are people who have chosen not to accept a party allegiance for a whole host of reasons. Some come from outside the realm of politics; some are actively involved in work away from Parliament and only come when issues arise where they feel they have specialised knowledge to offer. Others have been in political parties but want the independence that the crossbenches permit.

Many crossbenchers have specialist expertise drawn from diverse disciplines – including academia, science, industry, the countryside, the armed forces and the diplomatic service. Their contributions are always listened to with particular respect when they are speaking about their own discipline – and, indeed, they can have considerable influence on the outcome of debates.

There are about 180 crossbench peers (about 150 life peers and just under 30 remaining hereditary peers). The twelve Lords of Appeal in Ordinary (the Law Lords) are also included in the crossbench numbers (although their continuing future in the upper House is also now under review). In 2001 the government famously appointed fifteen individuals (selected by the House of Lords Appointment Commission) – dubbed by the media as the 'people's peers' – who also sit on the crossbenches.

The role of peers in scrutinising legislation, in a far less adversarial atmosphere than exists in the Commons, is clearly crucial. During 2002/3 alone some 9,782 amendments to Bills were moved in the Lords, many of which were either enacted outright or formed the basis for compromise agreements with the government.

Crossbenchers are uniquely placed in drawing together cross-party coalitions. They also take their own initiatives, such as sponsoring private members' Bills. They have also regularly chaired the many influential committees that have prepared reports that have then provided a framework for both legislation and the wider debate about public policy. One good example of this is the 1999 Protection of Children Act, which was introduced by my colleague Lord Laming. Coming from a distinguished social services background he was ideally placed to introduce a Bill that among other things provided for lists to be compiled of those who are unsuitable to work with children.

The Lords also takes very seriously its role as a scrutinising chamber. A series of committees evaluate all of the legislation that issues from the European Parliament while all UK primary legislation (with the exception of finance Bills) has to come under the glare of House of Lords scrutiny. This is work that will be deepened in the future.

The role of both Houses of Parliament, the devolution of powers to Scotland, Wales and Northern Ireland – and in the future, to some of the English regions – the role of local democracy and directly elected mayors and the redefinition of individual citizenship have been preoccupations of the past decade. Over the previous 25 years these issues were largely neglected. Apart from the abolition of the Greater London Council and the metropolitan county councils in 1985, governance issues were rarely concerns of the Conservative governments of 1979–97. While they were busy modernising industrial law and the British economy, the party of Burke and the constitution, the party also of Chamberlain's municipalism, was surprisingly uninterested in re-examining and reforming governance. In retrospect, and as they reflect on the nature of Lords reform and the introduction of measures such as the closed party list system of voting, they may come to see what an error this was.

That the way in which we govern ourselves has once again become a central political concern is something I welcome. What I regret is that tinkering around with the system now passes for reform, and that gaining a short-term partisan advantage has become a greater prize than entrenching sound democratic structures and real accountability.

Thoreau once said that if you cut down all the trees, there will be nowhere left for the birds to sing. In Britain, our great oaks of central and local government are something to prize and preserve. Before hacking away at their branches we need much greater thought and reflection.

SEVEN

Membership of the House of Commons and House of Lords: A Comparison and Discussion

Lord Howe of Aberavon

Your conclusions don't matter', advised Donald Maclachlan, first editor of the *Sunday Telegraph*, as I tackled the first mini-leader that I wrote for his new-born paper in 1961, 'so long as you ask the right questions.'

I often have the impression that academics have the same, rather semi-detached attitude to life. That, I am sure, is why I could never have settled for an academic career – nor even, in the long run, for a tenaciously forensic one: as a barrister, helping other people to achieve their own objectives; and later, as a judge, helping to clear up other people's messes.

And that, I am equally sure, is why I was determined, from a very early age, upon a career as a politician. I wanted to make a difference to the world in which I was going to live – a difference for the better, of course. (I've never been able to forgive C. H. Sisson for entitling one chapter in his book *The Spirit of British Administration* 'The politician as intruder'.) For all these reasons I was determined to approach the characteristic ('compare and contrast') question posed by Nicholas Baldwin with at least something of the same constructive zeal.

But it hasn't been at all easy, for two reasons.

First, because of the wide time difference between my experience of the two Houses. Out of four decades of almost uninterrupted membership of Parliament, the first three were in the Commons and only the last in the Lords. And over that period of time, there have been significant changes in the substantive role, the cultural style and the public perception of both Houses.

And second, because I have enjoyed very different viewpoints of the two Houses. All but three of my years in the Commons were spent on the front bench – all but five of them in government, while my eleven years in the Lords have all been as a backbencher.

Even so, it is more than possible to identify, in respect of the two Houses, huge (and to a large extent continuing) differences in almost every aspect of their existence. In the background, nature and behaviour of their inhabitants; in the work which they do and the effectiveness with which they do (or don't do) it; in the way in which, and extent to which, those differences are changing – and, more important still, in the constitutional and other implications of those patterns of change.

The crucial role of the Commons is to serve as the cockpit of democracy – the forum in which governments are created or defeated, in which political reputations and careers are made or destroyed. The political parties struggle there with a view to gaining power. Members, even of the same party, compete with each other with a view to gaining office. All the more so in our own system, with its traditionally two-party structure. Collectively and individually, it is a competitive and combative assembly. Its members, younger and still more personally ambitious than in the Lords, are easily fired by near-tribalistic instincts.

This is, of course, the classic reason for the establishment of second chambers. Concerns about untrammelled democracy shared by the Founding Fathers of the United States led to the creation of the US Senate – in order to bring different perspectives to bear and thus to 'prevent hasty or ill-considered decisions' by members of the first elected chamber.[1] (This, essentially, is the reason why no fewer than 67 of the 182 democracies recognised by the International Parliamentary Union have two-chamber parliaments).

What I have said so far might well persuade the reader that I have little, if any, respect for the working of our lower House. Not so. One of its more remarkable characteristics has been its ability, sensitively and completely, to change its tone, style and mode dramatically. I have particularly vivid memories of this quality from many weeks in 1970–72, which I spent (as Solicitor General) grappling with a committee of the whole House on the Industrial Relations and European Communities Bills.

For hours on end sometimes, the chamber would have all the intellectual tranquillity of a university seminar, as specialist insights were exchanged by real experts (trade union, managerial, agricultural or whatever, as well as legal). But then, as the hour for a timetabled division approached – and the bars and other haunts emptied – the chamber imperceptibly filled. And suddenly, the seminar had become a stadium – and the professor a gladiator (or worse still, a Christian), shouting to make himself heard above a baying mob!

And then, quite different again for the 'great' occasions – Budget day for example. In my time certainly, however gloomy the economic outlook or dismal the hopes, the House displayed a good-humoured sense of expectation and was ready to give the Chancellor a fair hearing. (I remember, for example, the general sense of shock, when Jo Grimond – of all people – attempted to intervene in the middle of my 1981 Budget speech).

I sensed something of the same atmosphere of silent expectation, and even respect, when I rose, rather nervously, on 13 November 1990, to make my resignation statement – my first speech from the back benches for more than quarter of a century. In sharp contrast with this, in a different way, was the warm-hearted and generous reception given by the House, just nine days later on the day of her own resignation, to Margaret Thatcher's dazzlingly confident swan-song speech as Prime Minister.

Such moments of drama and tension, of theatre indeed, are much less characteristic of the House of Lords. This is largely, no doubt, because the perceived 'big beasts' of politics are still mainly at the other end of the building. But it is also, I fancy, because the participating audience in the upper House is much less pervasively partisan than in the Commons.

Particularly now, since the built-in Tory (and hereditary) majority has been removed, one is very conscious of the presence in the Lords' chamber of an unpompous, and generally rather expert, jury of one's countrymen (and women) – sitting on the crossbenches. One has the feeling that, more even than the rest of the House, they embody the largely non-partisan instincts of the great bulk of the population – for whom the yah-boo style of much that now goes on in the Commons is deeply repellent.

It is this instinct – shared by almost all members of the Lords – which does so much to influence the courteous, thoughtful quality of most speeches and other proceedings there. On the rare occasions on which a peer makes what is described critically as 'a Commons speech', it may sometimes be seen as entertaining but is nonetheless unwelcome – and less persuasive than it otherwise might have been.

I had rather hoped that the televising of the Commons (which started during my time as Leader of the House) would have helped to persuade the Commons to change their ways in this respect. Sound broadcasting had sadly (but certainly) not done so. But there was surely some possibility that the actual display of noisiness and unruly behaviour might have a bigger effect? MPs might, I had hoped, be shamed into behaving better *devant les enfants*!

But the children, although themselves now able to watch, remained themselves unseen – and thus, alas, without any significant influence on behaviour in the chamber. So what has been described as 'the adversarial cockfight' of Prime Minister's Questions continues as another serial of television violence – the Punch and Judy show of British politics, much enjoyed by C-Span television viewers in the United States.

One other feature increasingly points up the contrast in the composition and performance of the two Houses. I have in mind the wide and growing difference in their diversity and expertise. There is, of course, nothing new about this. The Commons always consisted, by definition, of people who had deliberately chosen themselves to stand as elected politicians, while the Lords were simply a social class or 'estate of the realm', conscripted into political service of a kind, while free to pursue their other occupations (if any). So there was always likely to be a greater diversity of occupation in the Lords than in the Commons – and a greater preponderance of 'professional' politicians in the Commons than in the Lords.

But that difference has hugely increased in the four decades since I first entered the Commons. Even at the time when I first entered government, as Solicitor General in 1970, there was, for example, still a significant number of practising Queen's Counsel in the Commons – with at least half a dozen on the Tory side at that time competing for that job. The scene is very different today, when (in the absence of suitable candidates in the Commons) we have seen two successive Attorney Generals appointed from the Lords.

It wasn't just well-qualified lawyers who were once to be found in numbers in the Commons. On both sides of the House, opponents and critics of the controversial legislation which I handled as Solicitor General in the Heath government included many professionals – businessmen, leading trade unionists, farmers and, of course, ex-servicemen.

The contrast between the two Houses is much greater today. A few of the more eccentric occupations may have disappeared from the Lords, with the departure of the bulk of the hereditaries. But since 1958 more than a thousand life peers have been appointed (only a minority, of course, survive today); and the diversity of real expertise now available must far exceed that in any other legislative chamber in the world.

In one recent debate on the health service, for example, the nineteen speakers included two former deans of university medical schools, a practising dentist, a consultant obstetrician, a consultant paediatrician, a former GP, a former professor of nursing, a former director of Age Concern and the president of MENCAP.[2] Those speaking in the September 2002 debate on Iraq included three former Chiefs of the Defence Staff, three former Foreign

Secretaries, two former Home Secretaries, six bishops, two former ambassadors, two former defence secretaries and many others with service experience.[3]

And so on. It is this wide spread of experience that enables the Lords – not least in its network of expert select committees – to mobilise a really well-informed group for the scrutiny of any fresh legislative or policy proposal. And it is the knowledge that those participating in any debate are likely to include such independent expertise which helps to ensure that discussion is well focused. Whoever you are, you would be wise always to assume that there is someone in the chamber, who knows more about 'your' subject than you do!

Former MPs who arrive in the Lords do, of course, feel distinctly liberated in one respect – the disappearance of the familiar burden of constituency work. Some find it sad to be suddenly cut off from the flow of often friendly and always informative material, which has flowed in for many years. But the change is essential, given the disappearance of the substantial office staff to which today's MP can grow accustomed. It is remarkable to recall that when I was first elected in 1964, I was able to manage with only one-third of a secretary, whom I shared with two former ministers, Peter Thomas and Peter Thorneycroft.

In the Lords, one's secretarial help remains strictly limited – and office accommodation even more so. Like others, I share a tiny room with former Secretaries of State for the Home Office and Northern Ireland. And, again like others, I still hold more than one (unpaid) public sector job, and a clutch of charitable positions. Fortunately, however, for most of the thirteen years since I left government, I have been able to enjoy a wide range of business and academic posts in several countries besides Britain. This has not only kept me travelling but helped to keep me well informed about the rest of the world.

This is another of the most important differences between today's life in the Lords and in the Commons. As legislators we may be unpaid – but most of us are emphatically part time. We thus remain in touch with real life – much more so than during the years spent as a minister! And more too, certainly, than many members of the present House of Commons.

One contrasting, and remarkable, feature of life in the Lords (which I have never myself experienced, as someone who was glad to leave the front bench behind) is the huge burden of work now borne by those members of the House who have the duty of speaking from the opposition front bench. This work – like that of so many political offices outside government – is entirely unpaid and can be extremely onerous.

During the session of 2002/3, one Conservative frontbencher – Baroness Anelay, who led for the opposition on four major Bills (the massive Criminal Justice Bill, the Courts Bill, the Extradition Bill and the Crime (International Co-operation) Bill) – had to spend 48 full days in the chamber or Grand Committee, helping to process through all their stages more than 750 pages of complex (and often) ill-prepared legislation. During this time she estimates that she must have considered and debated at least 2,500 amendments or new clauses (having herself tabled about three-quarters of these).

Lady Anelay was, of course, very far from being alone in these proceedings. No fewer than 120 peers took part in the debates on one or other or all of these four bills. Seven (including the Lord Chancellor) were ministers, each with a heavy frontbench task to discharge. Ranged against them were 23 former ministers, thirteen of whom had served in Cabinet – two as Home Secretary and one as Lord Chancellor – and six others as junior Home Office ministers.

There was also a formidable array of legal talent, starting with the Lord Chief Justice and six former Law Lords – one of them the former Chief Justice of New Zealand – as well as six former Law Officers, two former Bar Council chairmen and fifteen other Queen's Counsel. Five Justices of the Peace and four solicitors (including one who had served on the Jimmy Young radio programme as its 'Legal Eagle' for eighteen years) spoke alongside two former Police Authority chairmen, a former Commissioner of the Metropolitan Police, a former chief executive of NACRO and two former chairmen of the Parole Board.

This diversity of wisdom was further extended by the participation of five professors, four each of bishops and former trade union general secretaries, three Oxbridge heads of college, two former European Commissioners, a former bank chairman and a former social services director. There is, no doubt, a little overlapping and double counting in this analysis – but not much. Taken in the round, it clearly demonstrates the range of expertise with which legislation is so closely scrutinised in the Lords.

The final contrasting irony is that the consideration given by the Commons to this quartet of Bills was cursory and superficial in the extreme. The two which started in the lower House were driven through under so-called 'timetable motions' (a.k.a. 'guillotines'). Well over half of each of these two Bills had received in the Commons no committee stage consideration whatsoever.

Why is it that so much of the real work of Parliament, as a law-making body, is thus being transferred from the elected to the non-elected House? Meg Russell has revealed the surprising – but highly significant – fact that exactly the same thing has been happening in other bicameral legislatures.[4] She has also explained why.

The essential difference springs from three features, which are common to all the relevant cases:

- The second chamber, unlike the first, has no power – through a no-confidence vote or in any other way – to end the life of the government.
- Correspondingly, the government has no power – through dissolution of the chamber or in any other way – to put at risk any member's continued membership of the legislature.
- The governing party does not have – and is not expected to have – a majority in the second chamber.

Meg Russell's conclusion is that 'this different kind of relationship between the second chamber and the executive has profound consequences'. Party discipline, for example, 'is less strict than in the lower house'; and in the diverse Parliaments which she has studied, it is 'a common pattern that the second chamber is less partisan and more deliberative than the first'. This in its turn is 'likely to lead to far closer legislative scrutiny'. She concludes that, as a consequence, in Australia for example, it is the upper chamber which has become 'the true site of negotiation between government and the legislature'. David Blunkett would not, I suspect, find it difficult, after his experience as Home Secretary, to recognise this as an accurate description of his relationship with Parliament in, for example, the closing stages of his 2003 Criminal Justice Act.

It is only fair to point out that this developing power of second chambers, to scrutinise legislation more closely and otherwise to hold governments to account, does not seem to depend, one way or another, upon the elected or unelected nature of the house. The crucial features are, first, the absence of a government majority and, second (and probably more important), the inability of executive or legislators to affect the political lifespan of each other. In these circumstances, the second chamber – much freer of executive or partisan control – can be an effective site for interparty negotiation and thus able to introduce an element of consensus politics, while also retaining the 'strong government' associated with an otherwise majoritarian system.

There are signs that this growth in the effectiveness of second chambers is giving them increasing confidence. In Britain, for example, the dramatic change in composition of the Lords since 1997 has greatly increased the practical, day-to-day confidence of that chamber. 'Ministers', proclaimed the *Independent* in mid-2003, 'have failed to intimidate Parliament.'[5] The paper was rightly applauding the repulse of David Blunkett's attack upon the jury system.

But which House was being applauded? The record speaks for itself. In the five sessions 1997–2001 there were 1,640 divisions in the House of Commons, without a single government defeat. In the same period in the Lords there were 639 whipped divisions, of which the government lost no fewer than 164 (25 per cent). On each of these occasions the government (and thus the Commons, in that order) has been obliged to think again about what might have been overhasty or misguided propositions. The House of Lords was thus fulfilling exactly the proper role and function of second chambers in many other Parliaments around the world.

There is more than one reason for this. The mounting confidence of the Lords is undoubtedly inspired by a growing sense of their own legitimacy – or, at the very least, a diminishing sense of illegitimacy. The disappearance of most, though not yet all, of the hereditaries is one powerful reason for this. The other is the matching removal of the formerly built-in Conservative majority. Neither opposition nor government can now be sure – indeed can no longer have a hope – of winning a division without the support of a number of crossbenchers and/or 'independents' (very often dissenting members of one or other of the main parties).

These ongoing changes are certainly having a positive effect on the morale of most, if not all, members of the House of Lords. And there are increasing signs – or so it seems at our end of the Palace of Westminster – of a decline in self-confidence amongst members of 'the other place'.

This is becoming apparent – for example and rather remarkably – from some recent observations by that Commons champion, Robin Cook.[6] He bewails 'the remorseless erosion of esteem for Parliament among the electors' and identifies 'the most visible measure of public disaffection with the parliamentary process' as 'the alarming drop in General Election turn out'. Hence what he graphically describes as 'today's disconnection between the electors and the elected'. Given this manifest and mounting reluctance by electors to enthuse over the outcome of the electoral process, it becomes all the more surprising that Robin Cook still feels able, as he does in the same article, to argue that 'legitimacy is conferred by democracy, and democracy is conferred by elections'.

He is not alone in continuing to assume – and to argue as though the world assumes – that overriding authority should, always and unquestionably, be accorded to 'the elected House'. Until recently at least, several distinguished commentators – for example, Donald Macintyre and Peter Riddell – have continued to assume that election is the only true passport to perceived legitimacy.

But the reasons for diminishing confidence are beginning to be recognised even in those quarters. The late Hugo Young, for example, in an important comment on the House of Lords' role in removing profoundly illiberal clauses from the Anti-Terrorism Act 2001, had this to say: 'Something important is being said about democracy when the only legislative chamber to perform the functions that people expect – deliberation, revision, improvement – contained not a single elected politician.'[7] And Peter Riddell has more recently acknowledged that 'representative democracy is on the defensive, if not on the retreat. The fall in electoral turnout is the most obvious sign.'[8] True, he goes on, as I am happy to do, to look for fresh ways of informing our governors about the currents of popular thinking – no one can object to that. But his expressed anxiety about the declining confidence of electors in traditional democracy should surely diminish the enthusiasm for introducing into the Lords one of the elements most likely to reproduce their the partisan structure, which makes today's House of Commons such a partisan battlefield.

There are signs that members of the House of Lords are becoming increasingly aware of the extent to which its acknowledged success in its presently wide role depends not only upon the diversity, expertise and experience of its present membership but also upon the continuance of the conventions and niceties of its present structure. It was clear, for example, from the recent debate about the Speakership of the House, that one reason for the success was the fact that the nominal 'chairman' of the Lords does not have – and never has had – any kind of authority over the House. In this long-standing absence of any kind of truly 'presiding officer', the House has been entirely self-governing in its management – almost, I suspect, like a Quaker meeting. In the words of a report of a House committee under the chairmanship of Baroness Hilton of Eggardon: 'The House should be proud of its capacity to combine good politics with good manners.'[9]

Against that background, many speakers warned of the risks involved in even the most modest steps towards the establishment of any kind of authority for its chairman. Shirley Williams (Baroness Williams of Crosby), for example, reminded us just 'how easy it would be to shift very slowly, gradually, little by little over the next few years to a situation where self-government was regarded as an anachronistic, out of date, no longer suitable, and we would find ourselves with the same kind of structure as the Commons.'10

This analysis may appear to have taken us some distance away from the subject of this chapter. But it underlines an important lesson – that the present role and performance of the House of Lords, and the quality and characteristics of its members, are very closely linked to the continuance of its existing rules and conventions. This means that the possible impact of any significant change in its arrangements needs to be very carefully considered, before such a change is sanctioned.

I do not here attempt to make any judgement about the comparative merits of the present structure of the House and of a very different one, which contained an elected element, of whatever size.11 But what one can say, with some certainty, is that the introduction of a significant elected element is bound to have some impact upon the manners, atmosphere and performance of the chamber. When life peers were introduced they were in effect 'drip fed' into the chamber, over almost half a century, and in practice were seen to enable the House to combine the best of what was new with the conciliatory traditions of the past. And it did, of course, add a distinctively positive new element, namely the availability of an increasingly wide and diverse stock of expertise. This surely is an important feature of the present House, which should not be jeopardised by whatever change may or may not be made in the direction of introducing an elected element.

This is why, as it seems to me, it is surely premature even for the most enthusiastic reformers to postulate anything like the overnight transformation, still less replacement, of the present institution – with the ejection of most, if not all, of the present members and their replacement by a wholly unpredictable tranche of elected politicians. Nobody would sensibly think of trying to transform the composition, nature and behaviour of the House of Commons by anything like such a mass upheaval of that institution.

Correspondingly, it must surely be seen as essential to the preservation of the culture, qualities and, above all, efficiency that are so widely commended in the present House of Lords, for even modest changes in its composition to be phased in over a significant period of time.

And so I have finished by asking what I hope are some of the right questions – and brought myself and the reader to at least one worthwhile conclusion. 'If it's a very long way from being broke, take great care before you begin to think of trying to "fix" it!'

Endnotes

1   Russell, M., 'Is the House of Lords Already Reformed?', *Political Quarterly*, Summer 2003, p. 311.
2   Hansard, House of Lords Debates, 21 November 2001.
3   Hansard, House of Lords Debates, 24 September 2002.
4   Russell, 'Is the House of Lords Already Reformed?'.
5   *Independent*, 17 July 2003.
6   Robin Cook, *Independent*, 18 July 2003.
7   *Guardian*, 18 December 2001.
8   *The Times*, 8 January 2004.
9   'Freedom & Function', HL Paper 34, 1 March 1999.
10   Hansard, House of Lords Debates, 12 January 2004, col. 390.
11   But see, for example, my articles in *The Times*, 2 August 1999, the *House Magazine*, 26 November 2001, the *Independent*, 12 November 2002 and the *Spectator*, 30 August 2003.

EIGHT

House of Commons Committees and National Security

Bruce George MP, J. David Morgan and Natalie Whatford

National Security is an evolving concept. There is now widespread agreement that it incorporates external defence, arms control, homeland security, the critical national infrastructure,[1] the fight against terrorism, threats from espionage and sabotage, actions intended to overthrow or undermine parliamentary democracy by political, industrial or violent means, and threats posed by the actions or intentions of persons outside the British Isles to the economic well-being of the United Kingdom.[2] Responsibility is shared between numerous government departments, devolved governments and legislatures and regional tiers of administration of government. In the last three years terrorism post 9/11 and the war in Iraq have dominated the agenda.

Parliament has never structured itself to deal with national security issues. Responsibility is spread as a result of an accumulation of decisions and practices from various times in our history. This chapter considers the work of House of Commons committees. The good work that has been done by House of Lords or joint committees is considered elsewhere. Information about the work of committees can be found in the various annual reports[3] and the sessional returns.[4]

The role of House of Commons committees in defence and national security

The role of parliamentary committees in defence, foreign affairs and warfare goes back to the medieval period, yet the UK today still exhibits the executive's dominance in decision-making.

Departmental select committees have greatly evolved since the current system was established in 1979. Their task is 'to examine the expenditure, administration and policy of the (relevant) government department ... and associated public bodies'.5 In 2002 core tasks were agreed for the select committees, and these were set out in a table produced in a Liaison Committee report.6

Committees have always enjoyed the power to send for 'persons, papers and records'.7 There are, however, four major areas of difficulty. Firstly, members of either House of Parliament cannot be required to attend. This has hindered some inquiries. Of greater concern on a regular basis is the fact that ministers can refuse a request from a committee to question a specific official. The third difficulty arises over the requirement to answer questions. *Erskine May* states that 'a witness is bound to answer all questions which the Committee sees fit to put to him.'8 Ultimately a witness who refuses to cooperate may be punished for contempt of the House. However, problems have arisen. For example, journalists have refused to reveal their sources,9 and, when the Maxwell brothers refused to answer questions before a select committee in 1991/2, no action was ever taken against them.

The House of Commons select committee structure largely mirrors the organisation of the executive in that each department has its respective committee. But a key feature of modern government is missing. The essential and timeless purpose of the Cabinet has been to coordinate policy across individual departments. Increasing centralisation to improve coordination has been a feature of British government for decades.

While terrorism is dealt with on an ad hoc basis by select committees, the government has a complex structure of ministerial committees with a secretariat provided by the Cabinet Office. There is now an intelligence and security coordinator at Permanent Secretary level in the Cabinet Office in addition to established secretariats for domestic and overseas affairs; intelligence and security; and civil contingencies.

House of Commons Defence Committee (HCDC)

The House of Commons Defence Committee clearly has a key role to play in the scrutiny of national security issues. Standing Order 152 makes it the committee responsible for the oversight of the Ministry of Defence's expenditure, administration and policy.

It has been the practice of the committee to undertake different types of inquiry. These can be categorised into ten major types.

Types of Inquiries	Examples
1. Government defence reviews, White Papers and policy	*A New Chapter to the Strategic Defence Review* (6th Report, 2002–03) *The Strategic Defence Review* (8th Report, 1997–98) Defence White Paper (current)
2. Proposed legislation (primary and secondary)	Draft Civil Contingencies Bill (7th Report, 2002–3) Arms Control and Disarmament (Inspections) Bill (3rd Report, 2002–3) Ministry of Defence Police: Changes in Jurisdiction Proposed under the Anti-Terrorism Crime and Security Bill 2001 (1st Report, 2001–2)
3. Defence procurement	*Defence Procurement* (8th Report, 2002–3) *Major Procurement Projects* (4th Report, 2001–02; 9th Report, 2000–01)
4. Combat operations involving UK armed forces	*Lessons of Iraq* (3rd Report, 2003–04) *Lessons of Kosovo* (14th Report, 1999–2000) *Iraqi No-Fly Zones* (13th Report, 1999–2000) *Peace Support Operations in Bosnia and Herzegovina* (1st Report, 1997–98) *Preliminary Lessons of Operation Granby* (10th Report, 1990–91)
5. UK defence	*The Threat from Terrorism* (2nd Report, 2001–02) *Defence and Security in the UK* (6th Report, 2001–2)

Types of Inquiries	Examples
6. International Defence and Security issues	The Future of NATO (6th Report, 2001–02)
	The Six-Nation Framework Agreement (1st Report, 2002–1)
	European Security & Defence (8th Report, 1999–2000)
	The OCCAR Convention (1st Report, 1999–2000)
	Inter-Governmental Conference – European Security and Defence (Current)
7. Personnel issues	*Armed Forces Pensions and Compensation* (1st Report, 2003–4)
8. Review of agencies	*The Defence Geographic & Image Intelligence Agency* (5th Report, 1999–2000)
	DERA (6th Report, 1997–8)
9. Appointments	*The Appointment of the New Chief Scientific Adviser* (6th Report, 1999–2000)
	The Appointment of the New Head of Defence Export Services (2nd Report, 1998–9)
10. Issues of Controversy	*Missile Defence* (1st Report, 2002–3)
	Gulf Veterans Illness (7th Report, 1999–2000)
	Defence Research (9th Report, 1998–9)
	Security of Supply and the Future of the Royal Ordnance Factory, Bishopton (5th Report, 1998–9)

In addition the HCDC was one of the first committees to produce an annual report on its work, a practice now widespread amongst the departmental select committees.

House of Commons Foreign Affairs Committee (FAC)

The Foreign Affairs Committee has responsibility for overseeing the Foreign and Commonwealth Office (FCO). It is unsurprising that this committee has also taken a keen interest in international issues relevant to Britain's national security. Since 2001 it has produced four separate reports entitled *Foreign Policy Aspects of the War on Terrorism*.[10] It reported on weapons of mass destruction (WMD) in August 2000[11] and on the Biological Weapons Green Paper,[12] and has produced reports on the conflicts in Sierra Leone[13] and Kosovo[14] and on the decision to go to war in Iraq.[15] It has additionally produced reports on private military companies.[16] It frequently takes evidence from the FCO's Defence and Intelligence Directorate and has occasionally taken evidence from serving or former officials from the Ministry of Defence.[17]

Quadripartite Committee

The Quadripartite Committee is made up of the Defence, Foreign Affairs, International Development and Trade and Industry select committees. Annual reports are produced by the government, setting out policy issues relating to strategic export controls and details of export licensing decisions taken that year.[18] The Quadripartite Committee is formally composed of all the members of each constituent committee, but in practice each committee nominates three members to represent it. In addition to considering the government's annual report, this committee has conducted inquiries into primary[19] and secondary legislation[20] related to export controls.

While the committee has been successful it has encountered difficulties. Arranging meetings convenient for the members and staff of four different committees is challenging. Unless there is a period of real crisis little is done. There are cultural differences between the committees. One such example is that the International Development committee does not need or want to sell arms to anyone. The Trade and Industry committee, however, discusses the security of exports. The Foreign Affairs committee has to be aware of our relations between countries and the Defence committee has to consider the MOD, jobs and the economy.

Intelligence and Security Committee (ISC)

Unlike the departmental select committees the ISC is the creation of statute.[21] It is resourced by the government and its secretariat is provided by the Cabinet Office. Although the requirement to examine expenditure, administration and policy is the same, instead of a single government department the ISC's remit covers the UK's three intelligence and security agencies: the Security Service (popularly known as MI5), the Secret Intelligence Service (popularly known as MI6) and the Government Communications Headquarters (GCHQ).

It is appointed by and reports directly to the Prime Minister. Consisting of parliamentarians, it produces an annual report which the Prime Minister publishes to the House of Commons. The ISC has produced a booklet explaining its role, and other matters regarding the oversight of intelligence.[22] The committee appoints an investigator to conduct research on its behalf where more detail is needed than the committee could do itself. In 2002/3 the investigator presented reports to them on the agencies' people policies, joint working in the agencies, the national intelligence machinery and the agencies' business planning processes.[23]

> The members are notified under the Official Secrets Act 1989 and, as such, operate within 'the ring of secrecy'. The Committee has also taken evidence from the Security and Intelligence Co-ordinator, the Chairman of the Joint Intelligence Committee (JIC), the Defence Intelligence Staff (DIS) and other organisations that receive secret intelligence from the Agencies. The Committee sees significant amounts of classified material in carrying out its oversight duties and it questions and has taken evidence from Cabinet Ministers and senior officials.[24]

The ISC sees every detail of the Single Intelligence Account – including how much they spend on staff, stationery and agents.[25]

Other House of Commons committees

There are other House of Commons committees which have responsibility for areas with national security interests.

House	Type	Title of committee	National security involvement
Commons	Select	Trade & Industry	The DTI has significant national security responsibility concentrated in its Offices for Export Control and Non-proliferationDirectorate; and its Office for Civil Nuclear Security. It has joined HCDC in inquiries into procurement and industrial policy. Currently looking at electricity supply contingency planning.
Commons	Select	International Development	The use of the military in humanitarian assistance has been a key theme throughout a number of the reports. In July 1999 it produced a report on 'conflict prevention and post-conflict reconstruction',[26] which dealt with such security issues as arms proliferation and the use of the military pre and post conflict. Studies have dealt with Iraq,[27] Afghanistan[28] and Kosovo.[29]
Commons	Select	Home Affairs	Internal security is largely the responsibility of the Home Office. While the 1st report of 2001/2, 'The Anti-Terrorism, Crime and Security Bill 2001,' and the 3rd report of 1998/9, 'Accountability of the Security Service,' seem to be the only recent reports clearly linked to Home Affairs national security, many of its reports deal with issues (border controls, asylum, immigration and extradition, identity cards) which are very relevant. In 2003 single-evidence sessions were held by the government's reviewer of anti-terrorism legislation, (Lord Carlile of Berriew QC). There was also an informal meeting with the director general of the Security Service.[30]
Commons	Select	Northern Ireland	*The Financing of Terrorism in Northern Ireland,* 4th Report, 2001–02.
Commons	Select	Transport	The DoT has its own security department (TRANSEC). The committee had not under taken any specific studies into security issues, for which there would be great scope, but references can be found in reports to transport security. Currently they are looking at the British Transport Police.
Commons	Select	Environmental Audit	Current inquiry into military operations and reconstruction: the environment in Iraq.

House	Type	Title of committee	National security involvement
Commons	Joint HoC	Liaison	Holds twice-yearly sessions of evidence from the Prime Minister to discuss international and domestic affairs. Its role as one of the engines of reform of Parliament and the select committee system makes it vital to improved scrutiny of national security matters.
Commons	Special	Science & Technology	*The Scientific Response to Terrorism*, 8th Report, 2002–3.
Commons		Public Accounts Committee	The National Audit Office reports to this committee. The chairman sees the expenditure details of the three intelligence and security agencies and can question the agencies on their expenditure through the NAO.[31]
Commons		Public Administration Committee	*Taming the Prerogative*, 4th Report, 2003–4 – includes the issues of making and ratification of treaties and the deployment and use of the armed forces.
Commons		Procedure	*Delegated Legislation: Proposals for a Sifting Committee*, 1st Report, 2002–3. *Parliamentary Scrutiny of Treaties*, 2nd Report, 1999–2000.

Primary legislation is considered by standing committees as part of the legislative process. Secondary legislation can come before the Select Committee on Statutory Instruments; the Joint Committee on Statutory Instruments or one of the seventeen standing committees on delegated legislation.

As evidenced by activity on the Anti-terrorism, Crime and Security Bill, departmental select committees and joint committees have also been involved in prelegislative scrutiny.[32]

Review of committee system

Autonomous working

There is no mechanism for allocating work to the committees other than each committee's interpretation of its own terms of reference. The Liaison Committee does not, despite its title, carry out this role. While committee chairs have amicably agreed to other committees undertaking studies which cross departmental boundaries, there is no one to provide a strategic vision for national security scrutiny.

Committees select their own issues for inquiries and tend to focus exclusively upon their own main department. Just occasionally a committee will comment on other departments; for example, the International Development Committee in its report Conflict Prevention and Post-conflict Reconstruction said:

> We find it ironic that in an administration supposedly committed to an ethical arms policy DESO's branch office in Indonesia has more staff and a higher budget (£190,000 in 1997–98 compared to £125,000 in 1996–97) than the FCO's Arms Control and Disarmament Research Unit.[33]

Primarily Reactive

Nothing shakes up a committee more than a war. This study has noted that the military engagements in the Falkland Islands, Kosovo, Afghanistan and Iraq have all led to a number of committees undertaking related inquiries. However, terrorism has held little interest for parliamentary committees. The events of 9/11 did provoke some committees to consider future threats to Britain, but there has never been a comprehensive, 'joined-up' study, to consider what are the United Kingdom's national security interests and vulnerabilities.

Recent Reforms

There have been a number of recent innovations within the select committee system for which the Liaison Committee has been the engine of reform. For example, it is now the practice of committees to produce both an annual report and a programme. This may aid Parliament to take an overview of the subject coverage and perhaps improve scrutiny of national security.

Committees are also undertaking more travel and making greater use of experts. Indeed, many committees have increased the number of specialist advisers. For example, the HCDC used six such advisers in its Iraq inquiry.[34]

Committee actions post 9/11

In the immediate aftermath of 9/11 the chairs of the Defence, Foreign Affairs, Home Affairs and Intelligence and Security committees were invited to a briefing from the Prime Minister. Subsequent to this meeting the chairs discussed how committees could cooperate and avoid overlap on issues raised by the terrorist attacks. No decisions were ever formally adopted, and committees took up reports on an ad hoc basis. There is informal liaison between committee staff,[35] and it has been noted that personal links, between staffs and between committee chairs, have helped to carry out work more effectively and cooperatively. There have been a number of occasions when a chair has proposed an inquiry and consulted other committees before starting. Few problems have been encountered. The Science and Technology committee went as far as to invite other committees to attend a debate in Westminster Hall after the publication of their report and the government response.

Post 9/11, the HCDC was first off the mark with its inquiry into the threat from terrorism, the first hearing being held on 7 November 2001. It was an 'attempt to examine how, as a consequence, our understanding of the threat to UK security and defence interests has changed'. It looked 'at how the implications of those events are being addressed by the Ministry of Defence (MoD) and our Armed Forces',[36] and reached some preliminary conclusions.

Two major themes have dominated the response of the HCDC. The first was a review of the Strategic Defence Review. The committee kept in mind some of the criticisms it had made of the review, particularly those related to the reserve forces. The MoD produced new plans for the role of the military in countering international terrorism, military action to be taken overseas and what the military has been doing and should be doing domestically. This process, like the original Strategic Defence Review, was closely followed by the HCDC.

The second theme concerned the threat to the UK from terrorism and Britain's preparedness to deal with such an eventuality. The committee's reports covered the armed forces, counter-terrorism, preparedness and resource and risk management. It questioned, amongst others, the head of the Civil Contingencies Secretariat, the Minister of State for Local Government and the Regions, the Metropolitan Police Assistant Commissioner and the director of the London Resilience Team.

The committee ended its report with the comment 'we have no doubt that Parliament and its committees will maintain a close interest in the consequences of the attacks of 11 September. There will be a continuing need for active scrutiny.'

The Defence committee, according to Bruce George and Natalie Whatford,

> has unashamedly broadened its terms of reference following the events of September 11 to include analysing and describing the role of other government departments, the Civil Contingencies Secretariat, briefly the intelligence services, transport security, nuclear installations, emergency planning, the health, fire and ambulance services, police, regional and local government, business and the private security industry. As it wrote so delicately, 'Our inquiry has taken us into many areas which are not normally the responsibility of the Defence Committee as we have tried to get a broad picture of what is being done by different Government departments and agencies, and to examine how all the different efforts are managed and coordinated.' The committee is now well placed to deal

with the entire spectrum of defence and security from nuclear strategy,
ballistic missile defence, through to security and policing and can
approach it in an integrated manner.[37]

The other committee which moved swiftly in response to 9/11 was the
Foreign Affairs committee. It began on 20 November 2001 a study into the
foreign policy aspects of the war against terrorism. Its ongoing inquiries have
involved detailed consideration of Iraq, Afghanistan, the Israeli-Palestine
conflict, other threats to security in the Middle East region, WMD and international terrorism, the work of multilateral institutions (UN, EU, NATO),
the International Criminal Court and Guantanamo Bay. There has been a
separate ongoing inquiry into Pakistan and WMD.

A speedy inquiry was held by the Home Affairs committee into the Anti-
terrorism, Crime and Security Bill 2001,[38] beginning with the first hearing
on 8 November 2001 and reporting on 19 November.

The House of Commons' Science and Technology committee has as one
of its core tasks 'to examine other Government Departments' expenditure
on research and advice on science and technology'.[39] It reported that

no fewer than 14 Government departments and agencies contributed to the
Government's written evidence to our inquiry into the scientific response to
terrorism. We subsequently took oral evidence from representatives of the
Home Office, the Department of Health, the Ministry of Defence and
Office of the Deputy Prime Minister (ODPM). We visited the Defence
Science and Technology Laboratory at Porton Down to examine the contri-
bution of that facility to combating the terrorist threat.[40]

But the report into the scientific response to terrorism highlighted some
key problems with cross-departmental inquiries and national security. In a
key passage from that report the committee stated, 'We have experienced
difficulty in receiving Government cooperation and several sessions have

been held in private.'[41] Table 5 in that report outlines a catalogue of problems, which included departmental complaints over the previously agreed remit and withdrawal of witnesses. The report continued,

> *Ministers seem to think they have a role in determining the remit of select committee inquiries. They do not ... just as Government should be joined up, so should departmental select committees. Government action does not always fall neatly within departmental boundaries ... This raises the further issue of parliamentary scrutiny of security arrangements. David Blunkett, former Home Secretary, believes that the ISC is the appropriate body to scrutinise government policy in this area. It should not be necessary to point out to the Home Secretary the difference between a parliamentary committee and a committee made up of parliamentarians appointed by government. As the Foreign Affairs committee has pointed out, when the ISC was set up in 1994 the House was assured that it would not 'truncate in any way the existing responsibilities of existing committees'. They concluded that the ISC be reconstituted as a House of Commons select committee, a view with which the Foreign Secretary has 'a great deal of sympathy'. The Home Secretary has been unnecessarily sensitive about this inquiry. It is perplexing and disappointing that he took steps, belatedly, to prevent us hearing from certain witnesses from his department and that he apparently sought to instill this uncooperative attitude in other departments. The Home Secretary's actions have sought to undermine the role of select committees.*[42]

Improving the effectiveness of committee scrutiny

The weaknesses of committee powers

The executive enjoys many advantages – of resources, of civil servants and advisers to advise ministers, of access to information not available to others.

The current administration has put a premium on 'joined-up government'. In addition to the long-established system of cross-departmental cabinet committees, there has been a concerted effort to solve problems through cooperation across the executive. Prime Minister Tony Blair, in evidence to the Liaison Committee, said,

> *If you actually look at the amount of work that is carried on by the Government through Cabinet committees or Cabinet Sub-Committees, it is actually probably more considerable and more extensive than it has ever been ... I think there are something in the region of more than double the number of Cabinet committees.*[43]

Later in his evidence he said,

> *This is a big issue for Government, as to how you make sure that departments join themselves up and do not end up in different silos with their own interests that do not come together in the common interest. That is absolutely right. The way of doing that is through the Cabinet committees that will look at these issues ... a lot of issues ... depend on more than one department working together. The only way you can do it is to bring it together in a Cabinet committee and look at it. The process by which we are drawing up the departmental plans that we are going to be publishing in the middle of the year from the main delivery departments is to a greater degree now involving the other departments ... I think one of the major issues for us as a Government, and what I say to the Civil Service is that this would be true whatever Government is in power, is how you reorganise the skill set of the Civil Service and reorganise some of these departments so that the focus goes away from the traditional Civil Service role, which is very much to do with policy advice, protection of ministers and so on, to delivery, project management and a whole set of different skills that require people to work across different silos and that*

require them to manage the delivery of projects in a way that a lot of the Civil Service is not used to doing.[44]

The executive enjoys other advantages also. It can use prerogative powers, impose a requirement for secrecy, rely on party discipline to mute criticism, take expert advice from within the country and benefit from talking to our allies. Most importantly it has experience of fighting wars and knows the value of centralisation and coordination.

Proposals for change

If Parliament is to follow the executive's move towards 'joined-up government' it must display deeper and more frequent cooperation between committees. There are at least ten different levels of cooperation:

1. Clerks meet regularly to exchange information about inquiries in progress.
2. Chairs exchange correspondence about their committees' intentions.
3. Chairs meet informally to update each other about inquiries and other activities.
4. Chairs meet formally.
5. Committees hold joint briefings and seminars.
6. Committees formally exchange evidence.
7. Committees hold joint meetings to take evidence.
8. Committees conduct joint inquiries.
9. Subcommittees which cooperate are established.
10. There is a concurrent committee on the lines of the Quadripartite Committee

There is evidence of limited cooperation within the first three levels, but this could be extended. There have also been a handful of joint meetings and briefings. While higher levels of cooperation may increase the workload for staff and highlight differences in the style, structure and culture of different committees, the prize of more effective scrutiny may be worth it. There are practical difficulties – as highlighted in our comments on individual committees – but these can be overcome.

In a House which is still centred primarily on the chamber, and in which heavy demands are made on individual members and a relatively small staff, cooperation will be a challenge, even if there is a desire for it. Attendance rates at committees in 2002/3 illustrate how committee members are already stretched:

Committee	Overall attendance
Defence	74.6%
Draft Civil Contingencies Bill (Joint)	64.4%
Foreign Affairs	78.8%
Home Affairs	71.1%
Human Rights (Joint)	62.8%
International Development	64.4%
Liaison	63.3%
Science & Technology	67.7%
Trade & Industry	60.9%
Transport	73.2%

In 1982/3 Bruce George – then an opposition backbencher – proposed an ad hoc national security committee to coordinate or even conduct inquiries. It would include the chairs and deputy chairs of the Defence, Foreign Affairs and Intelligence and Security committees. It could be a subcommittee of the Liaison Committee. Perhaps the experience post 9/11 suggests that it is time to resurrect this idea. It is also time to revise the rules for provision of government information. Alan Williams – chair of the Liaison Committee – told the Prime Minister that select committee chairmen were

> *deeply envious [of the Hutton inquiry] because none of them could have hoped to get a fraction of that information. I do not know whether you*

are aware that the rules that currently govern the access to information
for committees were laid down 20 years ago, not in consultation, but laid
down by the Government of the day, and they have never been revised.[45]

Conclusions

The so-called new select committee system is almost a quarter of a century old.
Is it a time for substantial improvement? Much good work is being done by
the Liaison and Modernisation committees. Other committees have enlarged
and improved their work of scrutiny, but it has been on an ad hoc basis.

A contrast can be made with US Congressional committees after 9/11.
Nearly 80 committees and subcommittees dealt with aspects of those events
and preparedness for the future. While many of these were single hearings,
that legislative body produced a wide-ranging scrutiny of executive actions
and inaction. The British House of Commons – with more members than
both houses of Congress combined – has been significantly less prolific.

Committees have performed reasonably well in examining national
security issues but they have been hampered by the culture and structure of
autonomy. Although there have emerged examples of cooperation and coordination through more joined-up committee work, much more could and
can be done.

Endnotes

1   The critical national infrastructure 'covers the infrastructure systems essential to national well-
    being: telecommunications, energy, financial services, water and sewerage, transport and govern-
    ment'. Intelligence & Security Committee, *Annual Report* 2002–2003, Cm. 5837, para. 15.
2   Security Service Act 1989, s. 1.
3   http://www.parliament.uk/parliamentary_committees/parliamentary_committees16.cfm
4   http://www.publications.parliament.uk/pa/cm/cmsid.htm
5   *Standing Orders of the House of Commons – Public Business 2003* (2), SO 152.
6   Liaison Committee, *Annual Report for 2003*, p. 7.

7   *Standing Orders of the House of Commons – Public Business 2003* (2), SO 152.

8   Limon, D. and McKay, W. (eds), *Erskine May's Treatise on the Law, Privileges, Proceedings and Usage of Parliament*, 22nd ed. (Butterworths, London, 1997), pp. 650–51.

9   Foreign Affairs Committee (FAC), *Evidence from Mr Andrew Gilligan to the Committee's Inquiry into the Decision to go to War in Iraq*, First Special Report of Session 2002–03, Appendix (letter from the Clerk of the Court)

10 FAC 7th Report, 2001–02, 2nd & 10th Reports, 2002–03, 2nd Report, 2003–04.

11 FAC, *Weapons of Mass Destruction*, 8th Report, 1999–2000.

12 FAC 1st & 5th Reports, 2002–03.

13 FAC, *Sierra Leone*, 2nd Report, 1998–99.

14 FAC, *Kosovo: Interim Report*, 7th Report, 1998–9 and *Kosovo*, 4th Report, 1999–2000.

15 FAC, *The Decision to Go to War in Iraq*, 9th Report, 2002–03.

16 FAC, *Private Military Companies*, 9th Report, 2001–02.

17 Air Commodore Dick Lacey, NATO Director, Ministry of Defence; Dr Thomas David Inch, OBE, Former Deputy Chief Scientific Officer, MoD at Porton Down.

18 See Export Control Act 2002, s. 10 [Explanatory Note: 'Section 10: Annual Reports. This provides for the Secretary of State to report annually to Parliament on the operation of the Act both as regards the export of objects of cultural interest and as regards other matters relating to the operation of the Act. "Other matters" are, in practice, likely to relate to the exercise of strategic export controls.'

19 2000–01 Report (7th FAC, 7th HCDC, 6th International Development, 11th Trade & Industry) on draft export control and the Non-Proliferation Bill.

20 *The Government's Proposals for Secondary Legislation under the Export Control Act*, 1st Joint Report, 2002–03.

21 Intelligence Services Act 1994 (relevant section).

22 *Intelligence Oversight*, available via http://www.cabinet-office.gov.uk/intelligence.

23 Intelligence and Security Committee, *Annual Report 2002–03*, para. 11.

24 *Ibid.*, paras 2 & 3.

25 *Intelligence Oversight*, p. 8.

26 International Development Committee, *Conflict Prevention and Post-conflict Reconstruction*, 6th Report, 1998–99.

27 International Development Committee, *Preparing for the Humanitarian Consequences of Possible Military Action Against Iraq*, 4th Report, 2002–03.

28 International Development Committee, *The Humanitarian Crisis in Afghanistan and the Surrounding Area*, 1st Report, 2001–02; *Afghanistan: The Transition from Humanitarian Relief to Reconstruction and Development Assistance*, 1st Report, 2002–03.

29 International Development Committee, *Kosovo: The Humanitarian Crisis*, 3rd Report, 1998–99.

30 Home Affairs Committee, *The Work of the Home Affairs Committee in 2003*, 3rd Report, 2003–04, para. 13.

31 *Intelligence Oversight*, p. 8.

32 Anti-terrorism, Crime and Security Bill: Introduction & Summary; House of Commons

Library Research Paper 01/101 D: Scrutiny by Parliamentary Committees, pp. 20–21.

33 International Development Committee, *Conflict Prevention and Post-conflict Reconstruction*, 6th Report, 1998–99, para. 148.

34 HCDC, *Lessons of Iraq*, 3rd Report, 2003–04, para. 9.

35 This point was made in a number of interviews with committee staff.

36 HCDC, *The Threat from Terrorism*, 2nd Report, 2001–02. para. 2.

37 'The Response to 9/11: Central-Regional-Local Public Sector Responsibilities and Resources', Chilworth Paper given by Rt Hon. Bruce George MP and Natalie Whatford for the ESRC Project on the domestic management of terrorist attacks in the UK.

38 Home Affairs Committee, 1st Report, 2001–02.

39 Science & Technology Committee, *Annual Report 2003*, Box 1, Task 5.

40 *Ibid.*, paras 13 & 14.

41 Science & Technology Committee, *The Scientific Response to Terrorism*, 8th Report, 2002–03, para. 226.

42 *Ibid.*, paras 226-8

43 Liaison Committee: The Prime Minister: Oral and Written Evidence, Thursday 3 February 2004, Q. 7.

44 *Ibid.*, Qs 86 & 87.

45 *Ibid.*, Q. 1.

NINE

The Role of Select Committees in the House of Lords

Lord Tordoff

At a time when the future shape of the House of Lords is under active discussion it seems sensible to pause a while to consider what it is that the House of Lords is supposed to do. Indeed, in order to map out future responsibilities it would seem to make sense to consider those things which the House does well or badly in its present incarnation. Consequently, in this chapter I focus on the select committees of the House of Lords, what they do and, perhaps more importantly, what they could, and should, do.[1]

There is, I believe, a widely held recognition that probably the most successful part of the work of the House is done by the select committees. Before going on to discuss why this should be so, it is worthwhile showing the extent of the work in hand. I accordingly cover the work of each committee (or group of related committees) in turn, beginning with the domestic committees and then moving on through those that scrutinise legislation and policy.

Key Themes

Underlying themes when looking at the functions of Lords committees are scrutiny and accountability. Lords committees have very little direct legisla-

tive power. They do, however, provide a meaningful opportunity to scrutinise the government, and, significantly, the European Union, and to hold
those who govern us to account for their policies.

It is an important feature of the work of Lords select committees that most
of the investigative committees do, at least in part, scrutinise and report on
legislation as well as considering and reporting on policy.

Two further key themes that will I hope emerge from this chapter are the
case for complementarity between Lords committees and those of the
Commons, and the particular effect that the current membership of the
House (with its range of expertise in policy areas) has on the work of committees. I touch also on the accountability of Lords committees themselves: to
whom are they responsible?

Domestic committees

The domestic (or administrative) committees are separate from the functions
of committees which scrutinise legislation or influence policy formulation.
But they provide something of the background to how the House's
committee system actually works.

The House's administrative committee structure underwent major change
at the start of the 2002/3 session. The House of Lords' Offices Committee
had, since it was first established in 1824, been the pre-eminent 'domestic'
committee of the House but had become an unwieldy body,[2] and, over the
years, most of the committee's responsibilities had been delegated to
subcommittees, working at one further remove from the House itself. As a
result, decision-making was inefficient, slow moving and opaque. Issues were
often debated at length in the Offices Committee after a subcommittee had
come to its conclusions based on precisely the same evidence. Indeed, no one
could even remember why the Offices Committee had that name!

The new structure, introduced in November 2002, is much more stream-
lined. The pre-eminent administrative committee is now the House

Committee, with eleven members: the Chairman of Committees serves as chairman; the leaders of the three major parties and the convenor of the crossbench peers sit *ex officio*; the remaining six members are backbenchers chosen by their respective parties. The committee is thus both representative of the House as a whole and has political clout. Indeed it represents one formal manifestation of the Usual Channels.

The House Committee is responsible both for the overall strategy of the administration and for finance. The committee agrees the House's strategic plan and approves the administration's business plan, which translates those strategic priorities into specific tasks and projects; and is responsible for approving spending plans and the bids for funding which are submitted annually to the Treasury.[3] Financial accountability has been further enhanced by the establishment of an Audit Committee, which oversees and examines the audit and accountability arrangements in the House in line with public sector best practice.

The House Committee is also developing an increasingly close working relationship with the Management Board,[4] which both advises the committee and provides strategic management for the administration.

Hence, the House Committee is an important factor in any examination of the committee work of the House. The House Committee controls the purse strings, including the budgets for committee activity, and oversees (and approves the priorities of) the administration, a significant part of which is devoted to serving select committees.

The House Committee does not, however, provide any strategic direction to the work of select committees. Decisions on which committees should be appointed (or even, although this a rarity, closed down) are matters for the House itself. The House has appointed a Liaison Committee to make recommendations on these matters as follows:

> *To advise the House on the resources required for select committee work and to allocate resources between select committees; to review the select*

committee work of the House; to consider requests for ad hoc committees
and report to the House with recommendations; to ensure effective
co–ordination between the two Houses; and to consider the availability
of Lords to serve on committees.

This means that the Liaison Committee reports to the House on bids for new committee activity, although the House is not bound to accept their recommendations. But, significantly, the members of the Liaison Committee are, once again, the party leaders and some backbenchers. So the Usual Channels have a key role here too and, hence, a rejection by the House of a unanimous recommendation of the committee would be unusual.

On my theme of accountability, however, it is interesting to note that the Liaison Committee has not set core functions for committees, nor does it regularly review the output, impact or effectiveness of committees.[5] It can also be questioned how far the Liaison Committee, in approving or rejecting new bids for committees, is operating on the basis of any vision of what the House or its committees should be doing. The committee tends to respond to events (such as a proposal from a member for a new form of committee activity) rather than attempting itself to set the agenda. This no doubt reflects a sense that this would be a matter for the House as a whole, although it is hard to see by what other means the whole House could come to a view on such matters.[6] The committee does examine in some detail the resource requirements for committee work, including the availability of members to serve.[7]

There are two further domestic committees which are significant in the work of select committees. The Committee of Selection proposes to the House the names of members to serve on select committees,[8] and the Procedure Committee advises the House on all matters of procedure, including the procedures affecting the work of select committees.[9] Both these committees include the Usual Channels among their members and indeed the Committee of Selection rarely, if ever, disagrees with proposals agreed privately by the Usual Channels.

Legislative committees

The House of Lords does not have standing committees on public Bills (as the Commons does) nor do the select committees currently established have any direct powers to amend public legislation as it passes through Parliament. The Lords' Grand Committee procedure is a stage in the legislative process but this comprises the whole House meeting away from the chamber to consider legislation. It is not a select committee so I say no more about it here.[10] But it is important to stress that Lords select committees do not have a direct legislative role, although reports of select committees can have a significant impact on the decisions of the House itself when considering legislation at the committee or report stages of Bills.

Hence a cynic might say that select committees are a convenient device for the executive, allowing Parliament to express a view without disrupting the flow of legislation. A more realistic view, however, is that the executive can find it hard to ignore the advice of a committee. But crucially, this depends on the committee's work being timely, focused, targeted and effectively delivered.

It is thus interesting to note that one of the most significant recent developments in select committee work in both Houses has been the examination of Bills published in draft by the government, ahead of their formal introduction to Parliament. One of the first examples was the joint committee of both Houses which examined a draft Local Government Bill in 1999, one of three Bills introduced for prelegislative scrutiny that year. Since then, the scale of this activity has increased dramatically: in the 2002/3 session no fewer than eleven draft Bills were published by the government, four of which were scrutinised by joint committees of the two Houses.[11] Similar levels of activity could be seen in 2003/4.

The government no doubt hopes that subjecting draft Bills to parliamentary – and public – scrutiny before they are formally introduced to Parliament will result in better law. The procedure allows proposals to be examined and fine-tuned at an early stage, before hard and fast political battle lines have been drawn. The choice of Bills so far selected to be published in draft has helped in this respect.

Parliament and the Lords have played their part, by attempting to create an atmosphere in which draft Bills are scrutinised in a constructive fashion, in contrast to the sterile confrontations which many think characterise debates in Parliament during the formal consideration of a Bill. Members of pre-legislative scrutiny committees have in general avoided seeking to make political capital out of shortcomings in draft Bills, and ministers have usually kept an open mind about possible alterations to draft legislation. It is often also easier for ministers quietly to accept the recommendations of a committee on a draft Bill than to be seen to be doing so during a Bill's passage, or to be forced into doing so by a defeat in either House.

Of course the government's aims are not entirely altruistic. In part it hopes to obtain an easier passage for its legislation when it is formally introduced, by ensuring that potential sticking points are identified and eliminated, and that a core of interested members in both Houses understand and are broadly sympathetic to the aims of the Bill.

These are early days, and the success of the experiment cannot be judged by whether the Commons and Lords are able to programme, plan and conduct large consultation exercises and then craft elegantly argued responses to the draft Bills. The key question will be whether the government is prepared to listen – and in some cases even substantially amend its proposals – or whether prelegislative scrutiny turns out simply to be an excuse to squeeze yet more out of the legislative sausage machine that is Parliament.

Human rights: the joint committee

A second area of committee activity concerned with legislation can be described as committees which comment on Bills as they proceed through Parliament. One such is the Joint Committee on Human Rights. The setting up of the Joint Committee on Human Rights, which was due to take place in 2000, was delayed for several months by protracted negotiations over the chairmanship. Agreement was finally reached in early 2001 and Jean Corston MP, a Labour backbencher representing Bristol East, took the chair. The concern over this issue perhaps reflected a feeling that the committee was likely to become influential. The first few years of its existence have indeed shown this to be the case.

The main business of the committee is divided between the scrutiny of Bills and general investigative inquiries, including inquiries into the UK's compliance with international human rights instruments. The committee also has certain functions relating to the technical business of scrutinising human rights remedial orders although these have so far been rare.

The committee scrutinises all Bills, including private members' Bills, which are introduced into either the Commons or the Lords. Since the passing of the Human Rights Act 1998, all government Bills are required to state that, in the minister's opinion, the Bill is compliant with the European Convention on Human Rights. The committee's function is to subject that assessment to critical scrutiny: the committee conducts a great deal of scrutiny and it is often critical.[12] These reports often contain clear recommendations that certain aspects of a Bill should be amended in order to make it compatible with the European Convention. The government is not obliged to act on these recommendations, but nor does it wish to be challenged in the European Court of Human Rights. It often, therefore, responds positively to the committee's recommendations. The committee has also expressed views on Bills presented in draft for prelegislative scrutiny.[13]

The committee's achievement in this area is not, however, to be measured by the number of occasions on which the government has changed legislation in line with the committee's recommendations. More fundamentally, the committee helps to ensure that the government maintains its commitment to human rights by checking that human rights issues are integral to legislation, rather than an issue to consider only after the meat of a Bill has been drafted.

The committee also conducts investigative inquiries – its major report to date, which took nearly two years to write, was on the case for a human rights commission. The committee has also investigated deaths in custody and the need for a children's commissioner.

The Constitution Committee

Another Lords committee which straddles both detailed examination of legislation and broader in-depth inquiries into policy is the Constitution Committee, appointed to 'examine the constitutional implications of all public Bills coming before the House; and to keep under review the operation of the constitution'. On being set up,[14] the committee's first task was to define what the constitution actually was. The committee was aware of the fact that the United Kingdom constitution is uncodified, and hence the sense of what is a constitutional matter is continually evolving. The first report of the committee therefore set out the five basic tenets of the UK constitution: sovereignty of the Crown in Parliament; the rule of law, encompassing the rights of the individual; union state; representative government; and membership of the Commonwealth, the European Union, and other international organisations.

In order to clarify its role, the committee has set itself the task of drawing attention to matters of constitutional principle which affect a principal part of the constitution. With this broad definition as its guide, the committee scrutinises all public Bills. The committee strives hard to remain impartial: it does not state whether a measure is good or bad, but draws attention to potentially significant changes in the constitution which a Bill would enact. The committee has no special powers to delay or amend legislation, and it does not report that a measure is 'unconstitutional' – indeed, in the United Kingdom this term is almost meaningless as the constitution is in a continuous state of flux. Instead, it draws matters of constitutional significance to the attention of those who are discussing the Bill in detail, and relies on them to give effect to the committee's conclusions as they see fit.

The committee has performed a similar function in reporting on the draft constitutional treaty for the European Union: without expressing a view as to the merits of the draft treaty, the committee published a report identifying fifteen separate areas of potential constitutional concern, but left it to others to draw their own conclusions.

The committee also carries out wider investigative reports. A report on the government's approach to constitutional change was followed by one entitled *Devolution: Inter-institutional Relations in the United Kingdom.* Following this the committee carried out an investigation into the accountability of regulators.

Delegated legislation: the DPRRC, the JCSI, and Merits

The Lords also has committees which perform a role in the scrutiny of delegated legislation at various stages. It would be open to the Constitution and Human Rights Committees to do so on matters within their terms of reference but the primary focus in this field has been the Delegated Powers and Regulatory Reform Committee (DPRRC).

Delegated (or secondary) legislative powers are principally legislative powers given to the executive[15] by primary legislation. Delegated legislation has been described as the 'Cinderella of parliamentary scrutiny'.[16] It is, however, burgeoning[17] and effective scrutiny of those powers is – and will become ever more – a critical task for Parliament in the performance of its more general purpose of holding the executive to account.

The House of Lords scrutinises delegated legislation at two points in the legislative process: on the creation of the delegated legislative powers (in primary legislation) and at point where those powers are applied (in the form of secondary legislation).

Creation of delegated powers

The committee which examines the parent primary legislation is the Delegated Powers and Regulatory Reform Committee. It was established (initially as the Select Committee on the Scrutiny of Delegated Powers)[18] following the report of the Select Committee on the Committee Work of the House, under the chairmanship of Lord Jellicoe, in 1992. The Jellicoe committee had noted that 'considerable disquiet' was developing 'over the problem of wide and sometimes ill-defined order-making powers which gave Ministers unlimited discretion'.[19] The DPRRC was charged with the task of considering whether the provisions of any Bill 'inappropriately' delegated legislative powers or whether the exercise of any delegated legislative power was subject to an 'inappropriate degree of parliamentary scrutiny'.[20] The DPRRC has achieved considerable influence in the House of Lords and amongst government departments.

Application of delegated powers

In scrutinising the ambit of powers granted by primary legislation, the DPRRC is the Lords' first line of defence against any unreasonable encroachment of the executive into the legislative dominion. The second line of defence is the Lords' scrutiny of the delegated legislation itself. Here there are two committees, one joint and one a Lords committee only, which undertake the complementary tasks of scrutinising the technical and policy aspects of delegated legislation.

The 'technical' committee is the Joint Committee on Statutory Instruments (JCSI), which was established in 1973.[21] Broadly, its function is to consider whether the primary legislation actually gives power to make a Statutory Instrument (that is, whether it is *intra vires*), whether it is drafted correctly and whether the instrument imposes a charge on the public revenues. The JCSI is expressly prohibited from considering the merits or policy behind an instrument.

The policy committee is a Lords committee only and is an entirely new weapon in Parliament's scrutiny armoury. Following a recommendation of the Royal Commission on the Reform of the House of Lords, under the chairmanship of Lord Wakeham,[22] the Select Committee on the Merits of Statutory Instruments was established in the 2003/4 session. The function of this committee is to draw the 'special attention' of the House to Statutory Instruments of particular interest. We wait with interest to see whether the committee is able to achieve the influence in the Lords that its scrutiny partner, the DPRRC, has achieved.

The European Union Committee

One of the most significant and long-established elements of the committee work of the House of Lords is the work of the European Union Committee. This was first established in 1974 but has undergone numerous changes and developments since then. The committee's formal terms of reference are 'to consider European Union documents and other matters relating to the EU'.

The Committee operates under the terms of the Scrutiny Reserve Resolution passed by the House in 1999, under which ministers cannot, subject to exceptions in special circumstances, give agreement to proposals in the Council of Ministers until the committee has completed its scrutiny of them. This is not a power to bind ministers or veto their decisions but an opportunity to influence ministers' positions in negotiations. The committee is treading a careful line between effective scrutiny on the one hand and the need to recognise the nature of intergovernmental negotiations on the other.

The committee has recently identified the following as the principal purposes of its scrutiny:

> We accordingly stress that national parliamentary scrutiny of EU legislation has a clear constitutional purpose. Scrutiny at an early stage is therefore essential and must be as effective as possible. To that end, scrutiny should include:
> • The accumulation, presentation and summary of relevant material, including information, statistics, explanation and analysis.

- *The provision of information to the House and to the public as a contribution to transparency.*
- *Drawing the attention of the House, the government, European institutions and the public to significant matters contained within that information and in particular making recommendations – 'focusing the debate'.*
- *Contributing to the law-making process by detailed analysis of draft texts, by exposing difficulties and proposing amendments.*
- *An examination of the government and its role in agreeing European legislation and, as part of that process, compelling the government not only to think through what it is doing or has done but sometimes to account for it.*
- *An examination of the Commission and the policies it formulates.*

Hence, although not subject to core tasks such as those agreed for Commons committees, it is clear that the Lords EU Committee has set itself the task of defining its role, not least as a contribution to its own accountability.

A second key feature of the work of the committee is that it operates through a series of – currently seven – subcommittees, each of which examines a range of policy areas.[23] This sets the committee apart from similar bodies in other national Parliaments (and the House of Commons), where a more usual model is for European scrutiny to be a function separated from scrutiny of (and expertise in) particular policy areas. This is one of the great strengths of the Lords system: that policy and European scrutiny are so closely linked, and that scrutiny of the European Union is thus mainstreamed, at least into the committee work of the House.

A third key feature of the committee's work is the balance between inquiries into matters of general policy and the scrutiny of particular legislative instruments. This has been a constant tension in the committee's work, particularly given the difficulties in scrutinising legislative texts. These can move very fast, and with the continuing growth of co-decision there is already an inbuilt mechanism for parliamentary involvement by the elected members of the European Parliament, who have direct powers to approve and amend such legislation.

The European Union Committee aims to square this circle by getting into the policy formulation process as far upstream as it can. The committee has always scrutinised Commission Green and White Papers but has recently begun also to examine the Commission's annual legislative work programme. The key to successful scrutiny of this kind is to identify and examine policy issues of concern at an early stage and seek to influence the policy before it is set in a specific legislative text. Hence scrutiny of the legislation when it emerges in draft form ought to be able to be conducted quickly and to focus on outstanding issues of serious concern.

The work of the committee is subject to a constant process of change and evolution – the committee is not complacent because of its history but is looking, to quote the present chairman, for 'continuing improvement'. At present outside pressures too are fuelling this drive: the draft constitutional treaty for the European Union would give new powers for parliamentary scrutiny and oversight of the EU, including more responsibility for national parliaments to operate collectively.

Thus the Lords European Union Committee, too, is involved in the scrutiny of legislation, albeit not of a domestic kind. However, it does not as a matter of routine examine the implementation of EU secondary legislation but has expressed a wish that this might be a function of the new committee on the merits of Statutory Instruments.

The Science and Technology Committee

The House of Lords moved to establish the Science and Technology Committee in 1979, following the rearrangement of the House of Commons select committee structure to reflect the remit of government departments. The committee has a wide brief to 'consider science and technology'. It conducts inquiries and reports on public policy relating to science and technology. It does not examine legislation of any kind. The Commons too has a committee on science and technology; hence two parliamentary select committees are dedicated to investigating this area.

The committee has a reputation for performing detailed and long-term inquiries, often lasting nine or twelve months. It specialises in identifying and pursuing issues that fall between the gaps of government departments. The committee seeks to balance life sciences and physical sciences across its programme. It does not often undertake inquiries based purely on social science or economics. Reports tend to be in one of the following categories:

1. Public policy areas which are, or ought to be, informed by scientific research.[24]
2. Technological challenges and opportunities which the government should address.[25]
3. Public policy towards science itself.[26]

The committee draws on the significant scientific expertise of some members of the House. This expertise, in addition to the normal powers of all parliamentary committees (that of being able to call in key players to give evidence and the fact that the government is obliged to respond to select committee reports), provides the committee with a unique and powerful position to raise the profile of science and technology.

The Economic Affairs Committee and the Finance Bill

The Economic Affairs Committee was set up on 7 March 2001, with the intention of monitoring the work of the Bank of England's Monetary Policy Committee. However, it was given wide-ranging terms of reference: 'to consider economic affairs'. Thus recent work includes not only a series of reports on the Bank of England's Monetary Policy Committee but also lengthy inquiries into globalisation and the economics of an ageing population.

The establishment of this committee prompts the question whether the Lords are departing from their traditional practice of complementarity with Commons committees – that is, not seeking to duplicate, replicate or overlap with the work of departmental select committees of the Commons. Can the Economic Affairs Committee find a meaningful role for itself drawing on the considerable expertise of the House while also remaining complementary to the Commons committees?

In 2003, the House of Lords asked the committee to set up a subcommittee to consider certain aspects of that year's Finance Bill. The subcommittee aimed to conclude its work before the final stages of proceedings on the Bill in the House of Commons, to stand some chance of influencing the provisions of the Bill, given that the Lords do not amend Finance Bills. Has this exercise been of value?

The subcommittee's report stated:

> All in all, we believe this has been a worthwhile exercise which should make a valuable contribution to parliamentary consideration of the Bill. We are encouraged by the wide and warm welcome given to it, especially in professional circles, and by the ready and invaluable assistance given to the inquiry by all our witnesses, both from the private sector and from the government Departments involved.

What can be said is that, for the House of Lords, the creation of a committee to examine the Finance Bill was an extraordinary step. Questions will surely have been asked about the propriety of such an exercise, given the Commons' primacy in financial matters. Leaving aside the purely procedural answer to this question (by which the committee and the House had of course acted entirely properly), there was a sensitive political question about how the Commons would react to such a development at a moment when the future of the Lords was largely in their hands. However, the presence in the House of a wide range of distinguished economists, former Chancellors of the Exchequer and finance ministers, together with the occasional ex-Governor of the Bank of England, provides a resource that Parliament would be foolish to ignore.

Ad hoc committees

A final feature of Lords committee work has been the establishment of ad hoc select committees to look at particular policy areas. The Lords tends to appoint only one such committee at a time, and they tend to run for a year or so. They have not usually scrutinised legislation directly, but have on occasion taken a Bill as a starting point for a broader inquiry.

Conclusions

As the House of Lords moves into the 21st century a number of key themes emerge from the role of select committees.

First is the broad terms of reference generally given to committees, showing the level of trust that the House places in them. But there is, as the European Union Committee has shown, a need to supplement this by self-analysis and reflection, by committees themselves if by no one else, on what they are there for. I suspect that an informed consideration of the future of the House, being predicated as it should be on an examination of the functions of the House rather than its membership, ought to go into this question across the board.

Is there not also a case for the House itself to take a more holistic and strategic view of its committee work, which absorbs so much of the time of many of its members and staff? In particular, there is the old buzzword of complementarity. Does the Lords really still believe – as it used to – that it should complement the work of the Commons? Or does a more assertive House, as we are now seeing, feel more confident in moving in on territory previously thought to be hallowed green turf? If so, what will be the consequences of that? Will the effect be a stronger Parliament, as the two Houses expand their work and take the executive more in hand, or will the result be that the Commons, with its majority drawn from the party which forms the executive, tires of these interventions and tries to rein their Lordships back?

It is clear that some at least of these deeply political questions are beginning to be played out on the once impartial field of select committee activity, and the work of committees may continue to evolve as a result. It is still the case, however, that there are a few cases of committee decisions dividing along party lines.

It is also clear that the majority of select committees focus at least a considerable part of their efforts on the scrutiny of legislation, whether domestic or European, but also seek to maintain an element of broad policy review. Once again, I look to the European Union Committee for an analysis of the effect of this combination of activity – they reached a clear conclusion that having the same members involved in both kinds of work strengthens both:

> We are not, however, complacent about the expertise of our members. Many Members of the House have been appointed because of their expertise in particular areas, but that expertise needs to be kept up to date. We accordingly consider that it is of positive benefit to those conducting scrutiny of specific legislative items that they have also conducted in-depth inquiries into general policy.

Across the board, however, it is clearly the case that the Lords has considerable resources in terms of experience and expertise across a wide range of topics, which in turn encourages witnesses of high calibre to give evidence on which reports are based. By operating in this spirit I expect that Lords Select Committees will continue to go from strength to strength whatever the parliamentary and constitutional turmoil around them over the coming years. What must not be lost sight of is the large number of peers (and other resources) needed to carry out these functions to a satisfactory level. This must have important consequences for decisions on the size and composition of a reformed House.

Endnotes

1   The views expressed in this chapter are my own, but the chapter would not have been possible without the very considerable help of the clerks of the House in providing me with the factual information I have used very extensively and for which I am most grateful.

2   In 2002 the committee had almost 30 members, although even this large number represented a drop from a peak of some 60 members in the more distant past.

3   As well as the House Committee there are now four 'domestic committees', responsible for administration and works, information, refreshment and works of art. These committees have certain limited decision-making powers, but are obliged to work within financial limits set by the House Committee. They also act in part as 'user groups', representing and responding to the views of members as a whole on issues of concern to them – for example, the provision of accommodation or of IT equipment.

4   The Management Board is an important part of management changes within the House designed to develop a sense of corporate identity and common purpose in the service of the House. It is a strategic decision-making forum within the House of Lords. The Clerk of the Parliaments is the chairman of the Management Board. The board is structured on the basis of the six main functions of the House's administration. These six functions are parliamentary services, information services, financial resources, human resources, committee services and support services. As there are fifteen departments and offices within the House of Lords admin-istration, not every head of department or office sits on the board. However, each department and office has a representative on the board.

5   Nor does it replicate two of the main functions of the Commons Liaison Committee, which is composed of committee chairmen, namely to micro-manage the budget for Committee travel or, at a more strategic level, hold the Prime Minister to account in an annual evidence session.

6   Occasional reviews have been set up to tackle such questions, including the review of the committee work of the House chaired by Lord Jellicoe in 1992 which led to the establishment of the Liaison Committee. It is interesting to note that a recent report by an ad hoc group chaired by the then Leader of the House (the late Lord Williams of Mostyn), which was primarily concerned with the procedures and sitting hours of the House, also made recom-mendation that the House's scrutiny of European legislation should be reviewed. This could be thought to imply that there is no systematic mechanism for such thinking.

7   The Liaison Committee has recommended recently for example that the number of members serving on subcommittees of the European Union Committee be reduced from twelve to ten. The European Union Committee has implemented this recommendation, although there is nothing in the standing orders of the House to oblige a select committee to restrict the size of its subcommittees in this way. The Liaison Committee is also responsible for setting the number of subcommittees the European Union Committee appoints and recently increased the number from six to seven (an attempt to reduce the number from six to five having been defeated by the House several years earlier).

8   Where a select committee appoints subcommittees it normally has the power to do so directly, although discussions would usually be held with the Usual Channels.

9   The Procedure Committee would, for example, report to the House on the kinds of formal powers select committees might have, or on the 'rotation rule', which sets limits on the period of service of many committee members.

10 The House has a number of other variants on committees on public Bills, and indeed does appoint select committees to consider (and amend) private Bills, but these are increasingly rare and are not covered further.

11 The four Bills in question covered corruption, mental incapacity, civil contingencies (i.e. disaster planning) and gambling. Various others were scrutinised by the appropriate departmental select committee in the Commons.

12 Only once has the ministerial statement on the front of a Bill stated that, in the minister's opinion, a Bill was not compatible with the convention. This was the Communications Bill, where the ban on political advertising and sponsorship in the broadcast media was thought to infringe human rights. Interestingly, the committee did not state that this was wholly unjustifiable, but did take issue with the government for not providing a better explanation for deciding to proceed in this way.

13 For example on the draft Gender Recognition Bill.

14 Since its inception the committee has been chaired by Professor the Lord Norton of Louth, Professor of Government at Hull University, and the members include academics, former ministers, a former private secretary to the Queen, and a former Law Lord.

15 Or, since the Government of Wales Act 1998, to the National Assembly for Wales.

16 Select Committee on Delegated Powers and Deregulation, *Special Report for 1999–2000 on the Committee's Work*, 37th Report, 1999–2000, HL 130, para. 1.

17 See House of Commons Procedure Committee, 1st Report, 1999–2000, HC 48.

18 The committee was later renamed the Select Committee on Delegated Powers and Deregulation, following the passage of the Deregulation and Contracting Out Act 1994, and then the Delegated Powers and Regulatory Reform Committee, following the passage of the successor Regulatory Reform Act 2001.

19 Session 1991–92, HL 35-I, para. 133.

20 Principally, this is a question of whether a power should be exercised subject to the affirmative (and therefore more rigorous) resolution procedure or the negative resolution procedure.

21 This replaced a similar committee, the Statutory Instruments Committee, which had been appointed by the Commons in 1944.

22 Royal Commission on the Reform of the House of Lords, *A House of the Future*, Cm 4534, January 2000.

23 With effect from December 2003, these are:
    - Economic and Financial Affairs, and International Trade (Subcommittee A)
    - The Internal Market (Subcommittee B)
    - Foreign Affairs, Defence and Development Policy (Subcommittee C)
    - Agriculture and Environment (Subcommittee D)
    - Law and Institutions (Subcommittee E)
    - Home Affairs (Subcommittee F)
    - Social and Consumer Affairs (Subcommittee G)

24 Science and Technology Committee, *Fighting Infection*, 4th Report, 2002–03, HL 138; *Therapeutic Uses of Cannabis*, 2nd Report, 2000–01, HL 50; *Air Travel and Health*, 5th Report, 1999–2000, HL 121.

25 *Chips for Everything: Britain's Opportunities in a Key Global Market*, 2nd Report, 2002–03, HL 13; *Resistance to Antibiotics*, 3rd Report, 2000–01, HL 56); *Managing Radioactive Waste: the Government's Consultation*, 1st Report, 2001–02, HL 36; *Human Genetic Databases: Challenges and Opportunities*, 4th Report, 2000–01, HL 57.

26 *Science and the RDAs: Setting the Regional Agenda*, 5th Report, 2002–03, HL 140; *Science in Schools*, 1st Report, 2000–01, HL 49; *Science and Society*, 3rd Report, 1999–2000. HL 38.

TEN (A)

Parliament, Parties and Whips: A View From a (Former) Whip

James Cran MP

Whilst many backbench members of Parliament are often in awe of the whips, their largely unspoken fascination with their work is only surpassed by that of the press. Despite the often determined attempts by experienced Westminster journalists, very few reports concerning the operation of either the government or opposition Whips' Offices are ever based on information acquired from within – unless it has been decided that this will be of assistance to the cause. However, deduction and speculation, based on discussions with MPs outside the office, are usually the reporters' key tools. Such press reports merely add to the mythology surrounding the whips, even when the reporter intended to try to break through it. Press fascination with the institution of 'whipping' comes about precisely because, uniquely in Westminster, it does not usually leak information. Government departments, 'spin doctors', backbenchers and select committees may leak information, but the Whips' Office does not. Thus the Whips' Office is the one watertight compartment within the parliamentary ship of state that keeps the ship afloat, especially in times of political crises. Of course, individual whips may peddle their own agendas but, if they do, it is done discreetly and fingerprints are usually never found. If they are, the chances are that the individual involved will be found a role outside the office.

History

The role of the whips has undoubtedly changed over the years. So it is important to understand how 'whipping' came about, in order to understand what they do now. It is somewhat ironic that Parliament, feverishly engaged in the abolition of hunting with hounds, should be destroying the sport from where the term 'whipping' originates. In each hunt someone has the responsibility for keeping the hounds hunting in a pack. That person is also responsible for rounding up those hounds which stray from the task, and is said to 'whip the hounds in'. It does not take a genius to work out the connection.

The main task of the government Whips' Office is to ensure that the government gets its legislation through Parliament – that of the opposition parties is to seek to amend or even frustrate it. The maintaining of discipline within the respective political parties is key to achieving these tasks. Hence the term 'whipping' came to be used to describe the process of maximising support in a vote, and the term 'whip' was applied to those who carried it out.

Politicians today are said, by prevailing wisdom, to be more in the control of the party whips than past generations. However, it does not always appear like that from inside Westminster, especially if one is a Prime Minister with a small majority and a determined band of your own backbenchers who oppose you on a particular policy. A classic example would be the Maastricht treaty votes during John Major's premiership. Indeed, it is fair to say that, given the strong views that were held on all sides of the Conservative Party on that issue, it was undoubtedly the skills of the Whips' Office that maintained John Major in office throughout the crisis. As one who opposed the treaty, I am better placed than most to be able to come to that judgement. More recently, the almost legendary discipline of New Labour has begun to break down under the strains of NHS reform, tuition charging and war in Iraq. Even with his massive parliamentary majority, it is doubtful whether Tony Blair, or his Chief Whip, will see their backbenchers as compliant stooges.

Members of Parliament, whatever their party, tend to be people of strongly held views and – often – independent spirit. Moreover, political parties have always tended to be coalitions, not united not by agreement on every detail of policy, but rather brought together by shared broad principles – and even by a simple loathing of the alternative. Thus, if anything, MPs – although not all – have just become more independent and, in these circumstances, whipping is a necessity. The role of the whips has therefore correspondingly become more important to their party leader, whether in government or not.

The 1970s saw an increase in dissent and rebellion, when compared to what had gone on before. The proportion of unanimous votes in line with the approved party whip declined significantly from 1970 onwards – although the first signs of a breakdown in the purely authoritarian style of whipping can be traced back as far as the 1950s. Before then, whipping had been based mainly on authoritarian lines, with duty and obedience being factors. Nowadays, the authoritarian element is less of a factor whilst intelligence-gathering and persuasion are more important, although there is always the exception – for example, during the Maastricht votes, bullying and persuasion were pretty evenly used, with the government Whips' Office using so-called loyal backbench members to cold-shoulder, or even harry, some of those who dissented from the government. At other times, parliamentary private secretaries were told collectively to ignore the recalcitrants. Soon thereafter, they were told to do the opposite. The government of Edward Heath (1970–4) marks the point where the percentage of unanimous party votes takes a noticeable drop, although it was even more marked on the Labour side during the Callaghan years (1976–9). Whips' Offices during these times would measure success not so much on unanimity on their back benches but on delivering a majority of votes for the government – or opposition – in any given vote. That remains their primary task. However, it is important to note that in the vast majority of divisions there are straight party votes with no dissent. Even if the Parliamentary Whip – the weekly notice of whipping – has been mislaid, all the member has to do is to establish whether his whips are at the mouth of the 'Aye' or the 'No' lobby. On most occasions, therefore, all that is required of the Whips' Office is to send out the weekly notice of whipping to their members. That alone is sufficient to produce a party vote without dissent. Nonetheless, the threat of rebellion is always there and, in a constant exercise of intelligence-gathering, the whips are looking for the early signs. Persuasion is initially exercised and, by this means, a rebellion may be headed off but, most likely, its effects reduced. The whips are therefore the leader's eyes and ears. Whilst this aspect of their role has always been important, it is now by far the most essential continuing role they have to play. The public image of party whips physically bundling reluctant MPs into the required division lobby, against their wishes, is therefore about as far removed from the truth as it is possible to be, although, in very tight situations, relatively good-natured cajoling is employed – often by the PM himself and his ministers, in addition to the whips.

How do whips maintain control?

It is a truism to say that incurring the wrath of the Whips' Office is generally not a good idea, and certainly not on a repetitive basis. In practice, however, it is not that easy to bring upon oneself. If relationships between the whips and a particular individual become so bad, then the whips would sometimes judge themselves to have failed – but more of them would judge the member involved to be a bad team player. If a member wants to guarantee incurring that wrath, there is one sure way of doing it. Voting against one's own party is not the ultimate sin, so far as whips are concerned – voting against one's party, but without telling the whips beforehand, definitely is a sin. They expect to be given the opportunity of persuasion. To deny them that opportunity is considered dishonourable. Repetitive absences from important votes, without the permission of the whips, would rank a close second.

The heavy hand is rarely used during the process of persuasion although, in general, whips will use whatever technique brings success. Reasoned argument on the issue is initially used. The potential rebel would be expected to speak to the responsible frontbench spokesman well in advance of the expected vote. The threat to the survival of the government, together with general appeals to loyalty, would probably come into play. After all, few politicians want to be seen as responsible for bringing their opponents into power, however strongly they might feel about the issue in question. The ultimate sanctions – withdrawing the whip or the threat of deselection by the rebel's constituency party – are weapons, but they are rarely spoken of, let alone carried out. Members know those sanctions do exist, and their awareness of them is not unhelpful to the whips' efforts to keep the more difficult members in line.

Whips have authority amongst their colleagues and much of this derives from three sources. The first is the widely held perception that whips are close to the Prime Minister or leader of the opposition, and are thus very much 'in the know' and have the leader's confidence. Moreover, because the Chief Whip is usually very close to the Prime Minister or leader of the opposition, the whips are perceived as being very influential and so must be kept on side by any reasonably ambitious MP.

The second source is undoubtedly the patronage within their gift. Members are well aware that whips monitor their performance and have input into the leader's choices for ministerial and shadow ministerial advancement. This is a powerful disciplinary tool, since many MPs will judge their success by whether or not they get to the front bench. Continuous indiscipline will almost inevitably put a block on this aspiration, although not necessarily forever. Appointments to select and standing committees are also within the whips' gift. Whilst it is rarely the case that rebellious members will sell their principles in direct return for lesser favours, members are aware that patronage exists and that they may have need of it at some time in the future. Indeed, whips will rarely offer such favours as bait, but their use has been known. It is not, however, unheard of for such past favours to be recalled for the rebellious to consider. Much of this remains unspoken, but its effect is real.

The third source derives from the fact quite simply that the whips are a mine of useful information, and its distribution builds up goodwill. The question most asked of them is 'what time will the vote be?'. Imparting guidance to members on such practical matters is part of the everyday routine of being a whip, but is invaluable in allowing members to order an otherwise disorderly existence. Whilst many votes in Parliament are set for particular times, many are not, and thus information concerning the timing of the next vote – which can only come from the whips – is invaluable. Occasionally a member has a genuine need to leave the House for a short while, and it is the pairing whip who decides whether absence can be permitted. The member requesting a short absence is well pleased it has been granted, and is doubly pleased he has not missed the vote. That is but one example of building up goodwill. The simple act of approaching a newly elected colleague, and offering help and advice whenever it is needed, gains goodwill for the whip early in the relationship. Above all, whips need an ability to listen. Members may be unhappy with some aspect of policy, and the whips' ability to listen in such circumstances is vital in collecting intelligence and judging the mood of the party. However, it is just as important in building up that vital goodwill. Members want to know they can impart their concerns, that they will be listened to, and that their views will be reported back to those taking decisions. A whip who listens is looked upon sympathetically. Indeed, the member may feel that the whip is 'on his side'. Respect and even friendship can follow. It would take a particularly strongly held point of principle to stop a member heeding a request for reasonableness from such a whip, although for those who are independently minded enough, this would not be enough to change minds.

Whips also act as social workers to their flock, and especially when a member has personal, family or even financial difficulties. It follows therefore that, in some circumstances, a member may want advice and help, and is only prepared to talk to someone who can be trusted, in the knowledge that it will go no further. The Whips' Office would be the natural place to go, precisely because it 'does not leak'. By such methods that vital goodwill is established.

Party similarities and differences

The most obvious difference between the government Whips' Office and the official opposition – and, for that matter, the Whips' Offices of the other parties – is that the former is government and the latter are not. This brings an intensity to the government whipping operation that the others do not experience. The government's business is at stake – a very serious matter – and it follows that no government whip wants to be responsible for its loss and would not want to have to explain the reasons to the government Chief Whip. HM Opposition is simply not in this position although, if the whips can engineer a government defeat, this is most welcome – and therefore good for morale – but relatively rare.

Another difference between the two main Whips' Offices is the different methods employed by the parties in choosing their Chief Whip. The Conservative Chief Whip is the direct choice of the party leader, both in government and opposition. The same applies to Labour – but only when in government. In periods of opposition, the Labour Chief Whip is elected by the parliamentary party. Conservative whips therefore exclusively derive their formal authority 'from above', whilst Labour's system means that their whips derive their formal authority, at different times, from 'above' and 'below'. The minor parties also have whipping operations, and by far the most significant is that of the Liberal Democrats.

When the chips are down, the whips are the leader's servants. In any crisis, they are his Praetorian Guard, even if their operational methods are somewhat more subtle than those of their Roman predecessors. Nonetheless, they are a channel between their leader and the back benches. Technically, in government whips are ministers of the Crown and in opposition are classified as frontbenchers, but their role in Parliament means that they spend most of their time at Westminster in the company of the backbenchers. Generally, they are therefore neither leaders nor followers, but can appear at times to be both. An ability to carry out apparently conflicting activities – sometimes simultaneously – is therefore a necessary quality for a whip to operate successfully.

Being operationally separate from both their front and back benches does, however, give the whips the unique status I mentioned earlier. Because they spend so much time at Westminster – often the first to arrive and the last to leave – they spend more time with each other than they do with anybody else. As a group, they take on the characteristics of a family. Strong bonds of loyalty exist between them. There is much mutual support, both personally and in their daily operations. 'Once a whip – always a whip' is a commonly expressed sentiment, certainly by those who have served in the Conservative Whips' Office. They are usually very aware of their unique status and are generally proud of it.

We have established that the demise of the purely authoritarian method of whipping began in the 1950s, and accelerated during the 1970s – and so the brotherhood of the whips is the one continuing feature of the modern Whips' Office. On the Conservative side, the traditional postwar Whips' Office would still have been made up of ex-servicemen, mostly of the officer class. Their office would have had a distinct officers' mess feel to it. It was very much a club. The modern Conservative whip is more likely to be middle class, probably grammar school educated, but not exclusively, with a professional background. In other words, the make-up of the whips has mirrored the changes in the Conservative Party and, to a large extent, society outside. However, the officers' mess feel to the modern Conservative Whips' Office does survive. This is largely because of the unique identity which their role forces upon them. Were it not so, it is doubtful that a large number of essentially competitive people could possibly survive in such close and continuous proximity to each other. The theme that runs though the thoughts of ex-whips, as they relate their experiences of the office, is their common expression of the comradeship they experienced whilst serving within it. This can best be described as *esprit de corps*. The Whips' Office is perhaps the one place outside of the military where such an environment can still be experienced.

Ex-Labour whips express similar memories of comradeship. The unifying effects of such an atmosphere are common to both, but the roots from which the two offices derive it are quite different. As described above, the Conservative experience has military roots. Labour look to the trade unions and cooperatives for theirs. Labour whips tend to have the air of the shop steward about them, and indeed many of them were traditionally just that. Even these days, the percentage of Labour whips with a trade union or public sector background is still quite high.

Whilst, as has been said, both Whips' Offices have been moving away from the more authoritarian style of old, it seems to those of us who have watched the Labour Whips' Office from the outside that they are still more prone than the Tories to use the stick rather than the carrot. Perhaps the shop steward approach still holds sway, despite their efforts to work by means of the goodwill approach that largely characterises the Conservative Office.

The two Whips' Offices are also characterised differently in terms of how each party views them, not least by the differing attitudes of the respective leaderships towards them. The Conservative Office is viewed as a training ground for advancement to the front bench. A large percentage of those who serve in the Conservative Whips' Office go on to become ministers or shadow ministers. Indeed, some even rise to become Prime Minister – as with Sir Edward Heath and John Major. An appointment to the Whips' Office would not be viewed by all Conservative MPs as the greatest job in the world. Many would be mindful of the long hours and hard work that characterise the role. They would, however, view it as an undoubted opportunity to prove themselves to the leadership, with the corresponding certainty that their service within the office could prove a decisive factor in improving their prospects of further promotion outside it.

The Labour Whips' Office is different in this respect. Whilst it is not unheard of for Labour MPs to serve in their Whips' Office and then move on to significant frontbench roles, the incidence of such advancements does not seem to be as great as on the Conservative side. Advancement within the Labour Whips' Office seems to be viewed as a career structure in itself. Labour appears to take the view that the suitability of a member to serve in their Whips' Office is a definitive skill in itself. This, however, does not necessarily preclude a future high-profile frontbench role, and a recent example would be Geoff Hoon, who served as a whip in 1994–5 and went on to be made Secretary of State for Defence in 1999.

One change has taken place in recent years that has altered significantly the make-up of both offices. For years, both were male domains – indeed it would be fair to say that there seems to have been considerable resistance, on both sides of the House, to the inclusion of women in the respective offices. Perhaps in the past, those responsible for the appointing of whips feared that the majority of members – being males – would not readily accept being 'told what to do' by women. Whatever the reasons, prior to the mid-1970s, only one woman had served as a whip, Harriet Slater, appointed in 1964. That has now changed. Women have served in both offices – for example, Ann Taylor served as government Chief Whip from 1998–2001 – without any significant change to the basic atmosphere and culture of the whips. This may have to do with the fact that Parliament generally is still male dominated, despite the increase in female membership since 1997. For the moment, this has not resulted in any discernible changes to the nature of the whipping, whether administered by men or women.

'Usual channels' and the role of the whip in parliamentary procedure

Nothing is entirely predictable in any organisation, and in Parliament this is especially so. Any organisation that has institutionalised confrontation between large groupings of exceptionally opinionated – and generally ambitious – individuals is bound to have a strong element of the unexpected about it. The whips

on both sides of the House act as a counterbalance to that potential organisational anarchy. There is therefore much contact between the two offices. Those
contacts are known as 'usual channels'.

Most 'usual channels' contact at high level is undertaken by the Leader of
the House of Commons and his opposition shadow, along with the government and opposition Chief Whips. To provide for the smooth operation of
these potentially delicate relationships, a Civil Service intermediary is
appointed to the office of private secretary to the government Chief Whip.
Although working with the government Chief Whip, this civil servant
normally continues the same role whichever party is in power. The main task
of these contacts is to discuss the business of the week prior to it being
announced. Sometimes the opposition will want to discuss a particular matter
on a certain day, whilst the government would prefer a different date. By giving
ground on one point of business, the government might grant the opposition
its desires on one day, in exchange for getting what it wants on another.

In the past, discussions used to take place through the 'usual channels' on
the timetabling of specific Bills as they went through their parliamentary
stages. Government might have sought to have specific agreed timings on
when votes were to be held, and how long each clause or amendment would
be discussed. Opposition could decide formally to agree such an arrangement, or they could agree to cooperate and try to meet the timetable, this
second option leaving more scope for the opposition to decide which part of
the Bill it wanted to concentrate on, both in terms of votes and debate.
Alternatively, no agreement – formal or informal – was arranged. A general
'word of honour' indicated that the opposition wanted freedom of
movement, but would not be unreasonable in terms of time taken. This was
sometimes enough. At the other end of the spectrum – and only very rarely
– the opposition would withdraw all cooperation with the government,
usually because they thought that the government was riding roughshod over
its rights. This is known as a total breakdown in the 'usual channels'. When
this happens, Parliament ceases to operate in its normally ordered fashion.

Such periods of all-out parliamentary war are therefore usually short lived. Long periods when no one knows when votes are coming not only make life impossible for the government business managers – since part of the government's legislative programme may be at risk – but they also do so for the opposition. It becomes impossible to organise any life outside Parliament. Sense usually prevails fairly quickly.

Since 1997 this process has, however, changed significantly. The then newly elected Labour government changed the rules. The whole process has now been channelled into a formal procedure for programme motions, representing an allocation of time for each stage of a Bill. By this means, the opposition is deprived of the one weapon – time – which used to be its main bargaining tool. Obviously, this used to give government business managers a potential headache. However, the government removed that weapon from the opposition, thereby significantly increasing the power of the executive over Parliament. The time devoted to effective scrutiny of legislation was the second consequential loser. The role of 'usual channels' – and therefore of the two Whips' Offices – was also correspondingly reduced, as another consequence of this decision.

At lower levels, junior whips usually deal with their opposite number, to decide how many speakers from each side can speak in a debate and how much time each frontbench spokesman will take when winding up. This is done by the whip, consulting his own frontbench spokesman, usually in the chamber on the day of the debate. He then speaks to his opposing whip and, once agreement is reached, the Speaker is notified. It is then up to the whips on duty in the chamber to ensure that their own sides stick to the agreement, and that the wind-up speeches take place at the appointed time.

The necessity of whips to the functioning of the House is never clearer than when Parliament deals with a matter that is not subject to any party whip. This is usually termed a 'free vote'. It is not uncommon, during such a 'free vote', for members to come up to a whip and enquire which voting lobby they should be in.

Responsibility of individual whips

Government whips work from two sets of offices – one in the House of Commons and the other at 12 Downing Street. The opposition work from the opposition Whips' Office in the Commons.

The government Chief Whip maintains daily contact with the Prime Minister in a close working relationship. From his Downing Street base, the Chief Whip is also expected to maintain close contacts with other ministers, especially with members of the Cabinet. Although the Chief Whip attends Cabinet, he is not formally a member of it. The Chief Whip is thereby the key liaison between Cabinet and back benches.

Both government and opposition Whips' Offices employ staff, paid for out of the so-called 'Short money', voted by the House to provide administrative back-up. The staff, in both cases, are civil servants rather than political activists.

The number two in the office is the Deputy Chief Whip, who, essentially, is responsible for the day-to-day running of the rest of the office, organising and coordinating the junior whips below him. He is also the 'floor manager' in that, through the other junior whips, he is responsible for the smooth running of business in the House of Commons, and the exploitation of any advantage that can be gained on the floor of the House, although always under the discretion of the Chief Whip. He is also known as the 'accommodation whip', responsible for allocating office space to members of his own parliamentary party, and negotiating the position and amount of space available for him to allocate. This is a deceptively important element of patronage, since most members will always want a bigger and better office, as it confers prestige. Appointments to select committees, and some delegations, also come within his control.

The pairing whip, in both the government and opposition Whips' Office, holds a senior and important office, whose responsibilities include the agreement of officially sanctioned absences by members, and the appointment of members to standing committees. In the former case, he has the responsibility of ensuring that the number of absences does not threaten the government's majority or – in the case of the opposition – maintains a credible challenge in the division lobbies.

The practice of pairing used to allow one member from each side, by agreement, to be absent on business designated as 'two line'. This meant that an absence did not affect the government's natural majority, nor the opposition's ability to keep that majority down. Pairing simply allowed MPs to fulfil midweek engagements, or to have a free evening. However, after the 1997 general election, the opposition ceased the practice, since the government's majority was such that pairing gave no advantage to the opposition. However, in a parliament where majorities for the incumbent government party are smaller, it may make sense for the practice to be revived.

The whips' day is a long one, and probably begins with meetings of the frontbench team responsible for a particular government department or, in the case of the opposition, with the shadow team. If the department concerned has particular legislation or business before the House, it is the departmental whip who has the responsibility of ensuring that sufficient speakers are available for the debates at all stages, and for liaising with ministers and, where appropriate, shadow ministers for the smooth running of the business. This is achieved because both government and opposition whips are well placed to see each other, their frontbenchers, their back-benchers and the Speaker, with all of whom, at some time or another, they will be either interacting or speaking. From this position, they are perfectly placed to liaise, spot any unexpected difficulties, answer any queries from members about the business, deal with any frontbench concerns, and generally monitor what is going on. Being right next to the clerks of the House, the whip is also perfectly placed to check on parliamentary procedure.

Junior whips are normally responsible on an ongoing basis for groupings of 25 or 30 members, usually allocated on a regional or county basis. It is with, this group – although not exclusively – that the whip is expected to work closely. In addition, junior whips are expected to attend backbench committees relevant to their departmental responsibilities. In the case of Conservative whips, they are also expected to attend the weekly meeting of the 1922 Committee of Conservative backbenchers. They are not allowed to speak but they are certainly expected to listen. There is one exception, namely the whip who reads out the following week's business – and this is eagerly awaited by the parliamentary party. Junior whips are also expected to take their turn on the bench for routine business on each day that the House is sitting.

It is also the whips who act as 'tellers' at every official division in the House. Both government and opposition whips give the names of two of their number to the Speaker at each division. One pair are announced by the Speaker as tellers of the 'Noes' and the other pair as tellers for the 'Ayes'. One whip from the government then joins one whip from the opposition, and head for the exit doors of the 'Aye' division lobby. The remaining two opposing whips go to the exit of the 'No' lobby. As the MPs file through each lobby, their votes are first recorded by the clerks and then, as they pass through the exit doors, the two whips just outside the doors count them through. When both lobbies have emptied, the last whip from inside the lobby, having himself voted, announces 'all out' to the whips on the exit door, and thus the division is over. All that remains is for all four tellers to stand together before the mace and announce the result. The announcement is made by one of the tellers from the winning side – usually a government whip.

Conclusion

No organisation within the confines of Parliament excites as much interest as the Whips' Office. It is a club within a club, which only those who have served in it will ever fully understand. Consequently, an air of mystery surrounds its activities, leading to myth and legend being created to fill the vacuum of knowledge. It is this very air of mystery that is essential to its effectiveness in terms not only of party discipline but also of its other activities. These activities are essential to the working of a modern Parliament, without which it is doubtful such a procedurally complex place could operate. Here lie the roots of ex-whips' refusal to tell all. It is for this reason that the Whips' Office can truly be said to be one of the last refuges of kinship and trust. Maintaining that trust, whilst at the same time explaining the positive contribution of the Whips' Office to parliamentary life, is not easy, but it has been the key objective of this chapter.

TEN (B)

Parliament, Parties and Whips:
A View from the Lords

Lord Davies of Oldham

B ut what powers do you have? What are the sanctions?' These were not idle questions. They were addressed to me, newly arrived in the Whips' Office, by the then PPS to the Prime Minister, Bruce Grocott MP. He was anticipating that after the general election he might join us in the Whips' Office if he became a life peer. Some convincing answers must have been given to other questions on serving the government in the House of Lords for he is now Lord Grocott, Government Chief Whip. Given the fact that the Whips' Office is expected to be the engine room of power in any legislature, my answer to these cardinal questions must have seemed strange, namely, 'Nil'.

The House of Lords is a full-time House of predominantly part-time unpaid members. Scarcely any peer relies on its modest daily allowance for their total subsistence. Those who have not retired on pensions, a substantial number, are engaged in professional roles outside the House; indeed the very reason the majority are in the Lords is through distinction in these roles in the wider community. If not in remunerative employment, peers have time-consuming prominent roles in outside organisations. Regular attendance presents frequent problems. Members of the upper House who have political ambitions are only a small fraction. Political experience is at a premium. The main group with such experience is of course the former MPs and Cabinet ministers. For most of them, however, entry to the House signals the end of political ambition and distinguished achievement. Schooled as they are in the rigours of Commons discipline, one of the chief attractions of the upper House is to be free of it. The Labour benches can also call on the experience of trade union and local authority leaders. They share with the MPs a deep knowledge of the party, and are used to teamwork and disciplined commitment to a cause. If not retired, however, they are caught on the spikes of dual loyalties, to the Labour cause in the House and to their own organisations. Most Labour members, however, arrive in the House with limited or no political experience. Procedure in the chamber can appear both arcane and daunting. Used to commanding positions in their own chosen field of professional excellence, teamwork and discipline are to be learned often somewhat grudgingly, not readily assimilated. There are persistent, often infinitely more attractive, projects to be pursued outside the House than attendance in the House for hours on end to vote on issues which are of limited direct interest and at times of little appeal. The inevitable parliamentary grind of legislation weighs very heavily on those with a life to live elsewhere.

The opposition parties share these difficulties. The Liberal Democrats have a high level of peers chosen from their local authority ranks, some of whom retain extensive commitments. The Conservatives mirror Labour with their strong representation of industrialists and the City. Many of their members have widespread interests outside the House. Most of their political appointments were prominent in almost two decades of Conservative power. Advocacy in opposition has by contrast distinct limitations. Except for the leader and the Chief Whip, no one is paid to be at Westminster. For many of their number, the return to power looks well beyond their likely active political span.

Even the majority of the exiguous numbers of peers who are professionally paid as members of the House have extensive commitments elsewhere. The fourteen ministers in the Lords play the full ministerial role in the country. They inevitably struggle with the voting demands of the House.

The Lords operates continually on what the Commons has always abhorred, a three-line running whip. During the passage of legislation, committee stage, report and third reading, votes can occur at any time. An informal understanding keeps votes at the committee stage on the floor to the absolute minimum, and there are none at all if it is conducted in grand committee in a room away from the chamber. The report stage can be subject to multiple votes, and often is, as also can be the third reading. On the great contentious Bills therefore, the major parties have running three-line whips for hours on end. The government needs its members in attendance even at committee stage. These are big demands to make of elderly unpaid members. This is particularly true of the crossbench peers, who, in an age in which neither the government nor the Conservatives can command a majority in the House, play a sometimes decisive part in Lords votes on legislation.

More frequently, however, it is the Liberal Democrats who wield the decisive votes. As a result of this, the party is very committed in the Lords. Their single largest group consists of those with extensive experience in local authorities, which, although not always readily transferable to a national chamber, nevertheless means that an element of real political cohesion exists. Their attendance is high for it is in the Lords that they reach the summit of their present ambition, control of the balance between the major parties. They may flail somewhat ineffectively in the elected Commons in the face of a massive government majority but in the Lords, their votes are critical. Most calculations carried out by the government whips and to a lesser extent by the Conservatives are based on what the Liberal Democrats intend to do. Their support guarantees the passage of government proposals, their abstention is usually significant enough for the government to prevail, their opposition means trouble. The earliest bout of parliamentary ping-pong in the 2003/4 session on the European Parliamentary and Local Election 'Pilots' Bill was the result of intensive Liberal activity. The clash between the Commons and the Lords over the number of regions in which the experiment of postal voting for these elections should be conducted saw the Liberal Democrats leading the argument in the upper House. Five times the Commons insisted on its view before the Liberal Democrats and their Conservative allies yielded. Never has a Bill been batted back and forth between Commons and Lords to such an extent. Few would argue that this was a Bill of the highest political salience. Had it been so, the Conservatives would never have allowed the Liberal Democrats to make most of the running. It was a clear demonstration that the Lords felt confident and justified in challenging the elected government on a mainstream Bill.

Earlier in the same session the Conservative Party had demonstrated even more dramatically the problems facing a Labour government in the upper House. Having mobilised almost their full strength, and buttressed by their ability to pull in four-fifths of the crossbench vote, they had effectively wrecked the Constitutional Reform Bill. This measure was of high controversy, both in the abolition of the post of Lord Chancellor, and in the creation of the Supreme Court, but its opponents would be hard pressed to suggest that the nation as a whole was in riotous mood about the proposal. The Conservative Party, reduced to just a quarter of the House of Commons, wielded its full power as the largest party in the House of Lords to support an amendment consigning the bill to a select committee. The manoeuvre, executed only twice before in parliamentary history, was defined by the government as a wrecking amendment. The inevitable several months delay meant that the Bill, facing obdurate opposition in the Lords, probably could not be delivered before the next general election. This was the exercise of delaying power with a vengeance. Opposition claims that nothing so dramatic had occurred were specious. Of course the government could put off the general election until 2006, the end of its parliamentary span, and the measure could become law if necessary under the Parliament Act. In that sense, the Lords had delayed, not wrecked. The price to be paid, however, by the elected government was the choice of its election date!

For that highly significant vote, Labour brought in 69 per cent of its supporters, the Conservatives 75 per cent and the Liberal Democrats, who voted with the government, 66 per cent. The crossbenchers, much vaunted for their independence, joined the Conservatives in the ratio of nearly four to one. The contention was that this reflected a botched introduction of the measure with the constitutional changes appearing as a byproduct of a Cabinet reshuffle. Certainly the argument for a new Supreme Court and the separation of powers represented by the abolition of the post of Lord Chancellor had been much discussed in general terms, but never a full proposal open to consultation. The much more substantial constitutional point, however, was that an elected government with a huge majority in the House of Commons ran up against the full power of the unelected House prepared to set its will against the government of the day.

The House of Lords may no longer be at the beck and call of the Conservative Party, as it was in yesteryear when the massed ranks of Conservative hereditaries comfortably outvoted the life peers of other parties. Nevertheless, it is playing true to form. Throughout their history, Labour governments have been beaten vastly more often than Conservative admin-istrations. The Thatcher government, Conservative in name but radical and challenging in nature to many of the received pieties – for example she so alienated the universities that Oxford refused her an honorary degree – had little opposition from the upper House even with its notorious poll tax legis-lation, which sparked riots in the streets. Moreover, the first Bill to strike at the hereditary peerage, the Life Peerages Act 1958, sailed through the House in a fashion explicable only by the fact that it was introduced by Harold Macmillan's Conservative administration.

Government whips, therefore, appear to be facing a renewed challenge. In the House of Commons a Conservative Party revived in spirit under Michael Howard is still incapable of landing a glove on the government in the face of its huge majority. When Labour is in trouble in the lower House, it is its own backbenchers who create the problem. On issues such as foundation hospitals and the Criminal Justice Bill in the autumn of 2003, the Conservative oppo-sition in the Lords drew strength from Labour divisions in the Commons.

Moreover, it is clear that with the departure of most of the hereditaries and thus the destruction of the overwhelming Conservative majority, the House has begun to claim greater legitimacy from its more balanced membership. Labour reforms in 1999 have ended the gross abuse represented by the Conservatives' overwhelming power, but left the challenging situation of the government controlling less than 30 per cent of the membership of an increasingly assertive House. The Lords has been stripped of its most extreme absurdities whilst at the same time having an anti-government stance and greater preparedness to appear so.

What price the whips in such a scenario? Guidance they can offer in abundance. Pagers mean ready contact with colleagues prepared to carry them and switch them on. Positioned near the lobbies, whips make abundantly clear where government supporters' loyalty lies. Moreover as all votes are recorded, a post mortem is easily conducted and the Chief Whip is accustomed to having the analysis of the division only minutes after the result has been announced. Information, however, is only useful as a prelude to action. Unfortunately the whips have few carrots and fewer sticks. The Whips' Office can provide little in the way of patronage or promotion. Their charges are, with limited exceptions, quite immune to any such blandishments, any ambition still nursed being more likely to be fulfilled outside rather than inside the House. A small number aspire to join the government as a junior minister or whip. Vacancies are few; the total government payroll in the House is only 20 ministers and whips. Others may hope for goodwill from the whips in seeking a choice select committee position but these can be secured readily without truckling too extensively to the powers that be. Major government appointments outside the House, such as the chairmanship of a public body, are more likely to be on merit and personal patronage rather than a sound voting record and a clean bill of health from the whips.

The main sanction against extensive rebellion in an elected House is the threat of a general election, or at the least a vote of confidence, to bring government supporters to heel. The House of Lords is impervious to such considerations. Likewise the dreaded letter to the chair of one's constituency party or even the outright disbarring from candidature, which can strike such terror into MPs, has no application to their Lordships. Moreover, rebellion in the Commons is a highly political act subject to keen party and public scrutiny. Those of a regularly challenging cast of mind usually protect themselves against the charge of outright disloyalty by being the most regular supporters of the government in the lobby when the legislation carries no party problems. In the Lords, such considerations rank as naught.

The most persistent rebel may commit the ultimate crime of rarely bothering to attend until there is an issue sufficiently provocative as to warrant a speech and a vote in opposition to government proposals. The absence of sanctions is laid bare, reduced solely to the social ostracism which can occasionally occur. Yet this can be ignored by those whose independence of mind is often matched by their main preoccupations being well outside the House.

Nevertheless, party cohesion exists to a significant extent. In the vast majority of divisions, as many as seven in ten, all members of the government and also of the two opposition parties who vote follow the party line. Dissent on highly contentious issues is not markedly at variance with the level in the Commons.

The distinguishing feature in the House of Lords is turnout. A House whose average age is over 65 contains a number of infirm, either permanently or irregularly, who find it impossible to attend. Many others are elsewhere engaged on matters which they deem to take precedence over voting in the House. Thus the parties, even the government, struggle to achieve a 75 per cent turnout. In such circumstances, absence can be genuine or a mark of dissent. For whips it represents a bleak perspective.

Government whips have some compensation for achieving solid turnouts yet regular defeats. They are paid just below the ministerial scale. As the House is self-regulating, the chair in which the Lord Chancellor himself sits for usually less than an hour each day exercises no authority. Order is kept by peers observing the norms and gentle, occasionally forceful, interventions by the leading whip on the government front bench.

Most debates not centred on legislation are timed and run like clockwork, each contribution having an allotted span, with a whip to ensure that speakers observe the timetable. Whips in the Lords do not observe the monastic silence which is the rule for their counterparts in the Commons. They have significant speaking roles, frequently deputising for ministers unable to attend, and in the case of the Deputy Chief Whip taking responsibility for a department where there is no Lords minister. They therefore feature each week in debates or at question times. This goes some way to compensate for the unenviable nature of their main responsibility, ensuring the passage of government legislation.

There is no timetable mechanism or guillotine available to the government whips in the upper House. The number of days allocated to committee and report stage on a Bill are by agreement through the 'usual channels'. Committee stage on the floor usually passes without any division, and one is precluded if the Bill is referred to a grand committee off the floor. Nevertheless, the government usually guards against the unexpected by requiring a substantial number of its members to be present on a two-line whip.

On report and third reading attendance is mandatory on a three-line whip. Most often the obligation runs until 7.30 p.m., when the whip is lifted. On the most contentious measures, however, and particularly in June, July, September and October, when the number of Bills being considered by the Lords is at its most intense, the whip may be sustained until business concludes at 10 p.m. or even later. A whip stands or, more accurately, sits sentinel in the Princes' Room adjoining the Chamber. As long as this presence is manifest, government peers only leave with a bad conscience, knowing their colleagues are likely to vote at some later stage. Even after blessed release is obtained, and the whip is lifted, some government members are subject to further discipline. Whilst government business is on the floor it must 'keep a House' even if the 'usual channels' have indicated that no official votes will be called. Thus 40 members, including some ministers, commit themselves to remaining until the House rises, to guard against a 'maverick' vote which might occur, sometimes with the malign intention of counting the House out if fewer than 30 votes are recorded in any division. Such procedural parliamentary games are played rarely in the Lords but the Government Chief Whip is not prepared to be caught off his guard.

Not surprisingly the whips form no part of this voluntary force of 40, whose membership changes from evening to evening to share out the burden evenly. Whips are present mandatorily and leave only when the 'House is up'. In any case, one of their number is on the front bench as no business is conducted in the chamber without a whip being present, even if their sole duty late in the evening is to move the adjournment motion for the House so that all can go home. This frequently occurs some three hours after the Commons has adjourned as their reformed hours mean that they work a more conventional day.

The more part-time House of Lords is finding it more difficult to reform its hours, despite the fact that the absurdity of three-line whips demanding attendance late into the evening is the source of huge aggravation. The remedy is, of course, in the hands of the peers themselves but the auguries for radical reform, necessitating regular morning sessions, are not good. The House has adjusted the Thursday sitting to begin at 11.00 a.m. and end at 7.00 p.m. in order that distant peers can travel that evening, but extending that concept to the other working days still seems unlikely.

Opposition whips operate in a considerably more relaxed environment. Apart from their Chief Whip and leader, all are unpaid. They call in their members with great efficiency on the big occasions and the government accepts the inevitability of defeat if both opposition parties are united in three-line whips to vote against the government.

The House is managed by the three Chief Whips operating through the 'usual channels' to organise business. Contrary to public perception, senior politicians work honourably in their relationships with opposing parties. 'My word is my bond' is observed with total rectitude in the House. An added dimension in the Lords is that the government Whips' Office acts as the information and organising centre for official business. Peers register there to speak in debates and expect and accept helpful advice on most aspects of the progress of business in the chamber. Such a facility is advantageous to all. It is of particular help to crossbench peers and bishops, who have no party structure to which to relate. Crossbench peers have a convenor who plays his part in the 'usual channels' but of course it would be a contradiction in terms if he were to act like a whip of independent peers. His role is as a two-way conduit of information for a disparate group. There is, moreover, one inescapable requirement which brings crossbenchers as a group into the closest relationship with other parties: accommodation.

The majestic Victorian proportions of the House of Lords appear to afford room for all but in fact provide rooms for few. Lofty ceilings provide grandeur, but nearly every office in the House is twice as high as a modern one. Moreover, Victorian peers expected to spend most of their time in the spectacularly impressive public rooms, the library, the dining room and the bars. The modern peer expects a desk, a computer and preferably a room whose only other occupant would be their assistant. Just like their counterparts in the Commons, though less dramatically, the Lords have spilled out into the adjoining buildings in Millbank, Abbey Gardens and Fielden House. Nevertheless, provision falls significantly short of demand. Most peers tolerate rather than enjoy the accommodation they command. Each party has a whip, in the case of the crossbenchers the convenor, to represent their interests on accommodation, all too often finding that there is a fifth guest at the party, the formidable House of Lords administration, which has its interests too. As the present writer fulfils this role for the government, tears occlude any fuller description of the process of reconciling competing demands.

The concept of whipping in the Lords can often look like a pale shadow of the House of Commons. Votes in that House, always referred to as 'the other place', can several times a year be headline news. The government can be beaten in the Lords many times a week without it occasioning a rumble in the world outside. It was put most sardonically by a former Commons Chief Whip, Lord Michael Cocks. 'Every vote you lose costs the Commons one and a half hours of their time to put right – not too much, is it!' That was an astute and fairly accurate judgement during the 1997–2001 Labour term. Post 2001 the government, following the limited reform of the House, is having to face challenges which are far more substantial than that. The abandonment in the third year of a parliament of two key Bills suggests that both the composition, and even more so the powers of the Lords, will secure increasing government attention. Marginal additions to Labour's ranks may reduce the furrows in the Government Chief Whip's brow, but neither this, nor any future government, will ever have remotely near a majority in the upper House. Whether any government, least of all a Labour government committed to reform, will accept the present powers of the upper House in the face of that overwhelming fact is highly improbable.

ELEVEN

The Legislative Process – An Inside View

Lord Biffen of Tanat

I was asked to write about 'the legislative process' from the standpoint of 'an inside view'. I have drawn upon my experiences as Leader of the House of Commons, 1982–7, as a departmental Cabinet minister, Secretary of State for Trade, 1981–2, as a backbench member of Parliament, 1961–79 and 1987–97, and as a life peer since 1997.

The 'legislative process' in the Commons which functioned up to 1997 has been significantly changed since then by the reforms initiated by the Blair government. These are discussed at the end of this chapter, but the fundamentals of law-making have not been altered. The reforms have been tactical rather than strategic. The internal changes relate to 'programming', a more correct description of guillotining debate, and the potential, rather than actual, use of carrying over unfinished Bills into the succeeding session of Parliament. The internal factor impelling change has been the desire to have more 'family-friendly' working hours. Quite separately are external factors, namely, the impact not only of membership of the European Union but also of Scottish and Welsh devolution upon the responsibilities for the Westminster Parliament.

Time is the master of the sessional programme. It governs the number and character of the laws that Parliament can manage in a session that normally begins in October/November and effectively ends in the following July, with a clearing up of unfinished business in October.

Departmental ministers are invited to make bids for places in the legislative programme. They are encouraged to be modest by the Chief Whip and the Leader of the House, who have the responsibility of seeing that the overall programme can be managed within the parliamentary timetable. As trade secretary I provided few headaches for the business managers. There was no immediate demand for legislation as, mercifully, a complex Bill on Lloyds of London regulations and a Companies Bill had just been passed as I became trade secretary. I suggested to my team of trade ministers that we should make no bid for legislation, but I yielded to protests that we must bid for something or else run the risk of being regarded as a no-bid department. I then requested a measure that affected consumer protection and nationalised industries. In my austere view it was not necessary and was motivated by populist politics rather than sound economics. Nonetheless, Trade was unusual in being modest in its legislative claims. Environment and Health/Social Security made substantial claims with major Bills, some of which carried out the reform programme of the Thatcher government elected in 1979.

The decisions on the legislative programme were highly political but always constrained by time. The latter obliged a discipline and sense of priorities. In my period as Leader of the House, from 1982–7, I was partnered by Michael Jopling and subsequently John Wakeham as Chief Whip. We struggled with our Cabinet colleagues to keep the programme within bounds. It was an ironic situation considering we had a mandate for less government. Our invaluable ally was William Whitelaw, the elder statesman, troubleshooter and arch-conciliator of the Cabinet. Our bargaining hand was strengthened by the finite number of parliamentary draftsmen. These highly skilled legal experts were relatively few in number, and their work was almost a vocation in view of their pay and what their skills would have earned in the commercial market.

The agreed programme would usually provide for 35 to 45 Bills. The public Bills, in the name of the government, would be divided, very broadly, into Bills contingent upon manifesto commitments, major Bills, lesser Bills and measures arising from international obligations. Distinguishing between major and lesser was an art form. Departmental ministers would almost swear an oath that a Bill was so universally popular it would almost pass undebated; the business managers were nature's sceptics. They knew that it was more relevant to recall how often ministers having authority for a Bill would try and 'add on' clauses during its passage through Parliament. Finally, the public Bill programme would have to leave time for private members' Bills.

Once the programme had been agreed it was put into the text of a draft Queen's Speech. This was then considered by the Cabinet and, just possibly, there might be some adjustment to the programme, but it was already set in drying concrete. There was also concern about the style as well as the contents of the speech the monarch would deliver. There was no Milton lurking in the Cabinet Office who could render the speech into memorable prose, but in my Cabinet days, the task was referred to Lord Hailsham. He applied his formidable scholarship but the speech would still read rather like a laundry list.

That did not spoil the imposing ceremony of the opening of a new session of Parliament, with the Queen making the speech from the throne in the House of Lords. It remains, for me, a solemn but theatrical occasion redolent with history. It started the new session in great style. In the Commons, and the Lords, there would be two backbenchers who proposed and seconded a loyal address to Her Majesty. These preceded the general debate. I particularly remember the backbench speech made by Charles Curran in 1963/4. It departed from the usual anodyne travelogue description of constituency virtues. In Curran's case, this was Uxbridge. Instead he offered sharp and satirical references to his new leader and Prime Minister, Alec Douglas-Home. The House of Lords has always treated these occasions with bland decorum.

The business managers, meanwhile, were starting the task of seeing the programme was launched immediately the ceremonial and pageantry had been concluded. They were conscious not merely of the Bills listed in the speech but of its standard admonition that 'other measures may be laid before you.'

One of the early decisions is the allocation of legislation between Lords and Commons. Most major Bills are started in the Commons but in order to maintain a balanced use of parliamentary time, quite a number of substantial Bills are introduced in the Lords. Occasionally a contentious Bill, but not contentious on party lines, will be put to the Lords to test the degree of discord. Such was the Shops Bill, concerning Sunday trading, in 1985. The Lords committee stage revealed a warning of acute cross-party opposition. The measure was defeated in the Commons at second reading – by 296 votes to 282 – and only became law having been reintroduced in the subsequent parliament of 1990.

There is constant cooperation between the business managers of both Houses. John Wakeham and myself met Lord Denham, then Chief Whip in the House of Lords, weekly. The latter would be equipped with a board marked with arrows and squiggles which indicated the state to business like a piece of critical path analysis. It was slightly Heath Robinson but it worked surprisingly well, and the load was sensibly spread between both Houses and over time.

Traditionally a Bill would be given a first reading merely on the title being read aloud by a parliamentary clerk. The second reading and debate would follow soon after. It is now a growing practice to have 'prelegislative scrutiny'. Provisions for this have existed over 20 years and were used on two occasions when I was Leader of the House. The process then was not much favoured by the business managers or departmental ministers because it was judged to extend rather than shorten the committee stage. The Communications Bill 2003 is an excellent example of the valuable role of prelegislative scrutiny. It was a Bill including many technical aspects of the media industry as well as major policy issues such as ownership. Outside bodies, interested parties and lobbyists could all represent views with the object of influencing the Bill before it was introduced to Parliament for its general debate and second reading. There is no doubt that this scrutiny did enable critics of the original Bill to obtain amendments, a process effectively orchestrated by Lord Puttnam in the House of Lords.

The second reading of a Bill is still the usual first occasion when the legislation sees the light of parliamentary day. The minister opening the debate and explaining the virtues of the Bill usually speaks for about 30 to 40 minutes. This is traditionally in mid-afternoon, parliamentary prime time, and likely to obtain media coverage. The debate usually lasts six or seven hours and there can only be a limited number of speakers. Backbenchers are encouraged to limit their speeches to ten minutes. The two wind-up speeches, from the front benches, take about 30 minutes each, and when the issue is highly controversial can be laced with drama. For me the most poignant second reading debate was the 1972 European Communities Bill. The concluding speeches were delivered against a background of noise and the narrow majority for the Bill – a mere eight votes – was received in uproar. Most second readings, by contrast, are conducted earnestly and constructively in a sparsely attended chamber. The Commons now rarely sits up to 10.00 p.m. and the boisterous wind-ups from 9.00 p.m. to 10.00p.m. were encouraged by smoking room conviviality. In that respect the Commons has been tidied up.

Most Bills are then sent 'upstairs' for consideration by a standing committee of MPs who examine and amend them line by line and clause by clause. The standing committee, which should reflect the political balance of the House of Commons, usually numbers around sixteen or eighteen and meets in the suite of committee rooms on the first floor. A number of Bills have a committee stage comprising the full Commons. These are usually constitutional Bills, such as those establishing the Scottish and Welsh Parliaments and the Bill authorising membership of the European Communities, now designated the European Union.

I arrived at Westminster in November 1961 and almost immediately saw the full Commons considering the committee stage of the Commonwealth Immigrants Bill. The Macmillan government introduced legislation which defined the rights of immigration from the Commonwealth. It abrogated the principle of free entry and was considered constitutional. I suspect the business managers decided the issue was so politically contentious that they had no option other than to let everyone 'blow off steam'. They did that. I recall an impassioned speech by Fenner Brockway, a Labour veteran, which he concluded by dashing across the floor of the House and throwing his speech notes on the Home Secretary's despatch box. It made a lively interlude between endless and high-minded debating.

When I arrived at the Commons I was soon put on the committee considering the Transport Bill. The decision to do this was taken by the Committee of Selection, with a membership of nine and a quorum of three. It was chaired by a senior backbencher. The committee naturally works closely with the Whips' Office and I have no doubt the Conservative whips decided the Transport Bill would be a useful apprenticeship for me in the drudgery of standing committee work. The Bill was massive, including, amongst much else, the implementation of the Beeching report on the railways. It was just not of sufficient length and contention as to merit a guillotine. So for weeks I sat in Committee Room 14 on Tuesday and Thursday mornings (and later afternoons) whilst Labour railway-sponsored MPs mounted a relentless and verbose opposition. They moved many amendments, all of which had to fall within the 'long title' of the Bill. I do not disparage the detailed committee stage of a Bill. It enables lobbyists and interested parties to brief members of the committee so that the arguments are often well informed. The minister is required to see if they can be met. The atmosphere of debates on the committee floor tends to be wordy but serious with little of the histrionics that liven the proceedings on the floor of the House.

There is a convention that at least two weekends should lapse between the second reading and the beginning of the committee stage. This enables the opposition and the lobbyists to prepare their arguments. Often the latter will sit at the back of the committee room so they can assess the debate firsthand. This is usually conducted in a fairly conversational manner, but I remember one occasion, the committee stage of the 1966 Prices and Incomes Bill when Frank Cousins was a backbench member. He had just resigned from the government and had a senior official of his union, the Transport and General

Workers', at the back of the room to advise him. It all ended in tears: Cousins walked out of the committee whilst it was still in session.

When I began my Commons career the Finance Bill was taken on the floor of the House. It was a marathon and necessitated at least a couple of all-night sittings. Eventually the Bill was split, most of the clauses being discussed upstairs and only the major measures being discussed by the whole House.

The committee stage of a Bill is a major task for the relevant minister and his whip. Few Bills are wholly uncontroversial and the committee has a responsibility to examine the provisions in detail. Opposition members will not feel constrained to be brief. In order to keep things moving a minister should have a conciliatory and not a confrontational manner. He should carry a few concessions in his pocket, but ultimately he can depend upon the whip moving a motion to end the debate – 'the closure'. This was introduced in the mid- to late nineteenth century when the load of public Bills was increasing and the Irish Home Rulers were disrupting parliamentary proceedings. The closure is an arbitrary measure but the indignation it provokes is more synthetic than heartfelt.

A more extreme measure is the guillotine. This provides a staged timetable for the Bill and whenever a debate exceeds the allotted time it is terminated. The guillotine has become increasingly used, but it has to be authorised by a vote of the entire Commons. When it is moved there is the ritual indignation, but it usually conceals a great deal of relief that protracted debate will now be disciplined. As Leader of the House I had to propose a guillotine on several Bills, including that establishing the Single European Market. My heart was with its Eurosceptic opponents so I wrote my own opaque guillotine speech rather than accepting a Civil Service brief. A guillotine which did provoke a furious reaction was that designed to reform trade union law – the Industrial Relations Bill 1971. Labour insisted on voting on every measure that had been guillotined and we had a session of non-stop voting that lasted through the night. There are now moves afoot to put guillotines on a more permanent basis, described more delicately as 'programming'. I shall refer to this later.

Once the committee stage of a Bill is concluded it is 'reported' to the House. The report stage enables further amendments to be made. This is an invaluable process. Often the minister will be inclined to accept the spirit of an amendment but will be advised by his department that its wording is faulty and needs redrafting. Occasionally major alterations occur at report stage. In 1972 Nicholas Ridley and I joined the Labour and Liberal members of the Counter-inflation Bill committee stage and secured major amendments. Our victory was short lived. They were all reversed at the report stage when the whole House had a vote.

The third reading, which follows the report stage, is now somewhat of a formality. At a second reading one can discuss the topic very generally and refer to the Bill's omissions: at the third reading one is supposed to be restricted only to the contents of the Bill. It is a safety valve in that it provides a window of time for those who have not been able to speak on the subject hitherto. There was one occasion – untypical – when the third reading was put to political and controversial use. The issue of immigration and race relations was extremely sensitive for the Conservatives in 1968, and an attempt was made to reconcile viewpoints by tabling a reasoned amendment to the second reading of Labour's Race Relations Bill. The government carried the legislation through second reading, committee and report stages. Edward Heath and the shadow Cabinet were happy to let the third reading pass 'on the nod'; the whole topic was painful and divisive. Conservatives who wanted a more restrictionist policy decided to put down a reasoned amendment to the third reading in exactly the same terms used by Edward Heath in respect of the second reading. Of course the amendment was not called but it served the purpose of demonstrating a degree of Tory backbench discontent with its leadership.

Often Bills contain provisions that enable subsequent law to be made by order – namely Statutory Instruments. These are usually considered by a select committee of MPs and many are subject to the most peremptory attention – indeed it could not be otherwise considering the enormous number involved. Orders which are authorised by 'affirmative resolution' have to be debated by a full Parliament. They may be accepted or rejected: they cannot be amended. In the 1960s the Wilson government conducted their incomes policy by using affirmative orders. It meant that all decisions restricting prices, charges or incomes under the Prices and Incomes Acts of 1966, 1967 and 1968 had to be brought before the Commons, something that usually occurred late at night. It became a nightmare for the business managers. The Conservatives contested every order often in cahoots with Labour rebels. It is difficult to imagine such a device being repeated. Statutory Instruments, like European legislation, remain an area where Parliamentary control is difficult to exert given the disciplines of time which constrain the business of the Commons.

The work of Parliament is dominated by public Bills, giving effect to government policy; but provision is also made for Bills promoted by backbench MPs. MPs submit their names for a ballot which is drawn by a clerk of the House, not unlike shouting numbers at bingo. An MP lucky in the ballot will be wise to choose a modest and worthy cause. As a backbencher it is extremely difficult to secure the passage of controversial legislation without the assistance of whips. Usually 20 Bills are chosen by ballot, of which between ten and fifteen are likely to become law. The whips normally have a list of Bills which the government have prepared and would like to see enacted. Backbenchers lucky in the ballot often take advantage of this facility. Very occasionally the government will welcome a private members' Bill and, crucially, provide government time to ensure its passage. Recently this has been the case with the Bill to abolish hunting. Much of private members' legislation has involved modest matters but Leo Abse, legalising consenting homosexuality, and David Steel, defining and permitting abortion, introduced major laws that government preferred to leave to free votes.

The Lords' treatment of legislation is similar to that of the Commons, but there are significant differences. The membership of the Lords exceeds that of the Commons, over 700 against 659, but active peers number between

300 and 400. Party loyalties in the Lords are not subject to effective whipping and some 180 peers sit on the crossbenches. There is a convention that all Bills are given an unopposed second reading, and that opposition should be constrained to any Bills that had featured in the government's general election manifesto. Second reading debates in the Lords are calm, and ministers are hardly ever interrupted. Those wishing to speak submit their names to the government Whips' Office and the Lords 'usual channels' then publish a speakers list; there is none of the Commons agony of wondering if the Speaker will call you. There is much to be said for this procedure but it does undermine debating. Most peers read prepared speeches and neither accept or make interruptions. There are very few rules governing procedure in the Lords, presumably because their business in the nineteenth century was unaffected by Irish Home Rulers. It is a tribute to the civilised politics of the Lords that the government can usually carry their business without closures or guillotines and finish on the right side of midnight.

It has been Lords practice to take most Bills' committee stage on the floor of the chamber. The growing volume of legislation means that this custom is difficult to maintain. The Lords' equivalent for an upstairs Commons committee stage is the use of the Moses Room. This is now used for a number of Bills, and its use is likely to increase. There is some anxiety (misplaced I believe) that use of the Moses Room diminishes the scrutiny of legislation. The Lords' consideration of legislation has been intensified by the increasing programming or guillotining of so much legislation in the Commons. Despite the absence of closures the Lords committee stage debates tend to be disciplined and at least as well informed as those in the Commons.

Report and third reading debates follow the Commons pattern except that amendments are permitted at the third reading. The junior role of the Lords was clearly established in the Parliament Act of 1911, which limited their ability to reject Commons legislation; such power was further limited by the Parliament Act of 1949. In my view it is highly desirable that the Commons should have the decisive role in law-making. Equally I am convinced that the

Lords' ability to amend is crucial, and I think it might be extended to cover financial legislation, which is now beyond its authority. An enormous number of amendments are moved by the government to rectify situations that have been overlooked by the Commons or not even considered as the result of programming. The ultimate right to delay legislation for a limited period is rarely exercised. It would damage the customary good relations between the two Houses of Parliament if it were. On the other hand reforming the Lords and abolishing the hereditary principle, and ensuring that crossbenchers hold the voting balance, could change this. The Lords might feel it had greater authority for the use of its amending and delaying powers.

Since the election of the Blair Labour government in 1997 there have been three major reforms affecting or 'modernising' the Commons' handling of legislation. I regard two of these as admirable. The first is 'programming', which seeks to have an agreed timetable for the discussion of all major legislation. The Conservative Party continues to resist this and I have no doubt that it has resulted in a great deal of legislation being undiscussed until it reaches the Lords. This is a serious blemish, but I believe that the Conservatives, when eventually back in office, would see the merit of seeking predictability for law-making and ensuring a reasonable allocation of time for debates. Ironically the 'usual channels' – government and opposition – are ambivalent about the measure. It deprives them of powers of bargaining which they like to have across all aspects of parliamentary procedure. They live in the world of compromise which can best be secured over the widest political front.

The second admirable reform is to enable a Bill which has not been completed by the end of a session to be 'carried over' for completion in the succeeding session. The former practice was that a Bill collapsed if it could not be completed within the session. This was the fate of the original and complex Bill that privatised British Telecommunications. The session had been foreshortened by an early general election called in 1983 and the Bill could not be completed and had to start anew in the session following the election. Recently the Financial Services Bill, horrendously complicated, was run over two sessions, and was better handled on that account. There is an argument for a fixed-five year parliament with no sessional breaks. If such an innovation were accepted, I hope we would retain an annual ceremony involving the monarch and the pageantry we now have when a session of Parliament is opened.

The third reform has been to alter the working hours of the Commons to make them more 'family friendly'. The substantial increase in the number of women MPs has been a factor in this decision. It has meant that the Commons sits until 10 p.m. only on Mondays, rises early evening on a Tuesday and Wednesday, and effectively ends after lunch on Thursday. This impinges upon time – a crucial lubricant for parliamentary business, including law-making. I do not see why the working conditions of Parliament should be 'family friendly' any more than working on a North Sea oil rig or in the Merchant Navy is conducive to domestic life. Politics should be a vocation involving a reverence for the institution of Parliament and a commitment to a constituency. That necessitates a generous commit-ment to time and should be accepted by those who seek a Westminster career.

I hope my anxieties will be falsified, but I suspect the recent and sensible reforms in law-making will be vitiated unless time is treated as a generous and not a rationed commodity. Law-making is at the heart of Parliament. 'The redress of grievance' has increased with the growing concept of the protective role of the state. From the great reforms of the Liberal Parliaments of 1906 and 1910 the role of the state has expanded to cover social and economic issues that did not preoccupy the Victorians. It provides a heavy burden for MPs, often toil without drama; but for me it has been a matter of fascination and a bond which ties Westminster to the wider public it serves. As an MP I have often gone to the Lords to witness the conclusion of Parliament's law-making. A clerk would intone the titles of the Bills and a second clerk would respond, using Norman French, 'La Reine le veult.' Long may this quaint and archaic custom survive. The ability to make the laws of the nation is rooted in history.

TWELVE

The Prime Minister and Parliament

Graham P. Thomas

This chapter examines the relationship between the Prime Minister and Parliament – primarily, the notion of prime ministerial accountability. It starts with an examination of the concept of accountability and discusses the role of Parliament in holding the Prime Minister to account. The decline in the power of the legislature is outlined and the particular features which contribute to executive dominance in Parliament are examined. This leads into a historical overview of the relationship between Parliament and Prime Minister, with special reference to the post-1945 period. The various factors affecting that relationship are considered, of which personality is but one, and, it is argued, increasingly not the most significant.

Accountability

The accountability of those in positions of power and authority is a central aspect of liberal democracy. It is crucial to the notion of both representative and responsible government and it is a guide for ethical behaviour. It seeks to ensure that those in power will operate in accordance with a complex system of rules. These may be explicitly set out in written codes or be imbibed by some kind of socialisation process, which seeks to ensure that power is not abused and that the object is some concept of the 'common good', however that is interpreted in the light of the presuppositions of the holders of that power. Those subject to authority need to have confidence that the holders of power can be held to account, while those in authority need to be aware of the standards expected of them and of the sanctions that can be imposed. Thus the concept of accountability is one of the standards against which systems of governments and the individuals who make up those governments can be judged. 'Accountable government is deemed to be good government, and carries with it connotations of advanced democracy.'[1]

However, accountability is a highly complex concept, with many, often highly elusive and even contradictory, meanings. Accountability is the requirement for the representative to answer to those represented how they carry out their duties and responsibilities, to act upon criticisms or requirements made upon them, and to accept at least some degree of responsibility for failure, incompetence or deceit. Finally it involves facing the possibility of removal from whatever position of power is held.

In democratic theory, accountability means that those who exercise power are in a sense stewards, and must be able to show that they have exercised their powers and discharged their duties properly. It requires that the duties, powers and functions of government bodies are defined in such a way that the performance can be monitored and evaluated by a 'higher' body, which may be Parliament, the courts or the people through the process of a general election. Accountability limits government power by establishing mechanisms of political control in which one institution (or a range of institutions) oversees the working and performance of another, scrutinising policy proposals and monitoring political performance. When this is achieved through regular and competitive elections, it amounts to a system of public control, what Pyper calls the 'inchoate generality'[2] of the public as the consumers and clients of services provided by those in authority. In this sense, public accountability is the practical face of democratic rule.

However, to be effective certain conditions need to be present. The mechanisms for monitoring performance need to be rigorous. The 'higher' institutions or bodies must have sufficient access to information to make critical and informed judgements. Appropriate sanctions must be available and the will to apply them in the event of underperformance and, most crucially of all, in the event of abuses of trust must be present. Critics of the degree to which British Prime Ministers are held accountable for their actions by Parliament point to deficiencies in all these conditions. Tony Wright, the independent-minded Labour MP and chairman of the Select Committee on Public Administration, argued that the environment of the House of Commons 'is that of a dominant executive and a legislature disciplined by partisanship';[3] it is unlikely that this judgement has been altered by the practices of New Labour in government or by Wright's time as an increasingly critical observer of the Blair government.

Accountability and the British Prime Minister

Given the uncodified nature of the British constitution and the absence of any 'official', generally accepted, definition of the role and position of the Prime Minister in the British system, prime ministerial accountability is an essentially political concept, not one enshrined in law or even embodied in constitutional theory and practice as is the case with the American President. In the USA, the written constitution provides several legal restraints on the President, including the threat of impeachment by Congress and the power of the Supreme Court to control his actions and those of his subordinates. This was most clearly seen in the resignation of President Richard Nixon in 1974.

Such a situation, the driving from office of the head of government by legal action (albeit in the context of intense political pressure caused by the scandals surrounding Nixon and his entourage) is highly unlikely – if not impossible – in the United Kingdom. Clearly the British courts do not possess the power to scrutinise the Prime Minister's conduct as head of government, especially given that the Prime Minister does not possess executive power. The Prime Minister is not responsible for legislation and so cannot be held *ultra vires*. Generally it is departmental ministers who answer to Parliament for things done in their departments and the Prime Minister does not have responsibilities for departmental matters. The Prime Minister is Minister for the Civil Service, although questions on the service are usually taken by the junior minister concerned, and has responsibility for various units such as the Cabinet Office, but is generally reluctant to answer questions on these responsibilities, again leaving it to junior ministers.

Of course, that does not mean that the Prime Minister is above either the law or moral censure. Prime Ministers remain responsible for their personal conduct in the same way as the rest of the population. It is entirely possible that private conduct could produce the sort of scandal which would make the premier's position untenable. It has been argued that had the news of John Major's former affair with Edwina Currie surfaced during his premiership, especially at the time of the 'back to basics' fiasco, his continuation in office would have been highly problematic.

There are various means by which Prime Ministers can be held accountable for their actions. Ultimately, the electorate is the primary source both of prime ministerial power and of the ending of a Prime Minister's career. Just as a general election is one of the two ways by which a person becomes Prime Minister (the other is succeeding a Prime Minister of the same party), defeat in a general election is a major cause of the end of a Prime Minister's time in office. Of the eleven people who have held the office since the Second World War, only Churchill in 1951 and Wilson in February 1974 came back after a previous defeat in a general election. However, there are other mechanisms for exerting some kind of check on prime ministerial power. These include the premier's colleagues, especially the Cabinet, his or her party, the media, and the focus of this chapter, namely Parliament.

There is a complex and shifting relationship between the Prime Minister and Parliament, government and party and the electorate. The ability of any part of the political process to hold the Prime Minister to account depends largely on the success of the administration in power and of the head of that administration. Success in one area usually leads to success in another. Electoral success usually leads to an increase in party support for the Prime Minister both in the country and in the House of Commons. Potential rivals for the leadership will be unwilling to put their head above the parapet. For the same reasons, government backbenchers (apart from the 'usual suspects') will support their leader and cheer him or her on during the ritual battles at Prime Minister's Question Time. The loyalty and vocal support of backbenchers are crucial to the Prime Minister's ability to dominate the Commons.

This dominance, this impression of a Prime Minister and government in charge of events, will then be picked up by the media and conveyed to the voters, who are likely to react favourably, always assuming that the impression created is one that accords with their own experience. Prime Ministers who dominate their party, the House of Commons and public opinion are hard to hold to account. They will be able to determine the direction the government is going and exert considerable influence over public policy and the nature of public discourse.

> *A Prime Minister's standing and hence his influence with his colleagues depends only partly on his personality; it depends also on whether they perceive his judgement to be good and his policies successful. A Prime Minister who transforms the latent power in the office into the successful exercise of power will grow in stature and that in turn will further reinforce his ability to wield power with his colleagues. His standing with the public is also crucial.*[4]

On the other hand, the process can be the reverse.

> *When things begin to go wrong, the mystical hold over the House which a confident prime minister might once have had can mysteriously*

disappear. Once again, the importance of the House lies less in its formal powers than in its informal influence, in the way it reduces the authority of the Prime Minister, and implicitly places on the public agenda the possibility of an alternative.[5]

A setback in relations with one group can lead to the loss of support in other areas. Loss of electoral support can lead to rumblings of discontent in the party. Cabinet colleagues begin to think of a change to the leadership and may think of themselves as possible successors or consider whom to back in the event of a change of leader. Government backbenchers begin to fear for their seats and their careers. Their support at Prime Minister's Question Time becomes less fervent, especially as the Prime Minister ceases to shine against a resurgent leader of the opposition. There will be mutterings in the corridors of Westminster that the Prime Minister is 'past his prime' and rumours of a change of leader will become more insistent, to be picked up by the media and conveyed to the voters. This process can be seen in the career of Margaret Thatcher.

After a long period in which she dominated British politics, during which time the Conservatives won three successive general elections – 1979, 1983 and 1987 – and she enjoyed the support of the bulk of the press, support which verged on the adulatory, Thatcher fell from power in 1990. A series of policy errors in the late 1980s contributed to a sharp decline in support for the Conservative Party at all levels of election. This was fuelled by growing disenchantment with her style of leadership, a disenchantment felt by many previously loyal Conservative voters, wide sections of the party and much of the media. Poll reversals became of such a magnitude as to lead many Conservative MPs to fear defeat at the next election. Opinion among many Conservative MPs grew in favour of a change of leader. The final blow was Geoffrey Howe's resignation as Leader of the House of Commons in November 1990 after his earlier demotion from the post of Foreign Secretary. His resignation speech was a devastating indictment of Thatcher's style of leadership and especially of her attitude to Europe, in which he accused her of risking the future of the nation.

Subsequently challenged by Michael Heseltine for the leadership of the party, Thatcher failed to gain the required outright majority in the first round of voting and withdrew from the contest, resigning as Prime Minister on the election of John Major as her successor. Yet despite losing power in this way, Thatcher did not lose her hold on the Commons. In the censure debate which followed she scored a triumph. Her claim that 'I sat down with the cheers of my colleagues, wets and dries, allies and opponents, stalwarts and fainthearts, ringing in my ears'[6] was endorsed by virtually all observers of one of the most dramatic episodes in parliamentary history. This unscripted performance was of such force that not a single Conservative MP failed to support the government.

The Prime Minister and Parliament

The relationship between Prime Minister and Parliament is highly paradoxical. On the one hand, premiers are totally dependent on the House of Commons for their continued existence, while on the other, they are usually in a position of dominance over the majority party in Parliament. This is the basic cause of control by the executive of the legislature and ensures that the government can usually get its way in terms of legislation and public policy generally.

Executive dominance over Parliament is a marked aspect of the British system of government. However, this needs to be seen in the context of a generalised decline in the ability of legislatures to control the executive branch. There are four major factors in this decline.

The first is the emergence of disciplined political parties. Especially in parliamentary systems, of which the British is the prime example, loyalty to party is usually of prime importance and outranks other loyalties, such as those to constituents, region, religious affiliation and so on. This means that where the government has a majority, especially if it is composed of a single party, when members are called upon to decide between various conflicting loyalties, party usually wins.

The second factor is the growth of 'big government', especially in the fields of social welfare and the management of the economy. The tasks undertaken by modern governments are so vast, so complex and so fraught with consequences that policy formulation and implementation increasingly requires the kind of specialised knowledge to be found in government departments, specialised agencies and so on. In these tasks the contribution of members of the legislature is limited to commenting on and scrutinising initiatives taken elsewhere.

Thirdly, for a variety of reasons, legislatures lack the capacity to provide leadership, to take concerted action and to respond to the vast varieties of pressure faced by the executive. Governments, because of their organisational coherence, expertise and experience, can provide the leadership required. One of the features of the British system so often adversely commented on is the unwillingness of MPs of the governing party to challenge executive domination, to provide leadership for those concerned at the growth of an 'elective dictatorship'.

Finally, legislatures have lost power, not just to executives, but to interests and groups external to government and in particular to the media, now a major political actor. Interest groups provide the public with an alternative form of representation, one that has proved of increased significance in recent decades, and can take up grievances and articulate the concerns not only of particular groups but to some extent of public opinion generally. Single-issue groups especially can be the vehicle for the kind of public debate that in previous generations would have been more likely to be heard in Parliament. Just as legislatures have seen their role in policy formulation decline, groups have become increasingly significant in terms firstly of drawing attention to problems and grievances and secondly of providing the expertise, advice and information needed to deal with the issues. The media takes much of the spotlight away from legislatures, having become in most countries the main arena for public debate and the most significant way for political leaders to communicate with the public. In Britain, the proceedings of Parliament are poorly reported even in the broadsheets and are treated with contempt by the tabloids. More recently, the British Parliament has lost power to the European Union and to the devolved assemblies and will increasingly face competition from the judiciary as a result of the Human Rights Act.

These general tendencies are accentuated in the British context by a number of factors. The dominance of the executive rests on the strength of party discipline and the willingness of government backbenchers to obey the party whip. In addition, the increase in the number of ministers and parliamentary private secretaries in the House of Commons, all bound by collective responsibility, means that there is a 'payroll' vote of around 120 which can be relied on to vote in the government lobby. Thus the executive decides what legislation is introduced (with the minor exception of private members' Bills, which in reality stand little or no chance of success without government support). Ministers decide the content of Bills and resist amendments unless proposed by the government itself and so government legislation is virtually always passed in the form the executive desires. The timetable of the Commons is decided by the government (in consultation with the opposition parties), although ministerial control of the Lords' procedures is less extensive; this control of the timetable is an essential element in executive control of the legislative process and of the other functions of Parliament. Departmental select committees, whose role is to scrutinise the executive, have a government majority (assuming the government itself has a majority in the Commons), and the executive has a degree of control over who sits on the committees in that the whips exercise back-door control of membership.

However, too heavy-handed executive interference in the work of these committees can face a backlash. When at the start of the 2001 Parliament government whips attempted to remove the chairpersons of the Foreign Affairs and Transport Select Committees (Donald Anderson and Gwyneth Dunwoody, Labour backbenchers thought to be rather too independent in their views), there was a revolt by MPs and the hasty reinstatement of the members concerned.

Nonetheless, there are limits to executive dominance. It remains the case that all governments depend on the House of Commons for their existence.

> *The Prime Minister and his Cabinet are accountable to Parliament. They have no fixed term of office, such as that of an American president, who is secure for four years though perhaps legislatively impotent for part of that time. They survive as a government just as long – not a day later – as they can count on a majority of Parliament, however small that majority.*[7]

In order for the government to pass legislation the consent of the Commons is required. Any Bill defeated in the Commons is lost. Should the government be defeated on a motion of no confidence or on an issue which it decides to treat as one of confidence, the Prime Minister would be obliged by convention to 'advise' the monarch to dissolve Parliament; the resulting general election would almost certainly result in defeat for the incumbent administration and hence a change of government. There were two such occasions in the twentieth century, in 1924 and again in 1979. However, both were minority (Labour) governments. Defeat on a motion of no confidence, or even the loss of a Bill, is unlikely to face a government with a majority, however small, in the House of Commons, even though there have been instances of measures being dropped or significantly altered in order to avoid difficulty or even defeat for the administration. Thus the reality of the relationship between the executive and the legislature in Britain is one of executive domination. It is this executive dominance which is the foundation of the power of the Prime Minister and the explanation for the weakness of accountability in the British system of government.

The Prime Minister usually has no difficulty fending off attacks by the leader of the opposition; even though William Hague often bested Blair in the 1997–2001 Parliament it had no discernable effect on the respective standings of government and opposition, as shown in the 2001 general election. Criticisms by MPs from the other side (and indeed from their own backbenchers) can in most cases be brushed aside as carping and misplaced. In many ways, premiers must take more care to placate their own side than to worry about the opposition. Usually that is not a problem; the loyalty of government backbenchers rests on a combination of party loyalty, sycophancy and a desire for a ministerial post. However, at times the knives are out for the Prime Minister from his (or her) own side. Then the Prime Minister must remember the adage: 'Your opponents are on the other side; your enemies are behind you.'

Although, as will be discussed later, recent Prime Ministers, especially from Callaghan onwards, have spent a decreasing amount of time in the Commons and have contributed less and less to its proceedings compared to their predecessors, parliamentary support is still a vital aspect of their survival. Control of the Commons, the ability to dominate in debate and at Prime Minister's Question Time, helps to create the image of a successful administration, of a government in control of events.

In parliamentary terms, the most successful Prime Ministers are those who can convince the opposition of its impotence and irrelevance; this in turn leads voters to the same conclusion. Various factors contribute to this dominance: the sheer authority of the office; the ability of the Prime Minister to hold the House's attention and respect; the support Prime Ministers have in their party, both in the House and outside; the ability of the leader of the opposition to match and even master the Prime Minister; and the morale of the opposition and whether it senses the possibility of victory at the next election. The degree of support or otherwise to be found in the media and the nature of electoral opinion are also vital factors.

The ability of the Prime Minister to dominate the House of Commons makes it harder for the opposition to probe and to reveal mistakes or abuses of power. For at least part of their period in office, some postwar premiers have been dominating parliamentary performers. Attlee, Churchill, Macmillan, Wilson and Thatcher all outshone their opponents. At other times Prime Ministers have lost their hold on the House. This most often happens when the premier is perceived to have mishandled a crisis or a scandal or when there is the general feeling that the government's time is up and that the next general election will bring a change of administration. Eden at the time of Suez, Macmillan following the Profumo scandal and Major for much of the 1992–7 Parliament are cases in point.

Blair is an interesting exception to most of these generalisations. He made his reputation in a series of shadow Cabinet posts – especially as shadow Home Secretary – learning the skills of media management vital for success in today's image-conscious climate. For much of his time as leader of the opposition he proved a more than capable adversary of the increasingly hapless John Major. However, as Prime Minister he has not been a dominant figure in the Commons. He rarely attends, largely restricting himself to the obligatory Prime Minister's Question Time – which he reduced from two sessions a week to one – and to the statements he is required to make after summit meetings or in the wake of events such as the attack on New York on 11 September 2001. At Prime Minister's Questions he was regularly outperformed in his first term by the more agile debater William Hague, whose ability to employ wit and biting sarcasm often had Blair squirming with embarrassment, and in the second half of his second term by Michael Howard. Blair's neglect of Parliament led to accusations from a variety of sources of arrogance and was taken as evidence of an 'elective dictatorship' and led to a partial reconsideration by 10 Downing Street of the importance of the Commons at the start of Blair's second term in office.

The pressure of modern government (plus fear of adverse publicity in the event of a setback in the Commons) keeps modern Prime Ministers out of the Commons except when there is no alternative.

An old-school Prime Minister gave first priority to winning the confidence of MPs in the House of Commons by attending debates and tending to the anxieties and egos of MPs. A new-style Prime Minister relies on television performances and favourable press coverage to keep MPs in line.[8]

Modern Prime Ministers rarely make speeches or intervene in debates, except on set-piece occasions such as the debate on the Queen's Speech. When they do so they give speeches which are assiduously worked on in advance by the Prime Minister and his team of Number 10 advisers and speech writers; speaking in an impromptu, unscripted debate is now very rare. More frequent prime ministerial appearances in the Commons come in the form of statements to Parliament, in the main about overseas summits, defence and security matters and suchlike. Depending on the circumstances, these can be moments of high drama for the premier, with opportunities for triumphs or disasters.

The most highly publicised occasion for parliamentary scrutiny comes in the form of Prime Minister's Question Time. This opportunity for members to question the head of government about virtually all aspects of government policy and actions was begun by Harold Macmillan in 1961, who confessed often to be sick with fear at such times. It is now the high point of the parliamentary week, especially with the televising of the duel between the Prime Minister and the leader of the opposition. It is an important factor in the political standing of the Prime Minister and the leader of the opposition (and increasingly, of the leader of the Liberal Democrats).

However, the value of Prime Minister's Questions as a way of holding Prime Ministers to account is limited. The parties attempt to orchestrate the occasion, even trying to persuade backbenchers to put down questions which have been 'planted' by the whips, either to show the government in as good a light as possible or, in the case of questions by opposition MPs, to try to embarrass the Prime Minister. Government backbenchers tend to ask questions (some of sickening sycophancy) which will provide their leader with the opportunity to shine, while opposition MPs tend to echo their leader's attacks. Many critics (including MPs from both sides of the chamber) see Prime Minister's Questions as a ritual, virtually meaningless, confrontation which contributes much more heat than light to the process of holding the Prime Minister and his government to account (and so as the low point of the week rather than the reverse), and clearly many voters are baffled by its arcane proceedings and are alienated by the often unruly confrontation. On the other hand, it does provide an opportunity to probe and to reveal both governmental deficiencies and opposition strengths.

Postwar Prime Ministers and Parliament

The amount of time spent in the House of Commons by Prime Ministers and their contribution to the proceedings of the House have declined in the postwar period. In the postwar period the parliamentary styles of Prime Ministers and the effect Parliament as an institution has had on their careers have naturally varied, both from Prime Minister to Prime Minister and within each period of office. 'Old-school Prime Ministers regarded the House of Commons as their political home, for before entering Downing Street, they had spent decades there.'[9] Winston Churchill was an MP for 39 years before becoming premier, Attlee for 23, Eden 31, Macmillan 32, Wilson 19, Heath 20 and Callaghan 31. Douglas-Home entered the Commons in 1931 and by the time he became premier in 1963 had been a member of the Commons and the Lords for 32 years.

What Richard Rose calls 'new-style' (post-TV) Prime Ministers have spent less time as an MP. Margaret Thatcher had been an MP for 20 years before entering Number 10. John Major had been an MP for only eleven years before succeeding her (all that time on the government benches and so without experience of being in opposition). Conversely, in his fourteen years as an MP prior to becoming Prime Minister in 1997, Tony Blair had never been a minister, answering questions from the government benches. According to some critics, this lack of ministerial experience helps to explain Blair's insensitivity in handling the ambitions of colleagues in the government and on the back benches. 'Less experience of life in the Commons goes along with a Prime Minister being less inclined to treat the House as his or her political home.'[10]

The decline in the extent to which Prime Ministers have been involved in the proceedings of the Commons dates from 1940; previously Prime Ministers who were MPs were simultaneously Leaders of the House (although Lloyd George was an exception to the rule), which involved sitting for long hours on the Treasury bench and working closely with the Chief Whip, taking account of the interests and concerns both of government backbenchers and of the opposition. However, when Churchill became Prime Minister in 1940 the position was taken by the Lord Privy Seal, Clement Attlee. The post was then held for a few months by another Labour MP, Sir Stafford Cripps, until Anthony Eden took over in November 1942, holding the post jointly with that of the Foreign Office for the rest of the war. In the postwar world the office of Leader of the House has been held by Cabinet ministers who have usually been senior figures in the governments concerned, although to date none have gone on to become Prime Minister. From the split between the two posts can be dated a general decline in time spent sitting in the House and in the level of involvement with most, though not all, of the activities of the Commons, as will be detailed later. This decline can be related to a number of factors. Rose comments,

> For the new-style Prime Minister, the box that counts is the television set rather than the despatch box next to the Mace in the House of Commons. What is said on television matches or surpasses in importance what is said in Westminster.[11]

Whereas old-style premiers saw the Commons as a forum for addressing the wider audience outside and as a way of influencing electoral opinion, their new-style counterparts are less concerned with the House, less aware of currents of opinion among MPs and less focused on Parliament as a way of influencing electors. This was clearly demonstrated by the way Blair shrugged off repeated maulings by Hague in the 1997–2001 Parliament. Thus this comparative disengagement from the Commons is not dependent on (although it many be related to) the personality of the various occupants of Number 10 in the postwar period but is the result of changes to the way premiers have gone about their business.

Winston Churchill 1940–45

Winston Churchill's parliamentary life spanned 65 years, apart from the two years between losing Dundee in October 1922 and being elected for Epping in October 1924, eventually becoming Father of the House. He was a minister for over 25 years, Prime Minister (in two periods) for a total of eight years and eight months. He served in the Cabinets of four Prime Ministers: Asquith, Lloyd George, Baldwin and Chamberlain, and held most of the great offices of state. He began his long parliamentary service in 1900, when Parliament was clearly at the centre of the British political system and retained a romantic attachment to the history and traditions of the Commons, refusing the offer of a dukedom when he eventually left the Commons in 1964. Even in wartime he was deeply sensitive to the mood of the House, insisting on debates and submitting to votes of no confidence even when the support of the overwhelming majority of members was obvious.

Clement Attlee 1945–51

Attlee is an example of someone who was a better parliamentary performer as Prime Minister than as leader of the opposition. His debating style, terse, never using two words when one would do, was in sharp contrast to his predecessor, yet exercising 'a quiet, almost schoolmasterly authority over the House'[12] and, especially in debates over domestic policy, generally getting the better of the leader of the opposition. He displayed competence and firmness of resolve, eschewing the oratorical flair and bravura of Churchill. His answers in Parliament were concise and clear, often with a leavening of humour, and his speeches were usually very short. Despite Labour's huge majority, Attlee was attentive to the mood of the parliamentary Labour Party and was firmly in the 'old-school' tradition of understanding the importance of regular contact with backbenchers in the tea and smoking rooms, especially as many Labour members spent much of their free time there.

> *In the last fifty years, perhaps for many years before that, the successful Prime Ministers have on the whole been those who spent hours each day in the smoke-room, tea-room or members' dining-room. Churchill, Attlee, Macmillan and others .... ; Douglas-Home and Heath much less.*[13]

Winston Churchill 1951–5

Churchill's hold over the Commons was based on force of personality, an unrivalled use of the English language and his place in history. However, opinions differed both at the time and subsequently about his effectiveness during his peacetime administration from 1951 to 1955. Some thought that his domination was undiminished: 'His complete authority over the Commons is one of the most important factors in the new round of the Parliamentary contest that is now beginning.'[14] However, others thought he was rather a spent force, except in set piece debates on foreign and defence matters, especially with the onset of illness and increasing deafness. Harold Wilson's judgement was that 'he was above all the great Parliamentarian.'[15] Few if any would disagree with that.

Anthony Eden 1955–7

The career of Sir Anthony Eden has about it the elements of Greek tragedy. He had made his name as a foreign policy expert and had been Foreign Secretary under Chamberlain and Churchill during the Second World War and after 1951. His parliamentary reputation when he became Prime Minister in 1955 was high but soon collapsed. During his brief premiership,

Eden rarely mastered the House and after Suez he was treated harshly by MPs. Eden, used to being listened to with due deference both by his own side and by those opposite, could not cope with hecklers; his inability to hold the attention of the House was compounded by continued ill health and, during the crisis which ended his career, lack of sleep. 'On a number of occasions he was so badly heckled by the opposition that he had to be rescued by the Speaker; his own side more than once sat in embarrassed silence.'16

Harold Macmillan 1957–63

For most of his time as Prime Minister, Harold Macmillan dominated the Commons, the parliamentary party and indeed the political scene generally. He was widely credited with having saved his government from collapse following the Suez debacle. Macmillan was one of the most intelligent and cultured of twentieth-century British Prime Ministers, and in debate was witty, erudite and polished. He was a masterly political actor, who cultivated a foppish, Edwardian languor in order to disguise a formidable intelligence and to hide the deep depression and personal unhappiness from which he suffered for much of his life. He accepted with relish his cartoon image as 'Supermac' (although was less happy when he was later renamed 'Mac the Knife', following the botched Cabinet reshuffle known as the 'Night of the Long Knives'). He regularly outshone the leader of the opposition, Hugh Gaitskell. But the collapse of the negotiations to join the Common Market and the growing economic gloom meant that unrest among Conservative MPs grew. The election of Harold Wilson as leader of the Labour Party, a formidable parliamentary performer, following the death of Hugh Gaitskell early in 1963, coupled with the darkening economic situation and a series of scandals such as that surrounding the war minister, John Profumo, left Macmillan increasingly exposed and floundering and he resigned in October 1963 on the grounds of ill health (although he lived another 23 years and survived to lambaste the Conservatism of Margaret Thatcher from his place in the House of Lords).

Alec Douglas-Home 1963–4

Despite his long parliamentary service, Alec Douglas–Home was Prime Minister for only one year, having renounced his earldom to re-enter the Commons after being appointed as head of the government by the Queen in controversial circumstances in October 1963. Given that much of his time had been spent in the gentler environment of the House of Lords and that his experience had been in foreign and Commonwealth affairs, he found it difficult to deal with the much more confrontational Commons, especially as the Labour Party under Harold Wilson was scenting victory at the next election. Thus he rarely dominated the Commons and left little mark on the chamber.

Harold Wilson 1964–70, 1974–6

Originally, Wilson's parliamentary reputation was as a dull, bureaucratic member of the Attlee Cabinet, but he honed formidable skills as a debater in a series of shadow portfolios. He proved a worthy opponent for Harold Macmillan, whose respect for him can be compared with the contempt he felt for Gaitskell. Wilson generally outshone Douglas-Home at the despatch box. As Prime Minister he initially dominated the Commons, towering over most of his less experienced colleagues and seeing off both Douglas-Home and then Heath, particularly at Prime Minister's Question Time. He was careful to keep in touch with opinion in the parliamentary Labour Party, using his office in the Commons to do much of his afternoon and early evening work before retiring to Number 10 for the rest of the evening. He took his parliamentary duties immensely seriously. He made an important personal input into the speeches he delivered in the Commons while increasingly leaving the preparation of speeches delivered outside Parliament to his Number 10 staff.

However, Wilson's hold on the Commons and on his own party declined sharply soon after the triumph of the 1966 general election as economic and other difficulties mounted and as criticisms grew of his style of government. He never regained his Commons predominance. He was surprised to win office again in February 1974 and found the problems involved in running a government which was actually in a minority from February to October 1974 and then with a wafer-thin and disappearing majority thereafter increasingly unbearable. He rarely dominated the Commons during this time as his physical and mental powers declined and as he grew disillusioned with tackling problems which seemed simply to recur and to be incapable of solution. 'He lost many of his parliamentary skills, the capacity to rally his supporters and to score off the opposition. His speeches lacked fire; they got longer, sometimes trivial and tended to bore the House.'[17]

Edward Heath 1970–74

Edward Heath will not be seen by history as one of the great parliamentary performers. This was partly because he spent nine years in the Whips' Office, serving as Chief Whip from 1955 to 1959, being precluded from speaking except on procedural matters. Thus he failed to gain experience in the parliamentary arts of persuasion, conciliation, charming those whose bruised egos needed some massaging and reacting to the subtle changes of mood in the Commons. He rarely shone as leader of the opposition in his duels with the quick-witted Wilson. However, he won grudging respect for the thoroughness for which he prepared for debate during his premiership, when the authority of the office was combined with the support of Tory backbenchers as the government's problems grew.

On the other hand, Heath showed little skill in managing his party. He increasingly neglected the backbenchers and spent little time talking to them or getting to know them, and he was niggardly with honours. In some ways Heath was not interested in politics at all, but in reaching the right, rational decision. Once he had done so, he tended to regard anyone, perhaps especially Conservative MPs, who disagreed with him as obstructive. He had little patience with the 'game' of day-to-day politics, and was more at home with civil servants than with Tory backbenchers, whom he continued to treat with a Chief Whip's functional attitude to getting the flock through the correct division lobby. The House of Commons environment of rather superficial and transitory personal contact was one in which Heath's distinctive personality and brand of humour were not best appreciated and he was often unambiguously rude. Philip Norton claims that his abrasive personality was the reason for the growth of dissent among Conservative MPs in the 1970–74 parliament. He and his Cabinet assumed that if they were convinced of the merits of a proposal, backbenchers would be of the same mind. Norton calls him a manager of measures not men. Heath seemed increasingly presidential in his relations with Parliament.

James Callaghan 1976–9

Jim Callaghan's parliamentary qualifications for the premiership were impressive. He entered the House in the Labour landslide of 1945, held junior office under Attlee and a series of increasingly prominent shadow posts during Labour's long exile from power between 1951 and 1964. His ministerial record was unique in that he held the three great offices of state: Chancellor of the Exchequer, Home Secretary and Foreign Secretary. As Prime Minister he often commanded the respect of the House, where he usually looked confident and in command.

> Callaghan's sang-froid stemmed in part from his unrivalled experience of government but also from the fact that he never (after Wilson's appointment as leader in 1963) expected to be made Prime Minister; [his period] in Number Ten was thus a windfall for him ... Callaghan had a natural dignity and exuded authority. His straight talking earned him the respect of all around him.[18]

Initially at least he dominated the then new leader of the opposition, Margaret Thatcher. He prepared carefully for Prime Minister's Question Time; as with all other postwar premiers he feared being caught off guard and made to look unprepared. He would see his parliamentary affairs private secretary the night before and go over all the issues that might be raised. The morning itself would be devoted to other matters while his staff continued work on the briefs being prepared. Before lunch Callaghan would be driven to the Commons where he would have a sandwich in the tea room, frequently joining the Welsh Labour MPs at their table. He would nap in his office for about 20 minutes before going into the chamber. Although he did not take the occasion lightly, he was almost invariably confident, especially if the whips had managed to ensure a supply of friendly questions from Labour backbenchers. Although in a number of respects the decline in prime ministerial involvement with the affairs of the House of Commons dates from Callaghan's time as Prime Minister, he was acutely aware of the need to keep in touch with the passing show. In addition to countless informal exchanges with Labour MPs in the corridors and tea rooms, he averaged some 50 formal appointments a year in the House.

Margaret Thatcher 1979–90

For most of her time as Prime Minister Margaret Thatcher was a dominant figure in the House of Commons. In this she was aided by a phalanx of backbenchers whose loyalty verged on the sycophantic and by the weakness of the opposition. Although Michael Foot, who replaced Callaghan as leader of the Labour Party in 1980, had a formidable reputation as a parliamentary orator, he proved no match for the increasingly confident Prime Minister. His successor as Labour leader, Neil Kinnock, was an often hapless figure, floundering in a sea of verbiage until he learned to shorten his questions and leaven them with humour and wit, qualities not even her most fervent supporters would claim were possessed by Margaret Thatcher.

In most respects, Thatcher's involvement in the work of the Commons and the time she spent in the chamber declined sharply. Overall, her record of activity in the Commons was consistently below the average for any previous Prime Minister. Several explanations for Thatcher's distinctive relationship with Parliament as an institution have been advanced:

- As with Lloyd George and to some extent Churchill, she saw her main role as one of running the government rather than appearing in the Commons.
- She became leader of the opposition during the time of Callaghan's premiership and may have been influenced by the trend towards reduced prime ministerial activity in the chamber.
- In general, she preferred to appear in public only in well-scripted, carefully rehearsed and tightly controlled situations so that she could avoid being caught unawares and thus not in control. This tendency, one shared by Tony Blair, can be seen in the rigorous preparations she and her advisers made for Prime Minister's Questions, usually a minimum of three hours for each fifteen-minute slot.
- She was the first woman Prime Minister, who found herself in an overwhelmingly male environment. She clearly did not find the clublike, almost public school atmosphere to her taste. She lacked the taste for repartee that characterised the Commons.

Several significant changes to the way the Commons went about its business occurred during her time as Prime Minister, although in all cases she was lukewarm or strenuously opposed. These included:

- the creation of a system of departmental select committees and the strengthening of the scrutiny of expenditure, both the work of Thatcher's first Leader of the House, Norman St John Stevas;
- the experimental televising of the Commons in 1988, which was later made permanent;
- the election of the Conservative MP Bernard Weatherill as Speaker in June 1983;
- the votes in favour of increases to MPs' pay and allowances for secretarial and research staff.

Although Thatcher vowed to learn from the mistakes made by Heath in his relations with Tory backbenchers, she came to forget, a failing which was to cost her dear in 1990. Some of her staff tried to ensure access for Tory MPs, and initially she met them for a drink if she was in the House for a late-night vote. But she was never a regular visitor to the tea rooms or bars of the House and more pressing matters always came first.

> *She also had little aptitude for small talk – one trait she shared with Heath. Attempts by her Parliamentary Private Secretary to counter this trend by guided tours of the tables in the Tea Room were often strained and embarrassing for all concerned.*[19]

Margaret Thatcher, like previous Prime Ministers, could never ignore Parliament. When she faltered, as over Westland and at times on health and social security issues, it reflected on her popular standing. The Commons remained an acute barometer of the mood both of MPs and of the nation generally. Thatcher's impact on Parliament was considerable but was essentially personal rather than institutional. She was dominant through her use of existing levers of power rather than by creating new ones.

John Major 1990–97

John Major had mixed fortunes as far as his relationship with the Commons was concerned. He was not a natural orator and his ability to dominate by force of personality was limited, especially as he and his government faced increasingly bitter hostility from his 'friends' on the benches behind him and as Labour became a more formidable opponent following 'Black Wednesday' in September 1992. His time in the Whips' Office, unlike that of Heath, proved a useful apprenticeship in terms of managing people. He was generally seen as a kind, courteous man, with an interest in others, and he consistently showed a preference for conciliation rather than confrontation. He was sensitive to the mood of Parliament, partly because his rapid rise up the parliamentary ladder was based on his ability to read the mood of his fellow Tory MPs. Initially at least he showed great skill in handling them and understood their personal and constituency needs. This whip's instinct, his willingness to pay genuine and close attention to the views of MPs, proved to be the bedrock of his support in the 1990 leadership contest, when he was the ordinary backbenchers' choice, although it was somewhat less in evidence during the 1995 contest, by which time the sheen had come off his leadership and he had acquired a range of enemies on the benches behind him and indeed in his own government. Hence Major's comment in July 1993 when he was asked why he did not sack some of his critics:

> *Where do you think most of this poison is coming from? From the dispossessed and never-possessed. You can think of ex-ministers who are going around causing all sorts of trouble. We don't want another three more of the bastards out there.*[20]

As Prime Minister he took a keen interest in what happened in the Commons. He remained at heart a whip *manqué*, and was accused of paying too much heed to the views of backbenchers, of making too many concessions and of failing to confront troublemakers often and early enough. Calculations of whether Tory backbenchers would accept some policy or other had constantly to be made and they showed their independence and assertiveness on a range of issues, including Europe, pit closures and their own pay and allowances. In particular, he was accused of delaying the final showdown over the Maastricht Bill for too long.

Major defended himself by pointing to his small and gradually eroding majority. However, this was not the only, nor possibly the most significant, factor. Major's background and temperament, his tendency to temporise, to want to be 'all things to all men', what the rebel Conservative MP Sir George Gardiner referred to as Major sitting with his buttocks firmly clenched on the fence, were other factors in his increasing difficulty. In any case, although the small majority was a constraint, it was not in a straightforward arithmetical manner. The Tories started the 1992 Parliament with a majority over Labour of 65, a larger margin than they had, for example, in 1970, and the opposition parties rarely combined against the government. The Ulster Unionists promised to support the government during the final Maastricht Bill crisis of July 1993. The real difficulty was the lack of cohesion in the Conservative Party, the culmination of ideological strains that had been building up during the Thatcher era, especially over Europe, the fact and nature of Thatcher's removal, and perhaps the strains imposed by a long period in office. For most of Major's premiership the Conservative Party was widely seen as divided. Major himself stated in October 1997 that open party divisions made his government's position impossible. He faced the most sustained backbench Conservative rebellion in postwar history against the Bill to ratify the Maastricht treaty. During the 1992–7 Parliament four Conservative MPs defected to other parties, the whip was removed en bloc from eight others. In 1995 he resigned the party leadership, triggering a leadership contest, in the hope of reasserting his authority. The overall effect, so cruelly identified by Norman Lamont in his resignation speech, was to give an impression of a government in office, but not in power, and of a Prime Minister lacking in authority, a view increasingly shared by the electorate and demonstrated in the Conservative electoral disaster of 1997.

However, although more care and attention had to be paid to managing the parliamentary party and doing deals with various opposition parties, the government got virtually all of its legislation through, despite some concessions, such as the abandonment of the plan to privatise the Post Office. As Philip Cowley pointed out,

> this is not to argue that Conservative MPs were not behaving rebelliously throughout Major's premiership, and especially after 1992, but it is to argue, however, that many rebellions took the form of conversations with journalists or appearances in the media, rather than in the division lobbies of the House of Commons.[21]

Thus it can be said that little of substance changed in the balance of power between the executive and the legislature during Major's time as Prime Minister. The crucial element was unrest among Tory backbenchers rather than pressure from the opposition or from Parliament as an institution, which was seen by ministers as something to be circumvented rather than as a body capable of obstructing the government. The executive continued to get its way even if it had to temper the wind to the shorn lamb rather more than ministers liked.

Tony Blair 1997 to date

In opposition, Blair appeared to promise a new era in the relationship between the executive and the legislature. In the 1997 manifesto, Labour attacked the Conservatives for appearing 'opposed to the very idea of democracy'. It declared that 'there is unquestionably a crisis of confidence in our political system, to which Labour will respond in a measured and sensible way.' Among several proposals for constitutional reform was that of reform of Parliament. The most substantial and far-reaching involved reform of the House of Lords, which saw the removal of most of the hereditary peers, although final agreement on the composition of the upper House has not – as yet – been achieved.

The manifesto also foreshadowed reforms to the Commons.

> *We believe the House of Commons is in need of modernisation and we will ask the House to establish a special Select Committee to review its procedure. Prime Minister's Questions will be made more effective. Ministerial accountability will be reviewed so as to remove recent abuses.*

Following the 1997 general election, Prime Minister's Questions was changed from two 15-minute slots on Tuesday and Thursday afternoons to one of 30 minutes, initially on Wednesday afternoon, although that was shifted in 2003 to the late morning in order to catch the one o'clock news on radio and television. The rationale for the change from two 15-minute slots to one 30-minute session was that it would allow for topics to be covered in greater depth. However, critics of what increasingly was seen as Blair's growing distance from Parliament argued that it would mean he would only have to prepare for questions once a week. It also gives the leader of the opposition – and indeed the leader of the Liberal Democrats – one opportunity rather than two to attack the Prime Minister.

Soon after the 1997 election the Select Committee on the Modernisation of the House was appointed 'to consider how the practices and procedures of the House should be modernised, and to make recommendations thereon'. Changes were made, firstly to the procedures for examining legislation and then to the way the House does its business.

However, despite claims by the Prime Minister that significant reforms had taken place, 'when put into a wider political context, the changes appeared limited and failed to change significantly the relations between the legislature and the executive.'[22] Although, when shadow Leader of the House, Ann Taylor argued that parliamentary procedures were defective both in ensuring that the legislative process worked properly and in holding ministers to account, little of real significance has so far taken place. Ann Taylor was replaced as Leader of the House by the traditionalist Margaret Beckett. In turn she was followed by the more reform-minded Robin Cook, whose attempts to complete the reform of the Lords by the introduction of a substantial elected element was resisted and eventually frustrated by Blair (something which may have contributed to Cook's decision to resign from the government over the issue of Iraq). Cook was followed by Dr John Reid, who was unconvinced of the need to redress the balance between Parliament and the government. After just a few weeks in post Reid moved to the Department of Health and Peter Hain was appointed Leader of the House, holding that position in conjunction with the Welsh secretaryship. Whether these weighty responsibilities will allow Hain time to reflect on the place of Parliament in a modern democracy remains to be seen!

Thus it has become clear that 'modernisation' means different things to the interests concerned. While reformers such as Tony Wright interpret the word to mean enhancing the ability of the legislature to hold the executive to account, ministers (and especially the Prime Minister, Tony Blair) see it in terms of facilitating the government's task of getting its legislation through speedily and unscathed. Although there have been changes to the way Parliament and especially the Commons does its work, these have been aimed at simplifying the legislative process, removing some of the more arcane practices which were widely thought to have contributed to the public's disillusion with Parliament. Another motive has been to make the Commons more 'family friendly' to suit the increasingly professional politicians who are elected as MPs, thus making the House more attractive to women, who will more easily be able to juggle family commitments and their work in Parliament. Critics pointed out that several of the changes, while ostensibly designed for the convenience of MPs and to enable them to do their work more effectively, in reality made it easier for the executive to get its business done. There was a widespread perception that Parliament had been further marginalised.

There were particular criticisms of Tony Blair's relationship with the Commons. As Philip Norton pointed out, parliamentary reform requires leadership, and it was clear that Blair was not prepared to provide that leadership. He largely ignored Parliament. In a speech to the parliamentary Labour Party after the 1997 election victory he stressed that the party was elected on the basis of the manifesto and that was what MPs had to deliver and to toe the party line. 'The Prime Minister's attitude towards Parliament was revealed both in his behaviour and in his remarks in the House of Commons on parliamentary reform.'[23]

- He devoted less time to parliamentary activity than his predecessors.
- Though turning up regularly to participate in Prime Minister's Questions and to make statements, he rarely participated in debates or in divisions.
- In the first two sessions of Parliament, he led for the government in only three debates, less often than any Prime Minister in recent history.

- His voting record was the worst of any modern Prime Minister – less than 10 per cent in the first two sessions.

To his critics, Blair's dismissive attitude towards Parliament indicated that he did not see it as having a central place in the task of governing and that it was under threat of marginalisation. Blair argued that concern about parliamentary reform was not shared by people in pubs and clubs. Although his attitude was not shared by all ministers, it seemed to permeate the government generally, leading, for example, to the Speaker complaining about ministers making statements outside the House before revealing their plans to MPs and so on. Accusations that the government was increasingly arrogant and dismissive of Parliament were reinforced by the way Labour MPs seemed to be dragooned into the voting lobbies and into displaying unquestioning support for whatever Blair dictated. Labour MPs were widely attacked as being supine loyalists, simply obeying the latest message on their pagers. This perception was reinforced by the behaviour of Labour MPs at Prime Minister's Questions, when congratulations to the Prime Minister grew markedly, leading to many accusations of sycophancy, although the extent was much exaggerated by the media.

Initially Blair refused to justify his record to MPs, arguing that this would be counter to existing conventions, especially that Prime Ministers did not appear before select committees, and that it would blur ministerial accountability for him to stray into matters which were the responsibility of his Cabinet colleagues. However, in early 2002 he agreed to meet the Liaison Committee twice a year, the first meeting taking place on 16 July 2002, and to incorporate the resolution on ministerial responsibility and any updating that might be necessary into the ministerial code relating to parliamentary accountability.

One of the themes discussed at the meeting was the Prime Minister's role at the centre of government and his relationship with Parliament. The Labour MP Barry Sheerman referred to the marginalisation of Parliament and asked whether the appearance of the Prime Minister before the Liaison Committee was to be his only contribution to improving the Parliament–executive relationship. The veteran Conservative MP (and noted rebel) Sir Nicholas Winterton asked whether under Blair's premiership Parliament was actually working and whether it continues to have a meaningful role or whether it is just some necessary inconvenience that he has to deal with in order to provide a façade for the democratic process. In reply, Blair defended his record. He argued that he had spent longer doing Prime Minister's Questions than his predecessor did in the same period of time and that he had given more prime ministerial statements than either of his two predecessors did in the same amount of time. However, he accepted there was a problem and that the government had to try and look for new ways of making Parliament relevant and capturing people's interest, although the problems were common to many other countries and were not the fault of his government.

Blair's second meeting with the Liaison Committee took place on 21 January 2003. Most of the session was taken up with foreign and defence policy matters, especially the looming crisis with Iraq. In answer to a question from Tony Wright, the Prime Minister accepted that in the event of military action, the House of Commons would be able to vote although he would not be drawn on when that vote would take place. He argued that he had never had difficulty at all with Parliament either being consulted and informed or expressing its view. Wright raised the issue of the royal prerogative and its relation to Parliament. Blair did not accept that there was any case for altering the position and refused to add to what he had already said.

In June 2003 Blair reshuffled his government and in so doing ran into a storm of criticism for what was seen as a high-handed and careless handling of parliamentary and outside opinion. It was announced that the office of Lord Chancellor was to be abolished and that in the meantime some of his duties would be carried out by the newly created Secretary of State for Constitutional Affairs and Lord Chancellor, a post occupied by Blair's one-time flatmate Lord Falconer of Thoroton. Amidst considerable confusion (shared by the ministers and civil servants concerned) the responsibilities and duties of the offices of Secretaries of State for Scotland and Wales were transferred to members of the Cabinet holding other responsibilities, who would in some unexplained way be responsible to Lord Falconer. It was clear that this fundamental constitutional change was not clearly thought through and had been announced with little or no consultation with opposition parties or with the legal profession. Anger was expressed, especially in the House of Lords, where it was not clear whether and under what conditions Lord Falconer would continue to act as Speaker, and among senior judges and other legal figures, concerned lest the independence of the judiciary might be compromised by the change.

In the wake of the furore Blair had his third meeting with the Liaison Committee on 8 July 2003. The session was dominated by the conflict with Iraq and by allegations that the Commons had been misled during the presentation of the case for war, something which, not surprisingly, Blair refuted entirely. In the course of the questioning, the Conservative MP and former Cabinet minister Sir George Young raised the issue of Blair's style of government and his relationship to Parliament. Blair replied that he believed he is the first Prime Minister to have gone to Parliament to seek specific clearance for a decision to go to war; he called the suggestion that Parliament had not been involved in the decision 'fatuous'. Later he conceded in an answer to Dr Ian Gibson, a Labour MP, that had Parliament voted against the war it would not have been sustainable, whatever the constitutional arguments, for the action to have gone ahead.

After a relatively long honeymoon period between Blair and the parliamentary Labour Party, relations cooled as Blair came to be seen as remote from Parliament and from his own backbenchers. He met the Parliamentary Committee every week after Prime Minister's Questions. He also regularly invited small groups of Labour MPs to meet him in the Cabinet Room, aiming to meet each one annually.

But these meetings have failed to stifle traditional complaints that the leader is remote from MPs. In contrast with Wilson (pre-1970), Callaghan, and reputedly Thatcher in her first years, he rarely visits the Tea-Room to mingle with MPs. He has never been a bar/tea-room man, has little small talk and was determined to find time for his wife and young children as well as for thinking about policy. When problems in the party arise, critics predictably complain about inadequate consultation and a centralist style of leadership.[24]

The rebellion of 139 Labour MPs over the decision to invade Iraq, followed by the resignation of Robin Cook and then (after a rather farcical delay) Clare Short, and other rebellions over foundation hospitals, university tuition charging and other aspects of the government's social agenda, were all seen as clear signs that Blair's credit with significant sections of the parliamentary Labour Party was declining. Whether this will lead to any significant moves, either by Blair or by his critics, to ensure greater accountability remains to be seen.

The changing pattern of relations between Prime Ministers and Parliament

Patrick Dunleavy, George W. Jones and others[25] surveyed the evolution of the four main prime ministerial activities, answering parliamentary questions, making ministerial statements, making formal speeches and intervening in debates, over the period 1868–1990. They pointed out that 'in the Westminster system the Prime Minister's active participation in parliamentary proceedings is a key mechanism for ensuring the accountability of the executive.'[26] This accountability requires the Prime Minister to be present in and involved in the operations of the legislature. In the period surveyed there was a long-term decline in Prime Ministers' speeches in the Commons, a stepped decline in debating interventions and a significant decrease in question-answering from the late nineteenth century to the 1950s. Prime ministerial statement-making increased after 1940 and then declined in the 1980s. The downward drift in question-answering was reversed with the introduction of Prime Minister's Question Time. Another important finding is that at the start of the period surveyed a Prime Minister such as Gladstone would undertake several different activities on the same day, while modern Prime Ministers rarely if ever undertake multiple activities on any given day. Blair follows the practice of his immediate predecessors of usually leaving the chamber immediately his contribution is over. Their general conclusion was that 'the direct accountability of the Prime Minister to Parliament has undoubtedly declined, a trend probably paralleled by decreasing indirect accountability. These findings raise fundamental questions about executive–legislative relations in the United Kingdom.'27 Dunleavy and his colleagues set out to test the evidence concerning this relationship of accountability.

Answering parliamentary questions

Questions in the House are the primary means by which MPs can try to hold the Prime Minister accountable. At the start of the period the practice of Prime Ministers answering questions was still developing. The number of questions grew and a place was found on the order paper. From Gladstone's second administration in the early 1880s until the Second World War Prime Ministers answered questions on between 90 and 100 days per session, although Lloyd George and Ramsay MacDonald (for different reasons) departed somewhat from that pattern. The appointment of Winston Churchill to the premiership in May 1940 marked the end of the pattern as he ceased to be Leader of the House and thus not involved in day-to-day management of Parliament. Postwar Prime Ministers answered questions far less frequently. By the 1959 session Macmillan answered questions on only 37 days, leading Labour MPs to complain that the Prime Minister was shielded from hostile scrutiny, especially as they suspected that Conservative MPs were using up the time to prevent questions to the PM being reached. Following a select committee investigation in 1961 the Commons agreed that two fixed fifteen-minute slots should be set aside, on Tuesday and Thursday at 3.15 p.m., following question time to ministers and just before ministerial statements. This pattern lasted until Blair combined the two slots into one 30-minute session each Wednesday the House sits. The 1961 change produced a change in prime ministerial behaviour, increasing the frequency of answering questions and largely standardising the pattern among all subsequent Prime Ministers. From 1961 until 1997 virtually all answered questions on between 47 and 53 days per session. This pattern has of course changed with the emergence of the single weekly slot under Blair, who now answers questions on considerably fewer days per session than his predecessors.

There have been significant changes to the form Prime Minister's questions take. At the start of the 1960s most questions focused on specific topics. When Wilson began to transfer many specific questions to the Cabinet minister responsible, a practice continued by Heath, MPs largely shifted to 'open' questions, asking about the Prime Minister's engagements for the day or, less commonly, when he or she would visit the MP's constituency. This would be followed by the oral supplementary, the real purpose of the question. More recently, MPs have been encouraged to forgo the 'open' question and ask the substantive one in order to end the time-wasting that accompanied the formal procedure. Another change has been the increased role of the leader of the opposition and, again more recently, the leader of the Liberal Democrats. In the late 1960s Heath alone regularly intervened, ending the practice whereby senior members of the shadow Cabinet would ask questions, and by the end of the 1970s this became the set pattern. Currently, the leader of the opposition is allowed six questions, and the leader of the Liberal Democrats is also allowed to ask questions. The broadcasting and especially the televising of Prime Minister's Questions means that the session is now of prime importance in the political battle between government and opposition, a significant measure of the standings of the respective party leaders and virtually the only part of the parliamentary week which regularly attracts media attention.

The utility of Prime Minister's Questions as a way of holding the Prime Minister accountable, both for his own actions and for the conduct of government as a whole, is widely thought to be limited. However, it should not be too easily dismissed as an instrument of accountability; the care successive

Prime Ministers have taken to prepare for what most have seen as an ordeal and the degree to which the performances of the Prime Minister and the leaders of opposition parties affect popular and especially media perceptions of their respective competence are clear indications that the weekly sessions are of enduring significance in the game of high politics.

Dunleavy et al. see question-answering by Prime Ministers as divided into two main periods. The first, from 1882 to 1940, saw most Prime Ministers answering questions on between 80 and 100 days. This coincided with Prime Ministers who were MPs normally also acting as Leader of the House. The second started in 1940 and is marked by a permanent decline in prime ministerial activity to around half the previous pattern. 'Inside this mould, further rapid institutional change has occurred, with Prime Minister's Question Time becoming more topical, gladiatorial and stylized.'[28] The major determining feature in this change has been institutional rather than the result of circumstances or the personality of particular Prime Ministers.

Making statements

Since 1868 Prime Ministers have made statements in the Commons about ten times less frequently than they have answered questions, although prime ministerial activity has varied sharply over time. The data shows three distinct periods. The first covers the alternation of Gladstone and Disraeli as Prime Minister, when the practice of ministerial statements was being formalised. Gladstone regularly made statements on more than ten days per session, considerably more than Disraeli. The second period covers the first four decades of the twentieth century, when, for a number of reasons, prime ministerial activity in this area fell sharply to a base level of one or two statement days per session, although this could rise sharply, partly depending on the international situation. The third period begins in 1940, when making statements revived as an aspect of the Prime Minister's activity in Parliament. This change was related to three developments in the role of the Prime Minister:

- Prime Ministers would make a statement following their attendance at international summits or heads of government meetings;
- they would make a statement about international crises, especially where British forces were involved;
- they would be expected to comment on negotiations or developments in domestic politics, especially ones with which they were personally associated.

These developments have meant that post-1940 premiers have made statements regularly, in the period covered by Dunleavy's survey virtually never slipping below a base level of between six and ten days per session and frequently considerably higher, depending on the political and diplomatic pressures. The peak came under Harold Wilson, who made statements on 44 days in the 1966/7 session and on 106 days from 1964 to 1969. This marked the period of Wilson's mastery of the Commons when he used statements to dramatise his domination of policy issues. There was a general decline following this burst of prime ministerial activity, but under Thatcher there was a longer and more significant period of decline. She made statements on only 79 days in her time in office from 1979 to 1990, and from 1985–90 made fewer than five statements per session, the lowest continuous postwar average. Her statements were confined almost exclusively to reporting on summit meetings, especially those concerning the European Community.

The conclusion is that this pattern of statement-making is largely a reflection of institutional factors:

- the early era of general parliamentary activism
- the dying out of significant prime ministerial policy statements from 1901 to 1939
- their emergence as a key Prime Ministerial activity from 1940 onwards.

However, changes in the postwar period alone show a different pattern, reflecting 'primarily conjunctural and personality effects'.[29]

Giving speeches

The institutional arrangements governing situations in which Prime Ministers make speeches in the Commons have remained largely constant over the period. Prime Ministers primarily attend and speak in debates on the Speech from the Throne and debates on very major pieces of legislation. They may also be forced to come to the Commons when an emergency debate is called; this may be as the result of the Speaker deciding that a matter is of sufficient importance, something usually resisted by the government of the day. The Prime Minister will also have to reply to any motion of no confidence proposed by the opposition. In all these circumstances, the Prime Minister will debate principally with the leader of the opposition.

Despite year-by-year and occasional cyclical variations the pattern has been for prime ministerial speech-making to decline over time. Four basic periods can be detected: the nineteenth century, 1906 to 1945, the postwar period and the 1980s.

Gladstone was an inveterate debater, as was Balfour. Prime ministerial speech-making then declined for a variety of reasons, including MacDonald's reluctance to face his one-time Labour colleagues following the formation of the National Government in 1931. Although Baldwin and Chamberlain made more speeches, mainly about the darkening international scene in the 1930s, and Churchill used the Commons to make speeches which have become part of British history, the postwar norm was for premiers to restrict themselves to only four to eight days per session. This reduced input fell even more under Thatcher. 'Although Margaret Thatcher was ready to lecture many audiences about her convictions, she was less inclined to attempt lecturing the Commons.'[30] Across eleven sessions she made speeches on only 36 days and after 1987 she spoke on only one day per session. She spoke only when it was unavoidable, leaving her Cabinet colleagues to speak on behalf of the government. Apart from debates on the Queen's Speech, she made only 23 speeches of fifteen minutes or more, half of them on foreign affairs. In contrast to her three predecessors, she spoke rarely on the economy or on social themes. Although Major faced a number of foreign policy crises such as the Gulf War and the Maastricht treaty, he continued the trend of avoiding debate. Speeches by Tony Blair similarly have been rare events, although the crisis over Iraq in 2003 led him to speak more frequently as unrest on the government benches increased.

The conclusion is that of long-run decline in this activity. This has been a fairly continuous trend, although the reticence of some Prime Ministers – Campbell-Bannerman, MacDonald and Thatcher stand out – has been rather more marked than that of others since the Victorian heyday of parliamentary activity.

Intervening in debates

This is a portmanteau category, including rising to pose a question to an opposing speaker, making a point of order and so on. When Prime Ministers were also Leaders of the House they often attended debates to see how colleagues were doing and to gauge the mood of the House; this often would lead to some kind of intervention. Even until the late 1970s, Prime Ministers were much more likely to make an impromptu intervention than to make a formal speech. However, this has largely disappeared; 'new-style' Prime Ministers are unwilling to spend time listening to a debate and then intervening when the occasion arises, preferring to leave immediately their contribution has been delivered.

Three periods can be observed: the late nineteenth century, with a transitional Edwardian era, a long trendless period from Lloyd George to the mid-1970s, and from the mid-1970s to the present. Gladstone constantly intervened in debates, averaging 75 days per session during his time as premier. Thereafter Prime Ministers were generally less active, although there were peaks and troughs. Premiers such as Churchill, Attlee and Eden intervened about once every ten days and Heath even more often. The final period started with Wilson's return to government in February 1974 and marked the almost complete disappearance of Prime Ministers' intervening in debate. Callaghan followed this trend and Thatcher intervened only sixteen times in her first five sessions. From 1985 onwards she failed to intervene at all until a solitary instance right at the end of her time as premier. Major's interventions were even less frequent, and Blair has largely avoided the cut and thrust of debate, failing to make a single impromptu intervention in his first eighteen months in office. As Dunleavy et al. point out, it is unlikely that the tradition of intervention in debate will be revived, given the declining involvement of Prime Ministers in the affairs of the Commons.

Conclusion

Although there are different explanations for the pattern of the various activities analysed by Dunleavy et al., the general conclusion is clear. There has been a decline in the overall activism of Prime Ministers in relation to Parliament and a consequent reduction in the ability of Parliament to hold the head of government to account.

There are some general factors which help to account for this decline. Some of these are institutional, for example that Prime Ministers no longer act as Leaders of the House and the decision taken by Blair to reduce Prime Minister's Questions from two sessions a week to one. To some extent, Prime Ministers have displaced some of their parliamentary responsibilities onto other ministers such as the Leader of the House. The size of the government's majority is another factor; part of the explanation for Thatcher and Blair's decreased involvement in the work of the Commons can be found in their large majorities. This can be compared with Major's need to conciliate his waning and fractious parliamentary party and to do deals with various opposition groups after 1992.

Some factors are clearly related to the personalities of specific Prime Ministers; the clearest example is the sharp decline in parliamentary activism by Margaret Thatcher, for the reasons outlined above, a pattern followed by Blair. However, it should be pointed out that Thatcher was following (even if intensifying) a pattern which had been gradually developing in the period since 1940. As Richard Rose has pointed out, 'new-style' premiers no longer see their political home as the House of Commons. They no longer regard the Commons as part of their lives, as a place to socialise, to share reminiscences of past political battles and victories won or defeats suffered. Whether Blair actively dislikes the Commons and its atmosphere and traditions can only be guessed at; clearly he does not share the affection and regard for it of a Churchill or even a Callaghan. Should the unthinkable happen and the Commons once again be destroyed by a bomb, it is unlikely that Blair would insist on it being rebuilt as a rectangular chamber, too small to accommodate all the members, as Churchill did following its destruction during the Second World War. Thus one factor in the story of declining accountability is a change in how Prime Ministers see their role as head of government, especially in relation to their responsibility to give an account of their stewardship to Parliament. To a considerable extent, the tribunes of the nation are no longer honourable members but David Dimbleby, Jeremy Paxman, John Humphrys and the *Today* team and that ilk.

Another possible explanation is the increasing 'complexity' of British government. But how to measure this 'complexity' is unclear; up to the post-Second World War period the British government was responsible for the largest empire ever seen, while at the end of the period studied its international significance had sharply declined. However, it is clear that modern Prime Ministers have many more calls on their time than was the case in previous generations. The Prime Minister spends much time abroad at international conferences, especially relating to the European Union, meeting foreign leaders and attending crisis meetings of one kind or another. On the other hand, even if the complexity thesis is accepted, it cannot account for the differential pattern of prime ministerial activity discussed above: a drastic reduction in the number of speeches and debating interventions, an increase in statements and what was from 1961 to 1997 a standardised level of answers to questions. Perhaps the most central explanation is the declining importance of Parliament in the British political system, the marginalisation of the House of Commons and of its members. If this is the case, it raises another question, which is why MPs have allowed themselves to become less powerful. But that is another story.

Endnotes

1   Pyper, R. *Aspects of Accountability in the British System of Government* (Tudor, Eastham, 1996), p. 1.

2   *Ibid.*, p.2.

3   Wright, T. *Citizens and Subjects. an Essay on British Politics* (Routledge, London and New York, 1994), p.47.

4   Hennessy, P. and Seldon, A. (eds) *Ruling Performance. British Governments from Attlee to Thatcher* (Blackwell, Oxford, 1987), p. 110.

5   Shell, D. and Hodder-Williams, R. *Churchill to Major. The British Prime Ministership since 1945* (Hurst and Co, London, 1995), p. 75.

6   Thatcher, M. *The Downing Street Years* (HarperCollins, London, 1993), p. 860.

7   Wilson, H. *The Governance of Britain* (Weidenfeld & Nicolson and Michael Joseph, London, 1976), p. 127.

8   Rose, R. *The Prime Minister in a Shrinking World* (Polity Press, Cambridge, 2001), p. 9.

9   *Ibid.*, p. 132.

10 *Ibid.*, p. 133.

11 *Ibid.*, p. 6.

12 Thomas, G. *The Prime Minister and Cabinet Today* (Manchester University Press, Manchester, 1998), p. 117.

13 Wilson, H. *A Prime Minister on Prime Ministers* (Weidenfeld & Nicolson and Michael Joseph, London, 1977), p. 224.

14 *The Times*, 4 November 1953.

15 Wilson, *A Prime Minister on Prime Ministers*, p. 240.

16 Thomas, *Prime Minister and Cabinet Today*, p. 117.

17 *Ibid.*, p.118.

18 Kavanagh, D. and Seldon, A. *The Powers behind the Prime Minister. the Hidden Influence of Number Ten* (HarperCollins, London, 1999), p. 143.

19 *Ibid.*, p. 197.

20 Kavanagh, D. and Seldon, A. *The Major Effect* (Macmillan, London, 1994), p. 50.

21 Cowley, P. 'Chaos or Cohesion? John Major and the Parliamentary Conservative Party', in P. Dorey (ed.), *The Major Premiership: Politics and Policies under John Major, 1990–97,* (Palgrave, Basingstoke, 1999), p. 23.

22   A. Seldon (ed.) *The Blair Effect: the Blair Government 1997–2001* (Little, Brown and Co., London, 2001), p. 48.

23   *Ibid.*, p. 54.

24   Kavanagh and Seldon, *Powers behind the Prime Minister*, p. 280.

25   Dunleavy, P., Jones, G., Burnham, J., Elgie, R. and Fysh, P. 'Leaders, Politics and Institutional Change: the Decline of Prime Ministerial Accountability to the House of Commons, 1868–1990', *British Journal of Political Science*, 1990, vol. 23, no. 3, pp. 267–98.

26   *Ibid.*, p. 267.

27   *Ibid.*, p. 267.

28   *Ibid.*, p. 276.

29   *Ibid.*, p. 280.

30   Rose, *Prime Minister in a Shrinking World*, p. 135.

NOTE

This chapter is an adaptation of an article that first appeared in a special edition of the *Journal of Legislative Studies* (winter 2004). Special thanks to the *Journal* and to the publishers, Frank Cass, for permission to include it in this collection.

THIRTEEN

Ministers and Parliament:
Responsibility and Accountability

Dr Nicholas D. J. Baldwin and Dr F. Nigel Forman

Ministers – both individually and collectively – are constitutionally responsible and accountable to Parliament. This is not only one of the key conventions of political behaviour in Britain but is also one of the key concepts in the British system of government. Under the doctrine of individual responsibility ministers have a duty to hold Parliament to account, and be held to account, for the policies, decisions and actions of their departments and next step agencies. As part of this it is seen as being of paramount importance that ministers give accurate and truthful information to Parliament, correcting any inadvertent error at the earliest opportunity. Ministers who knowingly mislead Parliament are expected to offer their resignation to the Prime Minister. A minister who no longer enjoys the confidence of Parliament – primarily the House of Commons, although this could apply to the confidence that the House of Lords has in a minister who is a member of the Lords – is expected to resign. Under the doctrine of collective responsibility ministers must not speak out in public against the policies of the government – if they do they would either be expected to resign or would be dismissed by the Prime Minister – and a government that no longer enjoys the confidence of Parliament – and in this regard this means the House of Commons – is expected to resign.

With regard to individual responsibility, the senior – and, increasingly, middle-ranking (ministers of state) and junior (parliamentary under-secretaries of state) – ministers in a department are theoretically responsible to Parliament for everything which happens or fails to happen within the department and, consequently, can be held to account by Parliament – and, increasingly in this day and age, the media – for acts of omission as well as commission. The classic view holds that ministers are responsible for every act of their departmental civil servants, regardless of whether or not they are properly aware of what is happening in their departments. The most often cited example of this doctrine was the resignation of the Minister of Agriculture, Sir Thomas Dugdale, in the 1954 Crichel Down affair.

Crichel Down was an area of land in Dorset that had been requisitioned by the Air Ministry in 1940 for use as a bombing range. At the time of its acquisition it was agreed that, when the ministry no longer required the land, the previous owner was to be given the opportunity to reacquire it. After the war, however, the Air Ministry offered the land to other departments and, as a result, it was taken over by the Ministry of Agriculture, who sought to develop it for agricultural purposes. Despite the fact that the previous owner claimed the land, the Ministry of Agriculture ignored the original undertaking and refused to relinquish its claim. Eventually, Sir Thomas Dugdale, the Minister of Agriculture, agreed to a public enquiry into the matter. In addition to revealing the lack of safeguards that were in existence for individual citizens when up against the machinery of government, the report – published in 1954 – also revealed that there had been a lack of contact between the minister and the department. As a result, Sir Thomas Dugdale resigned.[1]

Despite being the most often cited example, in fact this is not necessarily the best example of a resignation on the grounds of individual ministerial responsibility. It was originally thought that Sir Thomas Dugdale resigned because civil servants in the Ministry of Agriculture, Fisheries and Food had made mistakes of which he was not aware, but it was later suggested that he resigned because the government changed its decision on Crichel Down and he disagreed with that decision.[2]

Other examples cited usually include the resignation of James Callaghan as Chancellor of the Exchequer in November 1967, over his role in and responsibility for the devaluation of sterling (although it should be noted that he was immediately appointed Home Secretary),[3] and the resignations of Lord Carrington as Foreign Secretary and two of his ministerial colleagues – Humphrey Atkins, the Lord Privy Seal and spokesman for the Foreign Office in the House of Commons, and Richard Luce, minister of state at the Foreign Office – in April 1982 in recognition of the department's failure to foresee and prevent the Argentinian invasion of the Falkland Islands.[4]

Ministerial resignations can also result from what can be called political necessity, namely, when there is a perceived need to assuage party, Commons, media or public opinion – or, indeed, any combination of these. The resignations of Hugh Dalton as Chancellor of the Exchequer in 1947 after revealing Budget information to a journalist; of John Profumo as Minister for War in 1963 for lying to the House of Commons over his relationship with Christine Keeler; of Leon Brittan as Secretary of State for Trade and Industry in 1986 over the Westland helicopter affair (most particularly over the existence of a letter from British Aerospace and the apparent leaking of a letter from the Solicitor-General);[5] of Edwina Currie as Parliamentary Under-Secretary for Health in 1988 following an assertion that most of the egg production of the country was infected with salmonella; the resignations of both Peter Mandelson as Secretary of State for Trade and Industry and Geoffrey Robinson as Paymaster-General in 1998 over an undeclared home loan of £373,000 from the latter to the former; the resignation – again – of Peter Mandelson as Secretary of State for Northern Ireland in 2001 over the so-called Hinduja passport affair; the resignation of Stephen Byers as Secretary of State for Transport, Local Government and the Regions in 2002 after his department had announced the 'resignation' of Martin Sixsmith before it had been agreed, this coming in the aftermath of the so-called Jo Moore affair (an episode which highlighted that there had been a complete breakdown in trust in the department between the Secretary of State, senior civil servants and special advisers) and following months of pressure and having endured an almost permanent state of siege from the media; the resignation in 2004 of Beverley Hughes as minister of state at the Home Office over having 'unwittingly misled MPs' over the operation of immigration policy and the resignation in December 2004 of David Blunkett as Home Secretary following a string of allegations about his conduct as a minister, including that he had used his position as Home Secretary to 'fast track' and secure a visa for his lover's Filipina nanny are all examples of this – be they resignations resulting from personal scandals or from the concept of ministerial responsibility.

On the other hand, there are a large number of examples of senior ministers not resigning, even when their policies and personal reputations were in tatters. For example, John Davies did not resign as Secretary of State for Trade and Industry in 1972 after the failure of Vehicle and General insurance company. Similarly, Tony Benn did not resign as Secretary of State for Industry in 1974 in the wake of the collapse of the Court Line company. Equally, Norman Lamont did not resign as Chancellor of the Exchequer in September 1992 following the collapse of the government's exchange rate policy and the forced withdrawal of sterling from the exchange rate mechanism of the European Monetary System. Similarly, Michael Howard did not resign as Home Secretary in April 1995 when the courts threw out his cost-cutting Crime Injuries Scheme, even though he was accused of abusing power and flouting the will of Parliament. Neither did either William Waldegrave or Sir Nicholas Lyell resign following criticisms in the Scott report into the arms-to-Iraq affair in 1996. Nor did Robin Cook resign as Foreign Secretary despite damning criticisms of his department contained in a House of Commons select committee report into the arms-to-Sierra Leone affair in 1999. Indeed, Prime Ministers have often challenged the whole concept of ministerial responsibility. For example, Margaret Thatcher refused to accept the resignation of William Whitelaw as Home Secretary following a widely publicised breach of security at Buckingham Palace in 1982, or James Prior as Secretary of State for Northern Ireland following a mass escape from the Maze prison in September 1983.[6] Similarly, John Major stood by Kenneth Baker, then Home Secretary, when in July 1991 two Republican prisoners escaped from Brixton prison, and by Peter Lilley, then Secretary of State for Trade and Industry, following revelations in July 1991 that his department had sanctioned the sale of nuclear and chemical material to Iraq until three days after the August 1990 Iraq invasion of Kuwait. Finally, Michael Howard did not resign as Home Secretary in 1995 over escapes from Parkhurst prison, instead dismissing the chief executive of the Prisons Agency – in doing so highlighting an increasingly important distinction between the formulation of policy and the administration of policy.

A factor that should be noted, however, is that resigning (or in fact not resigning) at the moment in question, although the most obvious outcome, is not the only outcome. It may be that the minister concerned is not promoted in a subsequent reshuffle, or is moved sideways, or demoted or dropped altogether. For example, Nick Brown, as Minister of Agriculture, was the target for considerable criticism from the public and the media about his departments handling of the foot-and-mouth outbreak in 2001, and was subsequently demoted to minister of state in the department of Work and Pensions and later dropped altogether.

It is apparent, therefore, that there are no hard and fast rules which determine the nature of ministerial responsibility in all cases and the outcome depends on an unpredictable mixture of precedents and political circumstances. In contemporary conditions the factors which determine whether or not ministers resign from office seem to depend more on the extent to which they still command the confidence of the Prime Minister, the Chief Whip and their own backbenchers than on any objective assessment of the incompetence or impropriety of the action or inaction for which they may be criticised. In other words, holding on to ministerial office seems to have taken precedence over principled resignation in the majority of cases.

Nonetheless, it is argued that principled resignations do occur. Indeed, an example of just such a resignation is said to have occurred in October 2002 when the then education secretary, Estelle Morris, resigned, declaring that a succession of bruising rows – not least of all the A-level examination fiasco and the resulting resignation of Sir William Stubbs, the head of the Qualifications and Curriculum Authority, which led to accusations of ministerial incompetence – had destroyed her confidence to do the job, declaring:

> *I've learned what I'm good at, and also what I'm less good at. I'm good at dealing with the issues and the teaching profession. I'm less good at strategic management of a huge department and I'm not good at dealing with the media. In recent situations I have not felt I have been as effective as I should be.*[7]

Resigning for 'not being up to the job' is certainly unusual and this case – if taken at face value – is an interesting addition to the very short list of those ministers who have resigned from office solely as a result of failures in policy and delivery. Having said this, however, it should be noted that Estelle Morris had previously said that she would resign if the school targets were not met, which they were not, and that, however inadequate she may have felt, some suspect that her 'not up to it' interview was Downing Street 'spin'.

Resignations do of course occur as a result of policy disagreements within government (collective responsibility). Indeed, such resignations are more common than those over policy errors (individual responsibility). Examples would include the resignations of Michael Heseltine in 1986 over the Prime Minister's management of the Westland affair; of Nigel Lawson in 1989 over the Prime Minister's conduct of economic policy and the role of special advisor Sir Alan Walters; of Geoffrey Howe in 1990 over the Prime Minister's style of leadership on the issue of European cooperation; of Robin Cook in March 2003 over the government's failure to secure a fresh UN mandate for war in Iraq; and of Clare Short in May 2003 over what she termed the lack of consultation about the postwar reconstruction of Iraq. How such resignations play out within Parliament can be crucial. For example, it was Geoffrey Howe's resignation statement to a packed House of Commons (ministers who resign have the right to make a statement on the floor of the House) that 'lit the blue touch paper' under the premiership of Margaret Thatcher. During his statement Geoffrey Howe had declared that

> *the conflict of loyalty to the Prime Minister and the loyalty I perceive to the true interest of this nation has become all too great. I no longer believe it possible to resolve that conflict from within this government*[8]

and concluded by inviting his fellow Conservative MPs 'to consider their own response to the tragic conflict of loyalties with which I have myself wrestled for perhaps too long'.[9] It was an attack that not only made a leadership challenge likely, but also its outcome inevitable. As the *Independent* newspaper at the time observed,

> *the force of [the] attack lay in the breadth and the directness of the accusations made by the former Deputy Prime Minister – one of the chief architects of Thatcherism – against his leader, and in the measured manner in which this naturally loyal and patently long-suffering man delivered a fundamental critique, linking for all time the offensive style and the ill-considered and self-indulgent substance of Mrs Thatcher's rule.*[10]

This case showed the central significance of political parties in the British political system. An individual becomes Prime Minister – with very few exceptions, and then basically only technical exceptions – because they have the confidence of their party and, more especially, their parliamentary party. As such, an individual must work hard not only to obtain but to retain that confidence. In short, without the support of their party, and particularly the party in Parliament, a party leader – even if Prime Minister – is nothing. The case of Margaret Thatcher highlights this, as do both the example of the resignation of Neville Chamberlain as Prime Minister in 1940 and, although in entirely different circumstances, the resignation of Iain Duncan Smith as Conservative leader in 2003.

Ministerial resignations can also arise for personal reasons – business interests, career development, health, family factors and so on. For example, in June 2003 the then health secretary, Alan Milburn, resigned from the Cabinet, explaining that he was finding it hard to balance the demands of the job with the demands of having a young family (although he returned to the Cabinet in September 2004). In cases of resignation for personal reasons there can of course be a possible disparity between the officially stated reason for a ministerial resignation and the real underlying reason. For example, it may be in the best interests of all those concerned – the minister, the Prime Minister, the government as a whole – to mask evidence of either personal incompetence or policy disagreement which may in fact have been the 'real' reason for such a resignation.

The chain of responsibility in a department is hierarchical, which means that civil servants and junior ministers alike report to senior ministers at the head of their departments and it is the latter who have to take the ultimate responsibility for their action or inaction. Of course, there have been times when junior ministers have been so out of sympathy with a particular policy of their department or the government as a whole that they have felt bound to resign. This was the case, for example, with Ian Gow, who resigned as minister of state at the Treasury in 1985 in protest against the Anglo-Irish Agreement,[11] and with both John Denham (minister of state at the Home Office) and Lord Hunt of Kings Heath (parliamentary under-secretary at the Department of Health), who resigned in 2003 in protest over government policy in Iraq. Others have resigned in order to be free to criticise government policy more generally – as was the case over policies towards Europe and the resignation of David Heathcoat-Amory as Paymaster-General in 1996. Yet on the whole junior ministers stay at their posts and only tender their resignations if they are obliged to do so in the course of a ministerial 'reshuffle' organised by the Prime Minister of the day or as a result of political pressure arising from some scandal publicised by the media.

From all the available evidence it would appear that individual ministerial responsibility has been blurred and eroded in modern times by the size and complexity of modern government. Indeed, the traditional characteristics of the British system of government have been changed significantly in recent years and not least by the growth of so-called next-step executive agencies, which have had the effect of putting responsibility for the administration of public policy fairly and squarely on the shoulders of the much more visible chief executives who lead them and who can be sacked if their performance does not come up to expectations. Despite the fact that the position of executive agencies is very similar to that of the old nationalised industries – namely, that ministers are responsible for overall strategy but not for day-to-day operations – this has meant that it has been effectively impossible for senior ministers to be aware of, let alone control, everything which happens or fails to happen in their departments and the executive agencies that may come under it. For example, thousands of planning appeals have to be decided every year by the responsible secretary of state, be it the Secretary of State for the Environment (or Environment, Food and Rural Affairs as is its current guise) or a minister from the Office of the Deputy Prime Minister, many of them important and nearly all of them complicated and contentious. Yet no minister in that position can possibly hope to consider all of them personally, so junior ministers and civil servants effectively take the decisions in the senior minister's name in all but a few outstanding cases. Thus in most cases individual ministerial responsibility has become little more than a constitutional 'cloak', a convenient fiction for parliamentary and Civil Service purposes, but a convention which is put strictly into practice on very few occasions. Having said this, however, ministerial responsibility – especially individual ministerial responsibility – remains the basis for parliamentary scrutiny.

On the other hand, collective ministerial responsibility is more of a reality in modern political conditions, because it reflects the collegiate and usually cohesive nature of single-party government in Britain. It is really a way of expressing the fact that all ministers and whips – and, indeed, parliamentary private secretaries – are bound by government policy and are expected to stand by it and to speak and vote for it – or, at the very least, avoid criticising it publicly. While politicians cannot really be expected to believe totally in everything which they have to support in public for reasons of party loyalty, those whose activities are covered by collective ministerial responsibility are expected nevertheless to support the government on all occasions. If they feel unable or unwilling to do so, they are supposed to resign or can expect to be dismissed, as was the case in 1981, for example, when Keith Speed, the junior navy minister, was sacked for speaking out publicly against planned cuts in the Royal Navy budget, or in 1989 when Nicholas Ridley, then environment secretary, was sacked for speaking out against the Germans.

It should come as no surprise, however, that the convention of collective responsibility has not always been observed. Indeed, on those, admittedly rare, occasions when governments have been so split that enforcement has been effectively impossible, temporary suspension has become the only effective course. For example, in 1931 there was an open 'agreement to differ' in the National Government on the issue of tariff reform, and in 1975 during the European referendum campaign Labour Cabinet ministers were allowed to argue against each other on public platforms. It will be interesting to see if this convention will again be suspended during any future referendum on either approval of the European constitution or on any future British participation in the euro. It should also be noted that, for example, Frank Cousins never publicly supported Labour's incomes policy when he was a minister and that individual ministers – such as Tony Benn (Labour) and Peter Walker (Conservative) – have been especially skilled at letting their views be known without stepping formally out of line.

It is unwise, however, for those covered by collective responsibility to test the boundaries of the permissible too obviously or too often, since in doing so they are quite likely to invite dismissal by the Prime Minister of the day. On the whole, therefore, collective ministerial responsibility is a reality in modern British government, but it is no longer the effective mechanism of parliamentary accountability which it was originally meant to be.

In theory, the proper constitutional check on the power of the executive in Britain is to be found in ministerial accountability to Parliament. This is supposed to be achieved in three ways. None of these is adequate on its own, but taken together there are some safeguards for the public interest.

Firstly, there are the opportunities for MPs to hold ministers to account during proceedings in the chamber of the House of Commons (and, to a lesser extent, for peers to do so in the House of Lords) – that is, at question time, following ministerial statements and during debates. Yet the scope for effective parliamentary influence in such proceedings – through challenge, criticism and attack – is limited by the ability of most competent ministers to answer points in the House without revealing any new or substantial information if they do not want to do so. Experience also shows that such proceedings are often rather an empty ritual, since any attempt at a strong parliamentary challenge usually gives way to mere party political point-scoring. Also, the media have invariably discovered (or been briefed about) the points at issue long before Parliament gets its chance, in effect reducing the impact of Parliament.

Secondly, there are the opportunities for MPs and peers to probe ministerial thinking and government policy during select committee investigations and during the committee stage of government Bills. These have proved to be somewhat more effective mechanisms for parliamentary influence. Yet, in the former case, the usefulness of such investigations is limited by an unwillingness often shown by governments to act on the findings of select committees and occasionally even to allow key ministerial or official witnesses to appear before the committee at all.[12] In the latter case, legislative scrutiny by the opposition in standing committees has to be set against the normal voting power of the government majority, both in the committees and subsequently on the floor of the House at report stage and third reading. Such proceedings provide a form of parliamentary accountability and influence, but not effective parliamentary control, unless, of course, the government of the day has a relatively small or no majority in the Commons or a large enough number of its own backbenchers feel inclined to rebel.

Thirdly, there are the various opportunities for MPs and peers to use their power of publicity to dramatise the errors of ministers or the shortcomings of government policy. The principal effect of this form of parliamentary accountability has been to encourage an attitude of defensiveness on the part of civil servants and to reinforce the tendency for Whitehall departments to play safe in the conduct of government business. Indeed, it is the capricious and unpredictable quality of such parliamentary accountability which has led both ministers and officials to treat it with wary respect. This has had a marked influence on attitudes and working practices in Whitehall and has sometimes discouraged bold or imaginative decision-making by ministers. It may, therefore, have lowered the quality of decision-making in British central government.

Thus, if we examine the various forms of parliamentary accountability, we discover that none of them has proved to be a guarantee of representative and responsible government. The lack of proper accountability has been most marked in the detailed areas of policy covered by Statutory Instruments, the secondary legislation which is drafted by civil servants in the name of ministers and lawfully implemented under the authority of existing statutes. In effect, legislation of this type is no longer within the realm of effective parliamentary control. Although there is a joint committee of the Lords and Commons which has the task of overseeing the spate of secondary legislation which pours out of Whitehall, the problem has really become unmanageable now that there are more than 2,000 Statutory Instruments issued each year. The volume of such secondary legislation and the shortcomings of existing parliamentary procedures for dealing with it are such that genuine parliamentary accountability is really unattainable.

The other notable area in which parliamentary accountability is clearly defective is that of European legislation. Under the 1972 European Communities Act the British government is obliged to implement automatically the regulations issued by the European Commission, notably in the spheres of agriculture, trade and competition policy, and to find appropriate national means of carrying out the directives which flow from decisions taken by the Council of Ministers. In 1974 both the House of Commons and the House of Lords established special select committees to sift draft European legislation and to make recommendations as to whether or not the various items contained therein were sufficiently important to merit a debate on the floor of their respective chambers. As things have turned out, such debates (in the House of Commons at any rate) are normally brief and held towards the end of the parliamentary day, if and when the 'usual channels' find time for them at all. In some cases it has not even proved possible to find time to debate a particular draft European proposal before it is considered by the Council of Ministers or before it is promulgated by the Commission as directly applicable European legislation. This means that it may well become law in Britain before there has been any consideration of its merits or otherwise by MPs on the floor of the House of Commons or by peers on the floor of the House of Lords.

One answer to the problem of insufficient parliamentary accountability in this area of executive action is for the tasks of scrutiny to be performed by the directly elected European Parliament, which does have some enlarged rights of 'co-decision' with the other European institutions in specific areas of European Union activity. Yet this is not a complete answer, and in any case many of the national parliaments remain jealous of their historic rights to legislate and to hold ministers to account. The result is that there is what has been called a 'democratic deficit' in the European Union which could be closed either by a great leap forward towards fuller political integration in Europe with much greater powers for the European Parliament, or by a dramatic reassertion of democratic control by national parliaments, which seems both unlikely and possibly unattainable.[13] Other possible solutions would be to make at least some British members of the European Parliament also members of the House of Lords, or for the member states to create a second chamber of the European Parliament, made up of members drawn proportionately from the national Parliaments.

*

This is inevitably a difficult topic to cover, not least of all in a short chapter, partly because of the gap that exists between constitutional theory and political practice, but more particularly because it is complicated, especially over resignations on the grounds of individual ministerial responsibility. It is therefore not easy to make neat, watertight judgements. Because resignations, other than those on genuinely personal grounds (and even these sometimes, since in these days of 'spin' the personal grounds may be questioned), are mostly high politics, they do not necessarily provide the best criterion for judging the efficacy of ministerial responsibility. Besides which, it must borne in mind that ministers are constantly held accountable by the very fact of having to explain and defend their policies and actions in and through Parliament, and thereby bringing into the public domain much that would otherwise not be there.

Having said this, however, in reflecting generally upon the history of parliamentary accountability in Britain since the Second World War, we must conclude that it has been notable more for the tendency of ministers to escape the shackles of real accountability than for the ability of Parliament to impose its will and control on ministers. While there were the celebrated cases of the Crichel Down affair in 1954 and the Argentinian invasion of the Falkland Islands in 1982, each of which led to the resignation of the Cabinet minister considered most culpable, in modern times such cases have seemed to be exceptions to the general rule that ministers and civil servants can make grievous mistakes without ever really being subjected to full and effective parliamentary accountability. They may get sacked later on when the heat has died down and the public attention has turned elsewhere, yet at the relevant time, when they ought to be held strictly to account in Parliament, ministers are often able to get away with suffering little more than media censure – be it criticism or vilification – because their own party colleagues rally to their support within Parliament itself. On the other hand, if they lose such collective support from their own benches within Parliament – and particularly if they lose the backing of the Prime Minister – they have to go. Consequently, today, in most regards, it can be said that responsibility and accountability are played out rather more within party within Parliament as opposed to within Parliament as a whole.

Endnotes

1   See Nicolson, I. F. *The Mystery of Crichel Down* (Oxford University Press, Oxford, 1986) and Griffith, J. 'Crichel Down, the Most Famous Farm in British History', *Contemporary Record*, 1987, vol. 1, no. 1, pp. 35–40.

2   See Blackburn, R. and Kennon, A. *Griffith & Ryle on Parliament: Functions, Practice and Procedures* (Sweet & Maxwell, London, 2003), pp. 32–3.

3   See Morgan, K. O. *Callaghan: a Life* (Oxford University Press, Oxford, 1997), pp. 260–89.

4   See Lord Carrington *Reflect on Things Past* (Collins, London, 1988), pp. 348–72.

5   See Heseltine, M. *Life in the Jungle* (Hodder & Stoughton, London, 2000), pp. 293–333.

6   See Prior, J. *A Balance of Power* (Hamish Hamilton, London, 1986), pp. 232–3 and Whitelaw, W. *The Whitelaw Memoirs*, (Aurum Press, London, 1989), pp. 211–13.

7   Estelle Morris, letter of resignation, *The Times*, 24 October 2002.

8   Hansard, House of Commons Debates, 13 November 1990 .

9   *Ibid.*

10   *Independent*, 14 November 1990.

11   See Thatcher, M. *The Downing Street Years* (HarperCollins, London, 1993), p. 403.

12   For example, when the Expenditure Select Committee sought to cross-examine Labour ministers on public financial support for Chrysler UK in the 1970s, the then Prime Minister, James Callaghan, prevented any of his colleagues from appearing before the committee. Equally not all the key official witnesses were permitted by Margaret Thatcher when Prime Minister to testify before select committees in the wake of the 1986 Westland affair.

        Select Committees have also been denied access to material. For example, during their 1995–6 investigation into whether the Conservative MP and BMARC director Jonathan Aitken knew whether the company was selling naval cannons to Iraq, the DTI select committee was denied access to classified intelligence documents.

13   In 1989 the House of Commons began belatedly to address this problem when the Select Committee on Procedure considered the matter and issued a cautious report entitled *Scrutiny of European Legislation*, HC 622, 1988–89, vols I & II. See also the government's response, *Scrutiny of European Legislation*, Cmnd 1081 (HMSO, London, 1990).

FOURTEEN

Parliament and Devolution: Westminster in the Age of Multi-Layer Democracy

Barry K. Winetrobe

At the start of the 21st century, devolution to the nations and regions of the United Kingdom is still one of the most dynamic of the Labour government's package of constitutional changes. It seems to be bedding down in Scotland, less so in Wales, and, as part of the Northern Ireland peace process, is subject to the usual governmental rollercoaster in that territory. While not explicitly defined as devolution by ministers, the new forms of government in Greater London, and, embryonically, in the English regions, are also significant changes to British territorial governance. It may have been supposed that Westminster, as the Parliament of the United Kingdom, would have been significantly affected and altered by such profound constitutional change, especially when the two Houses themselves were in the midst of a substantial bout of internal modernisation and reform.

Yet, five years into devolution, the general verdict must be that Westminster has been relatively untouched by all these changes. As an expert text on Westminster has commented, 'as yet, the procedural consequences of [devolution] have been gradualist ad hoc adjustments dealing with relative jurisdictional matters and demarcation of administrative accountability.'[1] Is this because radical change was, and remains, unnecessary in Westminster's adjustment to devolution, at least until English regionalism kicks in? Or is it because both the UK government and Parliament have adopted an ostrichlike approach to these knotty and sensitive problems, for fear of opening what is often described as a 'Pandora's box' of much more radical constitutional change?

The British attitude to constitutional reform is often characterised as incremental and pragmatic. Perhaps it is more helpful to regard the dynamic of British constitutional change as an irregular series of sudden changes, followed by periods of consolidation and absorption. Devolution is clearly such a 'great leap', in so far as it has changed the constitutional and political landscape, most obviously in the devolved areas themselves. Yet it was intended, at least by Labour ministers, to be a strictly limited leap, one not designed as a first step to a federal UK or even to the unravelling of the Union. Seen in this light, Westminster symbolises not just the United Kingdom, but also its stability and permanence, and therefore the minimising of the procedural or structural impact of devolution on the UK Parliament emphasises these attributes.

This approach fits in neatly with the common perception (though sometimes a misconception) of Westminster being an institution resistant to change. It also chimes with the inevitable desires of those at Westminster, especially of MPs and others from the devolved areas, to protect and defend the powers and functions of the institution from seepage to devolved constitutions 'below', as well as to EU institutions 'above'. To describe Westminster as being so caught in this squeeze as to be in danger of withering away in the near future may be an exaggeration, but devolution does add to a sense of the UK national governmental tier becoming redundant.

Whatever the reason for Westminster's reaction to devolution thus far, this chapter argues that it cannot but be affected by it as time goes on, even if these changes may not be in the structural or procedural areas which are commonly discussed. Whether or not the Scottish Affairs Committee or the

Welsh Grand Committee continue, or even whether MPs from devolved areas continue to participate and vote in business not affecting the areas they represent, devolution's greatest impact on Westminster may well be as the catalyst for the development of a more modern and better form of Parliament. But first, devolution's existing impact on Westminster needs to be considered.

The procedural response[2]

Relatively little advance consideration had been given within Westminster to the potential impact devolution might have on it. One of the main exceptions was a thoughtful but relatively unnoticed report by the Scottish Affairs Select Committee published in December 1998, entitled *The Operation of Multi-layer Democracy*.[3] Among other issues it examined was the potential impact on the procedures of the House of Commons, raising most of the aspects which were to be addressed, even if not resolved, in the following years. These included the need for some protocols on the relationship between elected representatives, including MSPs and MPs, the notorious 'West Lothian question' and the postdevolution role (and number) of MPs from the devolved areas, as well as the more obvious issues of Question Time, the Scottish Grand and Standing Committees, the Scottish Affairs Committee and the rules of debate.

In a rhetorical flourish rare for a Westminster select committee, the report suggested that the novel situation of the UK having more than one Parliament required an attitude of 'thinking the unthinkable':

> *There is a tendency in any discussion of UK constitutional matters for people to claim that certain things do not accord with 'our' way of doing things (as, for instance in the argument that an 'in and out' solution to the West Lothian question is not possible because it is not the practice to have two classes of MP or Mr McLeish's comment that a step by step approach was in tune with the British Constitution) ... There has not*

*been more than one Parliament in Great Britain either recently, but there
is going to be one now, so that argument needs to be treated with a degree
of scepticism whenever it is used.*[4]

In early 1999, the House of Commons Procedure Committee examined the
procedural consequences of devolution in more detail, and made a number
of detailed proposals in its report in May 1999, just as devolution was
becoming live.[5] As an indicator of the priority given to devolution-related
procedural change, it may have been significant that these matters were
examined by the Procedure Committee rather than by the higher-profile
Modernisation Committee. Echoing the Scottish Affairs Committee's call for
goodwill as the key element in making devolution a success, the committee
trusted that the relationship between Westminster and the devolved legislatures would be one of 'mutual respect'. It then set out some common principles, taking into account the differences in the three devolution schemes:

- in passing the legislation which underlies devolution, Parliament has agreed
  that certain powers and responsibilities should pass from it to the devolved
  legislatures; parliamentary procedure or custom should not be called in to
  undermine that decision;
- there should be as few procedural barriers as possible to cooperation
  between Members of Parliament and Members of other legislatures,
  where such cooperation is desired;
- it is legitimate for all Members of the United Kingdom Parliament to
  have an interest in matters which remain the responsibility of the United
  Kingdom Parliament; however Members from an area to which powers
  have been devolved will have a particular interest in business affecting
  that area;
- even though uniformity is impossible, it is desirable that there should be
  as much consistency as possible in the way in which the House deals
  with matters relating to the devolved legislatures.[6]

The committee's proposals included:

- a narrowing of the admissibility rules for parliamentary questions and daily adjournment debates on devolved matters;
- a reduction of Scottish Questions to 30 minutes;
- the retention of the territorial select committees to scrutinise their respective UK secretaries of state and departments;
- the suspension of the territorial grand committees pending the outcome of the Westminster Hall experiment;
- procedures for dealing with legislation affecting only a specific part of the UK at second reading and committee stages;
- prevention of any formal joint meetings of house committees and members of the devolved legislatures without the express authority of the House.

Even this rather modest package was a little too much for a government apparently keen on a 'business as usual' parliamentary response to the advent of devolution, although it did support the committee's four general principles.[7] However, it rejected a suspension of the grand committees, believing them to be a useful means of additional debate on matters affecting the devolved areas. More significantly, it did not agree with the proposals for the differential handling of territory-specific legislation, especially 'England-only' legislation, believing them to be unnecessary and impractical.

The committee's report was not considered by the House until October 1999, though the Speaker had to provide some guidance on the admissibility of questions before the summer recess because of problems which arose during Welsh Questions on 7 July.[8] However, while little was happening within Parliament itself, this was not the case within government, where intergovernmental relations were formalised through an overarching memorandum of understanding and series of concordats (followed by bilateral concordats between the UK government and the individual devolved executives). The memorandum contained an important section on parliamentary business, which, among more general guidance, included a restatement of the 'Sewel convention', stating that Westminster would not normally legislate in devolved areas without the consent of the relevant devolved legislature:[9]

Parliamentary Business

13. *The United Kingdom Parliament retains authority to legislate on any issue, whether devolved or not. It is ultimately for Parliament to decide what use to make of that power. However, the UK government will proceed in accordance with the convention that the UK Parliament would not normally legislate with regard to devolved matters except with the agreement of the devolved legislature. The devolved administrations will be responsible for seeking such agreement as may be required for this purpose on an approach from the UK government.*

14. *The United Kingdom Parliament retains the absolute right to debate, enquire into or make representations about devolved matters. It is ultimately for Parliament to decide what use to make of that power, but the UK government will encourage the UK Parliament to bear in mind the primary responsibility of devolved legislatures and administrations in these fields and to recognise that it is a consequence of Parliament's decision to devolve certain matters that Parliament itself will in future be more restricted in its field of operation.*

15. *The devolved legislatures will be entitled to debate non-devolved matters, but the devolved executives will encourage each devolved legislature to bear in mind the responsibility of the UK Parliament in these matters.*

16. *These same principles will be applied to other aspects of each administration's responsibilities towards its Parliament or Assembly. The administrations will provide each other, so far as appropriate and practicable, with information necessary to meet these responsibilities.*

The practice and procedures of the House since 1999 have been shaped by these various rules and guidelines. Scottish, Welsh and Northern Ireland Questions remain in the regular rota, though the time for Scotland has been reduced to 30 minutes. Written questions to the Scottish and Welsh secretaries have been at least halved. The select and grand committees continue to meet, though also on a revised and reduced basis. The differential development of devolution in the three nations has had an impact on how Westminster has dealt with each of them, especially in relation to legislation. The intermittent nature of the Northern Ireland process has kept Westminster busy, both for day-to-day business in the periods of direct rule, and for primary legislation, often rushed through, reacting to the ups and downs of the peace process. As Wales relies on Westminster for its primary legislation, the main focus has been on the Westminster legislative process and the scope afforded for Welsh Bills, including those desired by the National Assembly.[10]

The House of Lords, no doubt due to its very different nature, composition and role, has not felt the need to adjust its procedures and practices in response to the advent of devolution, even to the limited degree introduced in the Commons. More significant change may come as part of any wider reform of the second chamber, especially if that includes some form of direct or indirect element in its composition explicitly representing the various devolved nations and regions. For example, all three presiding officers of the devolved Parliaments/assemblies in 1999 were members of the upper House, and they appeared to believe that this 'happy coincidence' should be made the normal practice for the future. The apparent suggestion by Donald Dewar, the Scottish First Minister, in 1999 that a reformed House of Lords could be used as a form of reviewing chamber for Bills of the unicameral Scottish Parliament was met with incredulity and was not pursued.[11]

One of the most significant innovations since 1997 in the Lords has been the establishment of the Constitution Committee, the first chair of which was the Conservative peer and noted political scientist Lord Norton of

Louth. Though its creation in 2001 was a response to wider constitutional change, and not just to devolution – it was originally suggested by the Wakeham royal commission on House of Lords reform – its first major, substantive inquiry was into interinstitutional relations under devolution,[12] and doubtless it will continue to regard devolution as a major subject of its scrutiny.

It is said that the distinctive nature of the House of Lords allows it to discuss important and politically sensitive issues in a full and measured way. This has been the case with devolution, both in its operation and in its impact. The Constitution Committee's report is one example; Lord Palmer's Bill on a referendum on the future existence of the Scottish Parliament was another,[13] and a cursory glance at most days' list of written answers suggests some peers appear to treat the House as a substitute for the Northern Ireland Assembly, especially during its periods of suspension.

Under present arrangements, elections to the devolved Parliaments/assemblies, held on a fixed four-year cycle, tend to occur in the mid-term of a Westminster Parliament.[14] Neither the 1999 nor the 2003 election campaigns had any significant impact on proceedings at Westminster, though there were protests by the SNP and others that the holding of the Budget in April 2003, in the middle of the devolved campaign, was inappropriate.

Interparliamentary relations

For the first two years of devolution, the most obvious sign of interparliamentary relations was the group of 'dual mandate' members, those who were both MPs and members of their devolved Parliament or assembly. However, with the exception of Northern Ireland (where such a dual mandate had occurred under previous devolved assemblies) and a few peers, this ended with the 2001 UK general election,[15] and is not likely to recur under current constitutional arrangements. From 1999 to 2001, other than in terms of standards regulation,[16] no special procedural or other arrangements appear to have been made to cater for this unusual representative situation, presumably on the basis that it was a limited-time aberration. From time to time, in the context of House of Lords reform, there is discussion of members of the devolved assemblies sitting in a reformed Westminster second chamber representing their nation or region, but this has generally met with a negative response from the devolved areas as an inappropriate and inefficient arrangement.

Notwithstanding their very different structures, functions and workings, relations between the various Parliaments and assemblies in the UK (and its near neighbours in 'these isles') have been going on happily and productively at various levels, both formally and informally, between members,[17] committees,[18] presiding officers and staff.[19] This has developed on a bilateral basis or a multilateral basis, and sometimes, when appropriate, even without Westminster's involvement!

All this has an impact on Westminster, because it is coming to recognise that, as devolution matures, it is no longer the only Parliament in town, but one of a family of four representative assemblies in the UK. If Westminster is (to use the common misquotation) the Mother of Parliaments, the other three (and others in London and the English regions) are not – or, at least, no longer – her children, dependent or otherwise. Of course, the newly established devolved assemblies looked to it for assistance, just as they and many Parliaments around the world (not all of them of the Westminster model) will continue to do. But this is no longer one-way traffic, as the new bodies increasingly have much to teach Westminster, as well as each other.

The future impact of devolution and territorial reform on Westminster

At the time of writing (mid-2004) we are perhaps entering the second phase of a postdevolution Westminster Parliament. The first period was marked by very limited change to procedure and practice in both Houses, as devolution was becoming established in Scotland, Wales and (in its own way) Northern Ireland. There was a palpable wish at Westminster not to rock the devolution boat by interfering in this process, at least publicly. This was helped no doubt by the general political compatibility of the three administrations in London, Edinburgh and Cardiff, and a strong desire within the UK government not to address the outstanding constitutional asymmetries and contradictions, especially as they relate to England, the sleeping giant of UK territorial governance.

As has already been noted, devolution, just like all the other elements of current constitutional change, has been marked by pragmatism, and by a desire within government for it not to lead to more fundamental territorial reform. This raises the whole issue of the stability of devolution reform – which is supposed to be both a 'settlement' and 'a process, not an event' – and even the more fundamental question of the future of the United Kingdom itself. Yet the period since 1997 has been remarkably smooth on the devolution front, both in its implementation and operation, perhaps because of the relatively auspicious political and economic conditions during these years.

This relative calm has been reflected at Westminster, where the impact of devolution on the Union Parliament has not yet been tested in any serious sense. This does not mean that the essential fault lines on territorial governance have gone away. The constant interruptions in Northern Ireland devolution put increasing strain on Westminster as the 'direct rule' Parliament for the territory. If, notwithstanding the proposals of the Richard commission, the National Assembly for Wales continues with its present structure and powers, there may be demands for a greater focus on Welsh business at Westminster. Much has already been speculated about intergovernmental relations if and when there are administrations of different political hue in London and the devolved areas. Would a Conservative UK government seek to rein back devolution, or create some form of 'English Parliament' either apart from or within the Westminster arrangements? Would an SNP Scottish

Executive pursue its policy of independence from the UK, through a referendum or otherwise?[20] Would independence for Scotland also trigger the departure of Wales and Northern Ireland from the present UK, thereby causing a complete break-up of the Union, rather than just a continuing Union without Scotland?

Even under the present constitutional arrangements, will the continued participation of MPs from devolved areas in issues affecting only England, and which they cannot deal with for their own constituencies because the issues are devolved, finally trigger some response in England? Despite much discussion in the media, in academic writings, and within the Conservative Party, the West Lothian Question[21] remains the dog that growls from time to time (most recently in 2003 on university finance, hunting and foundation hospitals), but has failed to bark decisively. Is this because, however much it may be a fatal flaw in theory, in practice it is just another example of British constitutional illogicality, asymmetry or unfairness which we accept and accommodate, however grudgingly?

Westminster has a long history of reinventing itself institutionally in line with the exact nature and membership of the Union, from 1707, 1800 and the 1920s. Presumably it could do so again, whether as a Parliament for, for example:

- an independent state of England;
- a UK of England, Wales and Northern Ireland;
- a federal UK; or
- a UK with some form of 'devolution all round'.

Territorial impacts may well be felt primarily through a second chamber, rather than in the 'lower House'. As with previous reconstitutions of 'these isles', the overwhelming representative predominance of England presumes that Westminster as a parliamentary institution can carry on regardless, whether or not it contains members from any of its neighbouring nations or regions.

If we assume that no such constitutional 'big bang' takes place in the foreseeable future, we can still imagine more practical impacts of devolution on Westminster. Even if the original devolution 'settlement' produces no more procedural change, further constitutional/territorial reform may well force Westminster to respond more substantively than it did in 1999. The latest example of this is the fallout from the UK ministerial reshuffle of June 2003, with the creation of a Department for Constitutional Affairs which incorporated the Scotland and Wales Offices; the proposed abolition of the Lord Chancellor; and the proposed creation of a Supreme Court which would replace the House of Lords in its judicial capacity and take over the devolution jurisdiction of the Judicial Committee of the Privy Council.[22]

Such effects may be felt mainly in scrutiny procedures, such as parliamentary questions and select committees. Changes in legislative procedure and practice at Westminster will depend, in part, on factors such as

- changes to devolved competence, such as the granting of primary legislative power to the Welsh Assembly (and the form of such a grant);
- more formal procedural arrangements, such as for Bills subject to the Sewel convention; certification of Bills and other business as specific to a particular territory within the UK, so as to be handled only by particular committees or MPs representing that territory; the development of joint legislative processes between the Welsh Assembly and Westminster, if primary legislative power is not granted to the assembly;
- developing conventions, such as any 'self-denying ordinance' by MPs over business that does not relate at all to their nation or region.

Other impacts on Westminster may be in more general reaction to devolution in practice. A possible example of this is in forms of representation at Westminster. Even now that the immediate issue of the decoupling of the numbers of Scottish MPs and of Holyrood MSPs has been resolved by legislation,[23] the devolved voting systems will influence the debate on electoral reform at Westminster. It seems that the lesson of devolved elections that is being learnt in Westminster and Whitehall is that mixed-member systems (especially those where both 'classes' of member represent distinct geographical areas, rather than, as with national lists, one class representing the whole territory) have not found sufficient legitimacy and acceptance from either public or politicians. If so, any change to the electoral system for the House of Commons, or introduced for a reformed second chamber, may become an even more distant prospect, or, at least, will not be on a mixed-member basis.[24]

If the House of Commons Procedure Committee ever does conduct the 'full review of the procedural consequences of devolution in due course' that it promised in its May 1999 report, some of the changes mentioned above, and others not contemplated or discussed here, may be proposed, and even implemented. The Westminster response to devolution will continue to be, like devolution itself, a process, and be one paralleling, albeit some steps behind, the development of devolved governance in the UK.

As has been suggested earlier, the major impact of devolution on Westminster may not be as a direct consequence of the structure of territorial governance. It may be more indirect, as the devolved Parliaments/assemblies demonstrate new ways of working within a Parliament, both procedurally and institutionally. This is considered in the final section of this chapter.

The 21st-century Parliament

The health and viability of Parliaments has been a common topic of discussion for decades, with views ranging from their inevitable and terminal decline to options for their revival and strengthening. The central institutional dilemma of the Westminster-model Parliament, that of the consequences of the executive within the Parliament itself, is encapsulated in the first chapter of the modern classic *Griffith & Ryle on Parliament: Functions, Practice and Procedures*. It describes the 'two confrontations' within the UK Parliament:

between government and opposition and between government and Parliament (i.e. between ministers and all other members). This formulation neatly highlights the main 'problem' of the Westminster model, that of the grip of political party groups within parliaments. It also expresses the duality of parliamentary politics that many media commentators fail to appreciate and often conflate when attempting to explain what is actually happening and why.

If this model of a democratic Parliament is to survive, and it is accepted that the central role of party within it cannot be so altered as to dilute its influence on how Parliaments work, then innovative strategies are needed. It is in this sense that the devolved Parliaments and assemblies can contribute meaningfully to the debate. Assuming party to be inherent in our forms of Parliament, perhaps its effect can be modified in institutions which are more genuinely multi-party and which involve the public in a meaningful way. For Westminster, the crucial comparator is the Scottish Parliament, which

- exhibits traditional party politics (unlike the Northern Ireland Assembly), if on a multi-party basis,
- has explicitly sought to work in ways that are different from Westminster (again unlike the Northern Ireland Assembly), and
- is clearly a Westminster-style 'Parliament' rather than some other form of elected representative assembly (such as the corporate Welsh Assembly).[25]

Differences between the London and Edinburgh Parliaments which stem from their powers and competencies do not necessarily affect how they operate in practice as institutions. Even the apparently essential distinction of the source of institutional power – Westminster's being inherent and expressed through notions of privilege; Holyrood's being granted by UK statute – may not be as important a factor as it could or should be in theory, because of the apparently inexorable decline of a strict or absolutist notion of parliamentary privilege.

The other major structural distinction between the two Parliaments is in their electoral system. At Holyrood, it provides more scope for multi-party and coalition outcomes, and produces MSPs elected by two different methods. These outcomes clearly have an impact on how the Scottish Parliament works, just as they do in Cardiff and, with yet another voting system, in Belfast. However, it may be difficult, if not impossible, to determine to what extent the different ways these Parliaments and assemblies work is due to their electoral systems rather than to other factors. Nevertheless, it does appear that the electoral system and its outcomes contribute, as was originally intended, to a political environment conducive to novel ways of doing parliamentary politics, albeit one where party remains of central importance.[26]

Westminster cannot help but be influenced by the existence and operation of other Parliaments and assemblies around the UK, including the Greater London Assembly, and any elected English regional assemblies that emerge. This is the case whether or not it wishes to be so influenced. Encouragingly, the lesson of the first four years is that Westminster is becoming increasingly aware of these new bodies, and more willing to acknowledge the potential they bring for analysis of different ways of working, both procedurally and institutionally. Such a development was assisted in the early days by the extent of dual membership, and through the positive approach of Robin Cook as Leader of the House of Commons (something that continued under one of his successors in that office, Peter Hain).[27]

Similarly, the devolved and regional bodies will continue to be influenced, whether they admit it or not, by Westminster, both positively and negatively. The sheer scale of the accumulated experience and expertise at Westminster, and the continuing relations between them, must make it an invaluable comparative resource, even if devolved eyes are also cast much further afield for suitable models for innovation and improvement.

If it is accepted that the Scottish and UK Parliaments are essentially similar bodies within the Westminster model, notwithstanding the differences already mentioned, then they face similar challenges in the 21st century. They both have to learn how to reconnect with their publics, in an age when new technology brings the potential clash between representative democracy and more direct democracy to the forefront of modern governance.28 They both have to find ways of establishing a sufficient degree of institutional and operational autonomy so as to be able to fulfil their constitutional functions, especially those which relate to the executive. They have to reconcile the complexities caused by *Griffith & Ryle's* 'two confrontations', including the central role of party, so as to make their proceedings meaningful.

The Scottish Parliament is a good comparator for Westminster for all these challenges.29 Public engagement is claimed to be an integral, essential factor in all its workings. Its rules and structures provide a greater degree of institutional and 'parliamentary business' autonomy from the executive than is the case at Westminster. It operates by reference to stated key principles, which embody a culture and ethos that Westminster is trying, albeit in a more ad hoc and irregular way, to evolve and apply. And it is having to grapple with the consequences of the 'two confrontations', even though much of its founding ethos was predicated on a simplistic, and optimistic view of the influence of *Realpolitik* and party competition, where the idea of 'confrontation' was itself to be replaced by notions of partnership and consensus.

In sum, the Scottish Parliament is the one product thus far of the devolution experiment which may have a profound effect on Westminster, as it provides the catalyst for the creation of a form of Westminster-model parliament that can work in the 21st century. This does not mean that it itself will be that model. Rather it suggests that a new or reinvigorated form of Parliament can emerge through a synthesis of what is best in the Scottish (and the other devolved and regional assemblies) and UK Parliaments. We may be at the point in our constitutional history where the future of the Westminster-model parliament is in such doubt that we need to decide whether it can be reformed or should be replaced by another model, perhaps one based on a more formal separation of powers. If so, the golden opportunity we currently have of examining a variety of Parliaments within our shores may provide us with part of the answer.

Endnotes

1   Blackburn, R. and Kennon, A. (eds) *Griffith & Ryle on Parliament: Functions, Practice and Procedures* (2nd ed.) (Sweet & Maxwell, London, 2003), pp. 756–7.

2   This section seeks only to outline how Westminster has adjusted itself to devolution. For a detailed running commentary and analysis, see the *Devolution and the Centre* quarterly monitoring reports posted on University College London's Constitution Unit website (http://www.ucl.ac.uk/constitution-unit/leverh/monitoring.htm#centre), and the yearly overviews in the unit's annual publication *The State of the Nations*: Russell. M. and Hazell, R. 'Devolution and Westminster: Tentative Steps towards a More Federal Parliament', in R. Hazell (ed.) *The State and the Nations: The First Year of Devolution in the United Kingdom* (University of London Constitution Unit, London, 2000), ch. 7; Masterman, R. and Hazell, R. 'Devolution and Westminster', in A. Trench (ed.) *The State of the Nations 2001: The Second Year of Devolution in the United Kingdom* (University of London Constitution Unit, London, 2001), ch. 9; Gay, O. 'Evolution from Devolution: the Experience at Westminster', in R Hazell (ed.), *The State of the Nations 2003: The Third Year of Devolution in the United Kingdom* (University of London Constitution Unit, London, 2003), ch. 7; and Lodge, G., Russell, M. and Gay, O. 'The Impact of Devolution on Westminster: If Not Now, When?', in A Trench (ed.) *Has Devolution Made a difference? The State of the Nations 2004* (University of London Constitution Unit, London, 2004), ch. 8.

3   *2nd report of 1997-98*, HC 460.

4   Op. cit., para. 10.

5   *The Procedural Consequences of Devolution*, 4th report of 1998-99, HC 185. See also an interesting Opposition Day debate on 11 May 1999, Hansard, House of Commons Debates, vol. 331, cols 174–224.

6   *Procedural Consequences of Devolution*, para. 5.

7   Procedure Committee, *First Special Report of 1998-99*, HC 814.

8   Welsh Questions and Points of Order, 7 July 1999, Hansard, House of Commons Debates, vol. 334, cols 1013ff, 1045–7; Speaker's statement, 12 July 1999, Hansard, House of Commons Debates, vol. 335, cols 21–2. The committee report and the government response were debated on 21 October 1999, Hansard, House of Commons Debates, vol. 336, cols 606ff, and the relevant changes to standing orders and related resolutions were debated and agreed on 25 October, Hansard, House of Commons Debates, vol. 336, cols 761ff.

9   December 2001, Cm 5240, paras 13–16. On the theory and practice of the Sewel convention see Winetrobe, B. 'Counter-devolution? The Sewel Convention on Devolved Legislation at Westminster', *Scottish Law and Practice Quarterly*, 2001, vol. 6, p. 286; Page, A. and Batey, A. 'Scotland's Other Parliament: Westminster Legislation about Devolved Matters in Scotland

since Devolution', *Public Law*, 2002, p. 501; Burrows, N. 'This is Scotland's Parliament: Let Scotland's Parliament Legislate', *Juridical Review*, 2002, p. 213.

10 See Welsh Affairs Select Committee, *The Primary Legislative Process as It Affects Wales*, 4th report of 2002–03, HC 79; the Government's response, *WASC*, 3rd Special Report of 2002–03, HC 989; the report of the (Richard) Commission on the powers and electoral arrangements of the National Assembly for Wales, March 2004, esp. chap. 8; Rawlings, R. *Delineating Wales* (University of Wales Press, Cardiff, 2003), esp. chap. 9.

11 Donald Dewar, John P. Mackintosh Lecture, 9 November 1999. <http://www.scotland.gov.uk/news/1999/11/se1244.asp

12 *Devolution: Inter-institutional Relations in the United Kingdom*, 2nd report of 2002–03, HL 28.

13 Scottish Parliament (Referendum) Bill [HL]. Though it failed to gain a second reading on 17 April 2002, it generated much interest in Scotland, and the Lords debate was interesting if a little idiosyncratic.

14 Again, this may not remain the case with Northern Ireland.

15 This was due to internal party selection policies, rather than any specific legal requirement.

16 See, in particular, Standards and Privileges Committee, *Remunerated Employment as a Member of Another Elected Body*, 12th report of 1998–99, HC 928.

17 MPs and members of devolved Parliaments/assemblies, especially those of the same party, often share their local office. See, generally, Russell, M., Bradbury, J. and Gay, O. 'Devolution and the Constituency Role of the British MP', paper presented to the Sixth Workshop of Parliamentarians and Parliamentary Scholars, Wroxton College, Oxfordshire, August 2004 (this is a preliminary report of current research in progress, expected to be published in 2005).

18 A recent innovation, which may presage greater cooperation between committees of the UK and devolved Parliaments/assemblies, is some joint work between Welsh Assembly and House of Commons committees. See Procedure Committee, *Joint Activities with the National Assembly for Wales*, 3rd report of 2003–04, HC 582, debated and agreed by the Commons on 7 June 2004, Hansard, House of Commons Debates, vol. 422, cols 73–90.

19 For details see B Winetrobe, 'Inter-Parliamentary relations in a devolved UK: an initial overview', *Devolution*, op. cit., Appendix 5, pp. 59–69.

20 See Murkens, J., Jones, P. and Keating, M. *Scottish Independence: a Practical Guide* (Edinburgh University Press, Edinburgh, 2002), especially Part 1.

21 Or, as some prefer to call it, the English Question.

22 The Constitutional Reform Bill, which implements certain of these, and related, changes, has been the subject of much dispute between the two Houses, and its enactment is far from certain at the time of writing.

23 Scottish Parliament (Constituencies) Act 2004. The practical impact of this decoupling, especially the voting system for the Scottish Parliament and the ending of coterminous electoral boundaries for Commons and Holyrood constituencies, is being examined by a committee set up by the Secretary of State for Scotland.

24 See generally *Changed Voting, Changed Politics, final report of the Independent Commission on Proportional Representation*, March 2004.

25 Winetrobe, B. *Realising the Vision – a Parliament with a Purpose: an Audit of the First Year of*

the *Scottish Parliament,* (University of London Constitution Unit, London, 2001).

26 See *Changed Voting, Changed Politics,* cited above.

27 See, in particular, Modernisation Committee, *Connecting Parliament with the Public,* 1st report of 2003–04, HC 368, in relation to aspects such as visitor centres, partner libraries, education services and public petitions.

28 See *Connecting Parliament with the Public,* cited above.

29 Winetrobe, B. 'Political but Not Partisan: Marketing Parliaments and Their Members', *Journal of Legislative Studies,* 2003, vol. 9, no. 1.

FIFTEEN

Parliament and the European Union: Refrigerators, Readings and Reforms

Dr Richard Whitaker

Membership of the European Union (EU) has profoundly affected the legislative process in the UK. Every department in British government now has to take account of legislation emerging from the EU's institutions. Westminster has adapted to this situation by developing mechanisms for scrutinising EU legislative proposals in an attempt to hold ministers to account and to ensure that the public is informed about EU measures likely to affect the UK. Scrutiny takes place principally through dedicated committees in both the House of Commons and the House of Lords. While the House of Commons examines a wide range of documents in brief, the House of Lords provide in-depth reports on areas of EU policy of significance for the UK. In theory, these two approaches complement each other but in reality there are problems with both. Suggestions for reform of this system range from procedural issues, such as the time allowed for discussion of EU documents, to fundamental changes, including the need for much more direct involvement of national Parliaments in the EU's legislative process.

The scrutiny reserve

The process of analysing EU documents in both the Commons and the Lords is underpinned by the scrutiny reserve, which holds that ministers must not agree to EU legislation in the Council of Ministers until the relevant proposals have completed their process of scrutiny at Westminster. Exceptions can be made for confidential, routine or trivial matters but in any other cases where ministers fail to ensure scrutiny is complete before making decisions on EU legislation, they must explain their actions to the relevant committees at the earliest possible opportunity. The Cabinet Office provides biannual reports of scrutiny reserve breaches and the Commons' European Scrutiny Committee, described below, calls ministers to provide explanations where necessary, as it did four times in 2002. Such requests of ministers were unnecessary in 2003, reflecting the higher priority given by members of the government to this issue and the efforts of the Cabinet Office in drawing attention to documents that may bring about scrutiny difficulties.[1] Both the Commons and the Lords view this system as working fairly well although its effectiveness is sometimes reduced by the nature of the co-decision procedure in the EU, discussed below.

Scrutiny in the Commons

The engine room of EU scrutiny in the Commons is the European Scrutiny Committee (ESC). The ESC receives copies of all of the European Commission's legislative proposals, each of which is accompanied by an explanatory memorandum (EM) from the relevant government department explaining the government's views on and the implications of the proposal. The committee's main functions are to sift these documents, to pick out any that raise questions of political and legal importance for the UK, to press ministers for further information on Commission proposals where this is necessary, and to select documents for debate. The committee can also ask other Commons committees to prepare an opinion on any EU document, a considerable power when compared with the abilities of other select committees.

The ESC receives an average of around 1,250 documents each year, of which typically about five will be recommended for debate on the floor of the House. However, such debates are often poorly attended and frequently attract the same group of interested individuals without engaging the wider membership of the House. In response to this problem the Commons established permanent European standing committees in 1991, of which there are currently three, each taking on a different set of EU policy areas. The ESC currently sends an average of 44 documents each year to the standing committees. Once a document has been discussed in standing committee, a related motion is moved in the House without debate. If this is passed, then the scrutiny process for that document is complete. The use of EU standing committees enables a broad range of MPs to be involved in the examination of EU proposals and provides an efficient method of debating their significance for the UK. The ESC itself has a diverse membership of sixteen backbenchers ranging from Eurosceptics to pro-Europeanists and includes a former member of the European Parliament (MEP) and one of Westminster's representatives in the European Convention.

In addition to its detailed examination of legislative proposals, the ESC draws up reports on matters of broad significance in the EU. In response to publication of the EU's draft constitutional treaty in May 2003, the ESC presented a critical analysis of the Constitutional Convention and its suggestions for the role of national Parliaments.[2] This followed a report on the wider issues of democracy and accountability in the EU.[3] Increasingly, the committee takes oral evidence as part of its investigations. In 2003, for example, experts gave evidence before the committee on several issues of particular interest in the UK, such as the European Convention's proposals on criminal justice, the draft constitutional treaty and reform of the Common Fisheries Policy. The ESC also questions ministers in writing before and after meetings of the Council at which EU legislative decisions are made. Improvements in the quality of ministers' answers mean that the committee is now well informed about the stances adopted by the government in Council negotiations.

The ESC has taken other steps to improve its scrutiny of EU proposals in recent years. Since 2002, it has undertaken detailed examination of the Commission's Annual Work Programme by taking oral evidence from Commission officials. Such activity allows the committee to gain an understanding, early on in the legislative process of the issues likely to be of concern to the UK in the forthcoming year. February 2003 also saw the ESC hold an informal meeting at Westminster, for the first time, with British MEPs, followed up with a second meeting later in the year. The committee's positive response to these events suggests they are likely to continue in the future, thus allowing the ESC to tap into a rich source of information regarding the EU's legislative activities and their consequences for the UK.

Scrutiny in the Lords

The House of Lords has similarly established committees for dealing with EU legislative proposals but these tend to focus their attention on a smaller number of in-depth investigations. The House of Lords has a European Union Select Committee with seven subcommittees, each covering a different area of EU policy. Each subcommittee includes members of the main committee and others who are coopted due to their expertise in a particular policy area. One of the major benefits of the Lords is its ability to draw on the knowledge of peers from a wide range of backgrounds including previous members of government, the Civil Service, the European Parliament and those with experience relevant to particular policy sectors.

Rather than considering all EU documents deposited at Westminster, the Lords' EU Select Committee chairman sifts the documents on a weekly basis and refers those of political importance to the relevant subcommittee. Around one-quarter of the documents received are referred to such committees each year.4 Such documents are either cleared from scrutiny with little or no comment or become the subject of an in-depth investigation that may involve taking a considerable amount of oral and written evidence and which will result in the publication of a report. Such reports, of which there are around 20 to 30 each year, have a reputation in Westminster and elsewhere in the EU for providing authoritative assessments of EU policy developments.5 Topics covered recently have included the EU's Working Time Directive, the future role of the European Court of Justice and developments in EU foreign policy. These reports offer opinions on the merits of proposed EU legislation, in contrast with the work of the Commons' ESC, which concentrates only on drawing attention to the significance of documents. As with the ESC, members of the Lords' EU Select Committee take part in meetings with MEPs and both committees further their work through collaboration with European affairs committees in other national Parliaments and the European Parliament, a process which is coordinated by the Conference of European Affairs Committees.

Problems with parliamentary scrutiny

The scrutiny of European legislation at Westminster has a number of shortcomings, some of which relate to the EU, others to the government. Since the Amsterdam treaty the EU has had to ensure a six-week period between the publication of a Commission proposal and any decisions on that proposal in the Council of Ministers. This is to ensure there is sufficient time for national Parliaments to examine legislation before Council decisions are made. However, the changing presidency of the European Council can lead to difficulties in this respect. Member states holding the presidency are often eager to ensure the passage of certain legislation prior to the end of their six months in the chair, thus leaving insufficient time for parliamentary scrutiny of proposals.6 This process is complicated by the EU's co-decision procedure, which involves the Council and European

Parliament. At its most lengthy, the procedure entails two readings, a conciliation committee and a final reading in each institution.[7] Legislative proposals can change considerably during this process thus decreasing the value of scrutiny carried out at the initiation stage. If the European constitution's proposals to extend co-decision come into force, this problem would be exacerbated.

Westminster-based problems include the late arrival of explanatory memorandums. This is rare but can cause difficulties for completing scrutiny before decisions have to be made in the Council. The ESC reported two occasions in 2001/2 when the Home Office and the Treasury were unable to agree on who should take responsibility for a particular EM, thus delaying its presentation to the committee by several months.[8] More serious questions were raised following the problems of implementing the EU regulation on ozone-depleting substances in 2002. A failure to identify the implications of this early on led to the growth of so-called 'fridge mountains' due to a lack of equipment for removing harmful gases from refrigerators prior to their recycling. The scale of this problem was not foreseen despite the regulation passing through the scrutiny process at Westminster.

Reforms

These difficulties have led to questions about the principles on which scrutiny of EU proposals are based in the UK. Comparisons have been made with the Danish system, which differs fundamentally in basing its scrutiny around meetings of the Council of Ministers rather than on examining documents.[9] Members of the Danish European Affairs Committee establish mandates binding on their ministers prior to Council meetings. Ministers are thus accountable to Parliament for their actions and must gain the European Affairs Committee's support before moving beyond the mandate agreed. Although this system is considered one of the most effective in the EU for ensuring national parliamentary control, neither of the EU committees at Westminster is in favour of adopting it in the UK. They argue that it would reduce the government's ability to bargain effectively, leave the EU committees with little time to consider proposals and would elevate the relevant committees to a position of power well beyond that of committees in general at Westminster.[10]

Further suggestions for reform include formalising the links between MEPs and their counterparts at Westminster.[11] Although meetings do take place between the two groups of parliamentarians, were these to be more frequent, they would allow MPs to obtain further advance information about significant proposals in the pipeline and to benefit from the insider knowledge of MEPs with direct experience of the EU legislative processes. The UK compares unfavourably in this respect with Germany, where the Bundestag's EU Affairs Committee includes fourteen German MEPs among its membership, although the latter do not have voting rights.

The ability to scrutinise proposals in detail and in the context of national legislation might be improved by channelling EU legislative proposals to the relevant select committee in the Commons rather than to a single European scrutiny committee. Such a system would allow the Commons to benefit from the expertise of select committee members in specific policy areas when examining EU legislation. A less dramatic change would involve retaining the ESC but encouraging the departmental select committees (DSCs) to produce more reports on EU-specific matters within their jurisdictions. As Lord Norton of Louth has argued,[12] select committees have a higher profile than the ESC and would therefore be able to bring EU matters to the attention of a larger proportion of MPs and the public than is currently the case. The ESC favours this option and, in particular, would like to see much more discussion of Commission Green and White Papers within DSCs.[13] Nevertheless, any moves in this direction are likely to be hindered by the current heavy workload of members of select committees, which makes finding time for scrutiny of EU proposals difficult.

This is related to a wider problem with European scrutiny at Westminster, namely that MPs and the media alike take little interest in the details of EU policies. As Peter Riddell argues,[14] procedural changes are unlikely to make a great deal of difference unless MPs are willing to take European scrutiny seriously.

The European Constitution and the role of national Parliaments

The difficulties for Westminster in influencing the EU legislative process may be slightly eased by provisions on the role of national Parliaments in the EU's draft constitution. Prior to the completion of the European Convention's work on the EU constitution, the ESC argued for a greater role for national Parliaments in the EU's legislative process.[15] Specifically, their report recommended that national Parliaments should be given more involvement in assessing the consistency of EU legislative proposals with the principle of subsidiarity, which refers to making decisions at the lowest appropriate level. The draft EU constitution goes some way towards implementing the ESC's recommendations in this regard and represents a step forward for national Parliaments' involvement in scrutinising EU legislative proposals. According to the draft constitution, within six weeks of the publication of a Commission legislative proposal, national Parliaments may indicate their opinion that the proposed legislation does not conform to the principle of subsidiarity. Member states with unicameral Parliaments will be given two votes each in this procedure, while those with bicameral legislatures will be assigned one vote for each chamber. If at least one-third of votes are in favour of a proposal's non-compliance with subsidiarity then the Commission must review the proposal. Thus, although national Parliaments would not be able to force the Commission to withdraw its proposed legislation, they would at least able to indicate their objections officially. Arguably, it may then become politically difficult for the Commission to maintain a proposal, especially if a large proportion of national Parliaments are opposed.

These provisions are certainly important in formally bringing the national Parliaments within the EU legislative process, but they are regarded by the

ESC as inadequate.[16] Although the committee is opposed to providing national Parliaments with a veto over EU legislation, it has argued for a strengthening of their role in applying subsidiarity. Specifically, the ESC recommends that the Commission should be forced to withdraw its proposal if two-thirds of votes among national Parliaments oppose a particular item. The committee would also like to see an opportunity for national Parliaments to submit opinions following the convening of a conciliation committee in the co-decision procedure. These changes have not been taken up in the constitution as agreed by the heads of government in June 2004 and only time will tell whether pressure from national Parliaments will bring about further change in the future.

Conclusion

Parliament has developed a thorough system of scrutinising EU legislative proposals with two contrasting and complimentary approaches, which together allow Westminster to keep abreast of the major developments in EU policy. Recent changes have seen increased links between Westminster and British MEPs, fewer serious breaches of the scrutiny reserve and more detailed examination of the Commission's annual plans for legislation. Nevertheless, the system suffers some defects. In particular there are occasionally restrictions on the time available for scrutinising EU documents, either due to their late arrival from Brussels or as a result of interdepartmental wrangling in Whitehall over responsibility for a particular policy proposal. Furthermore, the increased use of the co-decision procedure can mean that legislation changes substantially over the course of the legislative process, thus decreasing the value of scrutiny at the initiation stage. Changes introduced in the European Constitution may go some way towards improving the role of national Parliaments by allowing them to assess legislation against the principle of subsidiarity. However, substantial improvements in the scrutiny process may require not only stronger powers in forcing the Commission to withdraw proposals, but also renewed attempts to include a larger proportion of MPs and the public in debates on proposed EU legislation.

Endnotes

1   House of Commons, European Scrutiny Committee, *The Committee's Work in 2003*, HC 42-viii, 2003–04.

2   House of Commons, European Scrutiny Committee, *The Convention on the Future of Europe and the Role of National Parliaments*, HC 63-xxiv, 2002–03.

3   House of Commons, European Scrutiny Committee, *Democracy and Accountability in the EU and the Role of National Parliaments*, HC 152-xxxiii-I, 2001–02.

4   House of Lords, Select Committee on the European Union, *Annual Report*, HL 191, 2002–03.

5   Norton, P. 'The United Kingdom: Political Conflict, parliamentary Scrutiny', in P. Norton (ed.) *National Parliaments and the European Union* (Frank Cass, London, 1996), p. 102.

6   House of Commons, European Scrutiny Committee, *The Committee's Work in 2002*, HC 63-viii, 2002–03.

7   For a fuller description of the co-decision procedure see Judge, D. and Earnshaw, D. *The European Parliament* (Palgrave, Basingstoke, 2003), pp. 203–7, or Corbett, R., Jacobs, J. F. and Shackleton, M. *The European Parliament* (5th ed.) (John Harper, London, 2003), pp. 183–95.

8   House of Commons, European Scrutiny Committee, *European Scrutiny in the Commons*, HC 152-xxx, 2001–02.

9   Arter, D. 'The Folketing and Denmark's "European Policy": the Case of an "Authorising Assembly"', in Norton, *National Parliaments and the European Union.*

10 *European Scrutiny in the Commons.*

11 For example see Riddell, P. *Parliament under Blair* (Politico's, London, 2000), pp. 33–4.

12 Lord Norton of Louth, Memorandum, *Minutes of Evidence Taken before the European Scrutiny Committee*, Wednesday 7 November 2001, HC 152-xxxiii-II, 2001–02.

13 *European Scrutiny in the Commons.*

14 Riddell, *Parliament under Blair*, p. 38.

15 *Democracy and Accountability in the EU and the Role of National Parliaments.*

16 *The Convention on the Future of Europe and the Role of National Parliaments.*

SIXTEEN

Parliament and the Courts

Lord Norton of Louth

For much of the twentieth century, Parliament and the courts operated essentially as discrete entities. The courts operated independently of Parliament, though formally subordinate to it. Parliament made the law and, under the Diceyan doctrine of parliamentary supremacy, the outputs of Parliament could be set aside by no body other than Parliament itself. The doctrine was confirmed by the Glorious Revolution of 1688–9. If the King was bound by the will of Parliament, then so too were his courts. The courts were thus denied the power to engage in constitutional review. Their principal task became one of statutory interpretation. It was not their sole role. They interpreted and developed the common law, enabling them to protect fundamental tenets of human rights, such as the right to a fair trial. 'Such human rights as the law of this country recognises', wrote F. A. Mann, 'are almost entirely judge-made and in many instances involve no more than a rebuttable presumption to the effect that Parliament is unlikely to have intended to interfere with or destroy them.'[1] That presumption nonetheless enabled Parliament and the courts to operate independently of one another. Parliament enacted a growing volume of legislation, but as long as it did not conflict violently with the basic principles of the rule of law generated and protected by the courts, then there was no major clash between the legislature and the courts. Neither encroached on the domain of the other.

The only exception to the separation of the two branches was at the top. Parliament was the high court of Parliament and one chamber, the House of Lords, remained the highest domestic court of appeal. However, the reality was that the House of Lords operated as two bodies, one legislative and the other judicial. Formally, the House in its judicial capacity was the whole House. In practice, it comprised the Appellate Committee of the House. Only the Law Lords (appointed to the House to serve as judges) and other peers who had held high judicial office were eligible to hear cases. Decisions were still given in the chamber, but it was at a time separate from other sittings and with lawyers below the bar and usually only the Law Lords in the chamber.

It was thus possible for the courts and Parliament to be studied as distinct bodies, with little overlap between them. Law students could study the legal process with little or no reference to Parliament; to them, the House of Lords meant the Appellate Committee. Political scientists could study Parliament with little or no reference to the courts. To them, the House of Lords was one chamber of the legislature. The courts were not part of 'politics'. This distinct relationship existed within the context of what was seen as a settled constitutional framework.

That framework, however, did not remain settled. Over the past four decades, there have been significant constitutional changes that have affected the relationship between Parliament and the courts. The relationship is far less distinct than it was. In 2003, the government published its proposals to create a Supreme Court, separating the Law Lords from the House of Lords. The proposal could be seen as ironic given that the previous decades had witnessed changes that had rendered the separation between the two branches less clear than ever before. More precise institutional definition could not mask the fact that the courts were occupying a good part of the constitutional domain previously ascribed to Parliament.

The courts and the constitution

One of the most significant constitutional developments since the 1970s has been the extent to which the constitution has acquired a judicial dimension. The courts have, in effect, been brought into politics. The US Supreme Court, as James J. Magee observed, is neither a court nor a political agency; 'it is inseparably both.'[2] That now could be said of the higher courts in the UK. The constitution has acquired a new judicial dimension because of measures passed by Parliament. The three most important changes that have had this effect are membership of the European Community (now the European Union), devolution, and the Human Rights Act.

British membership of the EU

Under the terms of British membership of the European Union, European law takes precedence over UK law. This precedence was established by the European Court of Justice and was in place when Parliament enacted the European Communities Act in 1972. It is for the courts to interpret the law and to determine if there is a conflict. If there is a clash, then the UK law has to give way to EU law. Though the implications were not necessarily fully appreciated at the time of entry, they became more apparent as a result of a number of court cases in the 1990s. In 1990–92, in the Factortame case, the Divisional Court suspended the operation of an Act of Parliament until the European Court of Justice had ruled on the case. In 1994, in *R. v. Secretary of State for Employment, ex p. the Equal Opportunities Commission*, the House of Lords held certain provisions of the 1978 Employment Protection (Consolidation) Act to be unlawful.[3] In the latter case, *The Times* asserted that the country may have acquired, in the House of Lords, 'a constitutional court'.[4]

What the House of Lords may have acquired in its judicial capacity, it may have lost in its legislative capacity. The consequence of membership of the EC was to undermine the doctrine of parliamentary supremacy. Parliament was giving to the courts the power to strike down legislation deemed by judges to be incompatible with European law. Formally, the doctrine remains extant in that Parliament retains the power to repeal the European Communities Act. However, so long as the Act remains in force, the doctrine has been suspended by Parliament in respect of European law. The scope of European law has expanded with successive treaties: the Single European Act, the Treaty on European Union, the Amsterdam treaty and the Nice treaty have extended the sectors that fall within the competence of the EU. The effect of each has not only been to extend the domain of the EU but also of the courts. As the power of the courts has increased, so the independent capacity of individual national parliaments to affect EU decision-making has decreased. This has been the case especially with the extension of qualified majority voting in the Council of Ministers under the Single European Act.

Judicial involvement is also set to expand if the provisions of the Treaty Establishing a Constitution for Europe are ratified. The policing of the treaty will be a matter for the courts. The treaty not only embodies a primacy clause – 'The Constitution, and laws adopted by the Union's Institutions in exercising competences on it, shall have primacy over the law of the Member States' – but also incorporates the Charter of Fundamental Rights.[5] The provisions will serve to develop significantly the judicial dimension of the constitution.

Devolution

Devolution of powers to elected bodies in different parts of the United Kingdom has enhanced the position of the courts in that they have become, in effect, constitutional courts for Scotland, Wales and Northern Ireland. The devolved bodies are created by Act of Parliament and it is for the courts to interpret the legislation. A law passed by the Scottish Parliament, for example, may be challenged for exceeding the powers conferred by the Scotland Act. What are termed 'devolution issues' can be appealed to the Judicial Committee of the Privy Council. (Twelve cases had been considered by the committee up to the beginning of 2004.) The position gives great scope to judges, as they can give the legislation a narrow or broad interpretation.

The effect of devolving legislative powers to the Scottish Parliament has been to limit the Westminster Parliament's scope for legislating.[6] The restriction is a self-imposed one. The doctrine of parliamentary supremacy is embodied in the Scotland Act, enabling Parliament – should it so wish – to legislate in areas devolved to the Scottish Parliament. It chooses not to do so, unless invited to do so through what have become known as Sewell motions.

Devolution thus has the effect of contributing to the judicialisation of the constitution, conferring a greater role on the courts, while limiting Parliament in the legislative domain.

Human Rights Act

The Human Rights Act 1998 was the product of lengthy debate over the need for some greater judicial protection of human rights in the United Kingdom. In constitutional terms, it represents a significant shift in how the constitution is viewed. Traditionally, positive constitutionalism underpinned our constitutional arrangements: that is, the constitution was seen as enabling the will of the people to be paramount. That will was expressed through and, as necessary, tempered by Parliament. Parliament had the power to limit the liberty of the individual but at the same time was the ultimate protector of liberty in the UK. Parliament was viewed by supporters of the existing constitutional framework as fulfilling well its role as protector of liberty.[7] However, exponents of negative constitutionalism began to be heard: they viewed the constitution as a means of constraint and of embodying certain overarching prepolitical values. They took a jaundiced view of a political system in which a government, secure in a majority in the House of Commons, could achieve the enactment of legislation that could limit, even destroy, the rights of individuals. Calls for a Bill of Rights, embodying basic rights, began to be made in the 1960s and gathered pace in subsequent decades.[8] These calls, as David Feldman has noted, were reinforced by Britain's growing international obligations.[9]

The result of these pressures was the enactment of the Human Rights Act 1998, incorporating the provisions of the European Convention on Human

Rights (ECHR) into British law. The Act makes it unlawful for public bodies to act in a way that is incompatible with the provisions of the convention. A consequence is that the courts may on occasion have to determine whether some provisions of UK law are incompatible with convention rights. The change to judicial process has been substantial. In order to ensure judges were able to cope, full implementation of the Act was delayed until October 2000 in order to provide adequate training and preparation. The effect of the Act has already begun to be seen in a number of cases, though not as many as some critics had been expecting.

The effect on Parliament has been to limit the scope of its legislative capacity. It is expected not to legislate in a way that renders the measure incompatible with the ECHR. Formally, though, Parliament is free to do so. Under the 1998 Act, the courts are precluded from striking down a measure of UK law as being incompatible with the convention. What the courts are empowered to do is issue statements of incompatibility. It is then for Parliament to act in order to bring the law into line with the provisions of the ECHR. Parliament has introduced a fast-track procedure for changing the law in such cases. Though the minister responsible for the 1998 Act, the then Lord Chancellor Lord Irvine, stressed that Parliament was not bound to accept the statements by the courts, the presumption – borne out in practice – is that Parliament will normally legislate as a consequence of such statements. By the end of 2003, the courts had issued statements of incompatibility in fifteen cases, though five of these were overturned on appeal.[10] Of the ten not overturned on appeal, eight have already resulted in orders or legislation to bring the law into line with the declaration of the courts. In April 2003, for example, in the case of *Bellinger v. Bellinger*, the courts held that Section 11(c) of the Matrimonial Causes Act 1973 was incompatible with Articles 8 and 12 of the convention. In the next session of Parliament, the government introduced the Gender Recognition Bill – conferring rights on those who changed gender, including the right to a new birth certificate – to bring the law into line with the court's interpretation of the convention.

Parliament thus accepts some element of self-constraint as a consequence of the Human Rights Act. It can be argued that the greatest limitation imposed by the Act is on government. Government departments had to prepare for the implementation of the Act and to ensure that they were compliant with convention rights. The 1998 Act, under Section 19(1)(a), imposes a requirement on ministers to certify, on the face of a Bill, that in their opinion the measure is compatible with convention rights. Parliament has contributed to this constraint by creating the Joint Committee on Human Rights.

Parliament and human rights

The Royal Commission on Reform of the House of Lords (the Wakeham commission) recommended that the House of Lords create a constitution committee and that it have a subcommittee dealing with human rights. In the event, though the House did establish the Constitution Committee, both Houses agreed to the separate establishment of the Joint Committee on Human Rights. The members of both committees were appointed at the beginning of 2001.

The Joint Committee on Human Rights comprises twelve members, six drawn from the House of Commons and six drawn from the House of Lords, with terms of reference that permit it to consider 'matters relating to human rights in the UK' (though not individual cases) and proposals for the fast-track procedure and whether or not they should be drawn to the attention of the House. The committee has the usual powers of a select committee to require the submission of written evidence and documents and to examine witnesses, as well as to appoint special advisers. Where the procedures adopted by the two Houses differ, the Committee utilises Lords procedures.

In its first special report, the committee stressed the importance it attached to the scrutiny of Bills in relation to human rights issues.

We have therefore adopted a procedure whereby all Government bills (and possibly other categories of bills) will be examined by the Committee, taking advice from our Legal Adviser. Where appropriate our Chairman will put written questions to the relevant Minister in charge of the bill and we may, in the light of the answers we receive, decide to conduct a detailed inquiry into the bill.[11]

From 2001 until 2004, the committee's salaried legal adviser was a leading law professor, Professor David Feldman of Birmingham University. The legal adviser examines each Bill and reports to the committee on whether or not it has implications for human rights. The committee normally, though not always, accepts that advice. The committee itself benefits from having some senior figures among its membership. It is chaired by Jean Corston, who also is chair of the Parliamentary Labour Party, and among the membership is the Liberal Democrat peer and QC Lord Lester of Herne Hill, one of the leading lawyers in the movement to incorporate the ECHR into British law.

The committee's first report was into the implementation of the Human Rights Act. The committee examined the extent to which departments had prepared for the implementation of the Act and had begun to build a 'human rights culture', largely relying on the evidence to speak for itself. It then went on to consider a number of important Bills, including the Criminal Justice and Police Bill. Since its inception, the committee has been active and influential, the government variously acting on its recommendations. Perhaps the most high-profile success of the committee has been in successfully making the case for a human rights commission to promote and protect human rights in England and Wales.[12]

Parliament's role as protector of the rights of the citizen has thus changed. Parliament has enacted a measure of protection, in effect limiting its own capacity to determine rights, and then established a body to ensure that measures introduced into Parliament comply with those provisions. Despite occasional controversy – the committee attracted criticism for arguing that an amendment made to the Adoption and Children Bill in 2002 was incompatible with the ECHR – the committee has established itself as an important component of Parliament's scrutiny regime. It also shows the utility of drawing on the expertise of members of both Houses, something that is being built upon with the use of joint committees for the scrutiny of draft Bills.

The courts and parliamentary proceedings

The detachment of the courts from Parliament has also been eroded by a greater willingness on the part of the courts to look at what goes on within Parliament. The courts prior to 1993 held to the rule that in interpreting statute law they looked at the words on the face of the Act: they did not look at proceedings in Parliament as an aid to understanding the intentions of Parliament. That long-standing rule was set aside in 1993, in the case of *Pepper v. Hart*, when the House of Lords held that the courts could look at parliamentary material for the purpose of resolving any ambiguity or obscurity in the statute. According to Lord Browne-Wilkinson, reference to parliamentary material was permissible where 'legislation is ambiguous or obscure, or leads to an absurdity,' where the material relied on or consisted of a statement by a minister or promoter of the Bill, and where the statements were clear.[13] In practice, since that ruling, the courts have often applied a much more liberal interpretation than that given by Lord Browne-Wilkinson. As Kenny Mullan concluded on the basis of his study of cases where judges had recourse to parliamentary material:

> *Judges were ready to hear submissions on and view the contents of parliamentary material before they had made a decision to admit such material under the ruling in* Pepper v. Hart. *The courts were using the material to confirm the construction of the legislation which they had already discovered. The judges appeared to be willing to extend the meaning of 'ambiguity' and 'obscurity' and to broaden the range of admissible parlia-*

mentary material by arguing that it was necessary to understand the
statements of Ministers and their effect. Further, it was also clear that
judges were willing to refer to Hansard without giving a clear basis for
their decision and without indicating that the basis for that recourse was
the decision in Pepper v. Hart.[14]

Having previously denied themselves the opportunity to have recourse to parliamentary material, the courts have now embraced the opportunity to do so and on a scale not apparently intended by the House of Lords.

The ability to have recourse to parliamentary material has been further extended as a result of judgments in the case of *Wilson and others v. Secretary of State for Trade and Industry* (2003). The case involved the Consumer Credit Act 1974. The Court of Appeal in 2001 made a declaration that Section 127(3) of the Act was incompatible with the ECHR. In so doing, it had recourse to parliamentary proceedings, not as an aid to interpretation, but in order to determine why Parliament enacted Section 127(3). Although the parliamentary material was found to be inconclusive – the court said that the debates 'tend to confuse rather than illuminate' – the action of the court was challenged. By looking at debates to see if the policy behind a Bill was justifiable in terms of the ECHR and proportionate to the remedy proposed, the courts were in danger of 'questioning' what was said in Parliament, something that was expressly forbidden by Article 9 of the Bill of Rights 1689. The case was appealed to the House of Lords. Their Lordships decided that the Court of Appeal had gone too far in delving into the reasoning behind the provision.[15] They considered that it was permissible to look at debates to determine the mischief that the measure sought to address and that parliamentary material constituted one of several sources to determine compatibility. However, to consider parliamentary debates to see if they offered an acceptable justification was, in the words of Lord Hobhouse of Woodborough, 'an unacceptable approach and likely to give rise to abuse'.[16]

Though their Lordships adopted a robust tone in rejecting the approach of the Appeal Court, they nonetheless thus upheld the right of the courts to have recourse to parliamentary material in order to determine, along with other material extrinsic to parliamentary proceedings, whether a statutory provision was compatible with convention rights. As such, they were extending the right of the courts to examine parliamentary material.

The courts have thus been prepared to examine parliamentary material in a way that they were not prepared to do before 1993 (though ministerial statements were considered in cases of judicial review). It is arguable that in so doing, they have not so much strengthened their own position but rather that of Parliament. By examining Hansard, they are able to resolve ambiguities – ensuring that what Parliament intended is thus recognised – and to identify the mischief which a particular provision seeks to address. Had the Court of Appeal's approach in Wilson been adopted, then the situation would be very different.

There are dangers in eroding the dividing line between courts and Parliaments. Parliament has been sensitive to any moves that may lead to an encroachment of Article 9 of the Bill of Rights. In 1993, Lord Rees-Mogg sought judicial review of the government's power to ratify the Maastricht treaty. He was granted leave to seek a review by the High Court. This action was challenged in the House of Commons by Tony Benn MP on the grounds that it was a breach of privilege as the Bill giving effect to the treaty – the European Communities (Amendment) Bill – was still before Parliament. The Speaker, Betty Boothroyd, held that it was not a breach as the Bill had left the House of Commons. However, in an unusual move, she delivered a statement reminding the courts of the Bill of Rights and that the proceedings of Parliament could not be challenged by the courts. In the Wilson case in 2003, both the Speaker of the House of Commons and the Clerk of the Parliaments intervened to express concern over the 'wider significance' of the exercise undertaken by the Court of Appeal. The House of Lords has generally been sensitive to these concerns. The actions of lower courts in their interpretation of *Pepper v. Hart*, and the Court of Appeal in Wilson, raise concerns as to whether other courts share these sensitivities.

Parliament and a Supreme Court

The detachment of the judiciary from politics has been variously eroded. The measures we have outlined above have ensured such erosion. In June 2003 the government announced proposals for the creation of a distinct Supreme Court, in effect removing the Law Lords from the House of Lords. Though this can be seen as offering a physical detachment from Parliament, and thus arguably ensuring a greater degree of independence of the judiciary from Parliament, the effect may be to give the courts a much higher political profile.

The government argued that, in creating a Supreme Court, it would 'reflect and enhance the independence of the Judiciary from both the legislature and the executive'.[17] The proposal was supported by the senior Law Lord, Lord Bingham, and three other Law Lords. They said that they regarded the functional separation of the judiciary at all levels from the legislature and the executive 'as a cardinal feature of a modern, liberal, democratic state governed by the rule of law'.[18]

However, the proposals ran into opposition from other judges, including from six Law Lords. The Law Lords said that they regarded the creation of a Supreme Court as unnecessary and potentially harmful. Their position was summarised in the Law Lords' response to the government's consultation document:

> *The present arrangements work well. They believe that the Law Lords'*
> *presence in the House [of Lords] is of benefit to the Law Lords, to the House,*
> *and to others including the litigants. Appeals are heard in a unique, suitably*
> *prestigious, setting for this country's court of final appeal. The 'House of*
> *Lords' as a judicial body is recognised by that name throughout the common*

law world. Overall, it is believed, it has a fine record and reputation. The Law Lords who do not support the proposed change consider these real advantages need not be, and should not be, put in jeopardy.[19]

The implications for the relationship between the House of Lords in its legislative capacity and in its judicial capacity are of particular concern here. The retention of the Law Lords in the House of Lords arguably enables legislators to appreciate the work and role of the Law Lords. This helps reduce the potential for conflict between Parliament and the courts. The House of Lords in its legislative capacity can act as something of a protector of the House in its judicial capacity. The Law Lords, for their part, are better able to understand the role of the legislature. The interaction does not jeopardise the independence or the integrity of the judges but enhances their understanding.[20]

The creation of a Supreme Court, on the other hand, has the potential to widen the gap between judges and ministers. The Supreme Court will sit in splendid isolation from the legislature and the executive. Over time, the potential for understanding will decline as the existing Law Lords – with knowledge and experience of Parliament – are replaced by judges with no experience of Parliament. Recent years have seen some notable clashes between ministers and judges. The danger of having the highest court completely detached from Parliament is that those clashes will become more severe, as the means for tempering them disappear. There is also the danger that the sensitivity shown by the House of Lords in Wilson may be replaced by the more strident approach adopted by the Court of Appeal.

The creation of a Supreme Court was linked to the government's proposals to abolish the post of Lord Chancellor and create a judicial appointments commission. The decision to abolish the post of Lord Chancellor was challenged on the grounds that it would remove a senior figure from Cabinet who had been able to explain and defend the position of the judiciary. Following agreement with the Lord Chief Justice, the Secretary of State for

Constitutional Affairs, Lord Falconer, announced on 26 January 2004 that the Lord Chief Justice would become head of the judiciary and be titled President of the Courts in England and Wales.[21] There would be a statutory duty imposed on the constitutional affairs secretary to defend and uphold the continuing independence of the judiciary. The effect was nonetheless to sever the link provided previously by the Lord Chancellor. The change was justified in terms of the independence of the judiciary. The extent to which it did protect that independence was challenged by former Deputy Prime Minister Lord Howe of Aberavon:

> Does not that independence depend on, more than anything else, a network of conventions that have built up and observed with increasing good faith over the years? Is not the keystone of that arch of conventions the existence and presence of the Lord Chancellor? Do not all the changes that we have yet to consider in detail flow ... from the need to substitute for the existing structure of the constitution that has served us so well in so many respects?[22]

The effect of the changes is to raise the political profile of the courts. Who will be appointed to the highest court is likely to become a matter of political debate. Though the constitutional affairs secretary announced that his discretion would be severely circumscribed, the final decision on who to recommend to the Crown would rest with him. The more powerful the judiciary becomes, the greater the likelihood of the executive taking an interest in who is appointed to the highest court. The more detached the court is, the more vulnerable it is to attack from ministers.

Conclusion

The old certainties in the relationship between Parliament and the courts have given way to what amount to new uncertainties. O. Hood Phillips once wrote that the doctrine of parliamentary sovereignty 'may indeed be called the one fundamental law of the British Constitution'.23 That 'fundamental' law deter-mined the place of the judiciary in relation to Parliament. Parliament, largely by its own actions, has called into question the doctrine and, in so doing, has given a new role to the judiciary. The doctrine remains extant but disfigured. The relationship between Parliament and the courts has changed, is changing and, in the light of the government's reform proposals of 2003 and develop-ments in Britain's international obligations, will continue to change. The contours of the relationship are blurred and it may be some time before they can be seen in a clear, coherent light.

Endnotes

1 Mann, F. A. 'Britain's Bill of Rights', *Law Quarterly Review*, 1978, vol. 94, p. 514.

2 Magee, J. J. *Constitutional Vagaries and American Judicial Review* (University of Hull Politics Department, Hull, 1979).

3 See Maxwell, P. 'The House of Lords as a Constitutional Court: The Implications of Ex p. EOC', in P. Carmichael and B. Dickson (eds) *The House of Lords: Its Parliamentary and Judicial Roles* (Hart, Oxford, 1999), pp. 197–211.

4 *The Times*, 5 March 1994, cited in Maxwell, 'The House of Lords as a Constitutional Court', p. 197.

5 European Convention, *Draft Treaty Establishing a Constitution for Europe* (The European Communities, Luxembourg, 2003), Article 10 and Part II. On the constitutional implications, see House of Lords Constitution Committee, *The Draft Constitutional Treaty for the European Union*, ninth report, 2002–03, HL 168.

6 No legislative powers have been devolved to the Welsh Assembly. Legislative powers have been devolved to the Northern Ireland Assembly but, at the time of writing, it is suspended.

7 See, e.g. Butt, R. *The Power of Parliament* (Constable, London, 1967), p. 437.

8 For a summary, see Norton, P. *The Constitution in Flux* (Blackwell, Oxford, 1982), pp. 24–60.

9 Feldman, D. *Civil Liberties and Human Rights* (Clarendon Press, Oxford, 1993), pp. 62–9.

10 See www.humanrights.gov.uk/decihm.htm.

11 Joint Committee on Human Rights, *First Special Report: Criminal Justice and Police Bill*, Session 2000–01, HL 42, HC 296, para. 1.

12 Joint Committee on Human Rights, *The Case for a Human Rights Commission*, sixth report, Session 2002–03, HL 67-i, HC 489-i.

13 Cited in Mullan, K. 'The Impact of *Pepper v. Hart*', in Carmichael and Dickson, *House of Lords*, p. 214.

14 *Ibid.*, p. 237.

15 They also overturned the statement of incompatibility. The case is one of the five referred to above that have been overturned.

16   *Wilson and others v. Secretary of State for Trade and Industry (Appellant)*, [2003] UKHL 40, para. 143.

17   Department for Constitutional Affairs, *Constitutional Reform: A Supreme Court for the United Kingdom*, CP 11/03, July 2003, p. 4.

18   The Law Lords' Response to the Government's Consultation Paper on *Constitutional Reform: a Supreme Court for the United Kingdom*, p. 1.

19   *Ibid.*

20   See, for example, Lord Norton of Louth, 'The Proposal for a Supreme Court', evidence submitted to the House of Commons Constitutional Affairs Committee, 28 November 2003, HL 48–i, and, by the same author, 'Governing Alone', *Parliamentary Affairs*, September 2003.

21   House of Lords: Official Report, vol. 657, cols 12–17, 26 January 2004. Department for Constitutional Affairs, *Constitutional Reform. The Lord Chancellor's Judiciary-Related Functions: Proposals*, January 2004.

22   House of Lords: Official Report, vol. 657, cols. 26–7, 26 January 2004.

23   Hood Phillips, O. and Jackson, P. O. *Hood Phillips' Constitutional and Administrative Law* (6th ed.) (Sweet & Maxwell, London, 1978), p. 51.

SEVENTEEN

Parliament: Pay and Resources

Professor Michael Rush

The growth of government in the nineteenth and twentieth centuries inevitably increased the demands on Parliament. It sought to respond to these demands in a number of ways – by changes in procedure and operation, by meeting more frequently, and by increasing the resources available to members, both individually and collectively. Parliament became more and more professionalised, marked by a shift from part-time to full-time MPs and increasingly busy members of the Lords, the payment of MPs, expense allowances for peers, and the provision of a growing range of resources in the form of staff and various allowances, services and facilities in both Houses. However, these changes affected the Commons much more than the Lords and came much earlier in the lower House.

The payment of MPs

Members of Parliament were not paid a salary until 1912. In medieval times constituents sometimes paid their members and met some of the expenses of sending an MP to Westminster (or wherever Parliament was sitting), but the practice died out by the end of the seventeenth century and thereafter MPs needed personal wealth or a wealthy patron in order to sustain a political career. However, since the Commons normally met for six or seven months of the year, usually concentrated in the period February to August, membership could easily be combined with another occupation. This was also facilitated by the parliamentary day, which began in the afternoon, with the principal business being dealt with in the evening, when any important votes also took place. This particularly suited lawyers and those with financial or business interests. On the other hand, until 1918 parliamentary candidates were responsible for meeting the administrative costs in the constituencies they contested and, before the elimination of widespread corruption, following the passing of the Corrupt and Illegal Practices Act in 1883, contesting elections could be a very expensive business. As demands for working-class representation increased, so did demands for the payment of MPs. One of the earliest came from the working-class Chartist Movement in 1838 and proposals for paying MPs were debated five times in the Commons between 1870 and 1895 and formally adopted as party policy by the Liberal Party in 1891, but it was the rise of the Labour Party that gave the demand for payment its final impetus. Early Labour MPs were mostly supported financially by trade unions, but this was successfully challenged in the courts in 1909, leading directly to the introduction of a salary for MPs in 1912.

Table 1: MPs' salaries, 1912–2004 (selected years)

Year	Salary (£)	Year	Salary (£)
1912	400 (a)	1957	1,750 (d)
1931	360 (b)	1964	3,250 (e)
1934	380	1972	4,500
1935	400	1982	14,510
1937	600	1992	30,854
1946	1,000	2003	56,358
1954	1,250 (c)	2004	57,485

Notes: (a) From 1912 £100 was exempt from income tax, being regarded as an average allowance for necessary parliamentary expenses.

(b) In 1931 the salary was reduced by 10 per cent as an economy measure, half of which was restored in 1934, half in 1935.

(c) In 1954 the £100 tax-free allowance was abolished and a sessional allowance averaging £250 was substituted and included in the salary.

(d) The sessional allowance was abolished in 1957 and replaced by an additional sum of £750 to cover parliamentary expenses. This was included in the salary.
(e) £1,250 of the salary was regarded as an expense allowance.

However, as the notes to Table 1 show, pay became entangled with the expenses of fulfilling parliamentary responsibilities, although from 1924 MPs were able to travel free between their constituencies and Westminster. MPs' salaries almost inevitably became a political football – there was never a 'right time' to increase salaries and the decision ultimately lay with MPs themselves. In 1931, in fact, the salary was actually reduced by 10 per cent as part of a wider reduction in public expenditure during the depression of the 1930s. Extra-parliamentary bodies were twice set up to examine the question of MPs' pay and allowances, once in 1963–4 and then again in 1971. The first reported that many MPs were legitimately claiming expenses against their salaries for tax purposes, thereby significantly reducing their net pay. The second report reinforced this finding and recommended that a clear distinction be drawn between the member's salary and the expenses incurred carrying out parliamentary duties. This recommendation was duly accepted, but the Top Salaries Review Body (TSRB), now the Senior Salaries Review Body (SSRB), also made a crucial observation: 'By any reasonable standard ... most members must be considered as working on a full-time basis, and we consider that the level of remuneration should be assessed accordingly.'[1] Since its first report, the TSRB/SSRB has reviewed salaries and allowances once during every normal-length parliament, leaving MPs to vote on its recommendations at the beginning of a new parliament, but between general elections MPs' salaries have been linked to Civil Service pay and annual increases have therefore been automatic. However, during the 1970s, 1980s and 1990s governments limited or sought to limit increases, not always successfully. In addition, since 1965 there has been a parliamentary pensions scheme for all MPs.

Apart from ministers, who, of course, receive salaries in that capacity (in addition to their parliamentary salaries), the Speaker and the three Deputy

Speakers are paid salaries, as are the leader of the opposition, the opposition Chief Whip and one assistant whip, but in 2003 its was agreed that the chairs of select committees should be paid an additional salary of £12,500 a year. This applies to the chairs of all departmental committees and of the Environmental Audit, European Scrutiny, Public Accounts, Public Administration, and Regulatory Reform committees, and the Commons chairs of the Joint Committees on Human Rights and Statutory Instruments.

In contrast to MPs, members of the House of Lords (other than a small number of office holders) are not paid a salary, nor are they regarded as full time. This also contrasts with the members of second chambers in other comparable countries, such as Australia, Austria, Belgium, Canada, France, Ireland, Italy, Japan, Spain, Switzerland and the United States. In all these countries members of the second chamber receive a full salary and, with the exception of the Irish Senate, are regarded as and expected to be full-time members of the legislature. Members of the German Bundesrat are an exception in that they are not paid as members of the second chamber, but this is because they are 'nominated by and represent the Land governments and, as such, are paid salaries and provided with pensions schemes by those governments'.2

Resourcing Parliament

Both Houses of Parliament and their members are provided with a range of resources to enable them to fulfil their parliamentary functions, but there is a marked contrast between Lords and Commons. Not only are MPs paid a salary and peers not, but the level of resources for MPs is much greater than that for peers and the same is true of collective resources provided to each House. That said, extensive resources for MPs are a relatively recent development. Furthermore, although the two Houses cooperate in the provision of some services, such as telephone and postal services, and many aspects of security, most services and facilities are provided and funded separately.

The Palace of Westminster

Parliament has met at Westminster since medieval times, although it also sometimes met elsewhere – Winchester, Lincoln, York and Oxford, for example, and the old Palace of Westminster did not become the regular meeting place until the reign of Henry VIII. The old palace was almost entirely destroyed by fire in 1834 and the existing Palace of Westminster was built in the middle of the nineteenth century and officially opened in 1852, although the Lords' chamber was first used in 1847 and the Commons' in 1850. The new palace was purpose built to enable Parliament to fulfil its functions and MPs and peers their roles. Apart from the plenary chambers and a number of committee rooms for the two Houses, the Palace had the atmosphere and most of the accoutrements of a gentlemen's club: it had dining rooms and bars, smoking rooms, a chess room and two libraries. Living quarters were provided for the Speaker of the Commons and his counterpart in the Lords, the Lord Chancellor, and for the two senior officers of the two Houses, the Clerk of the House of Commons and the Clerk of the Parliaments. In addition, the Prime Minister had an office and the leader of the opposition had what a nineteenth-century MP described as 'a kind of small den'. However, there were no rooms or 'offices' for individual members of either House; none was thought necessary.

As a royal palace, Westminster long remained under the control of the Crown, represented by the Lord Great Chamberlain, although he delegated responsibility for some matters, notably office and other accommodation, to each of the two Houses. In 1965, however, control of almost all the palace was transferred to Parliament, but each House has its own arrangements. In the case of the Commons, control is vested in a House of Commons Commission, chaired by the Speaker, and consisting of the Leader of the House and his or her 'shadow' counterpart, and three other MPs. The commission is responsible for overall policy, with day-to-day running operating through a board of management and the heads of the various departments, advised by a number of specialised committees. Control of the Lords rests with the House Committee, chaired by the Lord Chairman of Committees, with day-to-day responsibility in the hands of the Clerk of the Parliaments and other senior officials, operating through a board of management.

The House of Commons

Table 2: MPs' allowances, 2003

Allowance	Date introduced	Provision in 2003
Staffing Allowance	1969	£66,458–£77,534 (linked to RPI) (a)
Incidental expenditure allowance (IEP) (b)	2001	£19,325
IT equipment (b)		£3,000 (centrally provided)
Telephone & postage	1969	Free on parliamentary business within the UK.
Travel	1924	Free to and from constituency and between home and Westminster, plus some provision for family, car mileage and bicycle allowance.
Subsistence (additional costs allowance)	1972	Allowance when the House is sitting: £1,618 London supplement (inner London MPs) or maximum of £20,902
Pension	(c)1965	Payable at 65 (60 with reduced benefit) according to length of service; minimum of 4 years' service.
Resettlement grant	1974	Lump sum equivalent to 50–100 per cent of salary, depending on age and service.

Notes: (a) Varying according to type of post and whether staff work in London or elsewhere. There is also provision for a contribution equal to ten per cent of each employee's gross salary to fund pensions.
(b) The IEP is intended to cover other expenses e.g. office rental, staff travel.
(c) Backdated to 1964.

As noted earlier, until 1972 no distinction was drawn between the salary paid to MPs and the expenses they incurred in carrying out their parliamentary responsibilities. The only allowance they received covered travel between London and their constituencies, introduced in 1924. Telephone facilities were limited to calls within the London area and postal facilities to communications with ministers, government departments and a number of public bodies. All other costs, such as paying for secretarial help, other telephone and postal costs, and subsistence while in London, had to be met from the member's salary or private resources. Although from the outset a proportion of the salary was treated as a tax-free allowance for necessary parliamentary expenses, in practice this became increasingly inadequate. This resulted in the ludicrous situation in which some MPs with sufficient income from other sources were legitimately claiming sums equal to their parliamentary salaries against tax. However, growing criticism of this state of affairs, both inside and outside Parliament, led in 1969 to the introduction of a secretarial allowance and free telephone and postal services for parliamentary business within the UK and, in 1971, to the setting up of the TSRB to review MPs' pay and allowances (and those of others such as senior civil servants, and senior members of the judiciary and the armed services). In addition to recommending a clear distinction between pay and expenses, the TSRB recommended a subsistence allowance to cover the cost of living in London during the parliamentary session. A pension scheme had already been introduced with effect from 1964 and this, with other changes, set MPs firmly on the road to professionalisation.

Even before the introduction of a secretarial allowance in 1969, only 12 per cent of MPs had no regular secretarial help, but only about a fifth had any full-time staff and two-fifths shared office costs and secretarial assistance with one or more other MPs.[3] After the introduction of the allowance the proportion of MPs with no regular secretarial help fell to 6 per cent and the proportion with full-time staff rose to more than a quarter, leaving two-thirds using part-time assistance.[4] By the early 1990s, over 90 per cent of MPs had one or more full-time staff and the average number of staff per member in 2003 was 3.5. This figure includes secretarial staff, personal assistants and research assistants.[5] In 1971 fewer than 10 per cent of MPs had a research assistant, but by the early 1990s three-fifths had. Some staff are located at Westminster, others in the member's constituency, with

Conservatives more likely to have more staff at Westminster and Labour MPs more in their constituencies.

There were, however, other developments in the provision of resources for MPs, particularly in the area of office accommodation for both members and staff and in extending information and research services. In 1950 few backbench MPs had even desk spaces at Westminster and none had offices. By 1960 the number of desk spaces had increased to nearly a hundred and about a dozen single rooms were available for backbenchers. Utilising space in the various nooks and crannies of the palace and taking over a number of nearby buildings resulted in 70 single rooms being available in 1971 and a total of nearly two hundred desk spaces altogether, two-thirds of which were outside the palace itself. By 1982 the comparable figures were two hundred single rooms and over six hundred desk spaces, two-fifths outside the Palace, plus more than 350 desk spaces for members' staff.[6] However, with yet further offices being provided in buildings near the palace and the opening of Portcullis House, the long-planned new parliamentary building, in 2000, individual office accommodation was available to all MPs.[7]

In addition to the provision of resources to individual MPs, there has been a considerable expansion in the staff of the House of Commons. Excluding staff in the Refreshment Department, for whom figures were not available in 1972, the Commons' staff increased by 168 per cent between 1972 and 2000[8] and the total in 2002 was 1,163. The total in 2002, including catering staff, was 1,430.[9] Apart from various ancillary staff vital to the operation and administration of the palace and its environs, these include clerks, who provide crucial procedural information and advice and are responsible for the running of committees, and the staff of the House of Commons Library, who provide MPs with invaluable information on all aspects of government policy and its implementation. The staff of these two departments in particular have risen from 95 and 55 respectively in 1972 to 282 and 209 in 2003.[10] The Clerks advise and assist MPs with the tabling of parliamentary questions, amendments to Bills and motions, and the library staff deal with reference enquiries from members and their staff (more than sixty thousand a year), longer research enquiries (some fifteen thousand a year), and briefing papers on almost all government Bills and a wide range of policy matters – some 96 in 2001/2. Apart from the services provided to MPs individually, the Commons' staff also play a major role in supporting the work of the House in the chamber, the additional debates since 1999 known as Westminster Hall sittings, and, of course, the extensive legislative and scrutiny work undertaken by committees.

Apart from the Public Accounts Committee, which is served by the 800-strong National Audit Office, most select committees engaged in the scrutiny of government policy and administration are assisted in their work by part-time specialist advisers, of whom there were 157 in 1999/2000 and 223 in the longer than normal session of 2001/2. They are drawn from universities, 'think tanks', various research bodies and the like. Some act as general advisers within a committee's remit, but most are engaged for particular enquiries.

All these services are provided on a politically neutral basis and, although they could be said to constitute the Commons 'civil service', the staff are not civil servants but employed by the House of Commons and have their own career structure. Nonetheless, there is also provision for supporting the various opposition parties. This is known as 'Short money', after the Leader of the House, Edward Short, who was responsible for its introduction in 1975. The amount allocated is related to the number of seats and votes won by each party at the previous general election. The bulk of it goes to the official opposition: in 2002/3 Short money totalled £5m, of which nearly two-thirds went to the Conservatives and nearly a quarter to the Liberal Democrats. The purpose is threefold – to fund the costs of the leader of the opposition's office, to provide research staff and other backing for opposition parties in carrying out their parliamentary responsibilities, and to assist with travel and other related expenses. This is, of course, over and above the payment of salaries to the leader of the opposition, the opposition Chief Whip and one assistant whip.

MPs, individually and collectively, and the House of Commons as a whole have undergone a professionalisation process which recognises that being a member of Parliament is a full-time job and that without adequate resources neither MPs nor the House of Commons as a whole can hope to fulfil their responsibilities. All services and facilities are subject to periodic review and most salaries and allowances are linked to the Retail Price Index. Whether they are adequate and whether additional resources are necessary will always be a matter of opinion, but one thing is clear – the professionalisation of the MP and of the House of Commons is an accomplished fact and any proposals for yet more resources should be seen clearly in that context.

The House of Lords

It would be easy to characterise the House of Lords as the amateur part of Parliament, more akin to the House of Commons of the nineteenth and early twentieth centuries, not least because, ministers in the Lords and a few other office holders apart, members of the upper House are unpaid. This, however, would be misleading, since, like the Commons, the Lords has been undergoing a process of professionalisation as a consequence of its increased activity and the role its has carved out for itself since the passing of the 1958 Life Peerages Act. Average daily attendance increased from fewer than a hundred in 1950 to nearly three hundred in 1980/81 and to over four hundred before the removal of most of the hereditary peers in 1999 – equivalent to more than a third of the eligible members. After 1999, average attendance fell back and in 2001/2 was 370, but this was the equivalent of more than half the membership. However, even before the 1958 Act, limited expenses allowances were introduced. In 1946 an allowance to cover rail travel between a peer's main place of residence and London was introduced, but was subject to an 'assiduity' rule that claimants must have attended at least a third of the possible sittings (though, after 1947, not applied to peers living in Scotland) and this was not abolished until 1972, it being argued that infrequent attenders could and did make a significant contribution to the work of the House. It was not until 1961 that a car allowance was introduced, but in 1957 an expense allowance to cover other costs – subsistence, secretarial help and the like – became available, but there was confusion about what it did and did not cover and this was not resolved until 1975. In due course the system was further refined, notably to allow some expenses for non-sitting days to be claimed for attendance at committees. In 2001 peers were allowed to claim free postage on parliamentary business and in 2003 some of the expenses arising from visits on parliamentary business to EU institutions and the national parliaments of EU members and candidate countries.

Table 3: Peers' allowances and services, 2003

Allowance	Provision
Day subsistence	£66.00 per day (a)
Overnight subsistence	£132.00 per day (b)
Office costs and secretarial assistance	£55.00 per day (c)
Travel – home to Westminster	first-class rail fares, air travel or car mileage allowance
Telephone and postage	Free on parliamentary business in UK
Visiting EU institutions and national parliaments	Various costs covered

Notes: (a) Maximum of £11,220.
(b) Maximum of £22,440.
(c) Maximum of £11,550 (170 sitting days, plus 40 non-sitting days for committees).

Just as office accommodation for MPs has, until recently, been a scarce resource, so it has for peers, but even more so: even in 1988/9 only 150 desk spaces were available, but the situation has improved dramatically since then and in 2003 desk spaces were available to 90 per cent of peers, although these are mostly in shared rooms.[11] In terms of staffing the Lords also provides a contrast to the Commons: as activity has increased, so have staff numbers, but in 2002 the House of Lords had only 404 staff (382 in 2001) compared with the Commons' 1,430, less than a third of the latter. It is, of course, important to remember that, unlike MPs, peers do not have constituents and the constituency role undoubtedly makes considerable demands on the time and resources of MPs. As with the Commons, the most important staff are the clerks and the library staff, both fulfilling roles similar to those of their counterparts in the Commons, though on a more limited scale, particularly in the case of the library. In 2002 the latter had a staff of 30, including two part time, compared with more than two hundred in the House of Commons Library. Even so, in 2001/2 library staff were able to deal with more than 17,000 enquiries from peers, but in other respects cannot match the scale of the services provided for MPs.

Again lagging behind the Commons, funds to support the opposition and, in the case of the Lords, crossbench peers in carrying out their parliamentary responsibilities were not introduced until 1996. Known as 'Cranborne money', after the then Leader of the House of Lords, it is on a smaller scale, amounting in 2002/3 to £621,000 (some 12 per cent of Short money in the Commons), with the greater part, more than three-fifths, going to the Conservatives and nearly a third to the Liberal Democrats.[12] Nonetheless, although the resources available to peers and to the upper House collectively are much more limited than those available to MPs and to the Commons, they have increased and will continue to do so, especially as the demands on the House of Lords and its members increase.

Financing Parliament

Institutions such as Parliament do not come cheap and the cost has inevitably risen with the professionalisation of both Houses, especially the Commons. In 1973/4 the House of Commons cost £13m, a figure not reached by the House of Lords until 1998/9,[13] but by 2002/3 the cost of the Commons had risen to £275m and that of the Lords to £57m. Of course, a significant part of that increase is accounted for by inflation, but the greater part is due to the expansion of the resources allocated to both Houses.

Table 4: Cost of the House of Commons and the House of Lords

	2001/2 (£) 2002/3 (£)	
House of Commons	254m (119m)	275m (134m)
House of Lords	56m (10m)	57m (13m)
Total	310m	332m

Note: The figures in parentheses exclude MPs' salaries and expenses for both MPs and peers.
Source: House of Commons Commission, Annual Reports 2001–02 and 2002–3 and House of Lords, Annual Reports and Accounts 2001–02.

As Table 4 shows, the House of Commons costs between four and five times as much as the House of Lords, but it is important to note that nearly half the cost of the Commons is taken up by MPs' salaries and expenses, whereas peers' expenses constitute less than a quarter of the Lords' total cost.

Between April 2003 and March 2004 the total cost of MPs' expenses was £78m. This averaged £118,000 per MP, the highest being Labour MP Claire Curtis-Thomas with £168,889. MPs' staff accounted for four-fifths of the total. As might be expected, travel costs tended to vary according to the distance between constituencies and Westminster, but other costs did not and, in some cases, MPs in neighbouring constituencies claimed markedly different amounts in expenses. There were also party differences, with Labour and Liberal Democrat MPs tending to claim more than Conservatives. Peers' expenses were considerably less, reflecting, among other things, the absence of contituency responsibilites and in most cases reflected attendence. A number claimed more than £50,000 and a significant minority £30,000–£40,000, but there was considerable variation.

Compared with lower chambers in other Parliaments, particularly those in comparable European countries, such as France, Germany and Italy, but less so compared with Australia, Canada and especially the US Congress, British MPs are about half-way up the international league in terms of salaries, services and facilities, better off in some respects, worse off in others.[14] The House of Lords, however, is less well resourced than a number of second chambers in comparable countries: 'There is no doubt that the resources available to Australian, Canadian, French and American Senators are extensive, especially to the latter in terms of staff.'[15] Of course, Australian and American senators are elected and have constituents, yet not only has the House of Lords become much busier in recent years, it also meets more often than any other legislative chamber save the Commons, and in 1999/2000 actually met one day more than the Commons. Given that its members are unpaid and are provided with much more limited resources than MPs, it can be argued that the UK gets its second chamber on the cheap. Were the second stage of Lords' reform to result in a fully or substantially elected upper House, the pressure for full-time, salaried, adequately resourced members would be considerable and resisting that pressure would be unwise, however tempted the Treasury or others might be. With an appointed second chamber appearing to be the most likely outcome of further changes in the composition of the Lords, it would be easier to leave the upper House resourced much as it is at present. However, the House of Lords as it is currently constituted has been experiencing professionalisation: some of its members are in practice full time; the demands on staff are less than in the Commons but growing; the services provided are more limited but expanding. In short, like the Commons, the professionalisation of the Lords is a continuing process. It is, furthermore, a process that is taking place in most modern legislatures, not only at the national level but the subnational level – witness the salaried, full-time membership and substantial resources of the Scottish Parliament, National Assembly for Wales and the Northern Ireland Assembly.[16] The history of the resourcing of Parliament as been haphazard and piecemeal and it is a history that shows every sign of continuing.

References

For the most recent MPs' and peers' expenditure go to http://.128.6350/.html.

Endnotes

1   TSRB 1971, para. 25.

2   Rush, M. 'Socio-Economic Composition and Pay and Resources in Second Chambers', in N. D. J. Baldwin and D. Shell (eds) *Second Chambers* (Frank Cass, London, 2001), p. 33.

3   Barker, A. and Rush, M. *The Member of Parliament and His Information* (Allen & Unwin, London, 1971), p. 171.

4   Rush, M. and Shaw, M. (eds) *The House of Commons: Services and Facilities* (Allen & Unwin, London, 1974), p. 276.

5   House of Commons Commission, *Annual Report 2002–03*, HC 806.

6   Rush, M. (ed.) *The House of Commons: Services and Facilities, 1972–1982* (Policy Studies Institute, London, 1983) , p. 82.

7   House of Commons Commission, *Annual Report, 2002–03.*

8   Rush, M. *The Role of the Member of Parliament since 1868: from Gentlemen to Players* (Oxford University Press, Oxford, 2001) p. 129.

9   House of Commons Commission, *Annual Report, 2002–03.*

10   Rush, *Role of the Member of Parliament since 1868*, p.129; House of Commons Commission, *Annual Report, 2002–03.*

11   Shell, D. and Beamish, D. (eds) *The House of Lords at Work: a Study Based on the 1988–89 Parliamentary Session*, (Clarendon Press, Oxford, 1993), p. 316; House of Lords, *Annual Report, 2001–02*, HL 153.

12   House of Lords, *Annual Report, 2001–02*, HL 153.

13   Rush and Shaw, *House of Commons*, p. 28; Shell and Beamish, *House of Lords at Work*, p. 313.

14   Senior Salaries Review Body, *Report No. 38: Review of Parliamentary Pay and Allowances*, Cm 3330-i–ii, July 1996, Sections 3a and 3b.

15   Rush, 'Socio-economic Composition and Pay and Resources in Second Chambers', p. 35.

16   Senior Salaries Review Body, *Report No. 42: Initial Pay, Allowances, Pensions and Severance Arrangements for Members of the Scottish Parliament, National Assembly for Wales and Northern Ireland Assembly*, Cm 4188, March 1999, Appendix E.

EIGHTEEN (A)

The Organisation and Management of Business: the House of Commons

Eve Samson

The organisation and management of business in the House of Commons is the domain of the government's 'business managers'; a loose term which comprises the Leader of the House and the government Chief Whip (and, in certain contexts, their staffs) and via what is known as the 'usual channels' – the business managers and their shadows from the official opposition (and sometimes from the other opposition parties). It is clearly impossible to set out all the political and procedural factors they need to take account of in so short a space as a single chapter. Consequently, this chapter gives merely the briefest introduction to a complex process in which there is constant interplay between what I will arbitrarily divide into the 'procedural arrangement of business' and the 'political arrangement of business'.

In reality, no such clear distinction can be made. The arrangement of business cannot be considered solely as something governed by rules and procedural conventions. Nor is it simply the product of intense political manoeuvring, itself governed by its own conventions. Those who set the business must be aware of both. Nevertheless it is easier to understand the complex interplay if procedure and politics are temporarily separated.

The rule book is far from simple, but while the procedural rules are set out in the standing orders and *Erskine May*, the political conventions are more fluid, and harder to assess. Although it is a truism that 'the government must always get its business,' experienced politicians will not necessarily agree what exactly that may mean in practice.

Procedural arrangement of business

Debate in the Commons has a simple default: debate on disputed matters must conclude by a particular hour – 'the moment of interruption' – and if at that point someone is still speaking or wishes to speak, the business is 'talked out' and must be dealt with on another day. It takes only a moment to see that this means a small group could prevent any decision ever being taken. The standing orders and conventions dealing with the arrangement of business can be seen as ways to deal with the practical problems that this default imposes.

It is worth mentioning one other default: notice of substantive business must be given, except in exceptional circumstances.[1] The government cannot ambush the House by bringing forward important measures unexpectedly, when only its own supporters may be present. Any member can ask to see the draft of the order paper on which the next day's business is set out, and it cannot be altered after the rising of the House.

In principle, the government has power to determine almost all the business before the House of Commons. Standing Order 14 says: 'Save as provided in this order, government business shall have precedence at every sitting.' It is for government to put propositions before the House, which has power to assent, dissent, or amend.

The only limitations on government power to dictate the agenda are the requirements that

- twenty days a year are for opposition business;
- thirteen Fridays are for the consideration of private members' Bills;

- three days have to be provided for debate on the estimates; in practice for select committee debates;
- time may have to be found for private business[2] (much is dealt with without debate, but the chairman of Ways and Means has power to set down opposed private business for debate on the second half of a sitting day when necessary);
- if the Speaker permits the application to be made, and the House approves it, backbench members can initiate emergency debates under Standing Order 24;
- each day's sitting ends with a half-hour debate 'on the adjournment of the house' initiated by a backbencher.

But control of the agenda is of limited use if one cannot ensure that decisions are made. The government has the power to invite the House to allow particular business to continue after the moment of interruption by the 'ten o'clock business motion',[3] decided without debate. However, although this enables debate to continue, it does not normally set a deadline by which a decision must be reached. Since time is finite, if debate continues beyond the point at which the next sitting day should start, then the business of that day is lost. Accordingly, lengthy debate on one measure may reduce the time available to deal with others.

Even with the advantages of control over the House of Commons time, and the ability to make sure business can be decided after the moment of interruption, government business managers find themselves having to juggle business to ensure that they get their programme through the Commons successfully, let alone the Lords, where government business does not have automatic precedence.

A range of additional measures has been employed to ensure that the will of the majority party, or even of the majority *tout court*, cannot be frustrated by a minority determined to extend debate, and reduce the parliamentary time available. Over many years, the procedure of the House has often been altered to seek a better balance between minority rights to debate and majority rights to come to a decision, and increasingly procedure has moved from the 'default position' of open-ended debate ending either in decision or in the business being talked out.

These measures can be roughly divided into five categories:

- Providing for certain types of business to be taken after the moment of interruption by standing order.
- Time-limiting certain types of business by standing order.
- Providing for certain types of business to be taken away from the floor of the House by standing order.
- Making particular provision for a particular piece of business.
- Time-limiting Bills.

Some of these devices have existed for over a century; some have been brought in as part of the process of modernisation of the House of Commons, and remain controversial.

Providing for certain types of business to be taken after the moment of interruption by standing order

Standing orders allow several types of business to be taken after the moment of interruption. However, simple exemption prevents the business being talked out but does not set a time limit for debate.

Time-limiting certain types of business by standing order

Given this weakness, it is not surprising that the standing orders provide that debate on Statutory Instruments (SIs) and on European Union documents is limited to an hour and a half. Debates on opposed nominations to certain select committees are also limited by the standing orders, and there are complex provisions allowing different times for debate on regulatory reform orders and human rights orders, depending on the view of the committees scrutinising them.

Providing for certain types of business to be taken away from the floor of the House

Taking business away from the floor of the House enables the business managers either to contain business within normal sitting hours, or to find space for additional business. The first business taken away from the floor of the House was the debate at committee stage of Bills; it is now the exception for such debate to take place in committee of the whole House, rather than in standing committee. More recently, debate on affirmative SIs, and on European Union documents, has taken place in committee automatically, unless other provisions have been made. Time has also been released by moving private members' debates out of the time for normal business; originally to special Wednesday morning sittings and, more recently, to Westminster Hall. This has been accompanied by an increase in the amount of time available for such debate, but the power of backbench members to put forward a substantive motion on which the House could make a decision which should be, in principle, binding on government was lost in 1995.

One rather specialised innovation in this category is the introduction of deferred divisions, a device by which divisions on business which can be decided after the moment of interruption are deferred until the subsequent Wednesday. The benefits are felt by government backbenchers who would otherwise have to remain in the House until late divisions were reached.

Making particular provision for particular pieces of business

Where there is no standing order provision, and when the ten o'clock motion is not adequate, more complex provisions must be made by 'business of the House motions'. These may provide, for example, that a particular amount of time should be given for a particular debate; that debate and decision can continue after the moment of interruption; that decisions will be taken on several related motions at a single time.

However, business of the House motions are ordinary motions and so governed by the 'default'; they are subject to no time limit themselves; they can be passed only if everyone is broadly in agreement with what is proposed, if debate comes to a natural end before the moment of interruption, or if the government secures the closure – and the closure is given only if the vote on it is won with at least one hundred members voting on the majority side.

Time-limiting particular Bills

These disadvantages mean there are other means for timetables to be set for Bills provided in standing or sessional orders. The older method of timetabling, the guillotine, or allocation of time motion, allows three hours for debate; the programme motion is made at second reading, and is essentially only debated by the House if the times originally imposed are reduced, although the timetables set for standing committee can be debated by the committee concerned.

Political arrangement of business

Since normally the government not only sets the agenda for the great majority of the House of Commons' business, but can reasonably expect to have the majority needed to use the various devices available to limit debate, one might expect the business managers' life to be easy. It is not.

In principle, each session should run to a predictable timetable. The government will need to find time for a series of set piece debates: the Queen's Speech is debated for six days; the Budget is debated for four days; there are five days for defence issues. There will be at least a day on local government expenditure. These should fall into a reasonably clear pattern: the Queen's Speech opening the session, the Budget taking place around March, the Finance Bill immediately after, and in autumn the House will debate the pre-Budget report. There will be a cycle of Consolidated Fund Bills, giving the government money it requires. As well as these, the business managers need to find time for other general debates: ministers may want a debate on a new policy; backbenchers may want a similar debate; the opposition may request that a particular subject be debated in government time, rather than in the more confrontational atmosphere of an opposition day.

Single debates are relatively easy to accommodate; the difficulties come in ensuring that the legislative programme is completed between one session and the next. Although the length of the session is in theory arbitrary, lengthening one session will squeeze the next, and ultimately risk reducing the amount of legislation a government can achieve over the course of a Parliament. New provisions such as carry-over of Bills, so that they are not automatically lost at the end of a session, may help, but may bring problems of their own.

The first problem for the business managers comes from government itself. The parliamentary session does not start with a clutch of fully drafted Bills, a similar clutch of prepared SIs, and a clear timetable from departments of exactly which further instruments will be coming forward and when, and the certainty that there will be no need either for further government measures. Instead, departments and ministers will have different priorities. Even when some consensus is reached, the flow of parliamentary business begins in departments, which themselves have to juggle different priorities and may not necessarily be alive to the difficulties their ministers can potentially cause parliamentary colleagues. And although the government needs parliamentary approval for the position it takes in European negotiations, European Union business will follow the timetable dictated by pressures in an international arena.

Governments make a great effort to control the legislative programme, which is of course the keystone of their business, but even here Bills can be ready late, put into Parliament less finished than ideal, or simply require extensive amendments to meet concerns expressed in one or other House of Parliament. Extra work on one Bill may have a knock-on effect on resources available for others.

While it is possible to keep some control over the 30 or 40 Bills per session, it is simply impossible for departments to forecast accurately exactly how many of the more than 1,500 SIs a year they are likely to be responsible for, or how urgently SIs will be needed. Unscheduled 'events', both fortunate and unfortunate, will add to the parliamentary burden; for example, break-through or setback in Northern Ireland may require emergency legislation.

The business managers cannot set their programme to suit the House of Commons alone. Legislation must pass through both Houses of Parliament before it is enacted, and each needs a steady flow of business. This cannot be secured simply by starting an equal number of Bills in each House. Firstly, there is a well-established convention that Bills of political importance should start in the House of Commons, so that the elected chamber gives its views first. Even if this were not the case, all money Bills would have to start in the House of Commons, as would any measure on which the government wished to retain the option of using the Parliament Acts.

These are the practicalities; business managers also have to handle parliamentary psychology. The first example of this is the need to manage their relationship with their opposite numbers very carefully. Their primary relationship will be with the official opposition, but smaller parties also have to be considered. If the usual channels are flowing smoothly, then there will be less likelihood of disruption. On the other hand, the government party will be discontented if business appears to be arranged simply at the behest of the opposition – and there will always be a fear that the opposition parties will seek to squeeze the most advantage they can out of any situation.

Government backbenchers also have to be satisfied. They will want to feel the government is listening to them (and they may not all have the same views). They will want business to be properly debated, but are likely to be impatient with procedural tactics that extend sitting hours to an extent they consider unreasonable. This is not necessarily confined to the government party and certainly not a new phenomenon; the establishment of the Select Committee on the Sittings of the House in the 1987 parliament showed a wish for reform of sitting hours. Even if all backbenchers were content to allow sittings to last as long as it took to get business through without recourse to any of the newer methods for timetabling and moving business off the floor of the House, the business managers would be aware that it takes only a few members of the opposition to prolong sittings, while a large number of government backbenchers have to attend for as long as the House is sitting, to ensure there is no ambush in the division lobby. Extreme tiredness undermines political effectiveness.

And there is a further constraint on the business managers; what they do must be defensible not only to their parties but to the public at large and, more particularly, to the House of Lords. That House has become increasingly ready to criticise the Commons' tendency to timetable business, and the adequacy of the timetables imposed. Haste in the Commons may simply lead to delay in the Lords, and squabbles between the two Houses as to which actually spends longer on legislation.

To take a simple example of the way that such complex considerations may have to be balanced in practice, let us consider how an SI might be dealt with. Unless specific provision is made, affirmative SIs are debated in committee; negatives are not debated at all. Affirmative SIs come to the House for a decision after the debate in committee or after an hour and a half's debate on the floor. Since they are one of the few types of business which can be decided after the moment of interruption, they are usually placed at the end of the day's business and if the House wants to vote on them after the moment of interruption, the division is deferred. It should be the business managers' dream: simple, usually taken off the floor of the House, time limited wherever it is taken, debatable at any hour and the deferred division means that members who do not wish to take part in the debate need not stay.

But even this most convenient type of business can cause headaches. Sending an instrument to committee requires time. If an instrument is required urgently, debate must be taken on the floor of the House. The instrument could be dealt with at the beginning of a sitting. If the day's main business is interesting, and the instrument is not, it may be approved without any debate or division. However, if the SI is debated, and even divided on, the time to debate the main business will be reduced. Alternatively, taking it after the moment of interruption would mean a lengthy sitting for many members, not just those who participated in the debate. Now that divisions after the moment of interruption are routinely deferred, there would also need to be an additional motion 'turning off' deferred divisions. Although such motion is not debatable, it gives the opportunity for an extra division, prolonging the sitting still further.

The business managers' decision will depend on the contentiousness of the SI itself, the nature of the other business available (Does it really need a full day's debate? Would there be an outcry if it was squeezed? Would squeezing it play well with the government's own party?) and the mood of backbenchers and the opposition (Will the government party object to sitting late? Is anyone likely to call divisions just for the fun of it? Will any opposition party consider a particular arrangement provocative? Would this matter?).

If this wasn't complicated enough, if an opposition party thinks a particular instrument is significant, they may request that it be debated on the floor of the House, and perhaps even for it to be given extra time. In general, providing extra time for debate will please opposition parties, but lifting the standing order time limit requires a business of the House motion. If the request is reasonable, and relations between the front benches good, the government may agree and the necessary business of the House motion may be passed without debate. However, the government is taking the risk that maverick backbenchers from either side could prolong debate on the business of the House motion, disrupting the substantive business of the day.

If experience shows that mavericks will talk on the business of the House motion, the government is likely to prefer to retain the normal time limit but to show its willingness to accommodate the opposition by referring the debate to the floor, which can be arranged without any substantive motion. If the government feels that the opposition is either exploiting procedural loopholes itself, or encouraging its mavericks to do so, it may be inclined to resist such requests altogether. However there is a danger even in this, because a frustrated opposition is more likely to exploit every procedural device it can to hamper business.

Even this example simplifies the real process, because the opposition participants in the 'usual channels' will themselves choose their position after considering the same kinds of variables as the business managers. Business can be arranged simply and straightforwardly; it can also be the result of extremely complex considerations on all sides.

Changing procedure

Because the government sets the agenda, it alone can propose changes to standing orders, which must be made as ordinary motions, subject to all the considerations explained above. Sometimes these changes are made on government initiative alone, and some minor tidying up may be suggested by the staff of the House, and put forward with other changes. Usually, however, procedural proposals come from a committee before they are put to the House.

The Procedure Committee is a backbench committee, with the power to set its own agenda, appointed by standing orders 'to consider the practice and procedure of the House in the conduct of public business, and to make recommendations'. In addition the Liaison Committee of select committee chairmen has suggested changes to improve committee workings, and individual committees or groups of committees may make recommendations. These recommendations do not always lead to standing order changes.

The government can also propose that there should be committees to look at particular problems. In 1991 the House set up a Select Committee on Sittings of the House, under the chairmanship of Sir Michael Jopling, which brought forward the 'Jopling reforms', designed to reduce what were generally regarded as excessively lengthy hours. After the 1997 election, the House established the Modernisation Committee, which has continued under the chairmanship of successive Leaders of the House, with the more general remit of considering 'how the practices and procedures of the House should be modernised'. It is unusual for a government minister to chair a select committee, but not unprecedented.

However they are set up, and whoever chairs them, select committees are nominated in proportion to membership in the House. Although this means that all parties have an input, this does not mean that their recommendations will be uncontroversial or universally acceptable. For example, successive governments have failed to put forward changes to the procedure for scrutinising delegated legislation recommended by the Procedure Committee, and the official opposition has rejected proposals from the Modernisation Committee.

The government's hidden power over procedure is that of keeping proposals it does not like off the order paper. Since the House can amend the government's proposals the procedural changes the government puts forward will be those to which it expects the majority of the House would agree. On some occasions, this may simply mean those that are acceptable to the government party, but wider support is preferable. Traditionally, the ultimate deterrent for government misuse of its power is the knowledge that, in the long run, it can expect to be in opposition once again.

The future?

Changes to procedure do not necessarily bring the benefits that their proponents hope. The need to keep all sides happy, and the impossibility of doing so, can be seen in the progress of programming. The idea that legislation would be better considered if all those involved in the debate knew how long scrutiny would last, and when particular provisions were likely to be reached, is far from new. Programming was recommended by the Modernisation Committee in its very first report. In 1998 some progress was made with agreed programme motions, which were signed by business managers from the three main parties, and were frequently altered during the passage of the Bill in question. Although the programme motions were in principle fully debatable, and could be talked out, debate was of the briefest, and some were decided without debate.

When consensus broke down, however, this model could not be followed. It is simply too risky for government to put forward debatable motions repeatedly on a single piece of business. The choice was between using the guillotine to provide a framework for programming, thereby risking being accused of heavy-handedness as almost every Bill was guillotined from the outset, and inventing a new procedure. Although the programming orders provided for less debate on the floor of the House than the guillotine, they were designed, in principle, to be flexible and to allow the kind of responsiveness to the course of debate that the original programmes had shown. The detailed timetable for debate in standing committee was to be drawn up by a cross-party business subcommittee, which would have the power to propose changes to the programme during the committee stage, and to propose that more time be given for the committee.

However, the advantages of programming could only be secured if all sides engaged with the new process, and if there was a certain minimal level of trust. It is clear that this was not always reached. If programmes were set loosely, and committees did not exercise self-discipline, then large parts of the Bill might not be scrutinised at all; on the other hand, if the government insisted on a very detailed and strict timetable, to ensure that Commons scrutiny could not be accused of being incomplete, the timetable might not give sufficient priority to matters which turned out to be important.

The Modernisation Committee's most recent report on programming concluded that although government bore the primary responsibility for programming, the opposition and backbenchers also had to engage with the process. The committee considered that changes to the standing orders would not, of themselves, improve the process; the system could be radically improved by using the existing framework more consensually. The experience demonstrates that rules alone will not produce consensus, but steady pressure from all sides may succeed in changing conventions.

Governments do not always control parliamentary business. It has been suggested that there could be greater consensus over the arrangement of business if the United Kingdom Parliament adopted the cross-party 'business committee' or 'bureau' that sets the programme in some other legislatures, such as the Scottish Parliament. Those in favour believe there would be less temptation for the opposition to ambush a programme in which it had clearly had a hand and that the government would be more receptive to opposition demands if they were made in a framework which acknowledged their legitimacy. The experience of programming potentially offers the chance to see whether, in a limited way, business committees can be made to work, or whether the procedural power that the House of Commons offers to government and the obstructive opportunities it offers to opposition are too tempting to be relinquished.

Endnotes

1 Consideration of Lords amendments to public Bills may be taken without notice if the House so orders. This procedure is only really likely to be used toward the end of a session when the two Houses are dealing with particular Bills, and particular provisions. The issues on which the House needs to agree, and the Bills in play, are clear, so that even though the business may not appear on the order paper, all sides should be alert to the possibility that extra business may be taken forthwith.

2 That is, business affecting particular places, organisations or people, such as a Bill dealing with a private development or, in earlier times, a Bill providing for a divorce.

3 The old name, since the moment of interruption normally fell at 10.00 p.m.; it now falls at 10.00 p.m. on Mondays, 7.00 p.m. on Tuesdays and Wednesdays, 6.00 p.m. on Thursdays and 2.30 p.m. on Fridays.

The Organisation and Management of Business: the House of Lords

Sir Michael Wheeler-Booth

The 2001 Labour manifesto stated: 'Labour supports modernisation of the House of Lords' procedures to improve its effectiveness' – an unusual pledge to make in a party manifesto, as normally the procedures of the two Houses are regarded as matters for the House concerned alone. It suggests a significant desire to move Lords' procedures closer to those adopted in the Commons in the last century and a quarter – namely to partially abandon the open and self-regulating system in favour of one where the government has some control of the legislative programme in the second chamber. In the debate on the Queen's Speech, the then Leader of the House, the late Lord Williams of Mostyn, amplified this by saying, 'We need to improve our working practice.' Subsequently he carried this through by setting up a group, under his chairmanship, and with the opposition leader on it, which consulted widely and reported in April 2002.[1] It recommended:

a. virtually all government Bills to be subjected to prelegislative scrutiny including taking evidence by Parliament;

b. that Bills subjected to prelegislative scrutiny should be allowed to be carried over in the following session;

   c. new procedures to enable the House to consider finance Bills, without encroaching on Commons' financial privilege;

   d. a new committee to examine the merits of Statutory Instruments;

   e. an extension of starred questions on Tuesdays and Wednesdays from 30 to 40 minutes, and the permitted number from four to five;

   f. ministers to be allowed one sitting a week free of having to answer questions (not accepted);

   g. the House to sit normally not later than 10.00 p.m., and this curtailment of time set to be coupled with greater use of grand committees;

   h. more prime time to be devoted to debates, for backbenchers, debates on select committee reports and on general topics;

   i. on Thursdays, the House to sit at 11.00 a.m. and rise by 7.00 p.m.;

   j. the House (and grand committees) to sit in September, and in return have longer recesses at Christmas, Easter and Whitsun;

   k. a review of the Houses' scrutiny of European legislation.

After debate, and some refinements by the Procedure Committee, the main proposals were all adopted: they represented a compromise between proposals which helped the government to legislate more easily and those which advantaged the opposition and backbenchers. Several of the more important changes were directly in accordance with the recommendations of the royal commission on Lords reform.[2]

It is too early to say how far they will have carried out the government's wish to 'improve the effectiveness' of the House's procedures – one thing that is quite clear is that they have not tilted the balance between government and opposition in the way that may have occurred in the Commons in the Modernisation Committee (and thereafter in the House on division) as a consequence of the failure by government and opposition to reach consensus on programming.

The present system

As background to the manifesto pledge, we need to consider briefly the wide disparities between the way in which business is managed, and procedures changed in the two Houses, where we find totally different systems. The Commons system and practice is described in the previous section of this chapter. We will delineate the Lords system[3] and provide a short account of the establishment of the Lords' government Whips' Office between 1960 and 1963.

In the Lords there is no concept of 'government time' as it exists in the Commons, where it is encapsulated in standing orders. Any member of the House can put down business on the order paper, for example, to give notice of a wish to hold a debate on a certain subject. But before putting it down for a specific date, it is customary to have gained the agreement of the 'usual channels' in advance.[4]

The 'usual channels' consist essentially of the three Chief Whips – Labour, Conservative and Liberal Democrat, although sometimes, in practice, this is reduced to the Chief Whips of the two major parties. The three are sometimes extended to include the convenor of the crossbench peers. For more significant issues, the Chief Whips are reinforced in discussion by the leaders of the parties. The 'usual channels' are served by the private secretary to the Leader of the House and Chief Whip, who is a Lords clerk on secondment for a period of about three years. Like in the Commons, there is no 'business committee' as exists in most other national parliaments in Europe. The 'usual channels' are answerable only to the House, which alone can overrule them, although in normal circumstances this should not and does not occur.

As previously stated, there is no 'government time', but there is a convention which is always observed that government business must be considered within a reasonable time and decided upon.

Unlike in the Commons, there are no procedures to expedite the consideration of legislation – no timetable motions or guillotines, selection of amendments or standing committees. Although a closure exists, it is officially recognised as an exceptional procedure and has only been used three times during the last three-quarters of a century. The only weapon available is a motion 'that the noble Lord be no longer heard', but it is debatable, and, if necessary, decided by the House on division. It only has the effect of silencing the member in question for that one occasion. It has only been divided upon six times in the last century, and its use is generally subsequently deprecated, as with the closure.

But apart from the procedural differences, there is a further and very practical reason why the House of Lords is not subject to government control, which stems from the party composition of the House. At present there are 182 Labour, 206 Conservative, 63 Liberal Democrat and 210 cross-bench and non-affiliated peers and bishops.5 It follows that the government has no majority, and can win votes only with the support of at least one of the other parties or the crossbench peers. A consequence of those figures is that the government is constantly under threat from an 'ambush', and therefore has to get its backbench supporters to stay, night after night, just in case there is a vote. Peers, unlike MPs, are not paid a salary, but may claim expenses within set limits: many have full- or part-time jobs, and many are elderly. The lot of the Lords government Chief Whip is not easy.

Nor do the Lords whips have the inducements of their Commons counterparts, the jobs or travel, or the weapons of coercion to make their members obey the whip. Withdrawal of the whip carries no near-automatic loss of membership at the next election – rather the offender continues to sit as a peer untouched.

With all these factors, why does the House in practice function and the government get the majority of its business? Partly at present because the Liberal Democrats more often side with Labour than with the Conservatives. And the majority of crossbenchers are patchy attenders and infrequent voters. Secondly, members of the Lords accept that the House of Commons is the democratically elected House, and that MPs are accountable, which peers are not. For this reason, they accept that the elected House should normally get its way. This applies more strongly in respect of mandated government proposals, endorsed by the Commons, where the 'Salisbury convention' inhibits the Lords from opposition on second or third readings of a Bill. But on many other issues in practice the opposition parties in the Lords allow the government to win in the end, even if they strongly disagree with Labour policies. On private members' legislation, some social issues and private and subordinate legislation, these conventions do not apply.

But the present freedoms and lack of procedural restraints depend on the realisation by all concerned that it is in the interest of all members of the House that the conventions should apply. Everyone is aware of the different system which rules in the Commons, and the majority want nothing of it. In the Lords backbenchers can introduce private members' Bills, introduce debates and ask questions freely. The opposition parties can, when they determine, inflict defeats on the government. But as the system and the members are self-regulating, they realise it will collapse if unduly abused. Any replacement system would be likely to be more restrictive – an example of this recently was in the Canadian Senate, where a prolonged filibuster resulted in the imposition of much stricter rules. It was lack of self-restraint in fighting for the cause of Irish Home Rule by Irish MPs from 1870 to 1914 that was the proximate cause of the old freedoms possessed for centuries by MPs being so drastically curtailed.

This background provides the basis for the existing system of negotiation on the arrangement of all business in the Lords. Despite the fact that these negotiations are conducted in private, it is open to anyone to observe the consequences. The process is essentially of give and take between government and opposition. The Chief Whips, the principals, are aided by the private secretary, who is supposed to act as an honest broker as a political neutral, and to be trusted by all sides, though he has a special responsibility to the government to get their programme through. The working of the 'usual channels' depends on good personal relations – but some of the bargaining is tough.

The system of checks and balances has as a longstop to the Parliament Acts, which ensures that the Lords can only delay legislation on which the Commons is determined. But in practice much of the hard slog of scrutinising legislation is at present carried out in the Lords, rather than in the Commons, where the large Labour majority ensures that, in practice, they do not lose votes. The opposition in the Commons cannot force the government to give ground. In the Lords, it is otherwise, because the passage of legislation demands cooperation, which is obtained through negotiation and compromise. Hence, for the present, in this era of half-finished Lords reform, the Lords have greater power than usual. It sometimes gives the opportunity for a mighty executive to be checked.

Procedures

The House is self-governing, where all its members are equal and there exist no powers of control by a Speaker. Procedural questions in relation to the conduct of business are decided by the 'sense of the House', within the ambit of the standing orders and the *Companion to the Standing Orders*, which respectively date from 1621 and 1862. The numbers of standing orders have grown somewhat recently and the length of the *Companion* markedly (up from 30 pages in 1955 to 265 in 2003) though this is much shorter than *Erskine May*. They do not codify all practice with the written word, and much continues to be governed by custom and common sense.

Procedural changes are suggested by the Procedure Committee, now annually appointed, and consisting of the leaders and other usual channels and crossbenchers and backbenchers. Where the House decides a certain procedural change, it is made and the government cannot block it. It is usual practice for such changes to be made by consensus, but on one recent occasion, a stricter Code of Conduct and Register of Interests was introduced following a vote, with Labour and Liberal Democrats favouring the change, and the Conservatives voting against. This was the first such change effected following a vote on party lines.

However, the procedural changes made as a consequence of the Williams report were adopted as an experiment by consensus among the front benches and following negotiation between the differing viewpoints, and this remains the norm.

Establishment of the Lords Whips' Office 1960–63

During the 'big sleep' of the House of Lords, from the 1911 Parliament Act to the 1958 Life Peerages Act, there was very little need for an active government Whips' Office in the House of Lords. The Conservatives had a large majority in party terms, and could always win votes if they wished. The fact that they chose not to reflected the political realities of predominantly Conservative administrations throughout much of this period and an unwillingness among Conservatives to use their automatic majority in the Lords when the lack of accountability of the hereditary-dominated House made it difficult to win in any appeal to public opinion. The House of Lords remained largely supine, and failed to copy the House of Commons in establishing an effective office of the government Chief Whips' private secretary to manage the government's programme of business, as was done between 1917 and 1961 in the Commons. This was the remarkable achievement of Sir Charles Harris (1901–86), which has been recently authoritatively described in an article by J. C. Sainty, 'Sir Charles Harris and the Management of the Business of the House of Commons'.[6]

In the Lords, by contrast, there was little organisation because it was not needed. In those far-off days, it was the Leader of the House who employed one of his own personal private secretaries to perform such business management work for the House as was required in addition to purely 'whipping'. This has been the system since before the passage of the Parliament Act in 1911. The files of the Leaders in the Lords' Record Office show a personal style, in which successive Leaders knew their flock and cared for them in a pastoral relationship, sometimes verging on the quaint.

Sir Charles Clay has described[7] the arrangements for organising the business of the House of Lords in 1908, when Lord Crewe, the then Leader of the House, appointed him as one of his four private secretaries at the Colonial Office. Lionel Earle (later permanent secretary at the Ministry of Works), a career civil servant, was the principal private secretary and would accompany Lord Crewe to be present at debates, but his Lords work was combined with his other Colonial Office work. As a consequence of this, and of the fact that the private secretary did not have an office in the Palace of Westminster, the parliamentary work for Lord Crewe was carried out in the Colonial Office, for example fixing dates for debates or for the answering of questions. Similarly, the Lords whips were constantly coming to see the Leader at the Colonial Office, although as Leader he had a room in the House, as did the leader of the opposition (Lord Lansdowne).

Clay moved with Crewe when the latter moved to the India Office in 1910, and thenceforth served him as Leader of the House, as well as on semi-private interests, distinct from the India Office work. He then worked from his India Office room, where he kept the Privy Seal in a safe, coming over to the Lords in the afternoon to attend to sittings of the House, where he had no room, but managed to arrange for an 'official's box' in the chamber, and for access to the library.

When Clay was appointed assistant librarian to the House of Lords in 1914, and thereafter, the system of personal, albeit temporary, appointments by the Leader of the House lasted until 1935, when Lord Londonderry appointed C. A. C. J. Hendriks, who had been in his previous private office in the Air Ministry. Hendriks remained private secretary to successive Leaders of the Lords – some nine in total – between 1935 and his death in January 1960.

The establishment of an efficient government Whips' Office in the Lords was the achievement in particular of two people – Lord St Aldwyn, Conservative Chief Whip 1958–78, and Peter Henderson (later Lord Henderson of Brompton), the first Lords' clerk (on secondment to the government) to fill the post of private secretary to the Leader and government Chief Whip, in the years 1960–63. Lord St Aldwyn at the time of his retirement gave a brief account of how it came to pass:

> *I shall ... say a few words about how the Whips' Office came into being. I think that that needs to be recorded somewhere and this seems to me as good a place and as good a time as any. When I was appointed by my noble friend [Lord Home] in 1958, I had an office, a telephone and a file, which noble Lords may have seen reference to in the* Sunday Telegraph, *saying 'Dead Peers.' But with no names in it. That is literally all that I succeeded to. The business of the House was then totally organised by the Secretary to the Leader of the House, Sir Charles Hendriks, a remarkable character who served this House quite brilliantly over many years. However, he was getting on in years and was due to retire at the beginning of 1960 ...*
>
> *I was then faced with the problem of what to do when Sir Charles Hendriks left, because I felt that the Chief Whip's job was to run the business of the House. I had many long discussions with the then Clerk of the Parliaments, Sir Victor Goodman, as to what was the best solution. He came forward with the suggestion, which I very readily accepted, that the government Whips' Office should be manned from the Parliament Office. I must admit at once that that seemed to me a thoroughly sound idea, for two reasons; first, because it meant that there would, over the years, be an increasing number of Members of the Parliament Office who really understood the government machine. In the past there has always been a slight tendency – I think probably in both Houses – for the Parliament Office to consider itself slightly remote from the government offices. This scheme has undoubtedly proved a great success and I think that most of your Lordships would agree that we have benefited from it. It also had the great advantage that various people were loaned for short periods only, which meant that no servant, either of the House or from anywhere else, rose to a position of extreme power.*

I am sure that it has been very much for the benefit of the House that
we have had this constant turnover. Really, the business has been in the
hands of the Chief Whip, assisted by his secretary, but not run by his
secretary.

Sir Victor suggested a young man to come and be the first of these secre-
*taries [Peter Henderson].*8

Papers in the National Archives and the House of Lords' Record Offices,9
now available under the thirty-year rule make it possible to describe the background to the rearrangements for a Lords Whips' Office set in place in 1960,
described by Lord St Aldwyn on his retirement quoted above.

Even before Hendriks' death there had been considerable discussion
between ministers and officials of what arrangements should be made to
replace him. On 21 September 1956, a Treasury official had reported to the
Cabinet Secretary, Sir Norman Brook, that Lord Home – Leader of the House
of Lords from 1957 to 1960 – 'will feel that Sir Charles Hendriks should be
put on notice now, but should not retire till August, 1957'. But there were
two big obstacles to such a change. As was reported on 5 June 1957,

when the Leader of the House of Lords was prepared to harden his heart
and give Hendriks the push – we would have a successor lined up. I am
*afraid that the successor*10 *has now slipped off the hook, having got a fat*
job in De La Rues. Would you wish me to make an alternative plan … ?
My only suggestion … is to revert to my original idea of looking among the
Clerks of the House of Lords for a suitable man. Coldstream suggested we
might do worse than Mr. A. P. D. Smyth or failing him Mr. E. D. Graham.

It is apparent that the reason for the delay in effecting Hendriks' retirement
was the financial difficulty of giving him a decent pension, as he was an
unestablished civil servant on a modest salary. It was for that reason, and
because of Lord Home's kindness of heart, that nothing was done.

Meanwhile officials continued to plan for a contingency which they believed could not be long delayed. Sir Norman Brook recorded on 22 April 1958 that he had

> *spoken to [Home, Leader of the Lords] about Sir Charles Hendriks ...*
> *[it was] plain Hendriks ought to retire before the end of the Parliament.*
> *[Home] asked me to speak to Sir G. Coldstream[11] about the possibility*
> *of finding a successor from among the existing staff of the House of Lords*
> *... possibly ... Burrows.... An alternative which has not previously*
> *occurred to me, namely that Sir Charles Harris might like to take this*
> *on. Harris was complaining of being tired and old and finding it increas-*
> *ingly difficult to cope ... The corresponding job [of Lords private*
> *secretary] was much less arduous ... I undertook to sound Harris about*
> *this.*

Treasury officials, including Mrs Abbot, had objections to this proposal. 'Harris would not find it easy to accommodate himself to the difficult atmosphere of the Lords ... the conclusive argument was that we had no successor in sight for No. 12 [the Commons Whips' Office].' A further possibility considered was to find someone already in the Civil Service, but the difficulty here was that no one was keen to find the pair of hands in their own department – there was little spare manpower either in the Treasury or the Lord Chancellor's Department, while the Cabinet Office had very few permanent officials, save either at the highest or lowest levels.

In the succeeding months, officials continued to discuss possible successors to Hendriks, but were stymied in their wish to make progress by Lord Home's unwillingness to 'grasp this nettle at all'. Meanwhile, the high Whitehall mandarins recognised that 'there is a considerable job of reorganisation to be done, in building up a proper government Whips' Office, now that the House of Lords has (as they say) taken on a new lease of life through the creation of life peerages.'

Coldstream had said, as reported to Brook on 13 May 1959, that

> *the revival in the Lords ... was quite remarkable and in his view*
> *stemmed from three different factors: the departure of Lord Salisbury, the*
> *arrival of the Life Peers and the enthusiasm and activity of Lord St.*
> *Aldwyn. All in all the Lords was a changed place. And the very amateur*
> *machinery which had passed unremarked previously was now creaking.*

What was needed now, in Coldstream's view, was 'a man with Whitehall experience to spend a period in the Lords, bringing the machinery up to date'.

In the event the nettle was never grasped until Hendriks died in office on 31 January 1960 at the age of 76,[12] and something had to be done as a matter of urgency to fill the vacancy.

It was at this stage that the then Clerk of the Parliaments, Sir Victor Goodman, on 1 March minuted the Leader (Lord Home) to suggest that the post of private secretary to the Leader and Chief Whip of the Lords 'should be permanently included in my office ... I could more easily than a government department provide someone to replace the existing secretary.' On the following day, Home contacted the Cabinet Secretary, forwarding Goodman's minute: 'I think this is an excellent solution. May I have your views?'

In his turn the Cabinet Secretary minuted the Treasury on 3 March (Mrs Abbot), asking for advice, in particular to

> *find out from people who are in daily touch with [the Whips' Offices]*
> *whether Whitehall will suffer if this post is held, on secondment, by a*
> *series of people who know a lot about the House of Lords' procedure but*
> *little about government departments.*

After consultation on 14 March Mrs Abbot was advised of the

*view ... it is more valuable for the holder of this post to know a lot about
the House of Lords and its procedure than it is for him to know a lot about
the government departments and the way in which Whitehall works.*

Four days later, the Cabinet Secretary was told:

*No one seems to feel that Whitehall experience is essential. [Coldstream]
says that Mr. Henderson filled the Bill very well indeed ... well liked ...
assiduous ... knows a great deal about the House and is setting out to
find out what else he needs to know ... very acceptable to Lord Home
and Lord St. Aldwyn.*

*For the future [we should] content ourselves with saying that [secondment
from the Lords] may well be the right answer normally but make no firm
commitment. Sir V. Goodman suggests the Private Secretary post be permanently included in his office – there may be constitutional objections to this.*

Goodman later reverted to his suggestion in 1961, when Mrs Abbot wrote
to him on 7 November to record their conversation:

*I should perhaps record that in our talk we touched upon the suggestion
that you should take the post of Private Secretary upon your establishment.
I explained that while it was accepted that there was a great deal to be
said for your regarding the Private Offices your responsibility in the sense
that you organise your recruiting, etc. arrangements on the assumption
that the Private Secretaryship be always filled by one of your men. There
were serious constitutional objections to you absorbing the Private Office
into your non-Civil Service establishment. I think you accepted this.*

The system thus established has continued ever since. The only two major
alterations suggested since have been that the Commons government Whips'
Office should take over the Lords Office as an outstation: this has never

found favour in the Lords. Secondly, occasionally there have been suggestions that the Commons should copy the Lords, by placing a Commons clerk in the Whips' Office on secondment, for a strictly limited period. This idea was nearly adopted in 1974, but fell by the wayside when the February general election resulted in a change of party in power. At the last occasion, in 2000, when the incumbent private secretary to the Commons Chief Whip retired, the post was filled after public advertisement by the Cabinet Office, and was open to the clerks in the two Houses as well as civil servants.

Additionally, as a halfway house, it has become customary for a Commons clerk to be seconded to work in the Cabinet Office for the Leader and the Chief Whip. The secondee is taken from a shortlist provided by the Clerk of the House, and chosen by the Leader, and only for a limited period – about two years.

An additional post of Assistant Private Secretary was created in 2000, first filled by a Lords clerk on two years' secondment. After two such appointments an interesting development takes place as I write: an assistant private secretary is about to move from the Whips' Office in the Commons to the Whips' Office in the Lords. This will be the first instance of an official having experience of both Whips' Offices. What the effect will be remains to be seen.

Conclusion

The quotations from the original documents of the period serve to substantiate Lord St Aldwyn's version of the birth of the Lords Whips' Office. Adopting Churchill's adage that 'we shape our buildings, and afterwards our buildings shape us,' the way in which the two Houses are run remain surprisingly distinct, and reflect the substructures provided by the respective Whips' Offices, which in the Lords were put in place by two men in the short spell of three years.

Endnotes

1   *Report by the Group Appointed to Consider How the Working Practices of the House Can Be Improved, and to Make Recommendations*, HL 111 of 2001/2.

2   Cm 4534.

3   See Walters, R. 'The House of Lords', in V. Bogdanor (ed.) *The British Constitution in the Twentieth Century* (Oxford University Press, Oxford, 2003).

4   I owe warm thanks to Mary Robertson, who as private secretary came to Magdalen College in 2002 to open a stimulating seminar on organising the government's business in Parliament, and on whose views I have drawn for a contemporary account of the 'usual channels' (my own experience dates from 1965–7). Rush, M. and Ettinghausen, C. *Opening Up the Usual Channels* (Hansard Society, London, 2002) provides a recent description of the system in the two Houses and, in Appendix 3, in some other Parliaments. Kennon, A. *The Commons: Reform or Modernisation* (University College London Constitution Unit, London, 2000) describes the government's control in the Commons over procedural change.

5   New creations announced on 1 May 2004 have added 23 Labour, five Conservative, eight Liberal Democrat and ten crossbench members to these totals. Thanks are due to David Beamish, Andrew Makower and David Jones for this information and other valuable comments.

6   *Parliamentary History*, 2002, vol. 21, no. 2, pp. 233–9. I am also indebted to Sir John Sainty for his assistance in identifying sources, especially in the National Archive, and for his notes on the private secretaries to the Leaders of the House between 1908 and 1960. For many years he has provided encouragement and support and discussions with him of problems concerning parliamentary history have been rewarding. Harris is included in the new edition of the *Dictionary of National Biography*.

7   Sainty drew my attention to, and kindly loaned me a note by, Sir Charles Clay which describes his period as private secretary to the Leader of the Lords between 1908 and 1914.

8   *Official Report*, 17 January 1978, cols 11–12.

9   TNA 199/628 and 199/909–912, and HLRO LH/3, LH/4, LH/9 and LH/10.

10 The successor designate was the then private secretary to the Lord Chancellor, Mr C. Rankin, who was described as 'particularly well suited to do this work'.

11 Permanent secretary to the Lord Chancellor, 1954–68.

12 His widow was left not well provided for and a total of £3,729 5s. was raised by private subscription by the Hendriks Memorial and appeal in consequence.

NINETEEN

Modernisation – Making the Commons Fit For the 21st Century

Oonagh Gay

Modernisation entered the parliamentary vocabulary with the election of the Labour government in May 1997, armed with a manifesto for major constitutional change. Parliamentary reformers had been making advances since the mid-1960s, notably the establishment of departmental select committees in 1979 and changes to sitting times and standards regulation in the 1990s. But the new term implied a shift of emphasis away from 'reform' to management concepts of 'efficiency' and 'fit for purpose'.[1] The unresolved issue with modernisation remains 'fit for whose purpose?'. This chapter offers a chronology of change, and then assesses the key components of the modernisation programme in the Commons.

The origins of modernisation

The speech to Charter88 by the then shadow Leader of the House, Ann Taylor, in May 1996 was the first indication of the new agenda.[2] This was presented as re-engaging with the public and making Parliament more effective at holding the executive to account. Liberal Democrat concerns with the public image of Parliament echoed many of these themes and reform was a major element of the Cook/Maclennan report on constitutional reform, launched in March 1997.[3]

Various themes can be detected in the modernisation process:

- Symbolic changes to achieve a modern Parliament, such as the abolition of arcane customs and improving visitor facilities.
- A genuine interest in improving the machinery for scrutiny, by giving select committees more resources and a more focused role, and offering different venues for backbench debates.
- A concern with processing business more efficiently, through programming legislation and adjusting sitting hours and the parliamentary calendar.

Some of the reforms fall into more than one category: for example, reform of sitting hours was also intended to improve the public image of Parliament, by making its work take place at more media-friendly hours. The Modernisation Committee did not explicitly articulate the potentially contradictory objects of its work, but these soon became apparent.

But the decisive element for change would be a new select committee, unusually chaired by the Leader of the House.[4] This was a double-edged sword; the Leader, as a Cabinet member, could guarantee some government buy-in for the proposals, and provide the motive force behind its work, but the close involvement of the executive would ensure that the major thrust of modernisation would be towards improving efficiency rather than achieving greater accountability.[5]

Ann Taylor – as Leader of the House following the 1997 Labour victory – worked swiftly to stamp her vision on the Commons. Initially, the committee met twice weekly, with the Conservatives offering pragmatic support for many initiatives. But there were some initiatives disturbing to parliamentary reformers even in May 1997, the most prominent being the unilateral decision of Tony Blair to move Prime Minister's Question Time to a weekly slot, with no attempt to obtain parliamentary input into the decision.6

The 1997 parliament – the agenda is set out

The first debate on modernisation took place as early as 22 May 1997. The Committee's first report was released on 23 July 1997, with a further six reports that session. There were only three reports per session in the two following sessions, and by 2000/2001 the only report issued was on the programming of legislation – the most controversial part of the modernisation package. A reduction in numbers is not on its own indicative of a slowing in the pace of reform, but illustrates how modernisation as a topic was moving towards becoming the work of just another select committee, not least of all once Ann Taylor had been moved to the post of Chief Whip in July 1998.

That first session set out the themes that still top the agenda eight years on. The legislative process was a priority concern – the government had a raft of constitutional legislation to get through Parliament, and some type of arrangement was essential to prevent opposition disruption. The first report of July 1997 called for programme motions to timetable bills, more prelegislative scrutiny, more explanatory notes on legislation and carry-over of bills from one session to the next. Programming was designed to inject consensus into the timetabling of bills and avoid the ritual time-wasting debates on a guillotine motion. The government was not entirely successful in introducing programming: guillotine motions were used four times on three major bills in 1997/8, but by the end of the session a real change was apparent. The opposition maintained a pragmatic stance; in effect, a tacit deal had been concluded: in exchange for keeping all stages of constitutional Bills on the floor of the House rather than in committee with less public attention, the spokesmen were willing to accede to their timetabling. The scale of their electoral defeat in 1997 ensured that the Conservative opposition had small enthusiasm for delaying tactics.7 Here, the contrast with the behaviour of the Labour opposition in

1979/80 is instructive – then the House suffered years of late-night debates and 'ambushes'. So devolution, human rights and Lords reform were achieved much more smoothly than commentators had expected in 1997.

But programming did not achieve its full potential. Its use was much more ad hoc than originally anticipated.[8] *Griffith and Ryle* suggests that the decision not to incorporate programming motions into standing orders depicted a failure of radicalism within the Cabinet and signalled that modernisation would not, after all, mean a new, more autonomous relationship between legislature and executive.[9] Prelegislative scrutiny suffered a similar fate: the initiative built on Conservative reforms of the 1990s, which saw eighteen draft Bills between 1992 and 1997 the subject of such scrutiny, but in the period 1997–8 only two Bills were presented in draft, and only one Bill submitted to the special standing committee procedure, which allows the taking of evidence at committee stage.

Miscellaneous reform proposals bore fruit. Explanatory notes for Bills and Acts were introduced to general acclaim: a more user-friendly order paper, greater flexibility on time limits for speeches, abolition of the opera hat formerly required for raising points of order during divisions, reforming the scrutiny of EU matters through removing some long-standing obstacles to the work of the European Scrutiny Committee, allowing standing and select committees to sit in recesses, deferring the divisions on less important business. All were sensible, but only the report on the Scrutiny of European Business actually boosted the scrutiny role of members.[10]

But the Modernisation Committee stopped short of radical changes; a consultation on electronic voting found a lack of consensus among MPs and the idea was shelved. Carrying Bills over from one parliamentary session to the next was proposed with little result;[11] changes to the parliamentary calendar were tentative, with the introduction of Thursday morning sittings from January 1999, but only at 11.30 a.m. The main proposal pushed the Commons towards a four-day week, with Fridays for constituency work, leaving the then Speaker, Betty Boothroyd, to express alarm about the significance for the Commons of the government's conception of the backbench role.

The final initiative of the 1997 Parliament was the introduction of a parallel chamber, in Westminster Hall, adapted directly from the experience of Australia's Main Committee and the House of Lords' Moses Room.[12] One of the original intentions behind its birth was to gain time for non-controversial government Bills. The Modernisation Committee confined the idea to using the hall only as an additional forum for the backbenchers, either raising matters of constituency interest, or debating on select committees.

Before this report was published in December 1998, Ann Taylor had been replaced as Leader of the House by Margaret Beckett, whose concerns did not appear to include the accountability agenda of modernisation.[13] Her focus was on the processing of legislation, and her viewpoint was straightforward. The Labour government had been given a mandate from the electors to carry out its manifesto – legislation should pass through both Houses as smoothly as possible. So programming passed from being a consensual planning instrument to a refinement of the 'guillotine' deplored by parliamentary reformers. Opposition unease was signalled by two minority reports to the Modernisation Committee under Beckett.[14]

The Conservatives established a commission under Lord Norton to call for improvements to scrutiny and accountability.[15] The Liaison Committee, composed of the chairs of Commons select committees, also lined up against the government priorities. In a series of reports entitled *Shifting the Balance*, they called for the second theme of modernisation – scrutiny – to be given the attention it deserved.[16] The Hansard Society Commission on Parliamentary Scrutiny added its influential voice to the growing debate about the Blair government's apparent disdain for Parliament.[17]

Nevertheless, Beckett continued with the modernisation agenda, concentrating on the more efficient management of business. The orders for the Westminster Hall initiative and the ending of Thursday's main business at 7.00 p.m. were renewed amidst initial scepticism about poor attendance.[18]

A majority committee report proposed that a number of divisions that would normally have taken place after 10.00 p.m. should be deferred to the following Wednesday, leaving the Conservatives to protest against making 'Parliament seem like a voting machine'.[19] The row over deferred divisions was illustrative of a perceived lack of consensus and imagination about the process of change.

The Cook approach to the modernisation agenda

The appointment of Robin Cook as Leader of the House in May 2001 revitalised modernisation. He relished the potential for creativity which the post of Leader offers, without the strain of running a major department. He established three reform objectives: more prelegislative scrutiny, a more media-friendly parliamentary timetable and calendar which would allow for Bills to be carried over from one session to the next, and revitalisation of select committees. He set out the reform agenda in December 2001 in a significant memorandum to the Modernisation Committee.[20] The Liaison Committee proposals, ignored under Beckett, thus began to bear fruit. But initially he did not appreciate the guile of the Labour Whips' Office, who were determined to frustrate his plans to allow backbenchers the final word in the appointment of chairs to select committees.[21] On a free vote on 14 May 2002 the House narrowly rejected these proposals, while accepting a package of other reforms as follows:

- Establishment of core tasks for select committees.
- Additional pay for select committee chairmen, combined with a two-term limit.[22]

Another package of reforms achieved a narrow success in a free vote on 29 October 2002. But the outcome was more partisan, since fewer than 30 Conservatives voted in favour. The main changes were:

- more timetabling of the introduction of Bills each session, and a greater use of carry-over and prelegislative scrutiny;
- the introduction of morning sittings for Tuesdays, and Wednesdays, finishing at 7.30 p.m., with statements and questions brought forward to more media-friendly lunchtimes and allowing more family-friendly hours to some members;
- an earlier end to the summer recess, with the Commons returning in September for two weeks;
- shorter notice periods for oral questions and time-limited speeches to ensure more topical debate;[23]
- debates in Westminster Hall became a permanent fixture.

But Cook struggled with improving the public face of Parliament, failing to solve the considerable difficulties of making an inward-looking body accept the need for change. After his departure in March 2003, there was a hiatus under John Reid, and limited resurgence under his successor, Peter Hain, who was interested in improving the public perception of Parliament.[24] Press briefings indicated that the Leader's office still hankered after more radical reforms, with the possibility of replacing sessions with one parliamentary term in which to pass Bills (as in the Scottish Parliament).[25] Amendment of the Parliament Acts would be necessary and looks unlikely at present.

The major themes of modernisation deserve greater scrutiny, and are set out below.

The impact on legislation

Prelegislative scrutiny is designed to discover the flaws in intended legislation at an earlier stage, and although it is not explicitly designed to ensure that the legislation can withstand less sustained attention later in the Commons this appears to be the result in practice, due to programming of Bills. The two reforms have become interlinked.[26]

Programming

Change to the treatment of legislation was the main preoccupation of the incoming Labour government of 1997. Their 1945 predecessors had found it necessary to expand the system of standing committees to deal with the legislation necessary to establish the welfare state.[27] The Hansard Society lent force to longstanding concerns with its report in 1992, *Making the Law*.[28] This was critical of the use made of guillotines to counter filibustering by the opposition, as limiting the quality of scrutiny.

The specially appointed Jopling Committee had made some progress with the introduction of voluntary agreements on the allocation of time to ensure scrutiny of all parts of a Bill from 1994–5.[29] But Taylor considered that a new approach was necessary. The Modernisation Committee borrowed the term 'programming' from *Making the Law* to apply to a new form of timetabling, designed to be more formal than the usual channels, but more flexible than the guillotine. As envisaged in its first report in July 1997, the programme motions would be introduced in the early stage of a Bill's progress, but in practice between 1997 and 2000 they were more often used later, to speed the passage of a Bill.[30] The reformers had hoped for a Business Committee model, to allow more transparency and independence in the allocation of time. This was vetoed by the whips.[31] Eleven programme motions were signed by all three parties, using existing standing orders established for guillotines in 1998, but by 1999 this had dropped to four, and programming ceased to be a consensual process.[32] A novel feature, the creation of programming subcommittees, did not in the event offer the type of dialogue with opposition interests that had been hoped for in 1997.[33]

A new set of sessional orders was introduced for one year on 7 November 2000 which applied programming to the great majority of public Bills.[34] All programmes were imposed by the government without consensus in 2000/2001. Sir Alan Haselhurst, a Deputy Speaker, commented that by this pre-election period:

It was difficult to escape the conclusion that a reform which had origi-
nally been proposed as a way of securing a fair balance between the
interests of the government, the opposition and other sections of the House,
and ensuring adequate consideration of all parts of each bill had become
just another weapon in the armoury for managing the business of the
House.[35]

From June 2001 a minister could move a programme motion immediately after second reading, without formal debate.[36] Programming was renewed on a sessional basis on 29 October 2002[37] and 6 November 2003.[38] The most recent Modernisation Committee review lamented its inadequacies, but could see no alternative.[39] A minority report continued to argue the case for abolition. Sir Alan continued to point out with some force that programming had led to less scrutiny than before – because of the truncation of debate particularly at the report and third reading stages.[40] He deplored the effect on minority and backbench interests as ministers and opposition spokesmen overran their time. In 2002 he concluded: 'If the basic idea behind the concept of programming has been to achieve balanced consideration of legislation, progress to date can frankly and brutally be described as nil'[41]

But the committee did not accept his recommendations for time-limited speeches from frontbenchers and an appeals procedure for backbenchers to plead for time to consider their amendments. It placed its faith in reducing the need for programming through more prelegislative scrutiny and making the process by which each stage is completed more flexible.[42]

Draft legislation

Pressure for more draft legislation has had an effect once government departments could be convinced that it was not wasted effort. Progress was haphazard until Cook's tenure as Leader of the House, when a real surge was evident:

Table 1: Draft Bills subjected to prelegislative scrutiny

Session	Session Leader of the House	Bills
1997/8	1997–98 Taylor/Beckett	2
1998/9	1998–99 Beckett	6
1999/2000	1999–2000 Beckett	6
2000/2001	2000–01 Beckett	2
2001/2	2001–02 Cook	6
2002/3	2002–03 Cook/Reid/Hain	8*
2003/4	(2003–4 as announced Dec 03) Hain	10

* In addition there were two sets of draft clauses to existing Bills.

Almost all draft Bills have subsequently been enacted.[43] Delicate negotiations with the usual channels have proved necessary for the allocation of prelegislative scrutiny to committees. Recently, there has been a tendency for draft Bills to be referred to ad hoc joint committees, with an instruction to report by a certain date. *Griffith and Ryle* commented:

> Select committees looking at draft bills seem to have steered a middle way between challenging the whole principle of the bill and minutely scrutinising the text of each clause ... Since committee scrutiny has often been conducted in tandem with public consultation on the bill, the whole process has subjected draft bills to more thorough public examination at an earlier stage than would normally occur. Arguably, at this stage, it is easier for Ministers to agree to make changes than when the Government's prestige is engaged as the bill goes through the formal legislative process.[44]

Timing has proved difficult, as committees struggled to meet the deadlines of the executive, a point picked up by the Liaison Committee. [45] But ad hoc committees offer real expertise, as demonstrated by the Joint Committee on the Draft Communications Bill.[46]

Some thought had gone into the question of resources for this new work. In 1998/9, the Procedure Committee considered that select committees would need additional help to examine resource accounting and budgeting, three-year spending plans and departmental reports in their scrutiny of departments. It suggested that 'a small corps of staff, available to all committees, would ensure committees had ready access to the expertise they need', to assist them in their scrutiny of estimates.[47] The Liaison Committee developed this recommendation and argued that the House needed to establish a special unit to support committees in prelegislative scrutiny work. The manner in which the Modernisation Committee built on this recommendation by ensuring that the House of Commons Commission provided funds illustrates its unique role in achieving implementation of proposals made elsewhere.[48] The Scrutiny Unit was established in November 2002 to assist with prelegislative and financial scrutiny.[49]

The impact on select committees

Scrutiny was slow to receive attention by the Modernisation Committee. It came on the agenda following pressure from the Liaison Committee when Cook became Leader of the House. The immediate impetus was a clumsy attempt by Labour whips in July 2001 to remove two long-standing select committee chairs, Gwyneth Dunwoody (Transport) and Donald Anderson (Foreign Affairs), who were not seen as 'on message'.[50] Labour backbenchers rebelled, and nomination arrangements were unsurprisingly found to be lacking in transparency.[51] The first Cook report set out a radical agenda to strengthen the committees – as with prelegislative scrutiny, it brought together a variety of existing proposals from reformers, especially the Liaison Committee. Its most ambitious proposal – to create a committee of nominations – was defeated in the debate on 14 May 2002. The defeat was a result of difficulties in transmitting the potential benefits of a nomination procedure independent of the whips, where the whips were the most usual channel of communication with backbenchers. The committee would have been drawn from backbenchers experienced in chairing standing committees, and perhaps suffered from being too divorced from party loyalties. Other setbacks included the failure to agree a larger membership of select committees, which would have meant that committee work was a major element of each backbencher's job. The Liaison Committee's opposition was influential, and also sound – there might well have been difficulties in operating committees of fifteen.[52]

Proposals which were successful were an additional salary for chairs of some select committees, combined with a limit of two parliamentary terms. The Liaison Committee supported the former but not the latter, arguing that 'effectiveness must be paramount'.[53] Of long-term importance was an acceptance of core tasks for select committees and a system of annual reporting to the Liaison Committee. This is designed to meet criticism of the uncoordinated nature of scrutiny given by the departmental select committees.[54] The adoption of these tasks has made select committees consider how their time is being spent. The creation of Westminster Hall debates has enabled committee reports to be debated and therefore increased their influence within Westminster. The Liaison Committee's encouragement to committees to return to previous inquiries to review the proportion of recommendations accepted has also helped to create more businesslike procedures.[55] Financial scrutiny has fared less well than prelegislative scrutiny in terms of profile. Attempts to improve the presentation of committee reports have had some impact, but there continues to be only sporadic success in interesting the media.

The missing element in select committee reform has been any rigorous attempt to introduce benchmarking on the effectiveness of the scrutiny role. Each committee now produces an annual report, based on the common core tasks, but this falls short of the recommendations of Hogg and Jenkins for audit indicators, related to the functions of Parliament.[56] One set of criteria might be: judging success by impact on government, impact on society and value to the House of Commons (in terms of producing suitable information and assessment to aid the scrutiny role).[57] Each committee could be audited on an annual basis by these performance objectives. National Audit

Office reports to the Public Accounts Committee are already subject to external appraisal, measured by a variety of indicators. It is perhaps a measure of the poverty of ambition for good scrutiny in the modernisation process that no serious attempt has been made to introduce performance assessment.

Impact on sitting hours

Experiments with sitting hours began in 1998/9 by advancing the hours on Thursdays.[58] But Cook made the more dramatic changes, extending these 11.30 a.m.–7.00 p.m. hours to Tuesdays and Wednesdays. The main rationale was to secure greater media interest in the Commons, as expressed by the Modernisation Committee report:

> *The problem with the traditional times of sitting is that major events such as statements, Prime Minister's Questions, or opening speeches come quite late in the normal working day. As a result parliamentary events do not set the day's agenda of public debate as often as they should, but frequently respond to an agenda that has already been set before the House meets. At the other end of the day the principal vote in the Commons comes at night. The consequence is that the key votes in the House of Commons cannot be adequately reported on the same day or be covered in most editions of the morning papers on the next day.[59]*

The changes were bitterly fought and did not achieve widespread acceptance, not least for some unforeseen consequences. The work of select committees has been disrupted by the need to attend divisions in the chamber, and MPs from outside the south-east consider that the utilisation of Tuesday and Wednesday evenings for parliamentary business would be preferable to the early starts now necessary for standing committees – not promoting family-friendly hours. Early in 2004 it became clear that compromises would be necessary if these changs were to become firmly embedded. There has been no programme of research to monitor whether media interest has in fact increased. Some indications are there, but the more partisan politics in recent years make it hard to separate out the particular role of revised hours in improving coverage.

Making Parliament more accessible

The weakness of the Modernisation Committee approach has perhaps been most palpable in its attempts to make Parliament more physically accessible. The committee has overlapping membership with the House of Commons Commission, which administers the House, but it does not have authority over the several vested interests at Westminster that delay reform.[60] The Commons has yet to establish either a crèche or a visitors' centre, despite well-established campaigns. More progress has been made with electronic accessibility – select committee hearings are now webcast.[61] But this followed an influential report from the Broadcasting Select Committee, which recommended joint Commons and Lords funding for the initiative.[62] The website is considerably improved after a relaunch in 2002. These changes have yet to transform the relationship between elected and the electors, just as new methods of voting have yet to galvanise the public into participation. But the widespread attention given to the Iraq debates in 2003 illustrates that the focus should lie with ensuring that parliamentary business is immediately relevant to public concerns.

The Modernisation Committee: a unique experiment?

It was immediately apparent that the new committee would have unique characteristics, compared with previous House committees charged with reviewing the working practices of the House. It was led by a senior government minister, and included in its membership the shadow Leaders of the House from the Conservatives and Liberal Democrats.[63] Although earlier committees, such as the Jopling Committee on sitting hours, had had unofficial government support, this was a step change. The executive, in effect, established a mechanism for directly influencing the development of the legislature.

From the start, the Modernisation Committee behaved differently from other select committees, rarely taking formal evidence or meeting in public. The process had moved on since Taylor's initial suggestions in her Charter88 speech for a 'special select committee with a panel of independent advisers'. It was apparent that the Leader's policy staff had a role in informally servicing the committee. Proposals also had to be taken through a Cabinet subcommittee, where more radical ideas tended to be repulsed. These characteristics meant that the committee lacked transparency. The Leader of the House has considerable sway over committee outcomes, but his proposals are mediated by the other members of the committee, so that its programme of work cannot be characterised as executive led in its entirety. The success of its proposals tends to depend on the uncertainty of free votes, so it must achieve reasonable 'buy-in' from backbenchers. This creates difficulties in attracting support in the absence of direction, and occasional hostility from the whips. Some aspects of modernisation have proved much more complex than originally expected.64

Surprisingly, pre-existing committees survived and proved a useful source for new ideas: the Procedure Committee's proposals on parliamentary questions were taken up by the Modernisation Committee; the Liaison Committee's proposals on select committees have been partially implemented. For some time there has appeared to be an overlap in the work of the Modernisation and Procedure Committees which looks messy: it was the latter committee which took the initiative in the review of sitting hours in January 2004 by its questionnaire to members. The future of the Modernisation Committee is uncertain, as it lacks any audit of its own work or any formal statement of its role. Neither the House nor the committee can establish the point at which modernisation has been achieved, or whether it is a continuous process. This makes it difficult to wind the committee up, but it may become marginalised, if other Commons mechanisms are used to take forward scrutiny debate post Hutton.

Conclusion: what has modernisation meant to the Commons?

Modernisation was more about the process of change – buying in support from both front benches to improve the efficiency of the Commons – than producing original reforms. The committee has not always proceeded by consensus, but neither has it always reflected the views of the Leader of the House. It has a higher success rate than the backbench Procedure Committee in securing the implementation of its proposals. This begs the question as to whether the Commons can reform itself without government initiative. The Scottish Parliament – based on the Westminster model – has abolished the post of Leader of the House, thereby achieving greater institutional autonomy.[65]

The area most affected by modernisation has been the organisation of business in the chamber. Programming has reduced the time spent on report stages and third readings; deferred divisions have reduced 'dead time' taken up by voting; Westminster Hall has reduced the need for members to stay in the House for evening debates on backbench business, whether constituency or select committee based. The changes in sittings hours did not reduce overall hours but it brought the parliamentary day forward and the reduction of business on Thursdays and its abandonment on Fridays have created an extremely truncated weekly plenary cycle.

Sitting hours' reform offered an opportunity for the House to develop into a more committee-based legislature, but leaving standing committee procedures untouched has prevented more radical change. Select committees have better resources, and more focus, but often do refuse the prelegislative burden. In their place, ad hoc joint committees draw on the expertise and manpower of the Lords, but do not remain in existence for the scrutiny of the final legislative product. The phased introduction of Bills throughout the session has only worked intermittently, in the absence of an effective system of carry-over. The absence of a transparent business committee may be responsible for the failure to achieve a more planned legislative cycle. Frantic negotiations to save prime government legislation at the end of the 2002/3 session appeared to indicate how little had changed in Parliament.

The scrutiny of legislation overall shows some signs of improvement, through the gradual adoption of the prelegislative phase. This at least allows backbench input, suppressed later through programming. The increase in the amount of legislation being processed through Parliament shows no sign of abatement, indicating continuing problems. It is often the most urgent Bills that receive the worst scrutiny. To put the modernisation package into perspective, consider the contribution of the Lords to reforms in the treatment of legislation; in the past decade, it has established two influential legislative scrutiny committees, one on Bills which authorise delegated legislation and one on constitutional legislation. These reports often do much more than the Commons to highlight inappropriate drafting.

The reasons for widespread unhappiness at Westminster at the changes in sitting hours are more fundamental than nostalgia for a lost age. The increased effectiveness of committees is not yet so marked as to justify the decline in plenary sessions. Greater media attention has yet to affect committees. The battle over the appointment of select committee chairmen is likely to flare again in the next Parliament, but this is not the most important issue. Attention has moved to the need for committees to be prepared to use their powers to demand information from government – the post-Hutton Liaison Committee review of the ineffective Foreign Affairs Committee inquiry involving Dr David Kelly is likely to demonstrate the lack of ambition displayed by most committees.

But the biggest effect of modernisation has been to speed up the change in the focus of the MP's role – discernible since the 1960s.[66] Put simply, more members now put the constituency first in their list of priorities.[67] The promotion of constituency weeks, constituency Fridays and more predictable timing of business, combined with greater office assistance, has enabled MPs to devote more resources and energy to constituency work. The reasons are well known: the route to preferment rarely lies through the exercise of an independent mind.[68] For the minority of backbenchers who prefer the option of enhancing scrutiny through select committee work, there are not enough places on prime committees to go round. The analysis in the Cook/Maclennan report that Parliament no longer holds ministers to account rings uncomfortably true seven years on. In 1998/9, the Modernisation Committee set out the functions of Parliament as follows:[69]

- The formation of a government and holding it to account.
- The scrutiny and passage of legislation.
- The authorisation of taxation and public expenditure.
- Debating issues of concern to the nation.

The Modernisation Committee has been reluctant to submit its work to formal audit, but the progress it has made towards improving the performance of the Commons in meeting these objectives is debatable. The only external evaluation undertaken is by Democratic Audit, and these reports range beyond the specific modernisation initiatives to examine the approach of the executive to Parliament.[70] A progress report on the implementation of recommendations by the committee is overdue, and might help with forward planning of objectives and even with the consideration of its future viability.[71]

Post Hutton, a reconstituted Liaison Committee is likely to appear as a more appropriate instrument for reform. The Commons cannot go back to a plenary-based existence; instead the future appears to lie in enhanced scrutiny of policy and legislation by backbenchers. Scottish reformers point to the introduction of a multi-party system as required to destroy the silent hegemony of the whips.[72] At present, both Lords reform and a new voting system seem a long way off for the Commons. If nothing else, it is time to be more precise about the language of change, to abandon the amorphous concept of modernisation, in favour of achieving more and better scrutiny, finally answering the question posed at the beginning – fit for whose purpose?

Endnotes

1   Richard Crossman, as Leader of the House, had made an intriguing comparison between modernisation and reform in the 1960s, cited in Seaton, J. and Winetrobe, B. K. 'Modernising the Commons', *Political Quarterly*, 1999, vol. 70, pp. 152–60.

2   'New Politics, New Parliament', 14 May 1996.

3   *Report of the Joint Consultative Committee on Constitutional Reform*, 1997.

4   Leaders of the House had chaired select committees previously, notably the Privileges Committee, but select committees do not normally contain government ministers.

5   See Kennon, A. *The Commons: Reform or Modernisation* (University College London Constitution Unit, London, 2000) for an analysis of the necessity for executive-driven reform in a Parliament that can act only rarely as a unified institutional force for decision-making.

6   He was not required to seek parliamentary approval for the decision. See Cowley, P. and Stuart, M. 'Parliament: a Few Headaches and a Dose of Modernisation', *Parliamentary Affairs*, 2001, vol. 54, pp. 238–56.

7   Labour enjoyed the largest majority since 1935. Philip Cowley in 'The Commons: Mr Blair's Lapdog?', *Parliamentary Affairs*, 2001, vol. 54, pp. 815–28 cites the comments of one Conservative MP on beholding them assembled: 'It's like that scene from *Zulu*' (p. 818).

8   See Seaton and Winetrobe, 'Modernising the Commons' for full details.

9   Blackburn, R. and Kennon, A. *Griffith & Ryle on Parliament: Functions, Practice and Procedures* (2nd ed.) (Sweet & Maxwell, London, 2003).

10   Modernisation Committee, seventh report, Session 1997–98, *The Scrutiny of European Business*, HC 791,. This built on proposals from the Select Committee on European Legislation in 1996. See Cowley and Stuart, 'Parliament: a Few Headaches and a Dose of Modernisation'.

11   First report, Session 1997–98, *The Legislative Process*, HC 190, paras 67–70 and third report, Session 1997–98, *Carry-over of Public Bills*, HC 543.

12   First report, Session 1998–99, *The Parliamentary Calendar: Initial Proposals*, HC 60, approved in debate December 1998.

13   Modernisation Committee, *Sittings of the House in Westminster Hall*, Session 1998–99, HC 194; *Programming of Legislation and Timing of Votes*, Session 1999–2000, HC 589.

14   Minutes of Proceeding, First Report, Session 2000–01, *Programming of Legislation*, HC 382.

15   *Strengthening Parliament: Report of the Commission to Strengthen Parliament* (Conservative Party, London, 2000).

16   Liaison Committee, *Shifting the Balance: Select Committees and the Executive*, Session 1999–2000, HC 300; government response, Cm 4737, May 2000; and committee response in

Independence or Control: The Government's Reply to the Committee's First Report of 1999–2000, Session 1999–2000, HC 748. See also its *Shifting the Balance: Unfinished Business*, Session 2000–2001, HC 321.

17 *The Challenge for Parliament: Making Government Accountable: Report of the Hansard Society Commission on Parliamentary Scrutiny* (Vacher Dod, London, 2001).

18 Modernisation Committee, *Sittings in Westminster Hall*, Session 1999–2000, HC 906. This recommended that the Westminster Hall experiment continue until the end of the first session of the next parliament. This duly occurred on 29 October 2002. The same approach was adopted in Session 1999–2000, HC 954 for Thursday sittings.

19 Sir George Young, Shadow Leader of the House, Modernisation Committee, *Programming of Legislation and Timing of Votes*, Session 1999–2000, HC 589, Minutes of Proceedings, para. 40. The types of vote deferred were mainly on secondary legislation.

20 *Memorandum Submitted by the Leader of the House of Commons: Modernisation of the House of Commons: a Reform Programme for Consultation*, Session 2001–02, HC 440.

21 Modernisation Committee *Modernisation of the House of Commons: a Reform Programme*

22 The House actually voted to refer the issue to the Senior Salaries Review Body, which reported favourably, and the new arrangements were adopted after debate in November 2003.

23 The Procedure Committee report on parliamentary questions (Session 2001–02, HC 622) was adopted by the government (HC 1121), but its proposal for a 30-minute topical question time in Westminster Hall was not taken up, and an amendment to introduce it was narrowly defeated on 29 October.

24 Hain has established a new website for the Leader of the House, hosted by the government network.

25 'Labour wants to downgrade Queen's role', *The Times*, 8 December 2003.

26 See paragraph 35 of the most recent Modernisation Committee assessment of programming in its first report of the 2002–03 session, *Programming of Bills*, HC 1222.

27 For a full discussion see Seaward, P. and Silk, P. 'The House of Commons', in V. Bogdanor (ed.) *The Constitution in the Twentieth Century* (Oxford University Press, Oxford, 2003).

28 Hansard Society Commission on the Legislative Process, *Making the Law*, chaired by Lord Rippon. See also the Procedure Committee report, Session 1984–85, HC 49.

29 The committee was nominally backbench, but it took account of frontbench concerns. Its main proposals are contained in its 1992 report HC 20, but the proposals were not implemented until 1994. See Hansard, House of Commons Debates,, 19 December 1994, cols 1458–1510. The experiment was made permanent in November 1995 (Session 1994–95, HC 491 and Hansard, House of Commons Debates,, 2 November 1995, cols 405–49).

30 *Legislative Process.*

31 See the Deputy Speaker Sir Alan Haselhurst's memorandum in the Modernisation Committee's second report, Session 2001–2, *Modernisation of the House of Commons: A Reform Programme*, HC 1168.

32 The motions were under SO 83, and were in procedural terms guillotines that had been agreed by the three major parties.

33 *Modernisation of the House of Commons: A Reform Programme*, Appendix 42, para 14.

34 The Modernisation Committee report *Programming of Legislation and Timing of Votes*, Session 1999–2000, HC 589 was debated and approved on 7 November 2000.

35 *Modernisation of the House of Commons: A Reform Programme*, Appendix 42.

36 Hansard, House of Commons Debates, 28 June 2001.

37 Hansard, House of Commons Debates, 29 October 2002.

38 Hansard, House of Commons Debates,, 6 November 2003.

39 *Programming of Bills*.

40 In 2002/3 only three out of 29 government bills received more than one day at report and third reading, compared with six bills out of 27 in 1998/9.

41 *Modernisation of the House of Commons: A Reform Programme*, Appendix 42, para 22. House of Commons Factsheet 10, *Programming of Government Bills*, gives information on the number of guillotines and programme motions from 1946/7. This was reproduced in the minority report contained in *Programming of Bills*.

42 *Programming of Bills*, para. 30.

43 For further detail see House of Commons Library Standard Note Pre-Legislative Scrutiny, 7 June 2004. <http://www.parliament.uk/commons/lib/research/notes/snpc-02822.pdf>

44 Blackburn and Kennon, *Griffith & Ryle on Parliament*, p. 624.

45 Liaison Committee, *Annual Report 2002*, Session 2002–03, HC 558, paras 33–6.

46 Toon, N. *Under Scrutiny – the Puttnam Committee and Successful Pre-legislative Scrutiny*, (IPPR, London, 2003) p. 1. http://www.ippr.org.uk/research/files/team34/Nick%20Toon%20article.pdf>

47 Procedure Committee, *Procedure for Debate on the Government's Expenditure Plans, Session 1998–99*, HC 295, paras 51–2.

48 Modernisation Committee, *Select Committees, Session 2001–02*, HC 224, para. 28.

49 House of Commons Commission, *Twenty-fifth report of the House of Commons Commission – Financial Year 2002–03*, HC 806, para. 70.

50 Hansard, House of Commons Debates,, 16 July 2001, cols 35–80. For a full account see House of Commons Library Research Paper 02/35 *Departmental Select Committees*.

51 See Cowley, P. and Stuart, M. 'Parliament: Mostly Continuity, but More Change than You'd Think', *Parliamentary Affairs*, 2002, vol. 55, pp. 271–86.

52 Liaison Committee, *Select Committees: Modernisation Process*, Session 2001–02, HC 692, paras 34–5.

53 *Ibid.*, paras 30–33.

54 See the useful summary in *Departmental Select Committees*.

55 Liaison Committee, *Annual Report for 2002*, Session 2002–3, HC 558.

56 Hogg, S. and Jenkins, K. 'Effective Government and Effective Accountability', *Political Quarterly*, 1999, vol. 70, pp 139–45.

57 These criteria are suggested by R. Kelly in 'Modernisation of the House of Commons and its impact on the effectiveness of select committees' M.Sc. dissertation, Birkbeck College, 2003. See also the Constitution Unit project on effective scrutiny, described on their website at www.ucl.ac.uk/constitution-unit.

58 *Parliamentary Calendar: Initial Proposals*.

59 Modernisation Committee, second report, Session 2001–2, *Modernisation of the House of*

Commons: A Reform Programme, HC 1168.

60 Administration of the palace and other infrastructure is shared with the Lords authorities.

61 Webcasting began on an experimental basis on 8 January 2002, and may be viewed at http://www.parliamentlive.tv.

62 Broadcasting Committee, first report, Session 1999–2000, *The Development of Parliamentary Broadcasting*, HC 642.

63 During the period of Eric Forth's appointment as shadow Leader of the House from 2001–3, he refused to serve on the committee, and his place was taken by his deputy, Greg Knight.

64 The failure to reform parliamentary privilege is a case in point. Taylor established the Joint Committee on Parliamentary Privilege in 1997/8. It reported in 1998/9, but its recommendations still await acceptance in 2003/4.

65 See Winetrobe, B. K. *Realising the Vision: a Parliament with a Purpose: an Audit of the First Year of the Scottish Parliament* (University College London Constitution Unit, London, 2001).

66 See Norton, P. and Wood, D. M. *Back from Westminster: British Members of Parliament and Their Constituencies* (University Press of Kentucky, Lexington, 1993) and Power, G. 'Party Politics vs People Politics: Balancing Westminster and Constituency', in G. Power (ed.) *Under Pressure: Are We Getting the Most from Our MPs?* (Hansard Society, London, 2001). See also Norris, P. 'The Puzzle of Constituency Service', *Journal of Legislative Studies*, 1997, vol. 3, no. 2, pp. 29–49, based on the British Candidate Survey 1992.

67 In a survey for the Hansard Commission, 67.6 per cent of MPs considered their geographical constituency very important in determining their role as a representative, compared with nation as a whole (58.1 per cent) and political party (26.8 per cent) (*The Challenge for Parliament: Making Government Accountable*, pp. 138–9).

68 Riddell, P. *Honest Opportunism: the Rise of the Career Politician* (Hamish Hamilton, London, 1993).

69 *First Special Report: Work of the Committee: Second Progress Report*, Session 1998–99, HC 865, para. 3.

70 Beetham, D., Byrne, I., Ngan, P. and Weir, S. 'Democratic Audit: Towards a Broader View of Democratic Achievement', *Parliamentary Affairs*, 2003 vol. 56, pp. 334–47.

71 It is not clear why the practice of regular progress reports has been abandoned by the committee since the 1998/9 session.

72 See Crick, B. and Millar, D. *To Make the Parliament of Scotland a Model for Democracy* (John Wheatley Centre, Edinburgh, 1997) and Winetrobe, *Realising the Vision*. However, the allocation of convenorships in the 2003 Scottish Parliament illustrated the ability of the major parties to frustrate the ambitions of smaller, less established parties.

TWENTY (A)

Reform of the Lords:
A View from the Outside

Dr Meg Russell[1]

L abour came to power in 1997 with a firm commitment to reform the
House of Lords by removing the hereditary peerage and creating 'a
more democratic and representative' second chamber.[2] The
Conservatives by contrast were committed to minimal change, describing
their policy as to 'oppose change for change's sake'.[3] Eight years later and
after two terms in office, Labour's promise remains unfulfilled. During this
same period the Conservatives moved from a position of defending the status
quo to proposing establishment of an 80 per cent directly elected second
chamber.

How has this situation come about? And what is likely to happen next?
This chapter reviews the developments since 1997 and asks what prospects
they suggest for the future. It concludes that the governing party is naturally
cautious about a reform that might strengthen the upper House, but that
reforms to date may already have had this effect.

The House of Lords has long been a target for Labour reformers. Through
much of the twentieth century the party had favoured abolition of the upper
House, this proposal last appearing in a Labour manifesto in 1983. In 1949
the Labour government passed the Parliament Act, which reduced the power
of the chamber to a delay of roughly one year over ordinary Bills.[4] In 1968

the Wilson government had also tried unsuccessfully to change the composition of the House and remove the automatic voting rights of hereditary peers.

Labour's traditional hostility to the upper House was fuelled by a strong dose of pragmatism, as well as principle. Even following the Life Peerages Act 1958, passed by a Conservative government, the chamber continued to be dominated by hereditary peers, the majority of whom took the Conservative whip. Immediately before the general election of 1997 there were 633 hereditary peers entitled to sit in the chamber, of whom 328 aligned themselves with the Conservatives and only fifteen with the Labour Party. Across the House as a whole the Conservatives could in theory attract 477 votes to Labour's 116, and although the chamber generally behaved with restraint, it had defeated Labour far more than Conservative governments.[5] For example, the 1974–9 government had suffered an average 60 defeats in the Lords per session, compared to the twelve defeats per session suffered by the Conservative government of 1992–7.

So for Labour the motivations were twofold. On the one hand the continued presence of legislators who sat in Parliament by virtue of their birth was clearly anachronistic at the end of the twentieth century. On the other, the removal of the hereditary peers would eliminate a potential obstacle to Labour in government. The Labour manifesto promised a two-stage reform, first the removal of the hereditary peers followed by a second stage to create the 'more democratic and representative' second chamber.

Eight years on, the principled case for removal of appointed members and their replacement with elected members (to meet the 'democratic' promise made) remains strong. However, this will prove difficult to achieve until the government of the day can see positive pragmatic advantages in democracy. And after eight years in office the attractions to the Labour leadership of building a stronger upper House to balance the executive have declined. Instead the most recent package proposed by government comprised a set of far smaller-scale reforms: the removal of the remaining hereditaries and tidying up the appointments process. With manifestos in preparation for a general election expected in May 2005, arguments in the Labour Party remain unresolved over whether an elected element in the second chamber is desirable, whilst some government ministers favour legislating to limit the powers of the upper House.

The House of Lords Act 1999

The government delivered on its promised first stage of reform with the publication in 1998 of the House of Lords Bill. This was a short Bill that simply sought to remove the rights of the hereditary peers to sit in the chamber (and in return gave them the right to stand for the House of Commons and to vote in general elections).

Although a simple Bill this threw up some difficult political dilemmas, for both the government and the opposition. For the Conservatives, who stood to lose the majority of their members of the upper House, the question was how to respond to the Bill. The party's political interest lay in defending the hereditaries, but the might of the government's huge majority in the House of Commons was against this. Also, for a party seeking to present a more modern image following a devastating political defeat public opinion was important. Polls showed strong support for Labour's first stage of reform.

For the government, the dilemma was how to get the Bill through the upper House, where the very members it sought to evict still comprised a majority. Labour ministers feared that if the Lords chose to make life difficult (with one hereditary member already proposing to behave like a 'football hooligan')[6] this could delay the implementation of the House of Lords Bill for a year, and possibly disrupt the remainder of the legislative programme until the hereditaries departed.

It was these pragmatic considerations on both sides which brought about a deal between Tony Blair and Lord Cranborne, the leader of the Conservative peers. In late 1998, Cranborne, without securing the consent of his party leader, met the Prime Minister, the latest in a series of covert meetings. They struck a deal whereby 92 hereditary peers would remain in the House of Lords in return for a commitment not to disrupt the passage of the Bill. In theory the Bill would therefore remove 90 per cent of the hereditary peerage (then standing at 759).[7] In practice, it only halved the active hereditary peerage, most of the rest being rarely seen or complete non-attendees.

The deal was unpalatable to Labour backbenchers in the Commons but the majority could be persuaded that an expeditious passage for the Bill, and removal of most hereditary peers, was preferable to possible legislative delays. Despite the displeasure of Conservative leader William Hague (he sacked Lord Cranborne) the deal also offered some compensation to the opposition. The Conservatives had alleged that the government would renege on its promise of second-stage reform once the hereditaries had been removed. But at least by retaining 92 of them there would be a constant reminder of the unreformed status of the chamber. When the amendment (moved by Lord Weatherill, convenor of the crossbenchers) was debated in the Lords, the Lord Chancellor stated that they would 'go when stage two has taken place and their presence is a guarantee that stage two will take place'.[8] Further, the deal would allow the Conservatives to retain most of their most active hereditary members. Of the 92 to remain, 49 would take their whip and just four would be Labour.[9]

However, the suspicion swiftly grew that although both the Labour and Conservative leaderships held to public positions supporting further reform, neither was necessarily eager. With the deal Labour got what many thought it wanted – a chamber that the Conservatives no longer dominated. Furthermore a large proportion of the remaining membership were on 'death row', knowing that rocking the boat too much could trigger further reform and their political demise.

For many Conservative peers the arrangements put in place by the deal also had their attractions. Legislation on Lords reform had historically proved very difficult to accomplish and the Weatherill amendment might last a long time. It was designed with that in mind (particularly by Lord Cranborne) with extraordinary arrangements to replace hereditary peers who died, using by-elections of their fellow hereditaries, divided into electoral colleges of each party.[10] Some peers explicitly stated their hope that no further reform should take place. Lord Weatherill justified his amendment by saying:

> *I believe if this works, as I hope it will work, it's within the bounds of possibility that the Royal Commission may say this has been working well – let's leave it alone. That would preserve continuity ... Surely a consummation devoutly to be wished!* [11]

With this single amendment, the Bill passed into law in 1999. When Parliament resumed that autumn it did so with a House of Lords that was stripped of more than half of its members, with roughly equal numbers of Conservative and Labour peers and the balance of power held by the Liberal Democrats and a large group of crossbenchers.

Election: the genie out of the bottle

At the same time that the House of Lords Bill was published, the government announced the establishment of a royal commission, to be chaired by Lord Wakeham, to make recommendations for the second stage of reform. The commission was established early in 1999 and reported in January 2000.[12] It invited written evidence, and conducted a series of public hearings with witnesses around the country.

The evidence received by the commission included submissions from all of the main political parties. In particular, attention focused on the evidence submitted by Labour. It was rumoured that Tony Blair had reversed his support for democracy and now favoured an all-appointed replacement for the current House, as he did not want to risk a chamber with elected members becoming a 'rival' to the House of Commons. When the Labour evidence was published it was widely reported as supporting this position. In fact the document – based on a series of meetings facilitated with Labour members by Professor Keith Ewing – did not explicitly support an appointed chamber but also did nothing to rule it out. It concluded that 'the composition of the House of Lords should be carefully tailored to its role and functions, and to the need to maintain the pre-eminence of the House of Commons' and that it 'must be a distinctive body, composed in a manner which is different from the House of Commons'.[13] The consultations inside the party had been low key and it could not be said that the issue was fully debated. Opinion was almost certainly split between this approach and the bolder position of replacing the House of Lords with the 'proper directly elected second chamber' that Tony Blair had promised in his speech to the Labour conference in 1995.[14]

The Conservatives likewise faced difficulties in presenting a united view. The party's submission to the royal commission instead referred to the commission it had established under Lord Mackay of Clashfern to look into the matter. The commission's report had proposed two alternatives, one an elected chamber and the other a mixed chamber of appointees, life peers, and indirectly and directly elected members.[15] Just as Labour's transition to government was inclining it towards a more cautious approach to Lords reform, the Conservatives' transition to opposition was inclining them towards a bolder approach. However, neither party had yet been able to find a settled view. The Liberal Democrats, meanwhile, favoured a wholly elected upper House based on regional boundaries and elected by a system of proportional representation.

Similar rumours to those that surrounded Labour's position also suggested that the royal commission was under significant pressure from the government to propose an all-appointed House. If this had been the unofficial brief given to Lord Wakeham he was unable to deliver it in practice. The commission's report strongly emphasised the need for the House of Commons to remain the supreme chamber of Parliament, and for the Lords to retain its distinct membership, ethos of expertise and independence, and capacity for detailed legislative scrutiny. However, it stopped short of concluding that this required a fully appointed House. Instead, it proposed a compromise, allegedly the product of vigorous exchanges between those on the commission, including Douglas Hurd, who leant towards democracy, and those wishing to retain an appointed House, including Gerald Kaufman. This compromise contained the suggestion that the chamber should in part reflect the new devolution settlement by including a minority of elected members representing the nations and regions of the UK. Failing to reach a single conclusion, the commission proposed that these members should compose between 12 and 35 per cent of the House. The remainder of members would be appointed by a new statutory Appointments Commission, with all powers of patronage removed from political party leaders.

Though the royal commission made 132 recommendations across the full range of issues concerning a reformed House, it was this point which attracted the greatest attention. As the House of Lords Bill passed through Parliament the public debate had quickly moved on from the merits of hereditary peers to the merits of election to the upper House. When the commission's report was published it was widely criticised for being too timid. The commission was also criticised for being out of step with public opinion. Polls on Lords reform consistently showed support for a largely elected House.[16] However, the government's response was to say that it 'accept[ed] the principles underlying the main elements of the Royal Commission's proposals on the future role and structure of this House, and will act on them'.[17]

The parties' responses to the royal commission were reflected in the manifestos produced for the 2001 general election. The Labour manifesto stated that 'we have given our support to the report and conclusions of the Wakeham commission and will seek to implement them in the most effective way possible,' also reaffirming the party's commitment to remove the remaining hereditary peers and to establish a 'more representative and demo-cratic' upper House. The Conservatives promised to create an independent appointments commission, and work towards 'a substantial elected element' in the upper House, whilst the Liberal Democrats repeated their commit-ment to 'replace the House of Lords with a smaller directly elected Senate'.

After the election the government attempted to move matters forward with the publication of a second White Paper in November 2001. This followed the Wakeham model in as much as it proposed a 20 per cent elected, 80 per cent appointed chamber, but it also dropped many of the commis-sion's other proposals such as long terms of office and the ending of party control over appointments, which were designed to enhance the chamber's independence.

The White Paper represented an uneasy compromise within government between those who were hostile to the notion of election and those that favoured a largely or wholly elected House.[18] The divisions on the Labour side became particularly evident at this point due to the tabling of an early day motion by a group of Labour backbenchers supporting a 'wholly or substantially elected' House.[19] This was signed by 305 members, including 139 Labour MPs – representing more than half of the back benches. 118 Conservatives also signed the EDM. This amounted to a transformation of Conservative opinion from that of 1997, when the overwhelming majority of the party was probably against any radical change. But it was consistent with an EDM sponsored by Conservative MP Andrew Tyrie in March 1999, which attracted over 140 supporters including a little under half the party's backbenchers.[20]

The White Paper was very poorly received. Issued as a consultation paper, there were over a thousand responses, 89 per cent of which supported a majority elected upper House.[21] The press were equally negative, and the paper also found few advocates in either chamber of Parliament. Responses in the Commons focused on the proportion of elected members, the overall size of the House (proposed to be 600) and the remaining presence of the bishops. In the Lords several members of the royal commission, including Lord Wakeham, criticised the proposals for diverging from their carefully constructed model. A House of Commons select committee published a unanimous report supporting many of the Wakeham principles, but calling for 60 per cent of members of the upper House to be elected.[22] In both of the two main parties, particularly Labour, the dilemma between wanting to support the democratic principle (and the politically popular option), versus the fears of boosting the chamber's constitutional authority if it were popularly elected, became increasingly explicit. There were open differences of opinion between the responsible minister in the Commons (the pro-election Leader of the House, Robin Cook) and the Lords (the pro-appointment Lord Chancellor, Derry Irvine), as demonstrated by their evidence to the select committee, and later public statements.[23]

'Let Parliament decide'

With the White Paper proposals doomed to failure, but with government unable to reach internal consensus on any other package, Number 10 brokered a compromise between Robin Cook and Lord Irvine whereby Parliament would be asked to resolve the dilemma. Thus in May 2002 the government announced the creation of a joint committee of both Houses which would be asked to come up with a range of options for the composition of the reformed House, to be put to the members of both chambers in free votes.

This was a highly unusual step, and was seized upon by reformers in the Commons as an opportunity to achieve the largely elected chamber that they desired. Judging from the mathematics of the recent early day motion this certainly looked the likeliest outcome. However, it also presented a challenge to Parliament of a magnitude not immediately appreciated by any of those involved. In recent years free parliamentary votes have generally been reserved for issues of 'conscience' such as laws relating to homosexuality, euthanasia and abortion, although they had also historically been used on constitutional matters, such as the 1917 Representation of the People Bill that would have changed the electoral system.[24] However, this time Parliament was being asked to resolve a matter where the governing party had been unable to reach internal agreement despite concerted attempts – indeed where the government's public position had already been rejected, and where views had become deeply entrenched.

In an era where the House of Commons is rarely asked to do more on major policy matters than endorse (on a three-line whip) the package decided in Whitehall this was a refreshing departure. However, it was perhaps unrealistic to expect party managers to allow matters to run their course on such an important political issue.

Attempts to ensure the votes were held before the summer recess by setting a deadline for the joint committee to report failed.[25] The committee, chaired by ex-Labour minister Jack Cunningham MP, did not produce its substantive report until December 2002. This proposed options on which the two Houses should vote, including a 20 per cent, 40 per cent, 50 per cent, 60 per cent and 80 per cent elected chamber. Together with the options of fully appointed and fully elected (which the committee had been required by its terms of reference to include) this created the potential for seven votes. It also created the possibility of splits between the advocates of a largely and wholly elected chamber.

The parliamentary votes were scheduled for February 2003. Aside from the political obstacles already discussed, other elements conspired against a clear outcome. Those wanting reform were dismayed by the plethora of options put forward, and there were some pressures to break convention and allow members to use a preferential voting system.[26] However, this proposal was rejected and instead all members were required to vote 'aye' or 'no' on each of the options. This created dilemmas for members about how many options they should support and how to put their votes to greatest tactical use. In principle, as this was to be a free vote, ministers could declare themselves to be on one or other side of the argument. Most held their silence, though the positions of Robin Cook and Lord Irvine became increasingly clear.

The most significant intervention, however, came from the Prime Minister himself, who declared to a packed House the week before the vote that he was opposed to a mixed elected/appointed chamber (the previous position of the government) and strongly implied that he therefore favoured appointment.[27] This ended Number 10's role as an 'honest broker', and sent a clear signal to loyal Labour backbenchers who wanted to support their leader.

In the event, the outcome of the votes was inconclusive. The Commons voted by a significant margin (325 to 247) to reject a wholly appointed House, but also voted against all of the elected options. The most narrowly defeated was 80 per cent elected, which fell by just 283 votes to 286. The minority elected options of 20 per cent and 40 per cent, closest to the previous position of the government and of the Wakeham commission, were defeated unanimously without a division. Meanwhile in the Lords the all-appointed option was supported (by 335 to 110) whilst all the other options were heavily defeated.

Given the earlier indications of the Commons' position, particularly through early day motions, the result there appears surprising. However, the analysis of the votes, and facts that became clear subsequently, show that there were many factors conspiring against the elected options.[28] Conservative members were evenly split on the 80 per cent option, which had been the official party position. Once this option had been defeated many Conservatives, and a small number of Labour members, voted against the 60 per cent elected option which remained the only one on the table. Given that this option attracted support from some members who thought 80 per cent too radical, it should have been expected to pass; but many opposition members decided they would rather scupper the government's reform than allow the Commons to support a compromise solution. The position of these members was relatively constructive, however, in comparison to the group of 20 MPs who voted against all options to ensure that no proposal had support. To this was added the confusion of some members about the sequence of the votes, which led to four MPs who voted for the 60 per cent and 100 per cent elected options voting against the 80 per cent option.[29]

A significant number of MPs were apparently swayed by the belief that any democratic reform of the Lords would diminish the authority of the Commons. These members actively sought to maintain a chamber with little moral authority or clout, which would protect the Commons' dominance and might even ultimately be abolished.

Perhaps most influential of all was the activity of the Labour whips on this ostensibly free vote. Until Tony Blair's intervention there was little sign of formal whipping activity, although there were campaign groups operating on all sides of the debate. On the Labour side the organisational and persuasive skills of the pro-election lobby was evident in the relatively little splintering between the 60 per cent and 80 per cent elected options. However, after Blair's preference was clear the whips themselves became more active, with one quoted on the front page of *The Times* on the morning after the vote boasting that 'the machine came through for Tony'.[30] Backbenchers themselves reported coming under significant pressure to back away from the elected options. Obviously in comparison to other campaign groups the whips (and the potential rewards and sanctions that they control) are a particularly potent force. It is therefore notable that even after their intervention fewer Labour MPs supported the all-appointed option than opposed it.[31]

The 2003 White Paper and (non-)Bill

This means of reaching agreement having failed, the expectation was that the government would seek to let Lords reform discreetly fade from the consciousness until at least the next general election. Some wanting elected members dared to hope that there would be future votes with clearer options that they could win, but the realists amongst them set their sights on the next Labour manifesto and beyond. Some who had favoured indirect election by local and regional government, or by other interest groups, urged this on government and the joint committee as a more palatable alternative to direct election. But this option had already been dismissed by the royal commission and most other bodies as unworkable. The likeliest outcome appeared to be a continuance of the status quo until the dust had settled and discussions could safely start again, with a largely elected chamber the most obvious alternative. The joint committee itself issued a report urging the government to state how it saw the way forward, and several members of the committee indicated their desire that it be shut down unless the government decided to back wholesale reform.

The government's responses to the joint committee, and to the subsequent White Paper published in September 2003, were thus surprising. They indicated the continued intention to press ahead with reform, and proposed a short Bill to remove the remaining 92 hereditary peers, and create a statutory appointments commission.[32] The commission would be empowered to decide the number of peers appointed by each party and the overall size of the House, with the balance linked in statute to the outcome of the most recent general election. The plans for such a Bill were reiterated in the Queen's Speech in November 2003.

There were many paradoxes in this position. First, the Bill would effectively create an all-appointed House, which was the least popular option when the House of Commons had voted. Certainly this option had been supported in the House of Lords, but the government had repeatedly defended the Commons' primacy over this matter, as it did over all other issues of policy. Second, the government's previous White Paper had failed not because the elected element was too large, but because it was too small. Yet the long and public negotiations that followed had resulted in a new set of proposals including no elected members at all. Third, the government had previously insisted that the 92 hereditaries would stay until 'stage two' of reform was complete. But since stage two was expected to deliver the 'more representative and democratic' second chamber promised in the manifesto, these proposals were not presented as stage two, but a temporary stopping point towards it. Further reform was promised, but with no clear objective or timetable. Yet it was stated that the hereditaries must go at this earlier point.

Like the previous proposals this package was not welcomed by any of the party groups in either of the chambers, with these objections and many others being made.[33] Indeed the resistance to the proposals proved so great that in March 2004 the government announced that it would not, after all, proceed with the Bill. This raises the question of what motivated government to present the proposals, rather than simply letting Lords reform run into the sand.

The answers are twofold. Most obviously, Labour had committed itself in its 2001 manifesto to 'the removal of the remaining hereditary peers'. However, this was only the smallest of its commitments, which also included implementation of the Wakeham proposals and creation of a 'more representative and democratic' House. Second, and more importantly, the government wanted to increase Labour's relative share of seats in the upper House. The Conservatives still had marginally more members than Labour (210 to 181 in January 2004) and the government was vulnerable to defeat. Indeed in the 2001/2 session the government was defeated in the Lords some 56 times, and 88 times in the 2002/3 session. The removal of the hereditary peers would evict 49 Conservative members and thus ensure a more comfortable passage for the government's legislation through the upper House.

Another irony, however, was that the government could have achieved its objective by non-legislative means. In 1999 an appointments commission had been created on a non-statutory basis to recommend independent crossbench members for the House. The government could easily have extended the reach of the non-statutory commission (and perhaps refreshed its members), giving it a remit to vet the political appointees and decide the numbers to be appointed, as had been proposed in the Bill. If the commission had been required to base the party balance on votes cast at the previous general election, it would have immediately appointed a large tranche of Labour peers. In the event, after the Bill was dropped, Tony Blair simply announced a new group of 46 new peers in May 2004, 23 of them Labour. However, he did not take the opportunity to announce any non-statutory limitations on his patronage powers to match those that had been proposed the previous autumn. This was a missed opportunity to avert the complaints of 'cronyism' that dogged Lords appointments, and enhance the image of the upper House.

The political difficulties encountered by the 2003 proposals centred on their failure to include any elected members. In the Commons it had been clearly demonstrated that election was more popular than appointment, even given the government whips' best attempts to win support for the Prime Minister's position. Ministers feared that they would not be able to fend off an amendment to introduce elections, and that this would be supported by numerous Labour backbenchers. In the Lords appointment was not necessarily unpopular, but the removal of 92 active members of the House when reform was acknowledged to not be complete was seen as a breach of trust. Additionally, exclusion of the hereditaries threatened to remove some of the most active members of the crossbenches, whom the government and others had stated they valued.[34]

Prospects

During this episode the government initially claimed its right to get its legislation through Parliament, particularly when implementing manifesto commitments. However, its later retreat demonstrated how the Lords was already showing itself to be a daunting opponent in defence of itself. Subsequent government pronouncements focused on the need to trim the powers of the Lords in order to allow government legislation to pass more easily. However, recent experience shows that such reforms would be extremely unlikely to win support in the upper House, and they might well prove very publicly unpopular. As the general election approached, the debate in the Labour Party about Lords reform was reignited, and at the party conference in September 2004 ministers were forced to accept a statement that the chamber should be 'as democratic as possible'. After a brief suggestion that government would embrace the peculiar 'second mandate' option proposed by the singer-songwriter Billy Bragg (whereby a proportion of the membership would be elected from regional lists based on a party's share of the vote at each general election), there was little sign of a new initiative on reforming the chamber's composition. Maintenance of the new status quo for the foreseeable future therefore appears likely.

The seemingly greater assertiveness of the Lords, as well as the perceived lack of legitimacy which comes from its undemocratic composition, make it certain that the chamber will remain the subject of controversy for years to come. It has significant formal powers which have been little used in practice, but reforms to date provide peers with arguments to justify more activism. Their Lordships can point to the fact that, following the 1999 reform, the balance between the parties in the Lords already more closely resembles the pattern of general election votes cast than does the House of Commons. Add to that the presence of independent members, and the removal of the bulk of hereditary peers, and there are reasons why the chamber can now consider itself somewhat more justified in questioning government policies.

Ironically, given the House's reluctance to embrace democracy, the Lords' best hope of influence lies in populism. This is the reverse of the role that second chambers theoretically perform – acting as a check on populism of the fully democratic House. Where issues are unpopular with the public the chamber can present itself as a champion of common sense over the executive-dominated House of Commons. It can also speak with authority on legal matters. In this way it has won significant concessions from government since 2001 over issues such as jury trials and treatment of terrorist suspects.

There are also some signs of a change in relations between the Lords and the Commons. There has long been a belief by government backbench MPs that the Lords will help sort out matters on which they do not feel able to rebel. But with the more restive nature of the parliamentary Labour Party new opportunities exist for collaboration between members in both Houses to extract concessions.[35] In 2003 the leading rebel over the controversial plans for foundation hospitals, Frank Dobson, announced that he had written to members of the Lords urging them to vote against the Bill. Following the rebellion of 60 Labour MPs (and abstention by a further 66) the Bill only narrowly passed the Commons on 8 July. It went on to be rejected by the House of Lords before the end of the session. Protests from government that the Lords should not stand in the way of the Commons due to its unelected basis found considerably less sympathy than they might previously have done, given that the Prime Minister's intervention had helped ensure the defeat of plans for elections. On this occasion the second chamber finally backed down (although there were some concessions) but the potential exists for greater disruption in future. The chamber may take up the issues on which MPs would like to defeat the government but can't (given the need to maintain a disciplined majority in the Commons), helping to focus media attention on these issues and sometimes encouraging government to think again. This threat applies equally to Conservative and Labour governments given the fine balance in the upper House.

It remains early days, but history may show that the reform to date, even if it only resulted in removal of around half the active hereditary peerage, was highly significant. It could be that it has revived the second chamber – through a rebalancing between Lords and Commons, and between Parliament and the executive – even without elections being introduced. If so, the classic view of the Westminster model whereby a disciplined party government gets its legislation through two compliant chambers may come to be seen as increasingly out of date. Yet if government is unhappy with this situation its options are limited. The composition of the House remains inherently unstable for so long as it is appointed. But responding to popular pressure to elect the members of the second chamber will do little to help a government seeking to get its legislation through unscathed. It is difficult for government to complain that the unelected Lords is unjustified in meddling in legislation and should be tamed, when a sceptical public can simply reply, 'If you do not like it as it is, then let us elect it!'

Endnotes

1   I would like to thank Andrew Tyrie MP for his input to an earlier version of this chapter.

2   Labour Party manifesto, *New Labour: because Britain Deserves Better,* 1997.

3   Conservative Party manifesto, *You Can Only Be Sure with the Conservatives,* 1997, p. 50.

4   The first Parliament Act, removing the absolute veto of the Lords and reducing it to a delay of roughly two years, was passed by the Liberal government in 1911.

5   Of the other members 57 took the Liberal Democrat whip (24 of them being hereditary) and the majority of the remainder were non–party-aligned members sitting on the 'crossbenches', including twelve acting and various retired Lords of Appeal in Ordinary. In addition the chamber included 26 bishops and archbishops. Note that figures on hereditary peers exclude roughly 120 on leave of absence.

6   The Earl of Onslow suggested that 'before I go, I regard it as my duty to do my level best to ensure that whatever comes after me is much, much better. If that means that I behave either, for the benefit of the intellectuals, like Fabius Maximus Cunctator, or, for the benefit of the tabloid press, like a football hooligan, so be it. I regard that as my duty.' Hansard, House of Lords Debates, 14 October 1998, col. 985.

7   In addition to retaining 10 per cent of each party group there would be fifteen members to serve as deputy Speaker and two royal office holders.

8   Hansard, House of Lords debates, 11 May 1999, col. 1092.

9   The hereditaries were to be chosen in proportion to their current party strengths in the House. For a detailed account see Shell, D. 'Labour and the House of Lords: a Case Study in Parliamentary Reform', *Parliamentary Affairs,* 2000, vol. 52, pp. 429–41.

10   The by-election provisions came into effect in November 2002 and their full absurdity was illustrated on the death of Lord Milner in August 2003, after which the three remaining Labour hereditaries 'elected' his replacement in the House from the ranks of the recently expelled hereditary Labour peerage – a group of about 30. These arrangements may be explicable but, in a democratic age, are hardly justifiable. Indeed when the deal was agreed Labour members were assured that they would never need to be brought into effect, as the second stage of reform would shortly be completed.

11   'A View from the Cross Benches', *House Magazine,* 11 January 1999.

12   Royal Commission on the Reform of the House of Lords, *A House for the Future,* Cm 4534, 2000.

13   *Reforming the House of Lords for the New Millennium, Labour Party evidence to the Royal Commission,* p. 40.

14   The 1992 manifesto had also promised 'replacement of the House of Lords with a new elected second chamber'.

15   *The Report of the Constitutional Commission on Options for a New Second Chamber* (Mackay Commission, London, 1999).

16   For example, a Gallup poll in June 1998 found that 52 per cent favoured public elections to the Lords rather than selection by party leaders or by an independent commission; an ICM poll for the Rowntree Trust in August 1999 found that 82 per cent favoured election over appointment for the upper House; an ICM/Guardian poll in September 2000 found that 78

per cent of those who expressed a preference said there should be a majority rather than a minority elected presence in the reformed upper House.

17 Baroness Jay, Leader of the House of Lords, Hansard, House of Lords debates, 7 March 2000, col. 912.

18 See the memoir of Robin Cook, then Leader of the House of Commons, *The Point of Departure* (Simon & Schuster, London, 2003).

19 EDM 226 of session 2001/2.

20 EDM 464 of session 1998/9, 'That this House believes that the composition of the second chamber of Parliament should be determined by election'.

21 *Reform of the House of Lords: Analysis of Responses to the Government White Paper 'The House of Lords – Completing the Reform'.* (Lord Chancellor's Department, London, 2002).

22 Public Administration Select Committee, *The Second Chamber: Continuing the Reform, fifth report of Session 2001–02*, HC 494-i.

23 See Public Administration Select Committee, *The Second Chamber: Continuing the Reform, fifth report of Session 2001–02, Minutes of Evidence and Appendices*, HC 494-ii.

24 This sought to implement the results of the Speaker's Conference which proposed use of the alternative vote in single-member constituencies and the single transferable vote in multi-member constituencies. See Curtice, J. 'The Electoral System', in V. Bogdanor (ed.) *The British Constitution in the Twentieth Century*, (Oxford University Press, Oxford, 2003).

25 See Hansard, House of Commons debates, 19 June 2002.

26 Although this would have been unprecedented on a policy issue, a new system for electing the Commons Speaker allowing an exhaustive ballot had been written into standing orders in 2001.

27 See Hansard, House of Commons debates, 29 January 2003, cols 877–8.

28 For a full analysis see McLean, I., Spirling, A. and Russell, M. 'None of the Above: The UK House of Commons Votes on Reforming the House of Lords', *Political Quarterly*, 2003, vol. 74, pp. 298–310.

29 The inclusion of an amendment in favour of Lords abolition, and the taking of two votes without a formal division meant divisions were not held in the expected order. This, coupled with the lack of the usual whips to guide people through the division lobbies, caused some confusion.

30 4 February 2003.

31 175 Labour MPs voted for the all-appointed option, and 181 against. On the 80 per cent elected option 153 Labour MPs voted aye and 197 voted no.

32 Joint Committee on House of Lords Reform, *House of Lords Reform: Government Reply to the Committee's Second Report*, HC 1027, 2003; Department for Constitutional Affairs, *Constitutional Reform: Next Steps for the House of Lords*, CP14/03, 2003.

33 See debates on the government statement in both Houses on 18 September 2003.

34 Some of these difficulties were discussed in detail in Russell, M. and Hazell, R. *Next Steps in House of Lords Reform: Response to the September 2003 White Paper* (University College London Constitution Unit, London, 2003).

35 For a discussion of changing party discipline in the Commons see Cowley, P. *Revolts and Rebellions: Parliamentary Voting under Blair* (Politico's, London, 2002).

The House of Lords and Reform: 'Building a house for the future' – A View from the Inside

The Rt Hon. Lord Wakeham DL

Reforming the House of Lords – reforming any second chamber – is not as easy as people like to think. If there is a second chamber, there must be a 'first' chamber, and first chambers, in parliamentary democracies at least, are very powerful institutions. Typically they are directly elected on a universal adult franchise, with seats distributed on a population basis. They determine which party forms the government. They usually control finance and supply. In most cases they have the final word over proposed legislation. Because, by definition, governments in parliamentary democracies control the first, or 'lower', chamber they end up in a very powerful position, with access to all the levers of power: executive, legislative and financial.

This gives rise to several fundamental obstacles to reform of the second chamber. Why should any 'first' chamber, or any government in a parliamentary democracy, want to initiate or support a process of reform which would be almost certain to cramp its own style? Why should the members of a lower chamber, having achieved victory in an often bruising battle to represent their constituents, agree to any enhancement of the status of members of the second chamber, who could become rivals for political influence?

It is no accident that second chambers in parliamentary democracies tend to have features which call their legitimacy and authority into question. This ensures that they cannot challenge the pre-eminence of the 'lower' chamber as the country's decisive political forum. The House of Lords, even after the 'first stage' of reform, retains a substantial number of members – 92 – who are there by virtue of being hereditary peers. Other second chambers may be wholly or largely appointed. Those which are elected usually use indirect election (as for example in France) or at least a different form of election from the system used to elect the 'lower' chamber. In general seats in the second chamber are not allocated on a population basis. The formal powers of second chambers in parliamentary democracies are usually less than those of 'first chambers'. But this is too intimately bound up with and justified by the lower degree of political authority and legitimacy which arises from their composition. As Australia has discovered, it is less easy for a government based in the 'lower' House to argue that the views of a directly elected second chamber should be overridden.

That may or may not be a good thing. The point is simply that, given a free hand, governments and lower chambers around the world are unlikely to support proposals to reform their second chambers unless their own pre-eminence is secured, both formally and in practice. That is a political reality with which all reformers must deal.

In retrospect, these factors contributed to the failure of successive attempts to reform the House of Lords throughout the twentieth century. The constitutional crisis of 1909–11 led ultimately to agreement on the Parliament Act 1911, under which any Commons Bill passed by the House of Commons in three successive sessions of Parliament would become law whatever the House of Lords thought. The length of the House of Lords' suspensory veto was subsequently reduced by the Parliament Act 1949 and the resulting balance has survived without serious challenge up to the present day. But attempts to reform the composition of the House of Lords – especially in 1918, 1948 and 1968 – broke down largely because of the failure to identify a satisfactory alternative.

By the end of the twentieth century, however, the situation had changed in two very significant respects. First, the introduction of life peers under the Life Peerages Act 1958 was a conspicuous success. By the late 1990s the House of Lords contained well over 500 life peers in addition to some 750 hereditary peers. The life peers were in the main people of great distinction and ability with a wide range of experience and expertise. Mainly due to their influence, the House had become more professional and effective, and played a larger role in revising legislation and scrutinising the executive, especially in those areas which were of less immediate political impact.

Secondly, the 1997 Labour Party manifesto committed the government to removing the right of hereditary peers to sit and vote in the House of Lords, and that commitment was largely given effect by the House of Lords Act 1999. That made it imperative to find a new basis for constituting the House of Lords, whilst avoiding the difficulties which led to the failure of previous attempts at reform.

It was in any event timely to consider the role and functions of the second chamber in the light of other elements of the Labour government's constitutional reform programme, including devolution, the enactment of the Human Rights Act 1998 and the United Kingdom's developing relations with the European Union.

Although the Blair government came to power in May 1997 with a clear mandate to extinguish the rights of hereditary peers to sit and vote in the House of Lords, there is evidence that they sought to explore the possibility of reaching an understanding with the opposition about the longer-term reform of the House of Lords; but the exercise revealed no basis for agreement with the opposition, and probably that there was no consensus within government either. The decision to appoint a royal commission was therefore far more than some kind of smokescreen or displacement activity.

Obviously, as the government moved to implement the 'first stage' of Lords reform – the expulsion of the bulk of the hereditary peers – the existence of the royal commission enabled them to claim that they were serious about moving on to 'stage two'. But all the members of the commission felt, throughout the process, that we had genuinely been brought together to exercise our collective judgement on what Sherlock Holmes would call a 'three-pipe problem'.

In fact, when the Prime Minister asked me if I would chair the commission, I had made two conditions: that the purpose of the exercise was indeed to come up with a workable and widely acceptable solution; and that the membership of the commission would be conducive to achieving that. The Prime Minister immediately agreed. I therefore believed from the outset that we had a real opportunity to lay the foundation for successful long-term reform of the House of Lords.

The 'stage one' reforms were going ahead anyway. The House of Lords was bound to change quite significantly, leaving the House made up largely of life peers created by successive Prime Ministers since 1958. There was a serious risk that the country would lose something rather important if we did not provide a blueprint to show where those changes should lead.

There was therefore both an opportunity and a real incentive to draw up a realistic and workable blueprint for a reformed House of Lords. We were also conscious, however, that some of the best political minds of the twentieth century had already tried – and failed. That is a tribute to the complexity and difficulty of the issues. If there had been an easy answer, someone would have found it long ago.

Our approach was to pose three questions:

- What is the purpose of a second chamber?
- What sort of people do you need to enable the second chamber to fulfil that purpose?
- What is the best way of identifying people with the right characteristics?

We immersed ourselves in the issues before we came to draw even preliminary conclusions. We reviewed the available academic literature, drew on the resources of the Constitution Unit, and invited submissions from a very wide range of academics, interested parties and those with a knowledge of particular issues. We studied the large volume of written evidence which we received. We initiated a programme of public hearings to ensure that we were exposed to the widest possible range of arguments and analysis.

Only then did we begin to look at the overall role and specific functions of the second chamber. We identified four main roles for the reformed second chamber. We agreed

- that it should bring a range of experience and expertise to bear;
- that it should be broadly representative of the modern United Kingdom;
- that it should provide a formal voice in Parliament for the nations and regions of the United Kingdom;
- that it should play a vital role under Britain's unwritten constitution in working with the House of Commons to hold the executive more effectively to account.

Our view of this fourth role reflected the fundamental principle of parliamentary democracy in the United Kingdom: governments are chosen in accordance with the will of the electorate as expressed in general elections to the House of Commons. Governments chosen in that way have a right to govern. They have a mandate to implement their policies. The will of the electorate, reflected in the composition of the House of Commons, must ultimately be decisive.

There are dangers and weaknesses in the system, which an effective second chamber can help to remedy, but it would be anti-democratic to reform the second chamber in a way which would enable it to frustrate the verdict of a general election. The reformed second chamber must therefore add value to the United Kingdom's system of parliamentary democracy, but without having a rival source of authority to that of the House of Commons. The House of Commons – and the government – derives its authority from its democratic mandate. The reformed House of Lords must derive authority from a range of sources without relying exclusively or even largely on the authority that derives from election. And it must play its part in a way that accommodates and acknowledges the decisive political role of the House of Commons.

The present system of parliamentary democracy in the United Kingdom has a number of weaknesses. The executive is perhaps overmighty. Formal or judicial controls are virtually non-existent. Party discipline, particularly in the House of Commons, is very strong and the party whips have an armoury of weapons at their disposal for ensuring party loyalty. This is reinforced by the fact that politics is nowadays a full-time occupation. MPs are professional politicians, dependent on their parties for their continued livelihood and for preferment. The House of Commons finds it increasingly difficult to balance its twin functions of sustaining a government in office and holding it effectively to account.

There are countervailing tendencies. The Human Rights Act will strengthen the position of the individual vis-à-vis the state. Devolution in Scotland, Wales and Northern Ireland and the extension of local democracy in London, perhaps other major conurbations and possibly in the English regions will bring power closer to the people. But there remains a vital role for the second chamber of Parliament in helping to exert a degree of restraint on the government of the day.

The second chamber's role should not be to confront or override the government and the House of Commons, but to challenge them to justify or reconsider their positions. Where this leads the government or the House of Commons to have second thoughts, legislation or other government business is improved. Where the government, with the support of the House of Commons, ultimately disagrees with the second chamber, so be it. It is their right to exercise such judgements and at least they will have been forced to confront the issue that gave rise to concern in the second chamber. The second chamber's position is also likely to stimulate media and other public interest, so it can exert a considerable influence even if it cannot ultimately enforce its objections.

This view of the overall role of the second chamber has several implications, both for its powers and for the characteristics of its members. The most important are

- firstly, that the second chamber should have a basis of composition which is distinct from that of the House of Commons;
- secondly, that is should have sufficient powers to force the government and the House of Commons to take it seriously;
- thirdly, that it should have the perceived legitimacy and authority to exercise those powers effectively;
- fourthly, that it should not be possible for it to fall under the control of the government, or indeed of any one political party.

The case for having a membership which is distinct from that of the House of Commons has several features. It avoids any element of competition, either between the two Houses or between individual members of each House. A different set of viewpoints can be brought to bear on the consideration of public policy issues.

The second chamber needs sufficient power that it will be taken seriously. Our proposals would leave the country with a moderately powerful second chamber, capable of exerting a significant influence on primary and secondary legislation and on the general development of public policy. Apart from the rare and exceptional circumstances in which the Parliament Acts may be brought into play, the positive approval of the reformed House of Lords would still be required for every piece of primary legislation.

The fundamental weakness of the former House of Lords was that it lacked legitimacy and authority. Because its members were there by birth or as a result of more recent prime ministerial patronage, they were often forced to pull their punches. The personal distinction of many members and the quality of the arguments they deployed often countered that disadvantage, but in general the House of Lords in recent decades has lacked the confidence to stand up for what it thought was right. Our recommendations would produce a second chamber that would have much greater authority and self-confidence.

The ability of the Conservative Party effectively to dominate the House of Lords throughout the twentieth century was another cause of its lack of perceived legitimacy. It was a fundamental recommendation of our report that no one party should ever again be able to dominate the second chamber. A chamber that could be dominated by the party of government would become a mere rubber stamp. A chamber that could be dominated by the opposition would become a source of constitutional conflict. Either way, it would become an extension of the political battlefield in the House of Commons and the political parties would try every trick in the book to gain control of it. We recommended that the political balance in the reformed second chamber should be set by reference to the proportion of votes cast for each party in the most recent general election. On postwar trends this would produce a situation in which the party of government was usually the largest party and all parties had a fair share of the seats, but in which no one party would ever have an overall majority. The possibility is further reduced by our proposal that there should be a statutory minimum of 20 per cent crossbenchers, or independents, in the second chamber. This recommendation would enhance the second chamber's reputation for independent judgement and thus enhance its legitimacy and its effectiveness.

Many people who had been sympathetic to much of the analysis in our report parted company with us at this point. They argued that by recommending a largely appointed House the royal commission undermined its own arguments and that the reformed House should have at least a majority of elected members if it is to have the authority and legitimacy to act as a real restraint on the executive.

It would inevitably be the case that a second chamber that sought to challenge the House of Commons on the basis of its electoral mandate would lose. It would be anti-democratic to suggest anything else. In any event, none of the political parties would support it, and the House of Commons wouldn't vote for it. So the reformed second chamber will have to rely on other sources of authority in any event. We believe these should include

- the extent to which the members of the chamber are broadly representative of the society they seek to serve;
- the breadth of experience and range of expertise they possess;
- their individual personal distinction;
- the quality of the arguments they bring to bear;
- their ability to exercise an unfettered judgement, free from partisan political control.

These qualities cannot be reliably delivered through any system of election. Those who would be willing to stand for election, or are likely to be successful in elections, are bound to be pretty well committed to a political party already. They would certainly be dependent on the political parties to secure election. Elections to the second chamber would therefore result in an extension of the power of the party machines, which is the very opposite of what most people want. Any system of election to the second chamber would also be unlikely to produce people who were broadly representative of British society, or who possessed the necessary range of expertise and of experience outside the relatively narrow world of politics. Crucially, they would lack the ability to exercise an unfettered judgement on the issues confronting them. A further consideration is that it is difficult to see MPs voting for a largely elected second chamber: they would not want to create electoral rivals and give them a national political platform.

For all these reasons the royal commission came down decisively in favour of a largely appointed second chamber. Crucially, however, we recommended that appointments should no longer be in the gift of the Prime Minister and the other party leaders at Westminster, but should be made by a truly independent appointments commission.

Of course the members of the royal commission were unanimous that there should be a significant minority of 'regional members' in the second chamber, chosen in a way which reflects the balance of political opinion within each of the nations and regions of the United Kingdom. A substantial majority of the commission favoured a model in which 87 'regional members' would be directly elected, by thirds, at the time of each European Parliament election.[1] But the crucial point to bear in mind is that our motive in recommending regional members was not just to incorporate an elected element in the second chamber. Our aim was to find a valid way of giving the nations and regions of the UK a formal voice in the second chamber alongside members reflecting other aspects of British society.

Another fundamental objective was to minimise any distinction between members selected by the appointments commission and those selected by the regional electorates. To that end we recommended that all members should serve fifteen-year terms.

We also argued for a total separation between the honours system and membership of the second chamber. The grant of a peerage should not confer a right to sit in Parliament, and no one should be required to accept a peerage in order to become a member of the second chamber.

Our recommendations would contribute to the stability of the present constitutional settlement. We argued against changes that could only have had a destabilising effect. We upheld the fundamental principles of parliamentary democracy while making recommendations which should have the effect of improving Parliament's ability to hold the executive to account.

The recommendations in our report are politically realistic, workable and achievable. Our recommendations took full account of the positions of all the main political parties and others with a significant interest in the second stage of Lords reform. But that does not mean that we trimmed our report in accordance with what we thought the parties wanted. On the contrary, our recommendations were not in line with the views of any of the main political parties. Everyone was challenged to some extent by what we proposed.

It is unfortunate that the present generation of political leaders have so far failed to rise to the challenge. I suppose that should not be a surprise. Previous attempts in 1918, 1948 and 1968 all failed because whilst most were in favour of ending the hereditary principle, they could not agree on what should replace it.

The Labour government accepted our report, and stated clearly in its 2001 election manifesto that it would implement our recommendations. From then on things went wrong. After the election they produced a White Paper called (in my view rather unwisely) *Completing the Reform*. This completely misunderstood that our report was an attempt at a compromise in which nobody got all they wanted, but all got something, and almost all agreed that even if they did not accept all our proposals, it was a move in the right direction. To call the government White Paper *Completing the Reform* sent a message of finality which upset a lot of people. I would have much preferred their White Paper to be called 'A Move in the Right Direction' or something similar.

The government proposals, although superficially accepting our recommendations, differed significantly. First, the government completely failed to appreciate the significance of the royal commission's insistence that anyone elected to the second chamber should be elected for a single long term and be barred from seeking re-election or from seeking election to the House of Commons. It is vital that the potential members of the second chamber should not aspire to a broader political career or be (or be seen to be) under the control of the party machines; and that they should not be come to be seen as rivals for local political influence by backbench MPs.

However, the government's White Paper proposed that regional members of the second chamber should be elected for short terms, at the same time as general elections, and should be eligible for re-election. As a former Chief Whip, I am certain that such proposals would result in candidates and members who were very much under the thumb of the political parties. And they would have raised the spectre of what I call the 'Manchester Gorton question': how could you prevent backbench MPs from seeing such people as serious rivals for local political influence, to the extent that they might oppose the whole reform in order to preserve their distinctive local power bases?

Secondly, the government did not accept our proposal that all appointments should be made by an independent appointments commission. Instead, the White Paper envisaged that 'political' appointments should continue to be made by the party leaders in the House of Commons, subject only to a probity check by the appointments commission, whose remit would otherwise be limited to selecting independent members. In practice, I doubt whether the party leaders would have lost much, as many appointments would have been people that they might otherwise have proposed. But perception is all, and the idea that the reformed House would be filled with 'Tony's cronies' and other political nominees was widely seen as no improvement at all on the hereditary House of Lords. For all its faults, the hereditary principle had thrown up many members who were seen to speak without fear or favour, being beholden to no one living for their place in the chamber.

Thirdly, the government did not accept our proposal to entrench the Parliament Acts, which set out the existing constraints on the powers of the House of Lords in relation to legislation. Our intention was to make it impossible for a future government to use its control of the House of Commons to further weaken the powers of the second chamber, and even to prolong its own life by deferring a general election. These are major constitutional issues and deserve a fuller consideration than the White Paper gave them.

It came as no surprise that the government's proposals got a rough ride in both Houses. Most people gave up any hint they would be prepared to compromise and most, including me, spoke against the government's proposals. A spirit of compromise was essential if progress was to be made, and it was in no way to be seen.

A joint committee of both Houses was set up and, interestingly, that committee seemed to accept broadly all the arguments for the type of second chamber we had advocated in our report, but it has so far failed to agree on the type of compromise that could bring about the second chamber they seemed to favour.

In effect Parliament was back where it had been in all the previous attempts to reform the House of Lords over the past hundred years. They had failed to agree the basis of composition that should replace the hereditary peers.

From the time I became chairman of the royal commission, I was always clear that a significant compromise by everyone was necessary to make progress. That spirit of compromise was not there and so the House of Lords continues doing the good work that it does, very little changed, except that the Labour government have significantly increased their representation by creating a large number of new Labour life peers. That was in my view perfectly reasonable, but it was no substitute for the long-term reform that we recommended.

Of approximately 750 hereditary peers, 650 have been excluded, but most of those did not in any event play an active part in the House, or in some cases come at all. Most of the hereditary peers who played an active part are still there, and by-elections will keep the number up to strength as individuals die.

In June 2003 the government announced plans for the establishment of a Supreme Court to replace the Judicial Committee of the House of Lords as the highest court in the land, for judges to be appointed by an independent commission, and for the abolition – after 1,398 years – of the post of Lord Chancellor and the creation of a new presiding officer for the House of Lords. Despite this, in September 2003, on the last sitting day in Parliament before the Labour Party conference, the government announced that there would be no radical second-stage reform of the House of Lords – there was to be no elected element for example – although they confirmed that it was their intention to introduce legislation to remove the remaining hereditary peers. These proposals, which will be hotly contested, will be brought before Parliament as and when parliamentary time permits. Part of what was proposed echoed proposals by the royal commission for an independent appointments commission who would have the task of determining the number and timing of nominations to the House of Lords, keeping the cross-benchers at around 20 per cent of the total. Other proposals differed from those of the royal commission, including no elected element and separating membership of the upper House from the honours system.

We shall see how the government's proposed legislation proceeds, but I am still convinced that what is needed is for the political parties and others to implement substantially our recommendations, even though they may not welcome all of them. If they don't, the risk is that the United Kingdom will be left with a second chamber – and a system of parliamentary democracy – which is less effective that it could be.

Endnote

1 At the time there were 87 British MEPs elected to serve in the European Parliament, the idea being that the same electoral boundaries could apply. With the addition of ten new member states to the membership of the European Union in 2004 this figure of 87 has been reduced to 78.

TWENTY-ONE

Parliament in the 21st Century: Concluding Observations

Dr Nicholas D.J. Baldwin

T he sovereignty of Parliament rests in the triumvirate of monarch, Lords and Commons working as one. However, and as outlined in Chapter 1, over the years power has not only moved from the monarch to the Houses of Parliament, but has moved within Parliament itself from the House of Lords to the House of Commons. Consequently, it is the House of Commons, at least in theory, that has power within the British body politic. Indeed, of the various interpretations of the British constitution which have been put forward over the years, the most traditional is the classic liberal view associated with the writings of Walter Bagehot and A. V. Dicey in the nineteenth century.[1] This view holds that it is the House of Commons which is the supreme political institution in Britain, with the power to make and unmake governments, to remove Prime Ministers, to safeguard the liberties of British subjects, to bring to light and remedy injustices, to pass any laws, to resolve the great political issues of the day and even to legislate itself out of existence or the country into a dictatorship if it so desired.

This view accords only subsidiary constitutional significance to the monarchy and the House of Lords. As R. H. S. Crossman pointed out, such a view could only have been valid for the period before any significant extension of the franchise and before the establishment of disciplined political parties with national organisations.[2] Consequently, if it applied at all, it applied only during the brief – atypical – era from the passage of the Great Reform Act 1832 until the passage of the Representation of the People Act 1867, an era when the House of Commons could be seen as supreme. (For example, it was during this period that no fewer than ten administrations fell because the House of Commons withdrew its support). However, by about 1868 – or very soon after – the main principles propounded by Bagehot and Dicey had already been eroded or overtaken by new political realities which became steadily more apparent during the last quarter of the nineteenth century. For example, and as outlined in Chapter 1, the legislative supremacy of Parliament was gradually overcome by the growing power of the political parties as they sought to appeal to a wider electorate which was extended in successive Reform Bills.

In modern conditions individuals interested in the British system of government and in the constitutional arrangements applicable in Britain need to make sense of a much more complex body politic in which parliamentary supremacy is only one important principle among many. The classic liberal view, although still regarded with respect and firmly established among the received ideas of British politics, is no longer particularly instructive as a guide to Parliament in the 21st century. It has been rendered rather obsolete by the enormously increased scope of modern government. Indeed, these developments have led to another well-known interpretation of the British constitution, which has been called the governmental view. This holds that the former power of the monarch has been passed not to Parliament but to the Prime Minister and Cabinet, subject only to criticism in Parliament and periodic confirmation or rejection by the mass electorate at general elections. It is a view usually associated with the writings of L. S. Amery and Herbert Morrison.[3] It maintains that the government has a clear responsibility to govern and that the essential form of political accountability is the responsibility of the governing party to the electorate. Accordingly the role of the opposition and all backbench MPs is to act essentially as filters or megaphones between the government of the day and the electorate. L. S. Amery was succinct when he wrote that 'the combination of responsible leadership by Government with responsible criticism in Parliament is the essence of our constitution.'[4]

Although this view, too, has to be qualified if we are to form an accurate impression of the position and role of Parliament in Britain in the 21st century, it undoubtedly has more validity than the classic liberal view, which is now characterised by sentimentality towards an era – perhaps more mythical than real – of so-called parliamentary government. In the legislative and administrative spheres at any rate, modern British governments have had virtually unlimited power, provided they have had a reliable working majority in the House of Commons and as long as they have been careful to keep their parliamentary supporters united behind them. Under the terms of the 1911 Parliament Act a government can retain this power for a maximum term of five years before it is obliged to seek a fresh mandate from the electorate. In view of the notable imbalance of political resources between government and opposition, there is some truth in Lord Hailsham's allegation that the British political system is 'an elective dictatorship' tempered only by the minimal restraints of constitutional conventions and the governing party's normal desire to get re-elected.[5]

More accurate still in modern conditions is the empirical view, which emphasises not only the weakness of Parliament in relation to the government of the day but also the weakness of the executive in relation to pressure groups, the media, public opinion and other actors on the national and international scene. It emphasises the way in which a deliberate extension of constitutional power can lead to a decline in effective power, no matter how great the parliamentary majority or the political momentum of the party in office. This is essentially because, if a government becomes over-extended in its ambitions or overloaded in its commitments, it is likely to encounter so many real-world obstacles and to create so many political enemies that it will be unable to achieve its objectives.

Indeed, a dispassionate reading of British constitutional history leads to the important conclusion that the most abiding political problem has been the gaining and retaining of public consent for the actions of any government. Stage by stage from the thirteenth century to the present time, governments in Britain, whether led by the monarch or by a Prime Minister in Parliament, have had to cede and share power with the other great interests in the land – and nowadays increasingly with their partners in the European Union. Effective government has only been possible with the consent, or at least the tacit acquiescence, of those most directly affected by it or involved with it. Against this background it makes sense to regard successive British governments as stable rather than strong, and to avoid confusing the concentration of responsibility with the concentration of power. Today public opinion, the influence of the media, the growth of European law and much greater judicial activism are all examples of the powerful forces which condition and limit the exercise of power by both Parliament and government alike.

Thus the contemporary situation within Britain is based on two key paradoxes. The first is the limited power of a theoretically supreme Parliament. This reflects the fact that, while Parliament is perfectly capable of passing any law, it is in practice able only to criticise and intermittently control the government of the day. It also reflects the growing political power and legal competence of the European Union, which has tended to reduce the power of the national governments within it and hence the national Parliaments which claim to control them. The second paradox is the limited power of the allegedly all-powerful executive, which reflects the fact that, while a government with a working majority in the House of Commons can invariably get its way in Whitehall and Westminster, little is achieved if its freedom of manoeuvre is unduly circumscribed by administrative constraints, media influence, interest group pressure, the impact of European law and much greater judicial activism – increasingly a factor since the 1960s, but undoubtedly enhanced by the Human Rights Act. This complicated network of informal checks and balances means that the system of government continues to develop organically, but provides few constitutional safeguards – be they parliamentary or otherwise – against the arbitrary exercise of executive power.

Formal limitation of the power of any British government is now more often sought and found in the rulings of the European Court of Justice or the European Court of Human Rights rather than through Parliament. On the other hand, informal constraints upon the power of all national governments are to be observed most clearly these days in the capacity of the global financial markets to discipline any national authorities which lose credibility in the eyes of global investors, and in the enormous power of the global media corporations.

In practice, the power of the Commons is usually subsumed in the power of the government of the day, which governs through Parliament as long as it retains the voting support of an overall majority in the House of Commons. It is usually misleading to refer to the powers of the Commons in any way which implies that such powers can be divorced from those of modern single-party government, which has been the norm in recent times. In normal parliamentary conditions, when one of the main parties on its own has an overall majority in the Commons, the power of the House as a representative institution seeking to monitor and control the government of the day is wielded principally by the opposition parties in their constant efforts to draw attention to the shortcomings of government policy and to criticise, delay and occasionally obstruct the progress of government legislation. There is, however, an important, if delicate, role for government backbenchers as representatives of those in the electorate who voted for the party in office and as critics of government policy when they believe it is reneging on party commitments or falling short of public expectations.

The House of Commons – unlike the monarchy or the House of Lords – still has real power in the British political system, at any rate on those occasions when it is willing and able to use it. Indeed, on a number of, albeit rare, occasions over the past 75 years the power of the House of Commons has really come to the fore and made itself felt. One of the most famous examples of this was on 8 May 1940, when the poor result of what turned into a vital confidence debate on the conduct of the war led Neville Chamberlain to resign as Prime Minister. Although the Chamberlain government won the vote with a majority of 80, this was down from the normal majority of 240 or more, while the division saw some 33 Conservative MPs vote against their own government and some 65 abstain; consequently, it was seen as having entirely lost the argument and the mood of the House. Chamberlain's resignation paved the way for Winston Churchill to succeed him as the country's wartime leader. As was observed,

> *it was certainly a decisive debate, for it altered the history of Britain and the Empire, and perhaps of the world ... Normally ... 'full-dress' Parliamentary debates are in the nature of oratorical or argumentative displays, intended not to sway votes inside the House so much as to influence opinion outside. These are contests of which the immediate result is more or less certain. But on this occasion everything was in flux.*[6]

Another memorable example was on 8 March 1979, when, at the end of a confidence debate following the so-called winter of discontent, enough of the opposition parties united to defeat what was by then a minority Labour government by 311 votes to 310 and so precipitated the May 1979 general election, which brought the Conservatives under Margaret Thatcher to power.

A more recent example of parliamentary power was the ability of the small band of Eurosceptics on the Conservative back benches to threaten and almost to defeat the government's legislation designed to give legal effect to the 1992 Treaty of Maastricht. In this case a disparate group of between ten and 20 backbenchers, often in tactical alliance with the Labour opposition, were able to alarm and annoy ministers for months on end while the Bill concerned was slowly grinding its way through the legislative process. The practical effect of this sustained parliamentary campaign – which had some powerful support in parts of the media and in many Conservative-held constituencies – was to debilitate and discredit John Major's administration and, in so doing, to sow the seeds of its subsequent loss of authority in the country at large and its eventual loss of office in 1997. On the whole, however, all such examples of raw parliamentary power have been rare in modern times, since on most occasions governments have been able to count on the voting support and loyalty of their own backbenchers in order to ensure their survival in office at least until the subsequent general election.

Yet the nature of the power of the House of Commons is different from what it was in the nineteenth century, when most of the traditional notions about the House were established. The House of Commons in the 21st century is neither the government of the country nor even the principal place where official decisions or legislative proposals are conceived. It is essentially the sounding board for popular representation and redress, one of the stages on which the party battle is fought, the principal forum within which legislation and other decisions of government are scrutinised, and the framework for parliamentary control of the executive – one of the tasks which it shares with the House of Lords.

The essential purposes of the House of Commons have not changed significantly since the last quarter of the nineteenth century. Sir Ivor Jennings described them as being 'to question and debate the policy of the government and in doing so to bring home ... the unpopularity (or popularity) of a particular line of policy'.[7] L.S. Amery described them as being 'to secure full discussion and ventilation of all matters ... as the condition of giving its assent to Bills ... or its support to Ministers'.[8] Such descriptions are still broadly valid today.

Today, the House of Commons has a range of powers and functions which can be formidable or merely nominal, depending on the parliamentary arithmetic at any time and the mood or inclinations of the 659 MPs. In what might be described as normal circumstances, when the governing party has an effective overall majority, the government of the day is able to get its way on the things which really matter, provided only that it retains the confidence and voting support of its backbenchers. In the rarer circumstances when the result of a general election has produced a very small majority for the governing party or even a so-called hung Parliament (in which the government has no overall majority), there can be a serious risk of defeat at the hands of combined opposition parties. Indeed, even when a government has a modest but sufficient overall majority, it can still encounter great danger in Parliament if a significant and cohesive group of its own backbenchers are in revolt on a political issue where they have a good slice of public opinion on their side – as John Major and his ministerial colleagues discovered in the early 1990s when the Eurosceptics on the Conservative back benches harried and nearly brought down the government during the passage of the legislation designed to bring British law into line with the 1992 Maastricht treaty.

In fact, even when a government has a large majority things may not always go its way. Take, for example, the loss of the Shops Bill at second reading by the Conservative government of Margaret Thatcher in 1986. Despite having a nominal majority of more than 130 at the time, in a division which saw a total of 72 Conservative MPs vote against the Bill and another fifteen to 20 abstain, the legislation was defeated by 296 votes to 282, a majority against the government of fourteen.[9] Equally, consider the Labour government of Tony Blair in November 2003, when the nominal majority of 161 for the government was reduced to seventeen on the issue of foundation hospitals, and in January 2004, when it fell to just five (316 votes to 311) on the issue of the introduction of variable university tuition charges, the biggest revolt on a three-line whip in more than 50 years with 72 Labour MPs voting against the government and a further nineteen abstaining. It was a victory for the government, but it was neither easy nor without political cost. In short, backbench dissent is a factor that governments ignore at their peril.

There are many paradoxical aspects of the House of Commons which ought to discourage sweeping generalisations. All that can really be said is that the House carries out its various tasks with varying degrees of efficiency and success. It is reasonably effective as a forum for popular representation and redress. It is best known as a dramatic stage for party political conflict, especially since it has been broadcast to a – potentially – large audience by first radio and then television,[10] as well more recently being available on the internet.[11] It is quite good at the detailed scrutiny of legislation (although it still does not make the most efficient use of this time), but almost incapable of modifying legislation against the wishes of the government of the day unless a large enough group of party rebels are prepared to stick to their guns to the point of defying the party whips. It is gradually becoming more effective as a mechanism for the scrutiny and control of the executive, although in this respect it is unable to emulate the power and independence of the American Congress, something that will continue to be the case certainly for as long as there is no formal separation of powers in Britain.

In short, while the House of Commons is theoretically supreme in the British political system, in practice it is usually controlled by the government of the day in tacit collusion with the official opposition. In other words, the power of all MPs – and especially that of the preponderance of backbenchers – is severely limited by the rules and conventions of Britain's 'frontbench constitution'. This position is unlikely to change significantly unless and until there is agreement to far-reaching reforms of Britain's constitutional arrangements – and, not least of all in this regard, the electoral system used for elections to the House of Commons. Such changes are unlikely to be made unless a new parliamentary consensus emerges to support them. However, the scope for delay and obstruction remains very great, especially since there are probably enough entrenched traditionalists in all parties to thwart the most ambitious plans of the parliamentary and constitutional reformers. In these circumstances it is unwise to make dogmatic statements about the House of Commons, not least because the mood and priorities of every parliament can change and in politics no one can necessarily accurately predict the future as things can change quickly. Indeed, as has been said, 'a week is a long time in politics' and, as has been observed, in politics 'while there is death, there is hope.'

The power of influence

In most normal circumstances the House of Commons has to rely on the power of influence – that is, influence on ministers in the government, influence on the policies of the government, and influence on the media and public opinion. Effective influence in the Commons is frequently exercised in a discreet manner before the event, whether in party committees, formal delegations or informal conversations. On the other hand, the exercise of overt parliamentary power (as in the previously listed examples of May 1940 and March 1979) is usually confined to the comparatively rare occasions when the authority of a minister or sometimes of the government as a whole is in jeopardy or may even have broken down. For example, when it became clear at the beginning of April 1982 that ministers in the Foreign Office and the Ministry of Defence had lost the confidence of the bulk of Conservative MPs following the Argentinian invasion of the Falkland Islands, Lord Carrington and two of his ministerial team at the Foreign Office resigned. The defence secretary, John Nott, despite offering his resignation, was not in fact 'obliged' to resign, not least of all because the 'demands' of the Commons had been assuaged by the departure of the ministers from the Foreign Office. Similarly, when in January 1986 the then Secretary of State for Trade and Industry, Leon Brittan, made a statement to the House of Commons on the matter of Westland, during subsequent questioning he was asked – by Michael Heseltine – about the existence of a letter from British Aerospace and in his answer he suggested – with the Prime Minister, Margaret Thatcher, sitting silently by his side – that there was no such letter. Shortly afterwards, however, Downing Street confirmed that a letter had been received. Leon

Brittan was later forced to return to the House of Commons – the opposition demanding a statement – and declared: 'If it is thought that I have misled the House I apologise unreservedly.'[12] There followed a number of interventions, one of the most devastating of which was delivered by Roy Jenkins, who stated that it was extraordinary that the Prime Minister had sat through the afternoon statement without intervening. He added: 'While Mr Brittan may just be within the formal bounds of truth, the margin was so narrow that we will count our spoons very quickly whenever they are together again.'[13]

This issue, (along with that of the leaking of a letter from the Solicitor-General), undermined any support that there might have been for Leon Brittan on the back benches and, when in it became clear that he no longer enjoyed the confidence of Conservative MPs, he was obliged to resign. In crude and capricious parliamentary conditions these are vivid examples of the power of the Commons or, more precisely, the power of government backbenchers when they are no longer prepared to support ministers because of grievous failures of policy – perceived or actual.

Other examples of what can be termed ministerial vulnerability to parliamentary displeasure – notably from the government back benches – can be provided; three will suffice, namely, the cases of Nicholas Ridley, Norman Lamont and Harriet Harman. Nicholas Ridley, Secretary of State for the Environment from 1986 to 1989, became increasingly accident prone and unpopular with the electorate because of his obvious disdain for the usual shibboleths of 'green' politics. His incorrigible attitudes made life very difficult for Conservative backbenchers, who conveyed their anxiety to the Conservative whips with increasing frequency and intensity. The result was that by 1989 Margaret Thatcher was left with no alternative but to move him from the Department of the Environment in her Cabinet reshuffle of July that year, even though he remained one of her personal favourites. During the long economic recession of the early 1990s Norman Lamont, the then Chancellor of the Exchequer, came to appear increasingly inept and accident prone. Against the backdrop of mounting criticism and speculation from the media seeking a (political) scalp, Conservative MPs were bombarded with demands from their constituents for the Chancellor to 'go'. The situation became even more embarrassing following Black Wednesday on 16 September 1992, when Britain was effectively ejected by the financial markets from the exchange rate mechanism of the European Monetary System, to which the government's entire anti-inflation policy had been anchored – at least rhetorically. Although Norman Lamont clung onto office for a few more months, his case became hopeless and his eventual fate was sealed. Accordingly, John Major unceremoniously sacked him in May 1993. Harriet Harman, when Secretary of State for Social Security in the Labour government which came into office in 1997, never recovered her authority after a major political row over cuts in lone parent benefit and the perceived threat of widespread withdrawal of some disability benefits and, as a result, was dismissed by Tony Blair in his first reshuffle in July 1998 (although she later returned to government as Solicitor-General). All three of these cases exemplify the political truth that when a minister becomes – or is perceived to have become – a significant liability or embarrassment to the party in office and especially to government backbenchers, sooner or later the unfortunate individual will either be moved, obliged to resign or will get the sack.

Over the long period since the Second World War such examples of raw parliamentary power have been relatively rare, although more recently in the febrile atmosphere of mass media politics the vulnerability of errant or fallible ministers appears to have increased. Certainly such things seem to happen faster and with greater sensationalism these days than was the case even 30 years ago and in this respect, as in many others, the nature of British politics has changed significantly over the years. Nowadays parliamentary reputations are built up and then demolished, sometimes with alarming rapidity. The more that certain ministers are thrown into the limelight, the more rapidly they seem to become vulnerable to destruction at the hands of the media and their own backbench 'colleagues'. This was clearly highlighted by the examples of Ron Davies, who resigned as Welsh secretary in October 1998 following a 'moment of madness' on Clapham Common; of Peter Mandelson, who resigned as Secretary of State for Trade and Industry in December 1998 following publication of details concerning a home loan he had obtained from Geoffrey Robinson; of Geoffrey Robinson, who resigned as Paymaster General in December 1998 when the Mandelson home loan raised one too many questions about his business dealings; and of Peter Mandelson – again – in 2001 when he resigned as Secretary of State for Northern Ireland over the so-called Hinduja passport affair. In all such cases the most decisive criteria for ministerial survival are the degree of political embarrassment caused to the rest of the government, the extent to which government backbenchers are prepared to weather the storm, the support that is to be found on the backbenches for the individual minister, and whether the Prime Minister eventually wishes to sacrifice or stand by the minister in question. In each and every case the chain of events and the eventual outcome is subtly different, although it may not seem that way to the victims of such political 'assassination'.

The background reality which lies behind all this is that at nearly every general election since the Second World War the electorate has voted and the electoral system has worked in such a way as to ensure that one of the main parties has had an overall majority in the Commons large enough to withstand most backbench rebellions and the political erosion which takes place due to death and retirement during the normal span of a parliament. In such circumstances the power of the Commons has not normally been manifested in successful attempts to censure ministers, still less to defeat governments. Instead it has been exercised through constant backbench influence on ministers and the constant interplay between governments striving to get their policy approved and their legislation onto the Statute Book and oppositions striving to criticise their actions and delay or frustrate their progress.

Scrutiny

A vital function of both members of Parliament and members of the House of Lords is to scrutinise and seek to control the activities of the executive. This is probably the most necessary, but also the most difficult, function to be performed in modern conditions, essentially because there is no formal separation of powers in Britain between the executive and the legislature, as there is for example in the United States. This means that in Britain the government of the day – provided it has a secure overall majority in the House of Commons – is more often able to dominate Parliament rather than the other way around.

Traditionally, it was assumed that ministers' responsibility to answer the questions and debating points of members of Parliament – and peers – constituted adequate and respectable parliamentary control of the executive. Yet with the remorseless extension of the perceived responsibilities of government over the last 60 years, it has become painfully clear that this traditional and complacent assumption does not meet public expectations and needs to be reinforced if central government and its agencies are to be properly scrutinised, let alone controlled by the elected representatives of the people in the Commons and by the membership of the House of Lords. The fundamental problem here is that with typical British ambiguity there is a clash between two different versions of democratic legitimacy – that of the party elected into office at the previous general election to govern the country for a period of years according to the principles and policies which it put before the electorate, and that of the House of Commons as a whole as the overall, democratic manifestation of the will of the people at a particular time.

In modern times parliamentarians (that is, members of both Houses) have sought to square this circle by making increasingly full and effective use of select committees. In the House of Commons these are committees reflecting broadly the political balance in the House at any time which are charged by the House as a whole with scrutinising and controlling the activities of the executive in given policy areas. Originally, in the nineteenth century, they were set up by the House ad hoc to look closely into particular issues of public concern – for example, Britain's military shortcomings in the Crimean War. They can also be traced back to the attitudes of William Gladstone and other parliamentarians in the 1850s, who, in their determination to guarantee the probity and efficiency of public expenditure, established the Public Accounts Committee as a permanent committee of the House of Commons designed to enable the House as a whole to be satisfied that public money was being correctly and properly spent.

From these nineteenth-century beginnings through to modern times, the fortunes of select committees have waxed and waned. They have tended to be more powerful when the government of the day has had only a very small majority in the Commons or no majority at all (as in the middle and late 1970s), but considerably less powerful when the government of the day has had a commanding majority which it could use, if necessary, to steamroller any flickering challenge from largely impotent select committees. Indeed, for many years there has been a whole school of thought – represented by people such as the former Labour leader Michael Foot and the Conservative politician the late Enoch Powell, for example – that holds that the correct way to scrutinise and control the executive is on the floor of the House and that select committees are little more than a self-important and time-consuming distraction from what should be the cockpit of parliamentary control in the chamber.

Against this background it was fortuitous and somewhat surprising that the incoming Conservative government in 1979 decided to propose a comprehensive reform of the select committee structure, which was willingly accepted by most government backbenchers and certainly by the opposition parties. Following this fundamental reform, there is now one of these all-party and largely non-partisan committees in the House of Commons for each area of central government activity, as well as a number of non-departmental committees, which have deeper roots in parliamentary soil as has already been explained. These select committees, each of which is usually composed of between eleven and seventeen MPs broadly reflecting the party political balance in the House as a whole, meet regularly (perhaps two days a week when the House is sitting and on other occasions as well) to oversee and investigate their particular area of government activity. In the course of their investigations, which can include foreign travel, they can call for persons and papers, and their findings are normally written up in substantial reports drafted by their clerks and expert advisers and usually redrafted and amended by members of the committee. Once published in the form of reports to the House as a whole, such documents are intended to inform both parliamentary and public debate. Occasionally, they can have real influence on the course of government policy.[14]

In normal circumstances select committees have no legislative role, so they are not really analogous to the congressional committees in the United States. However, on a few occasions they have been used as parliamentary mechanisms for the exploration of policy options at a prelegislative stage. Indeed, both the government of John Major (1990–97) and the government of Tony Blair (since 1997) made much more use of select committees – some departmental, some ad hoc, some joint – for examining draft Bills.[15] Whatever their shortcomings and inhibitions, they do represent a systematic attempt to improve parliamentary scrutiny and control of the executive and its agencies in Britain, which has come to seem all the more necessary as it has been increasingly recognised that the traditional forms of ministerial accountability to the House as a whole do not guarantee the achievement of this important parliamentary objective.

In recent years the influence (if not the power) of select committees has increased in that their public hearings are quite often televised and broadcast over the internet and hence attract a degree of extra media and public interest. This makes them more formidable interlocutors for ministers and senior civil servants and a more central part of the whole parliamentary publicity machine. The chairmen of such committees can become (or may already be) influential and newsworthy MPs who are often called to speak early in debates on the floor of the House and can be much in demand for media interviews – Gerald Kaufman as chair of the Culture, Media and Sport Select Committee and Tony Wright as chair of the Public Administration Select Committee for example. Yet it would be a mistake to believe that this extra visibility for select committees has altered to any real extent the fundamental imbalance of power in the House of Commons between a self-confident government with a secure parliamentary majority and the rest of the House, no matter how effective the opposition may be or how keen certain MPs may have become to use select committees and other parliamentary procedures more effectively to hold ministers and the executive to account.

The experience of the Westland crisis in 1986 and other clashes between members of Parliament and the executive before and since underlines the fact that parliamentary control of the executive in Britain is not, and may never be, as effective as its proponents or some members of the general public would like.[16] In the final analysis, select committees, and indeed Parliament as a whole, are likely to remain relatively weak when faced with a strong and determined government which is confident of its ability to use its voting support on the floor of the House to overcome any challenge. The only circumstances in which this situation might be changed would be if a government were committed to, or had imposed on it by dint of its minority status in the Commons, the introduction of proportional representation for elections to Westminster.

Parliamentary culture

The House of Commons and the House of Lords have sometimes been described as 'the best clubs in London', although doubtless there would be many members of other clubs, such as White's or the Garrick, to challenge this claim. However, it does say something about the parliamentary culture that exists in Britain. It is an atmosphere in which the cut and thrust of the party battle is balanced by a political camaraderie which often makes it easier to form friendships across the floor of the House than with other members on the same side.

The House of Commons is an institution which relies on the assumption that all its members are 'honourable' (although this may have become harder to sustain following various cases of what came to be termed parliamentary 'sleaze' in the middle and late 1990s) and all are equal in terms of democratic legitimacy. Yet in an institution in which there are supposed to be no second-class members, it is remarkable how some are more equal than others, and how frontbenchers and Privy Counsellors seem to get all the best parts. The main explanation, of course, is that traditional parliamentary procedure, much of which dates from the 1880s, assumes that debate and discussion will be conducted largely by the political giants of the day and that the rest will be content with minor roles as spear carriers or cheerleaders. This established tendency is reinforced by the simple fact that the chamber itself is rather small (deliberately so) and that no more than about two-thirds of those entitled can possibly find a seat on the green benches when the House is full – for example, on Budget Day or on Wednesday during Prime Minister's Question Time. In short, there are only limited opportunities for MPs to shine during prime parliamentary time at Westminster and most of these are taken by senior ministers and their 'shadows' on the opposition front bench.

Another interesting aspect of parliamentary culture in the House of Commons is the extent to which the institutionalised, almost ritual, party conflict is organised by the party whips working through what are known as 'the usual channels'.[17] This phrase is a euphemism for the sometimes heated and vigorous discussions which take place behind the scenes and off the record between the two front benches. Without the benefit of such discussions, which can include the Prime Minister and the leader of the opposition on occasions, the whole place would probably grind to a halt.[18] As it is, the essential deal between the two sides is based on two key assumptions:

- that the government must 'get its business' (that is, get its legislation passed more or less intact);
- that the opposition must have full opportunities to oppose and, within limits, to decide what is newsworthy and urgent or what is uncontentious and acceptable and hence suitable for full cooperation between the parties.

In support of this generally pragmatic approach to the conduct of parliamentary business is the basic British idea that it is the duty of Her Majesty's Loyal Opposition to oppose the government of the day, coupled with the understanding that there are few problems which cannot be solved in Parliament by the so-called business managers on each side acting in tacit cooperation.

Another aspect of parliamentary culture which is worth mentioning is the fondness of MPs in all parties for informal political groupings and gatherings of all kinds, the common denominator being the exchange of political gossip and ideas, something which is the very stuff of politics in all parliamentary assemblies around the world. For example, in the Labour Party there is the Tribune Group and the Campaign Group, while the Conservative Party has the '92 Group, the Reform Group, the Macleod Group, One Nation, The Progress Trust and the No Turning Back Group. All such groups compete for influence over party policy and appointments, while the views and opinions that emerge are propounded and taken forward by the MPs – and peers – concerned, who usually lose little time in passing on the essence of their discussions to their party whips and sometimes, in suitably veiled form, to lobby journalists. It is in these ways that much political opinion at Westminster is moulded and developed. If a full account is to be given of parliamentary life in the 21st century, attention should be paid to such activity.

Watchdog, poodle or incontinent Labrador?

In 1867 Walter Bagehot suggested that the House of Commons needed to perform the following functions if it was to do its duty: 'elect a Ministry, legislate, teach the nation, express the nation's will and bring matters to the nation's attention'.[19] If we were to translate his words into modern terms, we would say that the House of Commons has to provide most of the ministers in any government, to scrutinise and pass legislation, to give a lead to public opinion on the great issues of the day, and to seek redress for the grievances and concerns of the general public. There are, of course, other vital functions performed by the modern House of Commons, notably parliamentary control of the executive and party political conflict on the parliamentary stage. Yet the essential functions of the House have not changed very much since the time when Walter Bagehot made his authoritative observation.

With regard to the concept of parliamentary control of the executive, Professor Bernard Crick wrote – more than 35 years ago – that we should not read too much into the concept in Britain because it means 'influence not direct power, advice not command, criticism not obstruction, scrutiny not initiative, and publicity not secrecy'.[20] Yet even these attenuated forms of parliamentary control should not be under-estimated in a political system which has never been characterised by clear-cut and unambiguous power relationships. Furthermore, a degree of parliamentary control to match that exercised by Congress in the United States would only be possible in Britain if it were decided to move to an explicit separation of powers set out in a formal, written, codified constitution and guaranteed by an independent Supreme Court. (Despite moves to separate the judiciary from Parliament and to establish a distinct Supreme Court, it is nevertheless not envisaged that this would be one of its functions.) Such revolutionary change is unlikely to be brought about in a political system in which it is the government of the day and the official opposition front bench (the putative alternative government) which effectively control the nature and scope of parliamentary power. The irony is that it is in the name of 'parliamentary supremacy' that governments have come to dominate the political sphere in Britain.

In the 21st century, if no longer able to act as an effective watchdog, is Parliament merely the poodle of the executive? Let us look at recent events. In 2003 the prospect of a war against Iraq was a debate which touched not only on military strategy, diplomacy and international relations, but also on the power of the executive within the British system of government and the influence – or lack thereof – of the House of Commons over such matters. This again focused attention on the question of what the late Lord Hailsham had described as 'elective dictatorship', and what the Foreign Secretary, Jack Straw, had termed 'executive democracy', namely the powers of the executive vis-à-vis the legislature. As one observer noted:

> *Something is wrong in a parliamentary democracy when the greatest decisions about peace and war are made by the executive without reference to the legislature. ... Great issues ... are made not by Parliament or even the Cabinet, but rather under a convenient royal instrument that has descended down the centuries from the hands of an absolute monarch into the lap of an almost equally absolute Prime Minister.*[21]

The concept of an 'absolute Prime Minister' was, however, not one that the Prime Minister of the time, Tony Blair, readily recognised as he faced mounting criticism on a variety of fronts – for a failure to deliver promised improvements in the public services, for looking for a 'middle way' on the issue of hunting, for coming up with a scheme for reform of the House of Lords that pleased no one, and for identifying too closely with US policy (in the war on terror, with regard to the treatment of those held at the Guantanamo base on Cuba, and on the prospect of war against Iraq). Certainly – as was noted by Democratic Audit[22] – legally undefined royal prerogative powers give the Prime Minster and ministers executive freedom unchecked – in any formal sense – by Parliament; the Prime Minister may even wage war without consulting Parliament. However – and as was also pointed out by Democratic Audit – being strong, overpowerful, centralist and largely unchecked does not ensure effectiveness.

All of this notwithstanding, it should be pointed out that in the immediate run-up to the war against Iraq the government, breaking with precedence, was obliged – politically if not legally or constitutionally – to hold a vote on the issue of going to war. Although it was a vote that the government won, by 396 votes to 217, it was significant by virtue of the fact that it took place, establishing a precedent and, consequently, making it very difficult indeed for a government to go to war in the future without first holding a vote in the House of Commons. In addition, having 'forced' the hand of government into publishing intelligence information prior to the Iraq war, similarly, it is unlikely that the publication of such information could be withheld prior to involvement in military campaigns in the future.

Consequently, it is evident that, whereas the government may not lose sleep over the likely actions of the parliamentary 'watchdog', the House of Commons cannot be taken for granted – it is no executive 'poodle' – and that it can be, at the very least, an irritant to the government. In short, it does have both the capacity and the ability to be the political equivalent of an incontinent Labrador.

*

Legislatures have one thing in common, namely, 'they are constitutionally designated for giving assent to binding measures of public policy, that assent being given on behalf of a political community that extends beyond the government élite responsible for formulating those measures.'23 It is for this reason that legislatures have generally been categorised according to their capacity to influence policy. Consequently, four types of legislature have been identified:

- policy-making legislatures (sometimes termed 'active' legislatures);

- policy-influencing legislatures (sometimes termed 'reactive' legislatures);
- legislatures with minimal or marginal policy effect (sometimes termed 'marginal' legislatures);
- legislatures with no real policy effect (sometimes termed 'rubber stamp' legislatures).

Policy-making legislatures enjoy significant autonomy and can not only amend or reject measures brought forward by the executive but can substitute for them policy of their own. Policy-influencing legislatures react to executive initiatives in that they can either amend or reject measures brought forward by the executive but cannot – either formally or in practice – substitute for them policy of their own. Legislatures with only minimal or marginal policy effect have very little ability – in theory or in practice – either to amend or reject measures brought forward by the executive or to generate and substitute for them policy of their own. Legislatures with no real policy effect are under executive domination and, as a result, rubber-stamp executive decisions. The British Parliament – both the House of Commons and the House of Lords – is an example of a policy-influencing legislature.

There is, however, more to legislatures – much more – than either formulating policy or influencing the formulation of policy. Indeed, a wide range of functions – some intended and some unintended – can be identified:

Functions of a legislature

Representation, redress and express
On behalf of constituents
On behalf of interests
On behalf of causes
On behalf of party

Legitimisation
Latent – through meeting regularly and uninterruptedly
Manifest – the formal stamps of approval
'Safety valve' – as an outlet for tensions and an arena for resolving disputes

Recruitment, socialisation and training
Recruitment – of individuals into the political system
Socialisation – of individuals into the norms of political behaviour
Training – of individuals in political skills

Education and informing
Educating – to teach the nation what it does not know
Informing – to bring matters to the forefront through discussion and deliberation

Legislative
The scrutiny of legislation
The revision of legislation
The passage of legislation

Scrutiny
Of the actions (and inactions) of the executive
Of the activity of the executive

Source: Derived from Bagehot, W. *The English Constitution* (Collins, London, 1867); Packenham, R. A. 'Legislators and Political Development' in Kornberg, A. & Musolf, L. D. (eds), *Legislatures in Developmental Perspective* (Duke University Press, Durham, NC, 1970); Norton, P. *Legislatures* (Oxford University Press, Oxford, 1990) and Forman, F. N. & Baldwin, N. D. J. *Mastering British Politics* (Macmillan, London, 1999)

Against this backdrop it is interesting to note that one concept that appears to permeate the topic is the idea of 'the decline of Parliament'. Such a concept is not new. Writing in 1921, despite stating that legislatures were an indispensable part of the machinery of government, Viscount Bryce observed:

> The House of Commons seems to hold a slightly lower place in the esteem of the people than it did in the days of Melbourne and Peel. Its intellectual quality has not risen. Its proceedings are less fully reported. The frequency of obstruction and of the use of the closure to overcome obstruction have reduced the value of the debates and affected the quality of legislation, while also lessening respect for a body which is thought ... to waste time in unprofitable wrangling .... The independence of members has suffered by the more stringent party discipline. The results of these causes are seen in the diminished deference accorded to Parliament, perhaps also in its slightly diminished attractiveness for able and public-spirited men.[24]

Ever since then the literature has been dominated by the thought that Parliament has been in decline, not least of all in comparison with – and as a direct result of – the increased power of the executive.[25] Within the literature a variety of specific causes for this decline have been identified, including

- the emergence of organised, disciplined political parties;
- the growth in the activity and scope of government at both the national and international level and the resulting increase in the size of governmental bureaucracies;
- the greater capacity of the executive to respond to developments in a timely fashion, formulating policy and providing leadership on the national stage and in the international arena;
- the rise of pressure group politics;

449

- the power of the media, the impact of 24-hour news coverage and the media's tendency to portray politics in terms of personalities.

On the other hand, some of the available evidence does point to an increased ability on the part of Parliament to hold the executive to account. The extent to which this is possible, the extent to which Parliament is able to exercise power and exert influence on the government of the day is dependent upon a variety of variables, both 'general' and 'specific', including:

General:
- the institutional nature of the system within which a Parliament operates;
- the position of a Parliament within the framework of the constitution as it exists and the extent of its constitutional authority;

Specific:
- its working practices and the extent of its political independence from the executive;
- the extent to which it is affected by the nature of the party system;
- its standing in the eyes of the public;
- its organisational coherence – for example, the independence and strength of its committee system – and the professionalism of its membership.

The recent history of the working relationship between the British Parliament – House of Commons and House of Lords – and British governments certainly reinforce such an analysis as it points to the importance of such factors as

- the party balance;
- the size of the majority;

- timing – in terms of where one is during a parliamentary session as well as how close or otherwise one is to a general election;
- the perceptions among MPs of the authority and popularity of the Prime Minister;
- the skills of the Prime Minister in managing Parliament;
- the skills and abilities of parliamentary business managers (such as the Chief Whip);
- the prevalence of 'divisive issues';
- the quality of the institutional structures by which Parliament can scrutinise the executive;
- the unity and quality of the opposition;
- perceptions among MPs of the likely actions (and reactions) of members of the House of Lords on any given issue and, similarly, perceptions among peers as to the likely actions (and reactions) of MPs on any given issue;
- perceptions among both MPs and members of the House of Lords as to the status of public opinion;
- national and international events.

It is only by taking into account all such variable factors at any given time that one can assess the nature and status of the relationship between Parliament (the House of Commons and the House of Lords) and the executive and determine whether it is Parliament (particularly in this respect the House of Commons) or the executive that has the upper hand. In reaching a conclusion it is also necessary to recognise and to take account of the fact that influence can be exerted 'behind the scenes', something that makes analysis very difficult. For example, much executive leadership may not be directly observed or measured as it is often exerted primarily in private meetings with other political actors. Similarly, when the interests of the executive and Parliament align, it may be difficult to determine to what extent the executive is leading Parliament or responding to it.

To the list of variables affecting the ability of Parliament to exercise power over and exert influence upon the executive should also be added the fact that the very shift in emphasis to executives – the fact that voters have increasingly looked to executives to provide solutions to problems – may in itself prove to have adverse consequences for executives themselves as they may not be able to meet, let alone satisfy, heightened public expectations. This can cause a loss of faith not only in the government concerned but also in political actors as a whole, indeed, in the political system itself.

As Forman and Baldwin have argued,[26] against the backdrop of the growing complexity of modern, global society, the policies and aspirations of even the most powerful executives are vulnerable to developments and decisions elsewhere over which they have little influence and even less control. For example, the free movement of capital around the world, the growing interaction between computer, phone and television technologies, and the tendency for hundreds of thousands of people to migrate across national borders in search of a better life, all pose significant threats to the ambitions and jurisdictions of national executives. The dilemma for executives is that if they stubbornly persist in making claims to exclusive competence and control within their national jurisdictions, they are likely to discredit themselves in the eyes of their electorates because of their almost inevitable inability to deliver all that they have promised. On the other hand, if they give up most of their traditional pretensions, more and more people in their electorates may begin to look elsewhere for satisfaction of their material needs and aspirations.

The reality is that the situation in which Parliament finds itself in 21st-century Britain is dependent upon the history, traditions and special circumstances that are to be found within the British body politic. What is clear is that any analysis illustrates, to one degree or another, the complexity of the relationship between Parliament and the executive. It is not simply the case of Parliament controlling the executive or of the executive controlling Parliament. Even in those instances where the balance of power undoubtedly favours the executive it is not to the point of total subordination, as there are examples, even in these instances, of Parliament – both Commons and Lords – being able to have an impact.

In conclusion, what can be seen is a complex set of interrelationships involving, in most cases, the capacity to influence, as opposed to determine; the ability to advise, rather than to command; the facility to criticise but not to obstruct; the competence to scrutinise rather than to initiate; and the desire to ensure that light is shed upon what is going on rather than to have things covered by a veil of secrecy. In short, the ability to hold the executive to account and ensure that it is required to explain and justify its actions – and inactions – not least of all before the House of Commons, in which sit the representatives of the people, but also before the House of Lords.

The 21st-century House of Commons and the 21st-century House of Lords are both better equipped than previously to scrutinise and oversee the executive and they possess a unique authority not only to force the executive to account for their actions but also to hold them responsible for those actions. Consequently, to focus on 'the decline of Parliament' is too simplistic. Indeed, despite the fact that Parliament may be weaker in its capacity to influence policy today than previously, it has been growing in importance in a variety of ways, not least of all as a raiser of grievances, as an agent of oversight and, above all, as a forum for scrutiny of the executive.

Writing in 1921 Viscount Bryce observed:

> *Representative Assemblies must remain the vital centre of the frame of government in every country … The people as a whole cannot attend to details, still less exercise over the executive the watchful supervision needed to ensure honest and efficient administration.*[27]

This was true in the 21st year of the twentieth century and it remains true in the early years of the 21st century.

Endnotes

1   See Bagehot, W. *The English Constitution* (Collins, London, 1963) and Dicey, A. V. *The Law of the Constitution* (Macmillan, London, 1959).

2   See R. H. S. Crossman's introduction to Bagehot, W. *The English Constitution* (Collins, London, 1963), p. 35.

3   See Amery, L. S. *Thoughts on the Constitution* (Oxford University Press, Oxford, 1947) and Morrison, H. *Government and Parliament* (Oxford University Press, Oxford, 1959).

4   Amery, *Thoughts on the Constitution*, p. 32.

5   See Lord Hailsham *The Dilemma of Democracy* (Collins, London, 1978) for an exposition of this argument.

6   Macmillan, H. *The Blast of War* (Macmillan, London, 1967), p. 67.

7   Jennings, W. I. *Parliament* (2nd ed.) (Cambridge University Press, Cambridge, 1969), pp. 7–8.

8   Amery, *Thoughts on the Constitution*, p. 12.

9   See Brown, F. 'The Defeat of the Shops Bill, 1986', in M. Rush (ed.) *Parliament and Pressure Politics* (Clarendon Press, Oxford, 1990), pp. 213–33.

10 The proceedings of Parliament have been broadcast via radio since 3 April 1978. Since 23 January 1985, the proceedings of the House of Lords have been televised – an experiment that was made permanent from 12 May 1986. The proceedings of the House of Commons were televised on an experimental basis from 21 November 1989; an arrangement that was made permanent from 1 May 1991.

11 See http://www.parliamentlive.tv.

12 L. Brittan, Hansard, House of Commons Debates, 13 January 1986.

13 R. Jenkins, Hansard, House of Commons Debates, 13 January 1986.

14 For example, the Foreign Affairs Select Committee published a very influential report on the misuse of Overseas Development Administration support for the Pergau Dam project in July 1994, the Social Security Select Committee had a good deal of influence on the reform of the Child Support Agency in 1993–4, and the Treasury and Civil Service Select Committees helped to shape the code of the Civil Service between November 1994 and January 1996.

15 The practice of committing legislation itself to a select committee has been very rarely used in respect of government Bills (though it is not unusual in respect of contentious private members' Bills), with precedents for so doing by agreement to be found in the period during and just after the First World War. During the 1970s select committees were involved in investigating ideas for fiscal legislation – for instance, corporation tax in 1970/71, tax credit in 1972/3 and wealth tax in 1974/5. In the 2003/4 session during consideration of the Constitutional Reform Bill – legislation making provision to abolish the office of Lord Chancellor, to establish a Supreme Court for the United Kingdom and to abolish the appellate jurisdiction of the House of Lords, to establish for England and Wales a Judicial Appointments Commission to recommend appointment of all judges (other than those of the Supreme Court), and to introduce new arrangements for judicial discipline was introduced into the House of Lords – the Bill itself was committed to a select committee. Although some aspects of the policy of the Bill had been under consideration by the government for some time, the immediate catalyst for change was the specific announcement by the government on 12 June 2003 of its intention to abolish the office of Lord Chancellor and establish a Supreme Court. There followed a period of public consulta-

tion on the three principal elements of reform (Lord Chancellor, Supreme Court and judicial appointments), and the government published summaries of the responses on 26 January 2004. Meanwhile the Supreme Court and judicial appointments issues were also considered by the Constitutional Affairs Committee of the House of Commons, which reported on 3 February 2004. One of its recommendations was that the Constitutional Reform Bill would be 'a clear candidate for examination in draft' and a number of speakers in a keenly argued debate in the House of Lords on 12 February 2004 made the same point (Hansard, House of Lords Debates, cols 1211–1344). The government, however, took a different view and the Bill was introduced into the House of Lords on 24 February 2004. During the second reading debate on 8 March a number of speakers advanced the case for referring the Bill to a select committee (there having been no opportunity for prelegislative scrutiny) and following a vote the Bill was committed to a select committee (rather than to a committee of the whole House, which would have been the usual course). See House of Lords Select Committee on the Constitutional Reform Bill, *Constitutional Reform Bill [HL], vol. 1: Report*, Session 2003–4, HL 125.

16 The different, but overlapping aspects of the Westland crisis were examined by no fewer than three select committees – Defence, Trade & Industry and Treasury & Civil Service. See especially the Defence Select Committee report entitled *Westland plc, the Government's Decision Making*, Session 1985–86, HC 519 for further details.

17 For a detailed account and explanation of 'the usual channels' see Rush, M. and Ettinghausen, C. *Opening Up the Usual Channels* (Hansard Society, London, 2002).

18 Indeed, following the Conservative government's decision to guillotine the Statutory Sick Pay Bill in December 1993, the then leader of the opposition, John Smith, withdrew all official pairing for divisions in the House and became uncooperative in dealings through 'the usual channels'. This gesture of opposition displeasure with the government lasted only until the following spring, but it did serve as a reminder of the extent to which the House of Commons can only operate satisfactorily by consent and tacit cooperation between the two front benches.

19 Bagehot, *English Constitution*, p. 170.

20 Crick, B. *The Reform of Parliament* (rev. ed.) (Weidenfeld & Nicolson, London, 1968), p. 80.

21 A. Howard, *The Times*, 17 September 2002.

22 Democratic Audit, *Executive Democracy in Britain* (Democratic Audit, Colchester, 2002).

23 Norton, P. 'General Introduction' in P. Norton (ed) *Legislatures*, (Oxford University Press, Oxford, 1990), p. 1.

24 Viscount Bryce, *Modern Democracies* (Macmillan, London, 1921), p. 370.

25 For examples see Wakeland, S. A. 'Whither the Commons?', in S. A. Wakeland and M. Ryle *The Commons in the Seventies* (Martin Robertson, London, 1977), pp. 238–56; Riddell, P. *Parliament under Pressure* (Victor Gollancz, London, 1998); and 'The Decline of Parliament', in *Strengthening Parliament: Report of the Commission to Strengthen Parliament* (Conservative Party, London, 2000), pp. 10–19.

26 See Forman, F. N. and Baldwin, N. D. J. *Mastering British Politics*, (Macmillan, London, 1999), pp. 533–4.

27 Bryce, *Modern Democracies*, p. 370.

INDEX